MW00464336

The Lunda-Ndembu

The Lunda-Ndembu

Style, Change, and Social Transformation in South Central Africa

James A. Pritchett

The University of Wisconsin Press

The University of Wisconsin Press
1930 Monroe Street
Madison, Wisconsin 53711

www.wisc.edu/wisconsinpress/

3 Henrietta Street
London WC2E 8LU, England

Copyright © 2001
The Board of Regents of the University of Wisconsin System
All rights reserved

5   4   3   2   1

Printed in the United States of America

Library of Congress Cataloging-in-Publication Data
Pritchett, James Anthony.
    The Lunda-Ndembu: style, change, and social transformation in South Central Africa/
James A. Pritchett.
        pp.   cm.
    Includes bibliographical references and index.
    ISBN 0-299-17150-7 (cloth: alk. paper)
    ISBN 0-299-17154-X (pbk.: alk. paper)
    1. Ndembu (African people)   2. Ndembu (African people)—Social conditions.
    I. Title.
    DT3058.N44 P75   2001
    305.896'3977—dc21   00-012230

Contents

Maps, Tables, Figure, and Illustrations

FIGURE

ILLUSTRATIONS

Preface

"Ma-skirt!" "Ma-skirt!" the young girls carefully enunciated while pointing to their colorful cotton skirts. "Ma-blouse!" "Ma-blouse!" they
shouted in unison, now showing off their printed tops. My wife, who had
left the comforts of Boston, U.S.A., only a few days earlier to join me in
Mwinilunga, Zambia, was receiving her first lesson in the Lunda language.
"Oh," she countered, "and I suppose we are all ma-people, and we live in
ma-houses!" The young girls, who spoke not a word of English, responded
with puzzled silence. I struggled to stifle my laughter. I had had a similarly
amusing moment three years earlier during my initial visit to Mwinilunga.
That first cold night I had overheard one man ask another for "i-fosforo"
to light the fire; he then removed his "i-sapato" and warmed his feet. For
just an instant I wondered if I had stumbled onto some joke, an African
version of pig Latin perhaps. Surely the Lunda language could not simply
be Portuguese with an "i" stuck in front of each word.

Embedded in those two moments are messages that I have spent more
than a decade trying to decode. First, they illustrate that the Lunda have
no aversion to cultural borrowing. Much of their material culture is based
on items from elsewhere. Much of their social organization and ceremonial
life is indistinguishable from that of other Central African peoples. Lunda
history is replete with examples of an almost fanatical pursuit of novelty.
Yet, borrowing seems to entail not simply taking but also transforming.
Foreign things must be refashioned into Lunda things. Foreign words, for
example, must be assigned to one of the ten Lunda noun classes, given the
appropriate prefix, and then subjected to the same rules of alliteration that
apply to all other words within that class. But what of other foreign things?
How are foreign tools and techniques, foods and fashions, philosophies
and frameworks, principles and precepts internalized, localized, and indigenized—in short, transformed into Lunda things? In this work I begin the
task of uncovering these processes.

Second, these two moments hold important lessons about the nature of
social change. The young girls, for example, knew nothing about the English etymology of the words they spoke. They had perhaps never heard the

traditional Lunda appellations for skirt and blouse, *chikovwelu* and *mukonzu*. And if they had, they most likely would have associated the terms with old-style raffia or skin clothing, certainly not with the modern apparel they wore. Likewise, fire-starting tools and shoe styles have changed along with the words for them. Before the coming of the Portuguese, the Lunda relied on *mukalula* (flint) rather than boxes of matches for starting fires, and they wore handmade *nkwabilu* (sandals) rather than machine-made shoes. Again, few today have ever heard the older terms. To members of the younger generation, the words my wife and I could easily spot as foreign in origin are Lunda words, pure and simple, which they use to describe their current reality. What reflected a change in style or technology for one generation has become the taken-for-granted tradition of the present. Once grappled with and localized, change often becomes banal, requiring no explanation, unworthy even of contemplation. Unless, of course, an anthropologist shows up and pokes around looking for explanations.

I have been periodically poking around Mwinilunga, in the northwestern corner of Zambia, since 1982. The people of that area, variously called the Lunda, the Lunda-Ndembu, or the Kanongesha Lunda (I use the names interchangeably), are well known to the anthropological community through Victor Turner's writings, particularly *Schism and Continuity* (1957), *The Forest of Symbols* (1967), and *The Drums of Affliction* (1968). The scope and clarity of Turner's work resulted in the Lunda being placed in the center of anthropological discussions on topics ranging from the principles of matriliny to the meaning of symbols in rituals to the impact of the sexual division of labor on political culture and social organization. Introductory courses in anthropology almost always cull some examples from Turner's works. The unfortunate result of this popularity is that the Lunda people themselves have, in a sense, become frozen in time, forever spoken of in the ethnographic present. But it has now been almost half a century since Turner did his seminal research, and much has changed in northwestern Zambia. Wars in the neighboring countries of Angola and Congo have affected the demographics of the region. The spread of Christian missions and mission education have led to new ways of viewing the world. A postcolonial government has been trying to impose new forms of political and economic organization. What has been the cumulative impact of these and other forces of change on the Lunda systems so eloquently described by Turner?

After spending three months in Mwinilunga in 1982, I conducted dissertation research in Zambia from March 1984 to December 1987. I returned to do follow-up research during the summers of 1994, 1995, and 1998. In my years in Zambia I have relied on the assistance of more people than I could possibly mention here by name. Even the list of my neighbors and close friends in Chifunga village who contributed daily to my survival by teaching me how to speak the local language, how to secure food, how to build a shelter, and how to avoid illness would be quite a long one, indeed. As a curious outsider who simply wanted to understand local beliefs and practices for their own sake, I apparently struck a responsive chord. There seemed to be no end to the procession of people offering assistance. My teachers, translators, interpreters, informants, and confidants, thus, number in the hundreds. A collective thanks, however, would be woefully inadequate. Some individuals deserve to be mentioned by name. They include Senior Chief Kanongesha Silas and his subordinate chiefs, the Ikelenge, the Nyakaseya, the Mwiniyilamba, and the Chibwika, who, along with the officials of the Mwinilunga District Government, gave me complete freedom of movement throughout Lunda territory; Senior Headman Isaac Nkemba (the Chifunga), who treated me as a son and who, along with Jake Smart, Chitambala (Kabubu), Tebula, Chimwasu, Izenzi, and the other *akulumpi* (elders), guided me through a wealth of esoteric material; Noah and Miri Kataloshi, Speedwell, and Greenford, who adopted me as a brother and thereby provided me with a position in the local system of kinship reckoning; Vincent Chiteka, Stone Mafulo, Gabriel Katoka, Kapala Sakuumba, Elias Kangasa and Tobias, Peter Lambacasa, Noah Wailesi, Jah, Ndumba, Josayi, Shimishi, Kakoma, Kalenga, Wishmeli, Kamau, Yowanu, Jacksoni, Jampari, Charles, Teddy, Joseph, Benson, Anthony, Sebe, and all the other *maguys* who provided me with companionship while teaching me the basic, and not so basic, physical and social skills expected of every competent male member of Lunda society; Yeta, Ifezia, Sombia, Mrs. Nkemba, Hilda, Ester, Dorothy, Betty, and the other women of Chifunga village who were my wife's constant companions through some of the most exciting and most difficult times of her life.

Also deserving of special thanks for their sincere friendship at all times and special assistance at key moments are the Franciscan friars Joe, Louis, Efisio, Werner, Fritz, Pete, Terrance, and Pio, as well as the ever-changing group of Catholic sisters at Lwawu mission and Mwinilunga Boma.

Dr. Elizabeth Swaine and Dr. Rennie and his family of Kalene Hills Hospital, who nursed me and my wife and daughter back to health from potentially fatal bouts of chloroquine-resistant malaria deserve more thanks than words could ever express. Their colleagues, the Bentleys, the Haigs, and the Rheas, will always be included among our most special friends.

Ilse Mwanza, the affiliate officer at what was then the Institute for African Studies at the University of Zambia, must also be singled out for special thanks. Without her dedicated and sustained effort this project would never have gotten off the ground.

Thanks also to my professors at Harvard University, David P. Maybury-Lewis, Sally Falk Moore, Pauline Peters, and Jane Guyer, who impressed upon this most difficult of students the importance of anthropological theory in explicating ethnographic data. And thanks to Edith Turner. I will always remember the time we shared in 1985 as among my most precious and informative moments in Mwinilunga.

I gratefully acknowledge the Wenner-Gren Society for Anthropological Research, the Harvard Sheldon Fund, and the College of Arts and Sciences and the Department of Anthropology at Boston University for their financial contributions to this project.

And finally, an extra special thanks to my family, my wife Joan and daughter Gina Kankinza, for enduring the hardships of the field experience. Their presence and their trials and tribulations were the clearest demonstration to the local folks that people everywhere are more alike than they are different, linked by common concerns with the existential problems of daily life. My son Nate provided a much-needed contrast on the differences between growing up here and growing up there, as well as many a necessary break from the tedium of the writing process.

With all the assistance I have received over the years there should be no excuse for errors of fact or analysis. Nevertheless, they will invariably occur, and I alone must take full responsibility.

The Lunda-Ndembu

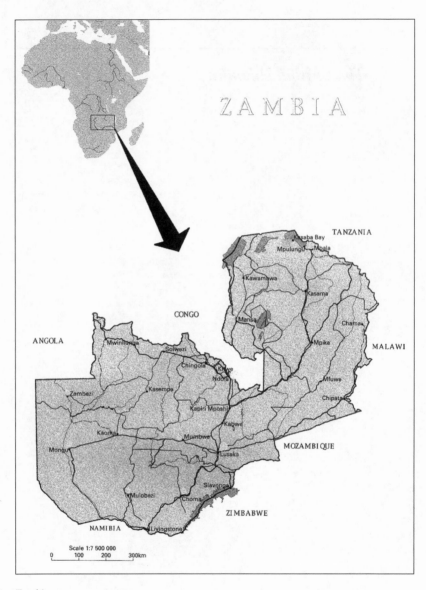

Zambia

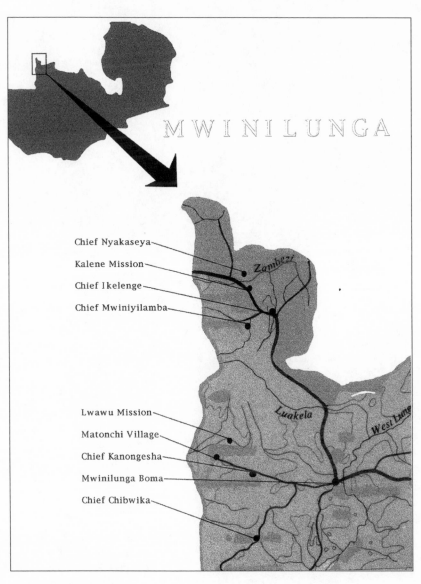

MWINILUNGA

Chief Nyakaseya
Kalene Mission
Chief Ikelenge
Chief Mwiniyilamba

Zambezi

Lwawu Mission
Matonchi Village
Chief Kanongesha
Mwinilunga Boma
Chief Chibwika

Luakela

West Lunga

Lunda-Ndembu Territory

Introduction

In this book I give an account of the Lunda-Ndembu people, who live on the Central African plateau in the northwestern corner of Zambia; I also reflect on general notions of continuity and change in Africa.[1] The account is based on a spotty but increasingly rich body of evidence that includes archaeological data; descriptions from travelers such as David Livingstone, Richard Burton, V. L. Cameron, and Alexandre Serpa Pinto; colonial field reports from generations of district commissioners; and the scholarly studies of Victor Turner, C. M. N. White, Robert Schecter, and Achim von Oppen. Where my own reading of the evidence allows me to speculate about gaps in the Lunda-Ndembu story, I do so; I also contribute my own observations, gained over fourteen years of intermittent contact with the region.

My first objective is to show how a group of people who have been at both the center and the periphery of movements that transformed the fundamental character of Africa and its relationship with the world nevertheless emerged with an image of themselves as essentially unchanged. To the outside observer, the contemporary Lunda lifestyle would appear to be very different from that revealed in past accounts. To the Lunda themselves, this is only superficially so; they speak of themselves as a people who have successfully maintained their traditions. In a sense, this account is about taming history, internalizing change, justifying the present. I digress frequently into history—oral and written, local and global—with the goal, however, of understanding the present.

My second aim, to reflect broadly on notions of continuity and change, extends from the recognition that lessons from the Lunda resonate loudly with emerging theoretical themes in Central African studies. For some time now the tendency of the 1970s and 1980s to avoid localizing, particularizing, and grand-theorizing has been giving way to renewed interest in regional and continentwide processes and in frameworks for meaningfully interpreting those processes. We find increasing attention paid to Jan Vansina's notions of deep tradition, Igor Kopytoff's ideas about a pan-African ecumene, Robert LeVine's contentions concerning widespread patterns of African personalities, and Achim von Oppen's thesis of continuities within historical oscillations.

5

In some respects, much of the newer work runs counter to the anthropological project of the 1970s and 1980s, which trounced stereotypes of an undifferentiated Africa. It was thought then that a normalizing, essentializing anthropological discourse overlooks the role of position. Individuals live their lives as positioned subjects firmly embedded within grand social processes, not outside them, where they would have the overview and analytical hindsight of the anthropologist. Each individual has a unique set of opportunities and constraints. Position within society shapes experience. Experience shapes interpretations, expectations, and, perhaps more important, strategies. As a result of these views, the anthropological exercise became focused on translating local experiences and on revealing those experiences through representations and literary devices. This process did not go unnoticed within academia in Africa. Indeed, African intellectuals applauded and assisted in the project. Samuel N. Chipungu, the noted Zambian historian, reflects:

In the 1980s, shifts in African historiography have again become discernible, now particularly away from the general theoretical and conceptual "group" analytical frameworks of "systems and modes of production," "the state," "class, race and consciousness," and "peasantisation" to understanding the articulation of the individual within these broader theoretical constraints. This trend of writing "people's history" seeks to discuss Africans, often by name, in their daily life as professionals, elites, farmers, ordinary villagers, and in general as participants in various activities, who also ultimately belong to and are influenced by wider realities of race, class, state and other structures. The "people's history" approach is, indeed, welcome in African history, particularly as it promises to make Africans visible again in "their history," showing their actions as part of rational ambivalences or ambiguities that existence reproduces. (Chipungu 1992, 2)

The center of history and anthropology moved toward highlighting complexities and exploring the multiplicity of sociocultural forms in Africa, with a focus on struggle and resistance to both internal and external forces. Yet within the social sciences, paradigmatic shifts are rarely complete. Some scholars continued to work on regional and continentwide processes, even after the modes of production arguments of the neo-Marxists became increasingly less satisfying throughout the 1980s and the death knell of the last grand theory sounded. Those still working within the earlier tradition have perhaps been out of vogue but were never completely out of sight. The contemporary effort to direct our attention again toward broad syntheses is, in some sense, a recognition that genuinely interesting work is taking place within that arena which merits evaluation by those of us whose work has been more localized in place and perspective. But the approach to grand theories need be different this time around. I suggest approaching theory through accounts of specific people. This would compel us to pay attention to local responses and to the ideologies that underpin those responses. This method keeps Africans visible in their own history, showing their actions as part of rational ambivalences or ambiguities yet guided by deeply held, long-standing notions. It keeps us centered on life as a lived experience, rather than on the interaction of depersonalized historical forces.

Perhaps the resurgence of synthetic approaches is also an inevitable result of the massive increase in historical and ethnographic works with a local orientation. The major contribution of the age of antitheoreticism in anthropology was the abundant production of material on local constructions of African social formations, widely dispersed in time and space. Yet, if read rapidly and in great quantities, and with a little imagination, this outpouring might appear to show an Africa of perhaps no more than a handful of archetypal cultures, endlessly rearranged. While we marvel at the cleverness of each particular local configuration, we continually encounter the feeling of déjà vu. Individual traits that form integral parts of the cultural milieu of a particular group are always present elsewhere; it seems that only the local mix is unique. Widespread clusters and constellations of traits hazily appear, particularly to the eyes of scholars such as Vansina, Kopytoff, and LeVine. If these scholars, working on a grand scale, can discern plausible evidence of long-standing continuities despite the traumatic forces to which Africa has been subjected, then we who do research on social change at the local level must assume the responsibility for illustrating and illuminating the local mechanisms by which change is grasped, harnessed, explained, and made to resemble, at some level, that which existed previously. To us lies the task of filling in the outline of the indigenization of social change. This book sketches out the broad dimensions of that new outline.

The Central African Ecumene

Jan Vansina's work has been central to the development of the idea that an ecumene of shared traditions exists in the plateau region of Central Africa. For several decades, Vansina has been reconstructing the broad contours of the sociopolitical history of different parts of Central Africa. Vansina's work is notable for its attempt to go beyond written sources, archaeological objects, and oral memories. He has called our attention to the fact that words carry imprints from the past into the present, imprints that can be interpreted historically. His use of historical linguistics has enabled him to make reasonably convincing pronouncements about long-standing continuities that link groups of people who have been most often noted in the anthropological literature for their differences. In *Paths in the Rainforests* (1990), for example, Vansina sought to demonstrate that the inhabitants of the vast Central African rainforest can be treated as a single cultural unit. He showed that the image of the rainforest as an impenetrable green belt occupied by scattered and isolated groups of people is a myth. Ease of communication is a major feature of the rainforest: no population was ever really isolated. Barriers exist around the edges, where plants have access to ample sunlight and thus grow quite dense, but inside the forest, under the canopy, the vegetation is less dense and movement becomes easier. Furthermore, the vast Congo River system forms one massive transportation network. Most villages are located near a tributary that gives them access to thousands of miles of navigable waters. Additionally, the myriad groups of forest dwellers are heirs to a single ancestral society and culture that expanded into the area from West Africa four to five millennia ago. Everything from word usage to aesthetic frameworks shows this to be the case. Vansina concluded:

Despite all the internal differences, the cultures and societies of the area constitute a unit when compared with the outside. The area contrasts with all the surrounding ones by its system of food production. Its decentralized, yet large-scale, social and political institutions strongly contrast to those of the great lakes to its east and the savanna to its south. Its overall pattern of settlement in villages rather than in dispersed settlements contrasts with the savanna to its north and the great lakes to the east. Moreover almost all the people of the rainforests speak related languages of a group called western Bantu. Their northern and eastern neighbors do not. Their southern neighbors do, but those languages show a strong influence of eastern Bantu languages. (1990, 5)

Vansina went on to assert that Equatorial Africa's most original contribution to the institutional history of the world was its unique effort to maintain local autonomy while enlarging the scale of society and creating the institutions necessary to accommodate the rise of a single huge economic space around an integrated system of distribution. There was a continual drive to keep authority local and to maintain the political integrity and independence of small social units, while at the same time building up widespread social, economic, and political linkages. The Lunda-Ndembu and their neighbors are essentially Equatorial Africans who migrated south out of the rainforest, climbed up to the Central African plateau, and constructed a savanna lifestyle. With time they acquired an overlay of the chiefly tradition that spread across the plateau from the East African highlands.

In an earlier work, *Kingdoms of the Savanna* (1966), Vansina presented a rudimentary outline of a political tradition that dominated much of the savanna region of Central Africa south of the rainforest. Additional work by J. C. Miller, Thomas Q. Reefe, and others inspired by Vansina fleshed out the contours of that tradition. These scholars noted, first, that the kingdoms of the savanna were in reality kingdoms of the interstitial regions: the interenvironmental zones that encompass savanna, forest, and riverine terrain. Although the kingdoms were situated on the savanna, their raison d'être was to control the movement of valued resources between diverse productive zones. Second, they noted the continuing dependence on rainforest products. The staple may have shifted to the savanna crops of millet, sorghum, and cassava, but the savanna lifestyle required steady and predictable access to goods from the rivers and rainforests down in the valleys beneath the plateau. Third, they noted the continuing presence on the savanna of cultural values developed during an earlier rainforest adaptation, particularly values associated with maintaining local autonomy while simultaneously developing widespread linkages. The chiefly tradition that emerged on the savanna took on a unique form when the incoming East African model was transformed by Central African culture. On the one hand, prestigious titles spread across the savanna, linking groups via supposed kinship relations among their leaders. Subsequent leaders inherited these titles and the preexisting relationships embedded in them. These features, known as positional succession and perpetual kinship, and which I address in more detail later, molded the Central African plateau into a vast intercommunicating zone of similarly organized polities, linked by a shared political idiom and a shared need of one another's productive capacity. On the other hand, the chiefly tradition was continually being contested on the plateau by strong centripetal forces, which tended to pull power to the lowest level. Many scholars of Central Africa, particularly historians, now speak of a Central African ecumene, a cultural tradition sufficiently widespread and long-standing to allow us to usefully delimit the plateau as a single an-alytical unit.

Tradition, according to Vansina's definition, is a changing, inherited, collective body of cognitive and physical representations shared by mem-bers of a society. It may flow out of a set of static principles about ultimate aims in life; the nature of the afterlife; the function of deities; the role of witches; the proper organization of space, time, and people; and so forth. Yet, traditions are processes. They continually change, but they also pos-sess the power to transform even the institutions in which they are embed-ded, while leaving their own basic principles unquestioned. Traditions have the capacity to recast history in their own terms. They can be pressed into service to justify events, attitudes, and aspirations that fall outside previous experience: "Traditions, as fundamental continuities, which shape the futures of those who hold them, are not just in the minds of observers. They are 'out there.' They are phenomena with their own characteristics" (Vansina 1990, 258).

We owe Vansina a great debt of gratitude for his pioneering efforts in un-covering deep similarities among widespread Central African societies. Yet, it is Igor Kopytoff, in *The African Frontier* (1987, 3–84), who goes the fur-thest in making explicit elements useful for deducing a Central African ecu-mene and the mechanisms by which it could reconstitute itself through time and space. Kopytoff places the notion of a frontier consciousness at the center of his thesis about pan-African political processes. But in contrast to those who view frontiers as natural forces for cultural transformation, Kopytoff asserts that the African frontier has most often acted as a force for cultural and historical continuity and conservatism. His focus is on local frontiers, those places at the fringes of established polities that are most often colonized not by utopian social transformers but by those seeking to replicate the metropole from which they came, in terms more favorable to themselves. Perhaps in the American west, and elsewhere, the frontier beck-oned to those desiring to construct a new lifestyle away from the social, po-litical, and economic constraints of their former urban existence. In Africa, however, the frontier was usually settled by those who had no basic gripe with the social organization of their world, only with their positions in that world. They came to the frontier to advance their status, not to transform society by experimenting with new social models.

The frontier consciousness that Kopytoff speaks of not only is present in the minds of those who actually move to the frontier, but also emerges from cultural elements that are deeply embedded in the societies from which the pioneers come. The first of those elements is a generalized tendency toward fission in African societies. Escape from famine, succession struggles, fear of witchcraft, and the desire for adventure all impel movement to the frontier. Concomitantly, high value is placed on being first in an area, establishing a new village, founding a new lineage, or simply bringing new physical space under social control.

Second, segmentation is usually carried out by a group: a lineage segment, a set of brothers, or another group linked by kinship, descent, or dependency. Once established on the frontier, a group typically attempts to rekindle links with family members back in the metropole. It may even seek formal validation of its newly independent status, perhaps through making concrete the political and personal relationships between the leaders of the new group and the original metropole. New titles may emerge which symbolize and express those relations in a kinship idiom.

Third, Kopytoff speaks of the constant drive to acquire followers, be they kin, subjects, slaves, or retainers. The expansion of one's following is, in a sense, the traditional method of constructing one's legacy, of seeking social immortality by leaving behind many who will perform culturally recognized acts of remembrance long after one has passed into the other world. But the indiscriminate recruitment of strangers can be dangerous. They may ultimately outnumber and overrun their original patrons. Kin, even if they are fictive, can be more easily controlled. Rights and duties can be more easily apportioned. The conversion of strangers into kin, even across ethnic boundaries, is thus a dominant feature of the Central African ecumene.

Clearly there are no external imperatives that require Africans to continually reproduce the above cultural elements throughout the continent. Rather, the process is propelled by widely internalized notions about the proper relations among people and things. Kopytoff's work, in many respects, builds on the work of scholars such as Robert LeVine (1976), who use psychological studies of personality and behavior to explain social adaptation to changing conditions. LeVine asserts that despite the fact that Africa possesses a wide range of individual personality types, certain strong central tendencies exist that may allow us to speak of a distinctive African personality. The uniqueness lies not in the individual traits themselves. Each, in fact, exists elsewhere in the world. Rather, a particular configuration of traits seems characteristic of Africa, and the African personality is

most clearly revealed in a certain uniformity of behavior. Although I seriously question the use of the term "personality" as a label for the assemblage of traits identified by LeVine, I nevertheless recognize this assemblage as a useful component in creating a working hypothesis regarding
Central African political and cultural similarities.

First, LeVine argues, powerful notions exist throughout Africa about
maintaining social distance between people who differ in age and sex.
There is pervasive institutional emphasis on avoidance, segregated activities, and formality of interaction even, at times, between members of the
same family, for example , husband-wife, parent-child, co-wives, and elder-
younger children. Second, this social distance is most often reckoned vertically. Differences in age and sex are key elements in constructing local hierarchies. Furthermore, variations in rank, status, and power at every level
of society tend to be the subject of much public elaboration. Third, material transactions are emphasized in interpersonal relations. That is to say, relationships can frequently be characterized in terms of the type of material
exchanges involved: who gives what, to whom, when, and under what conditions. Fourth, there is a functional diffuseness of authority relations.
Leaders, for example, may expect followers to obey commands that extend
far beyond those leaders' formal mandates. Followers, in return, may make
equally wide-ranging requests of their leaders. Additionally, the highest position in any social hierarchy is generally viewed as a terminal office, be-
stowing lifelong tenure on its holder. Fifth, Africans have a tendency to
personalize impersonal forces. Disease, accidents, infertility, miscarriage,
crop loss, or misfortunes of any type are often blamed on witchcraft, sorcery, or the violation of social taboos. The sixth trait that LeVine identifies
as characteristic of the African personality, which I find least convincing, is
the relative absence of separation anxiety. Youngsters move with relative
ease from household to household. Adult women frequently leave their
natal villages and embark upon new lives among the strangers of their husbands' villages. Adult men may spend much of their lives as long-distance
traders or migrant laborers away from the comfort of familiar faces. LeVine
believes that the openness of African societies, which do not require the individual to deny and repress hostility toward others, mediates against
strong feelings of anxiety, pity, and sentimentality that might be expected
to accompany separation. Last, LeVine proposes that the African personality tends toward concretizing abstract phenomena. Moral precepts and
philosophical concepts are understood through concrete examples embed-

ded in proverbs and fables. Life is guided by lived or inherited precedence rather than by extrapolations from abstract principles.

LeVine acknowledges that the "African personality" may be little more than a matter of statistical tendencies, whose importance depends largely on the level of analytical abstraction utilized. He further acknowledges that his proposed framework is applicable only to sub-Saharan agriculturalists, not to pastoral or hunting groups or to the urbanized elite. He admits that his suppositions lack depth because they are based on superficial, observable aspects of behavior rather than on their underlying dynamics. Nevertheless, LeVine contends that widespread similarities in behavior in so many varied contexts could be produced only by deep and shared similarities in basic personality structure. He therefore offers his framework as a starting point for more detailed structural analyses that will no doubt uncover localized variations.

The Lunda-Ndembu appear to conform to the generalizations put forward by these scholars. Until the seventeenth century, they were at the center of the most powerful savanna kingdom; they then moved to the frontier in stages seemingly consistent with Kopytoff's theories. Although cassava became their basic staple, they remained dependent on rainforest products. They conquered and/or integrated the peoples they encountered on their sojourns, through the dispensation of prestigious titles. Individual villages were linked by the supposed relationships among their leaders, and those links were maintained by positional succession and perpetual kinship. The Lunda-Ndembu have fought at every turn to maintain local autonomy. They have fought equally hard to establish widespread social, political, and economic networks. Segregation by sex and age is a dominant feature of their social organization. And at the surface level, at least, the cluster of behavioral characteristics outlined by LeVine does indeed appear to describe the Lunda-Ndembu.

How is it that scholars such as LeVine, Vansina, and Kopytoff, who have not studied the Lunda-Ndembu in any detail, are capable nevertheless of outlining the broad dimensions of their cultural history with such apparent accuracy? Is there a genuine Central African ecumene that circumscribes the locally available responses to historical forces? The object of this study is to delve deeply into these questions by observing the reconstruction of social life over time, to see how the Lunda-Ndembu have confronted and conceptualized the changes thrust upon them. The aim is to understand how a group of people who have experienced the disruptive impact of the long-distance trade era, the collapse of their empire, slavery, colonialism, missionary incursions, and postcolonial machinations nevertheless continue to speak of themselves as a people who have maintained their traditions. What, indeed, are these traditions? How have changing circumstances been internalized, indigenized, and justified in terms of a preexisting interpretive framework that is widely shared throughout the plateau?

Justifying Change

Objects, situations, or actions are not just mentally recorded as items; they are recognized and catalogued with the help of information already in the mind, and significance is attached to them.

Vansina 1990, 71–72

A tension always exists between the two realities people are acutely aware of: the cognitive reality that predicts how things should unfold, and the physical reality that actually does take place. Too wide a gap between these realities can be profoundly disturbing to individual consciousness and group cohesiveness. Discrepancies must be continually worked out. Movement away from that which is understandable must be reined in, harnessed, explained, and justified. This process is possible not only because physical reality influences the explanatory frameworks in the mind, but also because those mental frameworks influence how people actually experience physical reality. Cognitively, change can be made to resemble something known, something familiar, something justifiable. The justification of change is an indigenizing process that requires a certain degree of autonomous thought and action. But indigenizing change is also a way of regaining or reasserting autonomy. Even under the most oppressive conditions people endeavor to maintain autonomy of explanation. We are all innately endowed with the capacity to generate our own conceptual models of experience as well as to devise ways of modifying that experience, at least cognitively, if we are sufficiently dissatisfied.

Among the Lunda-Ndembu the formal gathering for discussing conflicts, disputes, law cases, or anything that deviates from the norm is called a *mulong'a*. The root of this term is *long'a*: things that are straight, righteous, in order. A *mulong'a* is, thus, a process for straightening things out, for placing things in order. It aims at reestablishing concordance between the cognitive and physical realms. It is at a *mulong'a* that one most readily observes the enormous amount of respect and social prestige accorded those individuals gifted with the ability to put forward persuasive rhetoric and logic. Here men and women vie for prominence and assert their worthiness for leadership. People collectively make and interpret their own histories. The most elegant arguments at a *mulong'a* are those cloaked in an idiom of tradition. Decisions about responding to past events or charting future courses of action are most easily embraced by the group if those interpretations and strategies can be justified as being in agreement with long-standing traditions.

The present, however, need not necessarily resemble the past in every detail. Indeed, cohort groups among the Lunda-Ndembu deliberately, self-consciously, and often with a great deal of flourish seek out new elements of style as visible, but superficial, markers of their separate identities within the larger group identity. Even in the absence of formal age-grades, Lunda-Ndembu society can still be visualized as layers of generationally based groups, with a mosaic of age-based styles appealing to commonly shared aesthetic choices. The manner of dress, greetings used, music preferred, dances developed, subsistence strategies devised, and so forth, vary noticeably from one generation to the next. This is not only accepted, it is widely expected. Changes of this nature, that is, modifications that remain within a particular cohort group, are acknowledged as purely a matter of style or fashion. Only when such modifications are intergenerational, adopted by all cohort groups, can we speak of social change. Even here, such changes are generally justified and naturalized by their conceptual or aesthetic consistency with long-standing cultural products that transcend generations. Only when the justifying principles themselves come into question and are modified can we begin to speak of social transformation.

The power differential between cohort groups would be expected to favor the elderly, giving them disproportionate force in producing social change by spreading their style to the younger age groupings. The elderly possess economic, ritual, and intellectual advantages to which the young aspire. But historically this has not always been the case; at certain moments the balance is noticeably shifted toward the young. Their physical strength, their facility in acquiring new skills, their exposure to new economic opportunities, and their adventurous spirit sometimes place them at the forefront of change. Social life can be characterized as a struggle between cohort groups to infuse the larger society with their own particular styles and interpretive practices.

In order to encompass and capture as much of the local dynamics of change as possible, this volume is organized around seven sets of relationships that cut across and link cohort groups:

- People and the environment
- The individual and the group
- The old and the young
- Females and males
- The rich and the poor
- Us and them
- This world and the other world

These sets of relationships are fragile and are continually debated and renegotiated even under the best of conditions. In a fashion reminiscent of Victor Turner, Max Gluckman, and other Manchester anthropologists, I take as my starting point that the natural state of society, if such a thing exists, is rife with fissures, schisms, and endemic oppositions. Societies are precariously balanced, at best, on the edge of delicate relationships. They are inherently ripe for change. These key sets of social relations have been shown time and again in the anthropological literature to be notoriously difficult to manage under conditions of even moderate stress. The shock treatments to which the Lunda-Ndembu have been subjected reverberate through all their systems: political, social, philosophical, economic, medical, subsistence, and so forth. But a focus on abstract systems is perhaps not the best vantage point from which to view change. The Lunda-Ndembu live in a world of immediate relationships, and it is at the shifting boundaries of these relationships that change is actually confronted on a daily basis, spoken about, and brought into cognitive conformity with widespread and long-standing traditions.

Following a brief overview of Lunda history, presented in chapter 1, subsequent chapters address each set of relationships in turn. Chapter 2 examines the relationship between the Lunda-Ndembu and their environment, addressing traditional ideologies and practices with respect to the environment and the place of humans within the environment. It details the new forms of environmental management that have emerged, particularly during the twentieth century, and the contours of their interaction with traditional beliefs and practices. It then shows how the new practices are ultimately justified and localized in terms of traditional beliefs about the relationship between humans and the environment.

Chapter 3 focuses on the relationship between the individual and the group. It addresses the tenuous balance between notions of individual autonomy, individual desire for freedom of choice, and control over one's own body, on the one hand, and notions about the group's need to control certain facets of the lives of its members, on the other. It lays out the new choices that emerged out of the colonial encounter, the subsequent penetration of the bureaucratic network of the newly independent nation-state, and the oscillating incursions by mercantile and productive capitalist agents. I propose that the traditional system of rewards and sanctions by which individual behavior was influenced weakened when it was confronted by new coercive forces and new sets of competing rewards.

Chapter 4 explores the relationship between the young and the old. It addresses the cultural underpinnings of traditional gerontocratic forms of local power, the means by which the differential distribution of privileges and duties was explained and given force, and the subsequent renegotiation of the relationship between young and old in light of external forces and new internal desires.

Chapter 5 examines the relationship between males and females. It discusses the delicately balanced relationship that derives from the differing positions of males and females within the kinship and descent systems, the cultural division of labor, and metaphysical notions about the separate existential status of males and females. It analyzes the historical interaction of males and females within new fields of constraints and opportunities.

Chapter 6 focuses on the relationship between the rich and the poor. It brings out the historically shifting differentials of wealth: the clearly observable differences in individual access to certain valued goods such as land, labor, cash, and commodities that have long characterized Lunda-Ndembu society. These differences were traditionally contained and made palatable by ideologies that sought to balance privilege with responsibility to the group as a whole. New definitions of wealth and new routes for acquiring wealth have continually reconfigured local notions of privilege and responsibility.

Chapter 7 explores the relationship between "us" and "them." It addresses ethnicity and the changing components and configurations of the notion of "Lunda-ness" as lateral linkages between peoples strengthened and weakened across the Central African plateau. It discusses the impact of expanding geopolitical boundaries and bureaucratic structures on local processes of identity formation, including currently emerging notions of "Zambian-ness."

Chapter 8 examines the relationship between "this world" and the "other world," addressing the impact of missionary, colonial, and post-colonial ideological assaults on concepts of the afterlife. It looks at the localized forms of strategic planning and positioning that people pursue within the physical world now, in order to secure a desired outcome in the metaphysical world later.

All of the above relationships are subject to much cultural elaboration among the Lunda-Ndembu. They are the dominant themes of many proverbs, they are animated in rituals, they are expressed daily in oral and physical enactments. The degree to which an ecumene or deep tradition persists is a reflection of the degree to which the outcome of struggles about relationships results in something that in some fashion parallels, at least at the conceptual level, that which it supersedes. This work lays out the tone and tenor of local debates about these relationships over time. In a separate work I will focus more specifically on the detailed articulation of these relationships within a single cohort group.

Storytelling, according to Roger D. Abrahams, "is of a piece with other African performance traditions based on the principles of opposition, overlap, apart-playing and interlock, inasmuch as it shares the aesthetic" (1983, 20). Abrahams's notions about oral performance can be extended to life itself. Life is the ultimate performance tradition. The African lifestyle, as a whole, shares the same properties as its more circumscribed components. African music is spoken of as polyrhythmic and polyphonic. African rituals have been described as polysemic and multivocal. African life can equally well be viewed as polystructured, polyconstructed, and multi-experienced. Among the Lunda-Ndembu opinions expressed in village-level discussions over what should be done and how it should be interpreted are rarely unanimous. They more often tend to be processes in which a range of opinions are heard and acknowledged. A general tone is established, a canon is constructed; not a canon beyond dispute, but a new canon to dispute. A consensus about the parameters of the next dispute is made explicit. There is a great deal of room for intellectual entrepreneurship in Lunda-Ndembu daily life, as this account will reveal.

Chapter One

Histories and Homilies

Pre-colonial Central Africa was a world curiously united by political experience. . . . Adaptability and innovation are the hallmarks of Central African history.

Birmingham 1983, 1

Older Americans most likely came of age with a uniform, shared vision of the African past. Before the coming of Europeans, many would have believed, Africa had been a vast and mysterious continent filled with separate, autonomous tribes, each with its own language, religion, and tradition, each living in harmony with its surroundings, each perhaps hostile and suspicious of other tribes. The younger generation, however, has a much richer and more regionalized repertoire of African stereotypes. Mention West Africa, and multitudes of American school kids will dutifully chant "Ghana, Mali, Songhai." North Africa for them evokes images of Islamic civilization. East Africa is epitomized by a string of Swahili city states. Southern African images are dominated by the militarism of Shaka Zulu and the massive stone ruins of Great Zimbabwe. But what of Central Africa? Here, it appears, is the last remaining refuge of the original stereotype. Central Africa for many is still the heart of darkness, the land least touched by the outside world, inhabited by the people least affected by global progress. It would be easy enough to simply dismiss this fatuity and move on with the story. But every story needs a context. And a place lost in time, a people isolated from history, is too decrepit a framework on which to base this one. The foundation must be rebuilt. The reader must realize that Central Africa has long been connected to the outside world, that it has long been a place of dynamic interaction among diverse cultures, and that it was the font of a political style that flowed outward for thousands of miles across geological and genealogical barriers alike.

Remarkable new information about Central Africa is continually being brought to light. More logical, sophisticated, and complex interpretations of old material are being constructed as well. Several synthetic histories of Central Africa have been published in recent years, and more continue to

appear. The information provided here is not intended to move forward the
process of constructing histories. Its purpose is to give the reader a taste of
Central African history, a sense of the themes out of which locals and foreigners have woven their separate tales, and of the conclusions that will no
doubt continue to be debated within both the halls of academia and the clay
walls of Central African compounds. The aim of this chapter is fourfold: (1)
to demonstrate the intensity of early connections between Central Africa
and global processes; (2) to present some of the evidence that suggests
movement and social reorganization in response to knowledge of and contact with external opportunities; (3) to lay out the features of a political style
that reconfigured the social landscape over thousands of miles; and (4) to
suggest some reasons why a people called the Lunda-Ndembu came into
being on the upper Zambezi River at a particular historical moment.

Archaeological Evidence of Foreign Trade

The archaeology of Central Africa is in its infancy, yet a few points seem relatively clear. Ironworking was well established, at least in the regions now
constituting southern Congo and central Zambia, by the second century
A.D., and there is evidence of widespread copper mining by the fourth century. The best-documented archaeological sequence, however, comes from
the great cemetery of Sanga around Lake Kisale in the southeastern forest
region (Nenquin 1963, de Maret 1975, Phillipson 1977). Between the
eleventh and twelfth centuries a remarkable amount of wealth had been accumulated in this area. Considerable variation existed among individual
graves excavated, with some of the wealthiest containing flange-welded
iron gongs, items that we know later served as symbols of kingship. Graves
radiocarbon-dated to between the seventh and the seventeenth centuries
contained large copper bangles and collars, ivory bracelets, iron pendants,
Indian Ocean cowrie shells, *Conus* shells, glass beads, decorated pottery
vessels from China, ceremonial regalia, and copper crosses of the type
known to have circulated later as money in Central Africa. Although there
are as yet no demonstrated links between the Sanga graves and the Lunda
per se, the graves say much about the early Central African social, political,
and economic cauldron out of which the Lunda emerged.

First, the items found at Sanga indicate links that extended to the Indian
Ocean and ultimately to the Far East. No one would suggest that Indian

and Chinese merchants were plying their wares directly. Nor do we have any reason to suppose that Central Africans themselves were then traveling as far as the Indian Ocean. But clearly, Central Africa did not exist in a realm apart from the Indian Ocean network, the greatest trading bloc in the world at that time. Through some mechanism or other, goods from halfway around the world found their way into the center of the continent.

Second, these goods suggest a capacity to produce surplus commodities deemed valuable by groups farther east. They also suggest a certain local security of subsistence, since surplus was being converted into items of limited use-value. We know little about the convertibility between glass beads, *Conus* shells, and Chinese pottery on the one hand, and subsistence goods on the other. Yet, the acquisition of prestige goods implies the sort of forward-looking, strategic investments that rarely coexist with deep concern for short-term subsistence.

Third, the buried items indicate the early existence of extensive social and economic differentiation. In life and in death, some individuals were treated with greater respect. The items also imply the presence of a complex social organization that guaranteed security of persons and products, provided for freedom of movement, and mapped out social spaces where differing groups could negotiate terms of trade and corresponding terms of trust.

Even the undisturbed condition of the artifacts excavated at Sanga gives pause for thought. Why had they not been plundered by grave robbers? Were they not of sufficient value? Were they too commonplace to merit much attention? Were they spared for fear of physical retribution or because they were thought to be metaphysically protected? Or was the problem one of convertibility? Perhaps, as will be more fully addressed later, the value of these items resided in acquisition rather than actual ownership. The capacity to acquire items of prestige from distant lands symbolizes knowledge of processes, embeddedness in linkages, and forethought. It is a demonstration of one's success at managing the present, one's confidence in negotiating the future.

Sanga was located perhaps 200 miles east of the areas where the Lunda Empire emerged. No major barriers exist that would have constrained the flow of goods or information between the two. In other words, there were no reasons for the early Lunda not to have known of the Chinese and Indian items at Sanga and something of the networks that brought them into Central Africa. These items would not have been hidden away as private capital for later use; they were quintessential African symbols of wealth and connectedness, whose possession had to be publicly proclaimed in order to attract dependents, the only real capital in Central Africa.

The Sanga excavation supports additional evidence from throughout Central Africa for a fourteenth- or fifteenth-century Central African explosion in the production of copper in standardized sizes and shapes: money. Archaeologists believe that every known mine was producing at full capacity at that time. The impetus for this monetary revolution is unknown, as is the question of whether this money was used to grease the flow of local or long-distance trade goods. Yet, from the fourteenth and fifteenth centuries forward, the evidence, although spotty, abounds with indications of groups jockeying for position, struggling for control of old copper regions, and striking out to discover new deposits of ore. One needs only a little imagination to envision a continuing process of reconfigurations of peoples and polities, identities and enterprises from the fourteenth century virtually straight through to the present. Nor would it take much imagination to envision these processes waxing and waning, erupting and evolving in tandem with global flows of goods and services, needs and desires.

The arrival of the Portuguese on the Kongo coast in the fifteenth century signaled the beginning of the rivalry between the Atlantic and the Indian Ocean trade blocs. All who have studied western Central Africa have noted the sustained and unquenchable African thirst for European imports. This thirst led to the breakup of long-established kingdoms and the emergence of new ones. It led to the development of new routes to the interior of Africa, and the flow of slaves, ivory, and rubber to the west coast. A parallel process must have occurred earlier on Africa's east coast when the Indian Ocean trade network expanded after the tenth century A.D. Little is known, however, about this process or about the extent of Central Africans' initial reaction to both commercial thrusts. Those who advocate the most narrow reading of the currently available evidence would have us believe that the great majority of Central Africans were unaware of or uninvolved in the mad scramble for foreign goods until well into the eighteenth century. Those of us who have lived and worked in Central Africa for a long time, who know the ease with which information and people flow across the terrain, who have seen Central African entrepreneurs search for opportunities through some of the world's worst war zones and local insurrections, cannot imagine that the years between the fifteenth and eighteenth centuries were anything other than tumultuous.

The impact of competing trade blocs on Central Africa cannot be measured in terms of distance from productive enclaves or numbers of foreigners trudging across the landscape. The impact would have been evident first in changing ideas about the relative value of things and second in changing forms of social and productive organization to acquire new things. Yet, unfortunately, ideas and economic strategies, particularly in their early stages, do not leave a heavy imprint on the historical record. Therefore, I implore readers to recognize that far more has transpired in Central Africa than we will ever know and that the impetus for much of the early dynamics is probably lost forever.

Early Lunda Social Organization

Historians believe that the basic social institution of the Lunda up until the sixteenth century was the segmentary matrilineage.[1] Each lineage segment occupied its own small territory, *mpat*, most of which were along the Kalanyi River in Congo. As anthropologists have often noted, the segmentation of lineages tends to work against the formation of strongly centralized political institutions unless there simultaneously exist powerful mechanisms for uniting people across lineages (see, e.g., Kelly 1985; Hutchinson 1996). Such mechanisms appear not to have been present before the sixteenth century, as each lineage segment had relative economic and political autonomy and divided frequently, giving birth to new segments. Like most Central African peoples at that time, the Lunda raised millet, sorghum, and other crops; all early European travelers to Lunda areas, however, noted the importance of fishing both for subsistence and trade. In all likelihood their most effective method for gathering fish was to build fish dams at narrow points in rivers, a technique that the Lunda still utilize today. Each *mpat* was probably centered on one of these ideal locations for fishing, with crops being planted in the fertile soil along the river bank. By all indications this system was extremely productive and, hence, Lunda territory was dotted with a rapidly expanding number of independent domains, each with its own headman.

The early Lunda also practiced positional succession and perpetual kinship; that is, each headmanship was a named position, and each successor to a particular headmanship would inherit not only the authority but also the name associated with that position.[2] Furthermore, relationships among headmen were more or less permanently expressed in a kinship idiom. For example, if an individual and his followers left group A and established their own *mpat*, not only would this group forever be considered the son lineage segment of A, but its headman and his successors would also permanently be considered the "sons" of whoever happened to occupy the headman-ship of lineage segment A. Therefore, segments and their leaders could stand in father-son relationship to one another, as well as grandfather-grandson, brother-brother, cousin-cousin, uncle-nephew, and so forth. Because of the relative economic autonomy of each segment, it is believed that perpetual kinship rarely affected daily life. The senior position of all the lineage heads was know as Yala Mwaku, who was historically remembered merely as the first among equals (Miller 1976, chapt. 5). Mobilizing the lineages for war or ritual is believed to have been his responsibility. But oral traditions of the Lunda concur that at a particular point when the Yala Mwaku was called upon to mobilize the lineages, it was in response not to an external threat but to an internal one. Once the lineages were mobilized they were, in a sense, forced to remain so until the dawn of the colonial era in Central Africa.

From the kingdom of Kansanje in central Angola to the Kazembe polity on the Luapula River in Zambia is a distance of over a thousand miles. Almost every ethnolinguistic group throughout this area, including the Luvale, Chokwe, Mbundu, Luchaze, and others, claims to have been founded by warriors or nobles from the central Lunda polity.[3] The oral traditions of nearly all these peoples point to a transformative moment, probably around the turn of the sixteenth century. A struggle for succession to the position of Yala Mwaku occurred. The previous incumbent had decreed that his daughter, Lueiji, would succeed him, and thus upon his death most of the lineage heads acknowledged her as the new Yala Mwaku. But Lueiji's two brothers, Kinguri and Kinyama, contested her appointment and mobilized their followers for war.

It is uncertain if the parties in this dispute were in fact the actual sons and daughter of the Yala Mwaku or if they were lineage heads who stood in father-child relationship to the old Yala Mwaku position. The Lunda system of positional succession renders us unable to separate biologically based kinship relations from politically based perpetual kinship relations in the oral tradition. Nor is it certain why the position of Yala Mwaku suddenly became so desirable that individuals were prepared to wage war to obtain it. Some evidence suggests that by 1600, through slow, steady improvements in technology, the Lunda were generating levels of surplus capable of sustaining widespread trade and occupational differentiation (Hoover 1978). The outgrowth of such developments would have been the need for more formal judicial structures to mediate conflicting interests in a society increasingly stratified economically. Augmented military capabilities might also have been needed to protect the trade networks on which local wealth was based. In any event, the density of population suggests that there was a need for political government on a larger scale than had previously existed in Central Africa. Historians believe that most other Bantu groups in Central Africa at that time lived in small, scattered agricultural communities where land was abundant and immovable assets few. Hence, antagonistic parties could easily resolve serious disputes by going their separate ways. But Lunda wealth was closely associated with control over a finite number of fishing spots that required considerable labor to develop. Since moving was no longer an acceptable solution to social stress, the Lunda needed stronger mechanisms of conflict resolution. Perhaps the position of Yala Mwaku had evolved into one that received tribute or fees for its role in mediating disputes and/or facilitating trade, and thus became increasingly desirable and contested.

Whatever the reason, it is widely proclaimed that a major conflict took place between the faction supporting Lueiji and the faction supporting Kinguri and Kinyama. What is salient about this incident is that in order to maintain the support of most of the lineage heads, to counter the threat posed by her brothers, Lueiji was forced to embark upon a new power-sharing relationship. She became the titular head of state, but a powerful new body, the council of headmen, known as the *tubungu*, came into being. Each loyal headman, with a detachment of young warriors, moved to and fortified Lueiji's *mpat* at Musumba, thus creating the first pan-Lunda capital city with a standing army. The heir apparent of each of these lineage headmen was then called upon to rule the local area in the headman's stead, in effect becoming the governor of the outlying province. Some of these leaders fortified their local villages (Dias de Carvalho 1890; Biebuyck 1957; Duysters 1958).

Lueiji's alliance provided an effective defense against her brothers' threat, but oral traditions note that she was not able to completely defeat them. They established their own polity on the western frontier of the central Lunda area, apparently biding their time, probing for any sign of weakness, ever ready to renew their attack on their sister's capital. Lueiji and the *tubungu* were, therefore, forced to continually expand their army and to establish a widening system of tribute collection to provision that army. The brothers also augmented their own forces by defeating and then incorporating the previously autonomous peoples on the margins of their new polity. A standoff existed for some years until Lueiji entered into an alliance with (or, some say, was defeated by) the Luba people on her eastern border, an alliance which temporarily merged the two peoples (Reefe 1981). The Luba were famous for their skills in hunting and metalwork. With their assistance the balance of power finally shifted in Lueiji's favor, and she began to push her brothers and their followers westward. In order to solidify the merger with the Luba, Lueiji expanded both the size and scope of the advisory council, placing many powerful Luba in key positions. Her position eventually merged with that of the Luba leader to create a new head of this expanded state, the Mwantiyanvwa.

Lueji's brother Kinyama organized a polity several hundred miles to the southwest of the Lunda capital (Papstein 1978). He eventually made peace by acknowledging the overlordship of the central Lunda polity, pledging loyalty and regularly sending tribute in salt to the capital. His people became know as the Lwena, or Luvale. Until this day their chief continues to be called the Kinyama. The fate of the other brother, Kinguri, is less clear. By some accounts he and his followers accelerated their westward pace, reaching the Atlantic coast just south of present-day Luanda, six hundred miles from the Lunda capital, around 1600 (Ravenstein 1901). Within a few years they are said to have moved several hundred miles inland to an area along the Kwango River in Angola, where they set up a trading state that became known as Kasanje and grew wealthy by monopolizing commercial exchange between the Lunda and the coast. Recent scholarship, however, suggests that tales of Kinguri and his followers have somehow become conflated with those of a late-sixteenth-century Central African military cult known either as Jaga or Imbangala (Miller 1988, 28). By other accounts, even Kinguri's association with the Lunda Center (the capital, or court) was a spurious eighteenth-century creation. Yet, even as an invention, it is a powerfully informative tale. For centuries, the path to power in Central Africa lay through claiming connections to the Lunda court. Scholars may long continue their debates about origins and evolution. But there is no doubt about the role of the Lunda Empire in generating wealth and validating political power throughout Central Africa.

During the eighteenth century a constellation of new political groupings arose to the west to take advantage of expanding Portuguese coastal trade. The Lunda were too numerous and well organized to be physically threatened by these small groups. However, the combination of constant pressure from the outside with their own desire to reap the benefits of the new goods now circulating in Africa led to new levels of centralized political organization. During the 1700s the empire was said to consist of a number of villages, each of which was ruled by a council of elders, the *ciyul*, and a matrilineally hereditary headman, or *Mwaantaangaand*. The headman was responsible for the supernatural well-being of the village, supposedly because his ancestors had founded it. Groups of headmen were ruled by an elder, the *mbay*, and groups of *mbay* in turn made up a district governed by the *cilool*, who was chosen by the collective *mbay*. The main function of the *cilool* was collecting taxes, which he forwarded to a superior residing in the Lunda capital at Musumba. Each district also had a resident representative of the emperor, the *yikeezy*, whose function was to oversee the honesty of the *cilool*. Tribute had become the lifeblood of the empire and, thus, numerous checks and balances were incorporated into the political system to insure the uninterrupted flow of tribute from the far-flung corners of the realm. The original *tubungu* that had shared national power at the time of Lueiji now consisted of fifteen headmen of the oldest villages and exercised only ritual duties. A new national council, the *citentam*, had come into being, consisting of the highest ranking titleholders from all the groups that now made up the greatly enlarged Lunda polity. The emperor, or Mwantiyanvwa, was also assisted by a number of titleholders linked to him through ties of perpetual kinship: the Swana Mulunda (perpetual mother of the Lunda), the Lukonkesha (perpetual aunt), the Swana Mulopwe (crown prince), the Mutiy (war leader), and so forth. In addition there were *kakwata*, chiefs who constantly traveled with a military force to collect tribute or carry out orders. The Lunda continued to expand, incorporating small groups on the frontier by following a dual approach of either offering positive incentives or threatening extreme violence (Vansina 1966; Miller 1969; Schecter 1976). In exchange for becoming vassal states of the Lunda Empire and sending regular tribute, which increasingly took the form of food, ivory, and slaves, the leaders of small groups received prestigious new titles linking them through perpetual kinship to the Mwantiyanvwa himself along with protection from the ever-increasing slaving activity. One had to acquiesce to Lunda overlordship, join the system, and send a few compatriots to the Lunda capital as slaves, or else feel the force of one of the Lunda armies and run the risk of having one's entire group reduced to slaves. Through this method a steady supply of people was funneled to slave markets at the Lunda capital, there to await the arrival of one of the numerous caravans that would transport them to the coast (Birmingham 1966, 133ff.; Thornton 1981, 7). Although the Lunda elites exercised a monopoly on the slave trade, commoners did a thriving business with the caravans that arrived from the west laden with trade goods, supplying them with food and other supplies and services for the return trip to the coast.

The 1730s saw the French and Dutch join in the action; their huge ships began to unload tremendous quantities of goods on the west coast of Central Africa, which they supplied on credit (Isaacman 1966). At the same time, advances in European industrial technology led to the wide availability of cheap firearms. Ships also began to arrive directly from Brazil, seeking slaves to fuel that country's rapidly expanding plantation economy. Central African long-distance trade grew dramatically. Caravans of up to a thousand porters and merchants regularly traversed the Central African plateau, most destined for the Lunda capital. In their description of Musumba, the capital city, in 1882, when the empire was already on the wane, Capello and Ivens wrote of "vast markets, true bazaars containing straight lanes or streets where flour of various kinds, ginguba, palm oil, fresh and dried meat, massambala, salt, tobacco, maluvo (palm wine), mabellas, and other articles are displayed, and are bartered for merchandise, such as blue and red baize, cottons, printed calico, large white and small red beads, powder, arms and bracelets" (1882, 1:389). The Lunda polity was virtually the only one that could produce enough slaves to make the thousand-mile trek profitable. Likewise, it was virtually the only one with surplus marketable commodities sufficient to provision such large caravans. Food emerged increasingly as the key to maintaining the caravan system, and, more and more, that food was being produced in the less densely populated margins of the Lunda Empire rather than in the center. This development is especially significant for our purposes because the Kanongesha established his polity in one of these marginal areas, the upper Zambezi region, around this time, that is, approximately 1740 (Schecter 1976, chapt. 5). By some accounts the original aim of this prince from the royal court had been to find new salt pans to claim in the name of the Lunda Empire, while at the same time to endeavor to bring groups on the south and southeastern frontier of the Lunda polity more directly under the control of the center. Eventually he founded his own polity, which became well known for its production of cassava for the marketplace. The Kanongesha was a loyal, tribute-sending subject of the Lunda Empire whose title stood in perpetual relationship to that of the Mwantiyanvwa as "son." Because of the distance separating his polity from that of the Lunda Center, however, he was able to operate in a rather autonomous fashion.

Cassava was a relatively new plant in Central Africa at that time, having been introduced at the west coast by the Portuguese around 1600 (Jones 1959; Miracle 1967, chapt. 2). It is unclear exactly when cassava arrived among the Lunda, but it is associated in oral tradition with subsequent Lunda migrations and conquests. Cassava seems to have jumped over many peoples situated between the Lunda and the west coast. Perhaps others did not find the plant appealing; perhaps they did not recognize its potential value. The Lunda, however, would ultimately take the new plant to heart.

The acceptance of cassava revolutionized the farming calendar and created levels of food surplus that bolstered trade. Without cassava, Central African agriculture could probably not have sustained the volume of slave and other trade in the eighteenth and nineteenth centuries (Miracle 1967; Harms 1978). Cassava is more disease resistant and higher yielding than either millet or sorghum. Furthermore, unlike millet and sorghum, which must be planted just after the rains begin and harvested precisely when ripe, cassava can be planted throughout virtually the entire rainy season and can be left in the ground and harvested as needed up to a year and a half after it matures. Thus, groups who subsist primarily on cassava are not faced with the problem of mobilizing a large labor force at particular times; nor are they forced to store and protect their entire year's supply of food. Cassava left in the ground would not be nearly as attractive a target for raiders looking for a quick and easy supply of food as would be a community granary full of millet or sorghum—digging up and processing cassava roots into food is a time-consuming and arduous task, with processing alone taking up to two weeks. Also, because the edible portion of millet and sorghum is the seed, a compromise must be struck between how much to eat in any one year versus how much to save for the following year's planting. Expansion in production may be limited by the availability of seeds. Indeed, control over seeds implies the possibility of control over people. With cassava, however, it is portions of the nonedible stalk that are planted, and one stalk may be cut into any number of small pieces. Hence, there is always an excess of planting material from year to year, with no compromise in consumption required. Among groups that depend primarily on cassava, then, control over labor through control over the inputs of agriculture is virtually impossible. Nor is cooperation on a large scale for planting and harvesting necessary. Cassava is, in a sense, a very decentralizing crop. It can also be planted on soil that is too infertile to sustain either sorghum or millet production, such as the savanna woodland south of the central Lunda Empire. The Kanongesha, as well as others, recognized the potential of this vast region, which became the "breadbasket" of the caravan system.

The Early Kanongesha Polity

Oral tradition describes the Kanongesha's arrival on the upper Zambezi as part of the second phase of the Lunda diaspora. The supposed departure from the Lunda Center of Kinguri, Kinyama, and others in the sixteenth or seventeenth century was designated phase one. During the second phase, in the mid-eighteenth century, another set of so-called Lunda noblemen— Kazembe Mutanda, Musokatanda, Ishindi, Kazembe Luapula, and Kanongesha—began establishing polities well beyond the previous limits of the Lunda Empire (Schecter 1976, chapt. 2). Among them, only Kazembe Luapula, who settled in a well-watered area with abundant fish, was able to develop a high-density, highly centralized polity, much like a miniature Lunda empire. All the other branches of the Lunda family settled in woodland savanna areas where fishing resources were limited but land for cassava production was abundant. A constellation of autonomous politics emerged with varying degrees of contact with the Lunda center. Many adopted local place names or the name of a political leader. The Kanogesha and his people acquired the appellation Lunda-Ndembu for supposedly having settled along a similarly named stream. The development of each largely paralleled the development of the Kanongesha Lunda polity.

According to the traditions of the Kanongesha Lunda, the upper Zambezi had been populated by groups of people known as the Mbwela, a hunting and gathering people who were small in stature and had no permanent settlements.[4] Through warfare and alliances, the Kanongesha was eventually able to establish himself as the overlord of a large territory. He used the same techniques as had his brothers of the first diaspora as well as the leaders of the central Lunda polity itself: dispensing prestigious titles that linked local headmen to himself and indirectly to the central Lunda

Empire. He extended an umbrella of protection from slavery in exchange for tribute, which initially took the form of wives and forest products such as meat, ivory, and skins. These products provided him with goods of immediate value on the caravan circuit. The wives served the purpose of immediately linking the Kanongesha and his followers to the preexisting lineages, but, perhaps more important, they provided the Kanongesha with a large labor force to plant cassava. For by this time the largest market for foodstuffs in Central Africa, catering to the needs of caravans heading for the Lunda capital, had sprung up at Nana Candundo in the Lwena (Luvale) territory of Kinyama (Papstein 1978). This market lay on the southern route to the capital, the route most preferred by the Ovimbundu, who were now the organizers of the largest caravans.[5] The Kanongesha evidently fought at least two unsuccessful wars with his Luvale brothers in an attempt to gain physical control over this market town, which was perhaps a two-day walk from his capital, before finally being content to be merely one of the major suppliers of cassava and other goods and services to that market.

By the mid-nineteenth century, the Kanongesha polity was well defined territorially and structurally. It consisted of lineage headmen possessing a wide array of titles and royal functions linking them to the Kanongesha at the center. These headmen periodically collected tribute in the name of the Kanongesha, keeping some for themselves and forwarding the rest to him. The Kanongesha in turn sent a portion of this tribute on to the Lunda Center, keeping some for himself. As a result, the Lunda Center with its roving armies of tribute collectors left the Kanongesha's polity in peace. But the slash-and-burn method of extensive cassava production in an area of abundant vacant land did not lend itself to the development of a high-density capital city, and the Kanongesha's royal functionaries continued to reside in their own areas. Thus he had no standing army, although he did have a war councillor who had the authority to raise sufficient personnel from the lineages to meet any outside threat (Schecter 1976, 203–5). But during this period there was apparently little need to mobilize an army. The Kanongesha's chief function seems to have been as final arbiter of disputes between lineages, keeping the peace so that all could prosper through the sale of cassava and other goods and services. As the individual with the most retainers, wives, and children, and hence the largest producer of cassava, the Kanongesha was the wealthiest man in his territory. The local caravans heading to the market at Nana Candundo traveled under his protection.

Meanwhile, on the coast of Angola, events were transpiring that would shake the Lunda Empire to its very foundation and eventually lead to its complete destruction. In 1836, after having outlawed the slave trade, the Portuguese attempted to stimulate the production of ivory as an alternative source of revenue. They abolished the previously imposed government monopoly on ivory, allowing the artificially low fixed price to rise. Immediately the price of ivory shot up by 300 percent, and it continued to rise in subsequent decades.[6] In Africa the ivory and slave trades had always gone hand in hand. The transport of ivory required much labor, and the cheaper the labor the bigger the profit realized upon reaching the coast. As the value of ivory skyrocketed, there appeared to be no end to the numbers of traders and raiders who were prepared to go any distance to find ivory and to any lengths to acquire slaves to transport that ivory. Central Africa became embroiled in war as groups fought one another in mad pursuit of slaves to exchange for guns with which to protect themselves against the slaving activities of others. An era of fear and instability set in. By the 1880s the Lunda capital itself was being overrun by better armed Chokwe groups from the west (Miller 1969).

The Kanongesha Lunda at first reacted defensively, concentrating themselves in large fortified villages in much the same way that Lueiji supposedly had done when threatened by her brothers Kinguri and Kinyama. But a different set of circumstances now prevailed. The Kanongesha Lunda soon found that large collections of poorly armed people served only to attract slave raiders. The Lunda political and economic structures completely broke down as people began dispersing into the bush to live in small mobile units, ever ready to flee at the approach of slaving parties. It would appear that the Mbwela heritage of the Kanongesha Lunda served them well during this period, when they were forced to survive by hunting and gathering (Schecter 1976, chapt. 8).

Somehow, in 1896, the Lunda were able to regroup and drive the Chokwe from their land. On the upper Zambezi, the effort was led not by a chief but by a commoner named Chipenge who traveled throughout the territory urging people to make a concerted effort to fight the invaders (Crawford 1912, 116; Tilsley 1929, 104–5). The Kanongeshaship and the prior mode of village organization had barely been reestablished before Great Britain and Portugal, in 1906, settled their lengthy dispute over the exact position of the border that was to separate the new colony of Angola from that of Northern Rhodesia. As it turned out, that line ran right through the middle of the Kanongesha's territory. The following year, when officers of the British South Africa Company arrived to begin administering the district they would eventually call Mwinilunga, the Lunda fled en masse out of the company's reach into Angola. But before long Portuguese troops began to arrive on their side of the border to assert control over eastern Angola, and some of the Lunda began to filter back to Northern Rhodesia. When the British South Africa Company introduced taxation in 1913, the Lunda fled a second time. However, the Portuguese soon began their own harsh program of taxation and forced labor, and, thus, many of the Lunda again returned to Northern Rhodesia. After nearly four decades of running, the Lunda finally began to resettle in villages. The remnants of the Central African long-distance trade network were eradicated through the combined effort of the various colonial forces.[7] This trade no longer served their interests, since their new agenda was to gain sufficient control over colonial territories to be able to expropriate labor and resources for the benefit of each individual metropole. Colonial territories were also expected to serve as captive markets for the surplus productive capacity of their European rulers.

The Lunda under British Rule

At the turn of the twentieth century the British government was extremely reluctant to become involved in the affairs of Central Africa. The region did not seem essential to British imperial interests, and it was felt that an infusion of taxpayers' money into an area with unknown potential was not justified. The British thrust into Central Africa was financed and organized by private capital in the form of a charter company, the British South Africa Company (BSAC) (Galbraith 1974). Formed in 1889 and headed by Cecil Rhodes, the BSAC held exclusive rights to all governmental and economic activities in the huge territory that became known as the colonies of Northern Rhodesia, Southern Rhodesia, and Nyasaland. Northern Rhodesia, the territory within which the Kanongesha Lunda resided, was regarded from the beginning as a vast labor reserve, best suited to fuel the economies of more developed British areas to the south. Taxation and brutal coercion were the primary tools used to wrench African labor power from village economies and redirect it to European plantations and mines elsewhere. The infamous hut tax was placed on the Lunda in 1913. Every adult male was required to pay a cash levy of ten shillings annually for his principle domicile and that of his wife or wives. To insure that the tax accomplished its objective of producing a steady stream of cheap labor, the BSAC eliminated alternative methods by which Africans could acquire cash. Hunting was banned in some areas and severely curtailed in others. The production of surplus agricultural commodities for the market was banned. The production of salt was stopped. Much of the local craft production was taxed out of existence (Hall 1965; Roberts 1976, 174–82). Furthermore, where employment was available, Africans were paid extremely low wages. It was a widespread assumption that Africans needed only enough money to pay taxes and perhaps buy a few clothes. Paternalistic employers urged Africans to maintain their traditional way of life, to look to their own tribesmen for basic support and security in sickness and old age. Long-term employment was discouraged or disallowed outright for fear that it would break village bonds and produce that most dreaded of all creatures, the detribalized African (see Berger 1974). Thus, while 30 to 50 percent of all able-bodied males were away from the village at any one time, their cash returns were too small to even maintain, let alone transform, the village economies from which they came. The process of rural decay set in.

In retrospect, it seems odd that missionaries and anthropologists following on the heels of colonial forces so brutally restructuring a continent could have proceeded to write about so-called timeless, traditional African societies. Many of the early characterizations of specific African groups as subsistence cultivators, hunters and gatherers, or herders, do not adequately reflect traditional pursuits at all, and certainly do not reflect desired pursuits. They simply indicate the limited options available after the cataclysmic upheavals of the eighteenth, nineteenth, and early twentieth centuries. Lunda history, replete with evidence of occupational diversity, is an apt example. Fishermen, hunters, traders, plunderers of caravans, commercial agriculturalists, and even cattle herders at one point,[8] they have come to be known through the anthropological literature as subsistence cultivators and hunters (Turner 1957, 20). Yet little has been written about the diminished diversity and impoverishment of Lunda society that resulted from the BSAC's policy of labor acquisition and control. These facts hold important implications for any analysis of the inner workings of Lunda social structure. History refutes the assertions of those who see the Lunda as an example of a closed predicament, cyclical society with rigid social and belief systems, composed of unreflective, nonexperimenting social actors (Gluckman 1956, 1963). Although Turner may initially have been allied with the group that shared this viewpoint, he ultimately concluded that no societies, including the Lunda, fit this model: "There never were any innocent unconscious savages, living in a state of unreflective and instinctive harmony. We human beings are all and always sophisticated, conscious, capable of laughter at our own institutions, inventing our lives collectively as we go on, playing games, performing our own being" (cited in Ashley 1990, xix).

The Lunda have demonstrated a remarkable capacity for experimenting with and modifying all their systems in response to both external pressures and internal desires. And as will be shown throughout this work, they have successfully maintained the capacity, in their own heads at least, to create autonomous conceptual models of their rapidly changing world and to generate responses informed and justified by long-standing traditions. As Fergus Macpherson showed in *Anatomy of a Conquest: The British Occupation of Zambia, 1884–1924* (1981), the Lunda found numerous ways of maintaining autonomy over various aspects of their lives even when confronted by the harshest British instruments of subjugation.

When the BSAC, as the result of numerous public scandals, was forced to turn its control of Northern Rhodesia over to the British Colonial Office in 1924, it left behind a legacy of rural economies so dysfunctional that becoming migrant laborers continued to be the only way for most Lunda males to acquire certain goods now deemed essential for the maintenance of village life. In the 1930s the Great Depression wreaked havoc on the fragile colonial economy, reducing the demand for labor. Migration did not cease entirely, but many more young men remained in the rural areas. The Kanongesha Lunda focused on developing a diversified subsistence-oriented economy. They planted cassava during the rainy season and practiced intensive horticulture in streamside gardens during the dry season. They hunted and trapped and fished. They collected wild fruits and vegetables, as well as edible insects. They made artificial beehives, gathered wild honey, and processed wax. They produced a small output of crafts both for local use and for sale to the increasing numbers of European missionaries and administrators flocking to the territory. This was as remarkably diversified a subsistence economy as any ever described in the anthropological literature. The capacity to produce surplus cassava remained greatly underutilized, however, and this factor would continue to loom large in the Lunda's economic relations with the world economy. We shall return to this point often as we continue our analysis of the changing patterns of Lunda social and economic structures.

An important development during the era of British rule was the reassertion of the Kanongeshaship as the focal point of Lunda political life. This might have occurred even without British interference; indeed, it was beginning to do so in the few years between the expulsion of the Chokwe and the coming of the British. The process was reinforced, however, by the British concept of indirect rule, which required strong chiefs and local headmen to cut the costs of colonial rule (see Gifford and Louis 1971; also Hall 1965, chapt. 3). British administrators and soldiers were relatively expensive. Wars of pacification against rebellious groups were even more so. If local areas could be left to produce their own leaders who could in turn be made to serve British interests, the cost of administering vast colonial territories would be greatly reduced. Initially, of course, it would be necessary for the British to demonstrate the overwhelming force at their disposal. So just as colonial powers did elsewhere in Africa, the British burned down some Lunda villages, shot some people, and occasionally held wives and children hostage in a calculated display to show the futility of resistance.

After 1924, however, the British moved quickly to establish peace under an indirect-rule system that supposedly would result in minimum interference in the day-to-day lives of people. Toward that end the British recognized the Kanongesha as the highest ranking Lunda chief in the district of Mwinilunga. The district was divided into administrative areas, and the senior subordinate of the Kanongesha in each area was allowed to rule under the title of Native Authority chief.[9] The Kanongesha himself was given a large area in the center of Mwinilunga as his personal realm. Furthermore, each of the colonially recognized chiefs was given a salary, which, although very small by contemporary British standards, roughly six pounds a year, was nevertheless a substantial sum in an area where British money had not previously circulated and yet was now desperately needed to pay taxes and to purchase goods—some novel, some previously acquired through trade with caravans from the west. Consequently, not only were the chiefs themselves spared the indignity of becoming migrant laborers seeking tax money, but they received sufficient cash to insure that many members of their families were spared as well. In addition, each chief was given a certain number of paid retainers, who could likewise safeguard individuals of their choosing from the drudgery of moving about seeking cash.[10] Around each chief's capital village gathered a large core of followers currying favors and seeking employment, trying to avoid the vagaries of the migrant labor system. There were of course many disputes in the early days over the process of selecting Native Authority chiefs. The Kanongesha had many subordinates who were of more or less equal rank. He lobbied heavily for the appointment of as many of those subordinates as possible. The British, however, had their own notions concerning the number of chiefs necessary to effectively administer a district as sparsely populated as Mwinilunga. A few changes were, in fact, made in the early years. Some chiefs were dismissed, either because they were felt to be redundant or because their loyalties or abilities were suspect. The boundaries of some chiefs' areas were changed as better estimates of population became available. Eventually the British settled on a five-chief system that to a large extent remains intact up to the present day. In addition to the Kanongesha, the other chiefs were the Ikelenge, the Nyakaseya, the Mwiniyilamba, and the Chibwika. The chiefs, in exchange for their salaries and retainers, were entrusted with the responsibility of maintaining an adequate census of their followers, making sure that taxes were paid in a timely fashion, and maintaining the peace in their areas by trying small offenses themselves and turning major offenders over to that now all-powerful figure, the district commissioner.[11]

If one were to evaluate the Lunda political system under British rule by listening to the Lunda's own oral history, one could easily arrive at the conclusion, as some have, that colonization had minimal structural impact—that the British merely recognized the system in place at the time of their arrival. The oral history of each of the Kanongesha's subordinate chiefs states that his own lineage ancestor arrived on the upper Zambezi with the first Kanongesha, fought side by side with him against the indigenous Mbwela, and was thus awarded his present territory. Without even questioning these statements of dubious veracity it is, nevertheless, undeniable that with the coming of the British, fundamental changes occurred in the nature of chieftaincy. Chiefly power not only extended from an entirely different source but manifested itself in entirely different ways in the day-to-day lives of the people. The power of the Kanongesha and his subordinates originally extended from their association with the mighty armies of the Mwantiyanvwa, which had the ability to destroy, enslave, or offer protection from the slave trade. But the British had abolished the Central African slave trade, and the Mwantiyanvwa, for all his symbolic value, had become a resident of a neighboring country, Congo, with little real power of his own. Previously the Kanongesha had been expected to remain an "objective outsider," dispassionately resolving cases brought to him by disputing lineage heads.[12] Now he became an extension of the British administration, forcibly intervening into the lives of his subjects, ensuring that British laws were followed and taxes paid. Individuals or entire lineages had in the past been able to move at will, establishing new villages in places they decided were advantageous. Under British rule, by contrast, vast tracts of land were set aside as protected forests and Crown lands, areas of possible European settlement. For taxation and labor control purposes, Africans were allowed to move only to registered villages. Chiefs were entrusted with enforcing these rules. Previously a chief's wealth had rested either on the receipt of tribute or the control of labor power to produce commodities for the caravan trade. Now it was based on the receipt of cash and the concomitant ability to protect chosen individuals from the harsher aspects of British rule and from the drudgery of life without money in an increasingly monetary economy.

Little about this system could be called traditional.[13] At Musumba during the height of the imperial stage, titled officials, not hereditary kin, were the foundation of the overarching structure that gave the Lunda their sense of unity. Although the relationship between many titled officials and the emperor was expressed in a kinship idiom, the emperor could create new positions or depose the holder of old ones. Hereditary relations were primarily used to reckon succession to ritual offices that were mostly concerned with appeasing ancestors. But the tribute collectors, the heads of the military force, and the councillors and advisors to the emperor—the backbone of the national structure—were unrelated people who had acquired titles through special service to the emperor or in exchange for tribute and pledges of loyalty that brought their followers into the Lunda fold. Once an individual received a title, future holders of that title would generally be chosen from among the heirs of that individual. Titles could be passed along either matrilineal or patrilineal lines. The title of emperor, or Mwantiyanvwa, was passed patrilineally, whereas most other titles were passed matrilineally. But all succession to major titled positions was subject to the Mwantiyanvwa's approval. The Kanongesha and a host of other Lunda émigrés had all attempted to use the central Lunda model in establishing their own independent, or semi-independent, polities on the frontier. We find among the Kanongesha Lunda individuals possessing titles virtually identical to those extant at the Lunda Center at the time the Kanongesha established his polity in the 1740s (see figure). These titles

Kanongesha titles	Musumba titles
Tubanji war leaders executioners	Tubanji war leaders executioners councillors
Tulula removes royal mats	Tulula councillors, various other roles
Chivwikankanu installer	Nswana Murund installer
Kalala war leader watches tribute	Kalala war leader
Ifota pathfinder, chooses site for capital	
Tubungu spreads royal mats keeps royal graves	Tubungu installation ritual leader
Kanampumba head of court	Kanampumb council head interregnal role
Mazembe resident of rear of capital	Mazembe councillors military functions
Nswana Mulopu heir apparent deputy of senior titleholder	Nswana Murop deputy prime minister war leader
Mwadi senior wife	Mwadi perpetual wife in charge of royal tombs
Chota builds council house, watches tribute	Chot chief of palaver house

Comparison of Contemporary Kanongesha Lunda Titles with Those Known to
Have Existed at the Lunda Empire Capital (see Schecter 1976, 203–4).

never achieved the level of prominence obtained by their counterparts at Musumba because the Kanongesha Lunda themselves were never able to achieve a comparable level of centralization or tribute flow.

For the better part of three centuries, the central Lunda polity pursued an expansionist agenda not just out of desire but, perhaps, also out of necessity. In many respects it was similar to those pyramid schemes that require the constant incorporation of new participants at the bottom in order to feed resources to those players higher up. Once a system such as the expansionist tributary system of the Lunda ceased to expand, those trapped on the bottom rung had little incentive to be totally loyal to the state; if they were numerous enough, controlling them could strain the military force of the state. There are many examples in Central African history of states that were able to achieve incredible levels of centralization and amass fabulous wealth as long as they were expanding (Vansina 1966; Miller 1969, 1988; Reefe 1981). However, once a state reached the limits of expansion either by exhausting its resource base or by not being able to retain effective military control, a process of rapid involution occurred and the polity quickly collapsed upon itself. The Kanongesha polity, however, constrained on three sides by other Lunda-style polities endeavoring themselves to expand and on the fourth side by the tenacious Mbwela group, was never able to cross the threshold to become a full-fledged tributary state. But evidence of the attempt to do so remained embedded in titles that, although conferring little power, were handed down from generation to generation as mnemonic devices linking the Kanongesha Lunda to their Musumban roots. The titles of the Kanongesha's four subchiefs, Ikelenge, Nyakaseya, Mwiniyilamba, and Chibwika, however, are a development unique to the upper Zambezi context. These positions did not exist in the Central Lunda polity, yet it was this relatively recent political innovation that was institutionalized by British indirect rule as "traditional."

The concept of tradition has long played an important role in legitimating authority in Britain. The monarchy, common law, and the class system all rest on the assumption that that which is traditional and long-standing is right and proper. British administrators, in their attempt to develop a framework for ruling Africa, were predisposed to seek out facets of African society that could be labeled traditional. Yet, in codifying and promulgating what they understood to be traditional, they were in effect replacing fluid and flexible custom with rigid unyielding laws. Many recent studies concur that the societies of precolonial Africa did not lack internal social and economic competition, and that the authority of chiefs and elders did not go unchallenged. Nor was each person firmly embedded in a rigid matrix of rights and duties, privileges and responsibilities, ordained by the ancestors and re-created in each succeeding generation. In fact the very concept of society or group is much more problematic than once thought. As Ranger noted,

Far from there being a single tribal identity, most Africans moved in and out of multiple identities, defining themselves at one moment as subjects to this chief, at another moment as a member of that cult, at another moment as part of this clan, and yet another as an initiate in that professional guild. These overlapping networks of association and exchange extended over wide areas. Thus the boundaries of the tribal polity and the hierarchies of authorities within them did not define conceptual horizons of Africans. . . . Competition, movement, fluidity were as much features of small-scale communities as they were of larger groupings. (1983, 248)

In freezing the flow of history and designating one particular point in time as traditional, the British were not acting alone. They sought and often received the assistance of local powerful figures. Chiefs and headmen, recognizing the limitations of the new colonial reality, would seek to lock in as many of their current privileges as possible. Collaboration was a practical matter of maximizing benefits. Once the new tradition had been established, it became the reality against which future local dynamics would be acted out. Males seeking privileges vis-à-vis females, elders vis-à-vis the young, long-term residents vis-à-vis recent arrivals would all cite the tradition as their authority.

The British did, for the most part, allow the Lunda to choose succeeding chiefs in their own manner. The district commissioner, however, could veto the choice if he felt that it was unsatisfactory. Nevertheless, the use of local titled chiefs as the agents of British policy played an important role in shaping the dynamics of political processes in Mwinilunga. Five chiefs operating alone could not possibly keep an eye on twenty thousand people in three thousand square miles of savanna woodlands. The chiefs therefore relied heavily on the cooperation of local headmen. Most local headmen in turn, either by virtue of belonging to a lineage that had formerly been invested with some title or by having established linkages via tributary wives, stood in relationship to one or more of the chiefs, or even to the Kanonge-sha himself, as either potential successor or royal functionary. Previously this had had only limited importance, for during the era of long-distance trade any headman, or any ambitious individual for that matter, who could assemble an adequate labor force could prosper through trade. But under the British, the options were severely limited. One had to either find a paid position in the new political structure dominated by the Native Authority chiefs or become a migrant laborer. As would be expected, the competition for any traditionally acknowledged headmanship, with its potential of succeeding to the salaried position of Native Authority chief, became fierce. The preoccupation with lineage affiliation and lines of descent grew into an obsession. Even men who spent a large part of their lives away from the village as migrant laborers returned as often as they could, strategically using their cash to gain supporters in an eventual bid for headmanship. This era was dominated by intrigue, collusion, and rampant accusations of witchcraft upon the death of any chief, headman, or potential successor.[14] The situation was further complicated by the fact that until the late 1800s the Kanongesha had succeeded patrilineally. Only recently had the mode of succession been changed to conform to the matrilineal succession pattern of lineage headmen.[15] Many argued for a return to the older system, where succession to offices was reckoned through either the male or the female line. By that system, nearly every man could make a claim on some traditionally royal position. Most, in fact, did.

The dynamics occurring at this particular time had a profound impact on Victor Turner's perception of Lunda processes and were instrumental in shaping the model he would present to the world as epitomizing the traditional Lunda way of life. In the following chapters I attempt to go beyond those early static perceptions by resituating Lunda processes within their larger Central African context.

Chapter Two

People and the Environment

Sambalu's House Burns
Dry Season, June 1992

Kenneth Kaunda's twenty-seven-year reign as president of Zambia had been brought to an end seven months earlier by the rise of Frederick Chiluba and his new party, the Movement for Multiparty Democracy. Exhilaration and anxiety commingled as debates raged over the precise meaning of democracy and what it would mean for the complex array of overlapping interest groups that make up the Zambian citizenry. Competing definitions vied for the spotlight. For many of the people of Mwinilunga, and rural dwellers elsewhere as well, democracy meant something quite basic and tangible: development. It was hoped that democracy would bring new flows of resources and opportunities into the neglected rural areas. For particular classes in the urban areas, however, democracy meant freedom of economic movement, freedom from the economic constraints of the old regime, and the opening up of new areas for investing capital. Government parastatals that dominated much of the economy under the old regime were being rapidly dismantled under instructions from the World Bank and the International Monetary Fund. Currency and import/export laws were being rewritten. A new regulatory environment was being created. There was much talk in the capital city of the need for land reform. The disposition of most of the available land in Zambia was still largely in the hands of government-sanctioned traditional chiefs. There was a major push in some quarters for the development of a new system of land dispensation and registration that would provide security of land tenure unrelated to the whims of the chiefs. A movement for a comprehensive process of land reregistration was gaining momentum, both as a prelude to a national conference on land policy and as a political tool for gathering information about the land holdings of former government officials and their associates.

When word reached Mwinilunga that the new government might soon require all individuals to officially register their land holdings, it was not well received. In an area where shifting cultivation is the norm and whole villages might change sites during the dry season, land registration seemed a needless constraint. Mwinilunga has an average population density of only six people per square mile and a long history of chiefs who understood the need and the desire for periodic change. It was generally felt that a land registration policy would be a transgression of the fundamental freedom of movement, as well as an affront to chiefly authority.

Brother Joe, an American Franciscan friar at Lwawu mission station, had a different set of concerns. The mission was perhaps the only entity in Chief Kanongesha's core area that actually possessed a freehold title to land. It had been registered when the mission was established in 1948. The mission's holdings had been surveyed and its title updated when the first independent government came to power in 1964. But since then, the mission had expanded greatly as each new friar and priest made his own mark on the landscape. Brother Tony had constructed fishponds along the Lwawu River. Father Efisio had built pigpens and chicken runs and had expanded the garden. Brother Louis, with external funding, had dammed the Lwawu River, installed a small hydroelectric plant, and run electricity to the dozen or so buildings that comprised the mission station. Brother Joe had taken up cattle rearing and had fenced in large grazing areas. The majority of the mission now lay outside the titled area, on land over which only usufruct rights had been granted by Chief Kanongesha. The expatriate-owned mission station had fared quite well under the old system. Brother Joe thus shared the local anxiety about the potential impact of a new land registration exercise. He decided to take the initiative by having the expanded mission property surveyed and attempting to gain a new freehold title in advance of any formal government action. He was well aware that both surveyors and government officials had a predilection for land bounded by straight lines. But the mission's boundaries had grown fuzzy over the years; they had become Africanized in a sense. Mission land abutted and intermingled with African gardens. African goats grazed on the mission lawns. In deciding where straight lines should be drawn, no doubt debates would arise from numerous sources. Brother Joe needed help. Clearly this was a job for Sambalu.

Jassman Sambalu was in his mid-thirties, married with two young children. He was tall, handsome, well liked by all, and extremely fortunate. He had come of age at a time when the mission at Lwawu first began offering high-quality secondary education to a select few African youths. Sambalu was among the first group to attend the Catholic boarding school, where all instruction was given by expatriate teachers, exclusively in English. He had been a top student in both academic and technical subjects, mastering English with fluency and style. After traveling and working in other parts of Zambia for years he had recently returned to Mwinilunga, where he had settled in as a lay leader in the local Catholic church and as the truck driver for the mission. He was perhaps the highest paid of the very few salaried workers in the area.

Sambalu was also extremely fortunate in that he was the grandson of the senior Lunda chief who had reigned before the present Kanongesha. Sambalu had been raised at the court as one of his grandfather's favorites, accompanying him virtually everywhere, and he had come to possess the old-style manners of a courtier, with the distinctive hand, head, and body movements that looked especially elegant when performed by graceful young men. Sambalu was well versed in proverbs, traditional jurisprudence, and royal diplomacy, and he was widely acknowledged as a "sweet talker." Brother Joe would need some sweet talk. He selected Sambalu to assist him in marking the mission boundaries.

After nearly thirty years in Mwinilunga, Brother Joe was as sensitive to issues of flexible access to land as any native-born Lunda. For him, the exercise in marking boundaries was merely a legalistic formality for securing documentation of the mission's right to remain in the area. It was not intended to signal any change in the mission's land usage. But at one point, Brother Joe and Sambalu were seen measuring a line that ran through the middle of Teddy Machayi's garden. Later, someone said that Teddy had been drinking heavily and complaining boisterously that Sambalu had no right to give away his land to the Catholics. Others saw Teddy staggering up and down the road shouting derisively that Sambalu was behaving as if he were the new chief. Late that night, the dry thatched roof on Sambalu's house near the mission ignited like a match. The family barely escaped with their lives. Most of their possessions were consumed by the fire.

No one actually saw Teddy put the torch to Sambalu's house. Teddy denied any involvement. Sambalu built a new house on his farm a mile away from the mission. Teddy fell seriously ill a few days after the incident and remained so for months. Some say Sambalu was responsible for the illness. The mission's application for a new deed is still pending.

Fire and Rain: The Seasons of Life

The environment from a Lunda-Ndembu perspective is first and foremost land, and all that affects the land. The environment is not simply the stage on which social actors construct their drama of life; it is an active participant in that drama. The environment reacts to human action and, at times, throws out its own surprises to which humans must react in turn. Thus, it is difficult to talk about the relationship that links people and environment, for in reality there is no way to separate the two. Inextricably bound, each changes only in tandem with the other.

The Central African plateau is a landscape largely shaped by fire. Centuries of slash-and-burn agriculture, as well as occasional naturally occurring dry-season fires, have resulted in a balance of flora and fauna that are adapted to, and dependent on, the actions of humans. For example, there has been a proliferation of tree species that are fire resistant but have extremely hard seed-casings that explode with the arrival of fire; the seeds then germinate in the rich ash deposits that blanket the earth after the fire. Many of these species are fragrant bloomers that attract bees, which support the local honey and wax industries. Annual fires in low-lying valleys with moisture-holding clay soils favor fast-growing grasses at the expense of trees, thereby satisfying the local need for thatching grass and for thicker reeds to use for making mats and baskets. Such grasslands also attract the animals on which Lunda hunters prey. Thus, the natural landscape has been shaped and conditioned in tandem with human action.[1] The environment, however, can pose challenges to people's customary ways of doing things. Oscillations in rainfall patterns or the sudden appearance of new pests may mandate new approaches. The revelation of new resources such as salt, iron, copper, or other valuable deposits may radically alter local subsistence strategies by presenting opportunities too precious to ignore.

The three-thousand-square-mile region that constitutes Lunda-Ndembu territory, which for the most part is equivalent to the western half of Mwinilunga District of the Northwestern Province, is situated on a plateau whose undulating surface rises and falls in altitude between four thousand and five thousand feet. The vegetation and soil types are generally described as northern *Brachystegia* woodlands on clayey plateau soils in the northern one-third of the territory, northern *Brachystegia* woodlands on Kalahari Contact soils in the central portion of the territory, and *Cryptosepalum* forest and *Cryptosepalum-Brachystegia* woodlands on upland

and central sands in the south (Trapnell and Clothier 1937). To the untrained eye the terrain of Mwinilunga appears to be a relatively homogeneous blanket of rolling forest, broken in places by streams, cleared land for villages and gardens, and the occasional stretch of grasslands. But to the Lunda, who know the names and characteristics of every tree, shrub, and blade of grass, the landscape is broken up into myriad microecological niches: *ivunda* is thick forest; *ikuna*, forest of low stunted trees; *itu*, gallery forest that grows along rivers; *chana*, grassy plains; *lusesa*, sparse shrub land at the edge of plains; and so forth.[2] With a detailed terminology that indicates minor variations in the landscape, the Lunda can navigate to or describe to one another discrete locations in the deep forest as precisely as urban dwellers might describe the location of a specific building in the city.

The most striking features on the landscape are the omnipresent termite mounds, ranging up to ten feet or more in height, and the human architecture which uses the clay in those mounds for the basic building material. Using hoes, people pulverize termite mounds into a fine powder which they mix with water and then mold into rather large bricks that are sun baked for a couple of weeks or more. The bricks are stacked up, with wet clay as mortar, to form square or rectangular houses. A wedge-shaped frame of wood and bamboo poles is affixed to the top, and an extremely fine grass thatching is attached using long strands of pliable tree bark fibers. The top ridge of a thatched roof is usually double or triple lashed with carefully trimmed bark fibers, insuring water tightness and imparting an appealing geometric design to the roof. The color of the clay and the shape of the roof combine to give a finished house the appearance of a gigantic mushroom sprouting from the earth. Situated beside or behind each house is usually a smaller structure that serves as the cooking hut. It may have the appearance of a miniature house or it may be a circular pole-and-clay structure, reminiscent of the Lunda's older housing style. For every collection of dwellings that constitute a village there is one centrally placed structure know as a *chota*. A circular arrangement of thick vertical poles, topped by a conical grass roof, it is the place to which men gravitate to talk, drink, and pass the time, and the place where the whole village meets when there are important topics to be addressed. In the past, villages were built as circles around the *chota* (Turner 1957, 10). Today, they tend to be lined up along roads and major paths, sometimes forming unbroken strings of dwellings for up to a mile or more, clustered at crossroads or, most often, around chiefs' capital villages, the villages of long-standing senior headmen, and

Christian mission stations. There are also collections of villages around the
district government administrative center, known as the *Boma*. But the residents of the Boma, with its collection of government offices, shops, markets, schools, and churches, tend to be government employees, a handful
of wealthy businessmen, and a few long-established missionaries, most of
whom are not Lunda.

There are three rather distinct seasons in Mwinilunga. *Nvula*, the rainy
season, runs from roughly September to April, during which time forty to
seventy inches of rain may fall. May to July is *chishika*, the cold dry season,
when the temperature regularly drops down to around forty degrees
Fahrenheit and night frost sometimes occurs in low-lying valleys. August
to September is *nonga*, the hot dry season, with temperatures regularly
soaring into the nineties.

The rainy season is the time for planting cassava. Most villages are virtually empty during the day as nearly every man, woman, and child who can
walk is busy in the fields hoeing up mounds and inserting cassava sticks.
Beans, groundnuts, pumpkins, yams, and other vegetable crops are typically planted around the base of cassava mounds. In all, nearly one hundred
different crops are grown in Mwinilunga. Hunting, the quintessential male
activity, becomes progressively poorer as the rainy season progresses. The
availability of green plants everywhere allows the animals to disperse widely,
and the tall elephant grass provides them with excellent cover. Most men
cease all attempts at hunting and focus primarily instead on cultivation.
Likewise, the swollen rivers and streams, loaded with organic matter, yield
poor fish catches. Thus, although the rainy season is a time of agricultural
abundance, as well as a time of plentiful wild fruits, berries, and mushrooms, it is also the time of *dikwilu*, meat hunger. April could be dubbed
the "illness season" or even the "fighting season." The combination of
sheer exhaustion from the long planting season, the low protein intake, and
the abundance of malaria-carrying mosquitoes takes its toll, resulting in an
unusually large number of individuals lying around the village incapaci-
tated.[3] Tempers flare, accusations are made, arguments ensue, fights break
out, and at times it appears that nearly everybody is dissatisfied with their
present living arrangements and is threatening to their leave village-mates
and build elsewhere. When the rains cease in May, it is time for those who
were serious about such threats to act. With only four months before the
rains begin anew, all new clay brick construction must be quickly completed. Those who procrastinate run the risk of having their unroofed or

half-completed houses reduced to useless globs of clay. Although far more people threaten to move each year than actually do so, an amazing rearrangement of villages and village personnel actually does take place each dry season. Whole new villages spring up; old ones are reduced to shadows of their former selves. Much time is spent merely keeping abreast of who is moving where, with whom, and for what reason.

For those not building new houses, the dry season can be a time of relative leisure. It is the period for visiting relatives in distant parts of the district, or even in Angola or Congo. Women have time to distill lots of alcoholic beverages. Boys' and girls' initiation ceremonies, curing rituals for those who are still ill, weddings, and other events, all of which are accompanied by great feasting and drinking, add a sense of merriment to the dry season. As the dry season progresses the tall grass turns brown, and eventually spectacular brush fires sweep across the landscape. Wild animals again become concentrated along the rivers where they are easy prey for Lunda hunters. As rivers and streams dry up, fish are more easily trapped in shallow pools by young girls with fishing baskets. Meat and fish, along with alcohol, are in great supply in every village, and people grow healthy and robust again. But by September, the prolonged heat, choking dust, and dwindling supply of vegetables have people again looking forward to the coming of the rains. Such is the annual cycle of life in Mwinilunga.

Fields and Forest: Commodities and Connections

The relationship between people and environment in Mwinilunga is immediate, direct, and complex. Few manufacturing processes or institutions of commercial exchange mediate between people and essential products. The need for poles, bamboo, bark fiber, thatching grass, good clays, and reeds for mats and baskets can be fulfilled only by direct access to perhaps a dozen different microecological niches. The environment is the source of nutrition in the form of meat, fruit, berries, mushrooms, honey, greens, tubers, caterpillars, and other delicacies. The environment is the local apothecary, fully stocked with health-producing and -maintaining substances extracted from plants, animals, and minerals. For those with the appropriate esoteric knowledge, the environment can also provide *yitumbu*, power substances—medicines used for doing or revealing evil, for attracting good fortune, or for communicating with those in the unseen world.

In the past, the environment was also the source of local currencies, which is in turn the provider of units of exchange, standards of value, and stores of wealth. It was directly from the environment that the Lunda extracted the commodities that linked them in networks of exchange with neighbors, adjacent peoples, and ultimately both the Atlantic and Indian Ocean trade blocs (see von Oppen 1993). Locally generated currencies identified by historians included at various times dried fish, copper, salt, raffia cloth, cassava, ivory, rubber, oils, dried meat, honey, and wax. The shifting nature of Central African currencies and their impact on local social formations and external relations cannot be stressed too strongly. Indeed, much of Central African history between the sixteenth and twentieth centuries was about articulating European economies, whose currencies were based primarily on precious metals, with African economies, whose currencies were based primarily on items of use-value (see Miller 1988; von Oppen 1993). The Lunda-Ndembu became active players in this search for modes of articulation. During the last three centuries they have been continually involved in the process of negotiating and renegotiating terms of trade with the outside world. This process has entailed both an external struggle for position within an ever-changing set of market conditions and internal struggles to redefine the division of labor between young and old, but perhaps even more especially between males and females.

Participation in the wide-ranging import/export economy required lots of male labor. Yet no shortages of food production are mentioned in the literature as a result of shifts in labor allocation. No doubt this is because of the exceptional productive capacity of women and the close link between male activities aimed at producing for export and those aimed at producing for the regional food supply. Although it was the product of female labor, processed cassava, that fueled those who conducted the trade, the most valuable items from the local area that flowed overseas via international trade networks were by-products of customary male forest activities. Male dry-season hunting expeditions produced meat and other wild foods for the village, as well as ivory, wild rubber, oil-bearing plants, honey, and wax for the market. Even today, when groups of men head out into the bush for a few days, they almost never define their aim as narrowly as "going hunting." They most often say *mwaya mwisanga*, "we are going into the bush."

Men almost invariably go into the bush in groups of five or six adults, with one or two young boys. The first order of business is shelter. Some men maintain semipermanent structures on a campsite to which they frequently return, but a structure sufficiently sturdy to provide protection from rain and wind can be put together in about an hour or so. Branches and bamboo for a frame, tall grass for covering, and bark rope for lashing the structure together are abundant materials in the bush. Even young boys are quite skillful at building different types of structures suitable for different seasons. Rarely do all the men hunt together as a group. While one or two strike out to track game, one might go fishing, one set up bird and rodent traps, and one remain in camp keeping a fire going, fresh water available, and a pot ready to cook anything his mates might capture. Duties rotate, sometimes interspersed with periods of gathering honey, digging up edible roots, or collecting insects, fruits, and medicines. Even if men are not successful in securing big game, which is frequently the case these days, their activities generally yield a varied and exciting diet. Men may subsist adequately in the village, but in the bush they feast. They also return with items desired by others that have a widely acknowledged exchange value. A favorite local saying is, "Only a fool leaves the forest empty handed, poorer than when he entered."

The switch to cassava from millet and sorghum greatly increased the local and regional availability of food. But its impact on the division of labor was equally profound. Cassava played a key role in freeing men from food production. What it has done to women is still very much in debate. On the one hand, women became less dependent on men for clearing, harvesting, building storage facilities, scaring away birds and browsers, and other tasks that had been required with millet and sorghum cultivation. Some women fared quite well selling surplus cassava to precolonial caravans (von Oppen 1993, 87–98), and women who provided cassava for the rapidly expanding body of Zambian mineworkers in the 1940s and 1950s reaped respectable profits (Turner and Turner 1955). But on the other hand, women's workload increased tremendously because of the amount of processing required. Thus, it has been argued that cassava either liberated Central African women or enslaved them (see Spring and Hansen 1985 for the latter view). Clearly, the absolute requirements of any particular crop do not determine the nature of male-female relations. Such relations are rather the outcome of a negotiated process that takes place in the context of newly emerging opportunities and constraints. This issue will be taken up in greater detail in chapter 5. For now, suffice it to say that cassava may indeed have been a double-edged sword. Men must plant suffiᴄᵢᴄnt cassava for their own subsistence needs, but only women process the roots. Removing the hydrocyanic acid, a poison which contributes to cassava's pest-resistant nature, is a tedious and laborious two-week-long process that locks women into a rigid triangular pattern of movement from village to garden to river and back to village again. A basket of fresh roots is dug up several times a week, year-round, and taken to the river to be soaked for a week or so before being transported to the village for several more days of pounding, sifting, and sun bleaching before it is transformed into an edible flour. Men's and women's differing spatial relationship to the environment acts as the grand metaphor for nearly all of male-female relations. But it is not a metaphor without debate, contestation, and historical realignments in tandem with the environment.

The Nation-State and the Cinderella Province: In Pursuit of Development

Four decades of independence have generated little tangible economic improvement in Zambia. A country that was substantially self-sufficient in foodstuffs in the 1960s is today a net food importer. A country that began its independent existence with a clean fiscal slate is now billions of dollars in debt to foreign lenders. A country that once consisted mainly of self-sufficient farmers, pastoralists, craftspeople, and traders is increasingly becoming a nation of shanty-town dwellers who precariously survive by engaging in marginal and sometimes illegal activities. Zambia was ranked among the twenty poorest countries in the world in 1990 (World Bank 1990, 178). While food production and external trade have stagnated, government expenditures on education, health care, housing, and other social services have declined precipitously. Total external debt for Zambia in 1990 surpassed the 8 billion dollar mark (World Bank 1990, 218). This state of affairs is not the consequence of benign neglect or inactivity on the part of Zambia's leaders, nor is it the result of indifference or inaction by the international community. Indeed, inordinate amounts of time, money, and intellectual energy have been expended attempting to foster development in Zambia. Like other countries in Africa, Zambia has long served as an arena where opposing development strategies compete for prominence. Successive waves of development fads have swept across the country, each with its own set of revelations about the necessary and sufficient requisites for development, each with its own hard core of advocates and opponents, and each claiming to have surpassed the previous paradigm in theoretical sophistication. But, as Stöhr and Taylor (1981) noted, the validity of development approaches will not be determined as a result of theoretical and ideological debate, but in the realm of practice. And it is precisely in the realm of local practice that we shall observe the impact of three decades of development efforts in Mwinilunga and their environmental implications. First, I show that these efforts have failed largely because those implementing them have not understood the historical relationship between the Lunda and their environment. As Porter, Allen, and Thompson contend, "The failure of a great many development projects to achieve even their most fundamental objectives is due to a reluctance on the part of development practitioners to appreciate the significance of history. Projects are frequently designed as if time began with the project implementation schedule. Past lessons are seldom examined and still fewer professionals bother to enquire into the historical circumstances of the people their interventions seek to assist" (1991, xv). Indeed, the Lunda have fundamentally different ideas of what constitutes the environment than do most foreigners working in Zambia; later in the chapter, I show how the Lunda regard the development projects themselves as environmental resources and have been able to divert the projects for their own purposes.

Development Schemes in Mwinilunga

After thirty years of independence, Mwinilunga is still one of the more isolated and underdeveloped districts of Zambia. According to the most recent government statistics, there are only forty-eight miles of paved roads in the entirety of Mwinilunga District (Central Statistical Office 1990). Public services are few and widely scattered. For example, the medical needs of roughly sixty thousand people are, during the best of times, served by only four doctors, three of whom have tended to be volunteers from overseas. But in Zambia the Mwinilunga District is seen as an area of immense untapped potential, in contrast to the more densely populated central region or the drought-prone southern region. The rainy season is rather long and predictable, and the area is well watered, being blessed with plentiful rivers and streams. In fact the northwest has frequently been referred to as the Cinderella province of Zambia, a thing of potential beauty hidden beneath a thin veneer of poverty.

Over the years many suitors have come courting the Cinderella province with glass slippers of economic prescriptions which would supposedly transform Mwinilunga into the financially radiant area many felt it was destined to become. The people of Mwinilunga are thus quite familiar with externally inspired and administered development projects. Nearly every year some new group, full of enthusiasm, arrives with new projects aimed at improving social and economic conditions. During my initial periods of field research (1982, 1984–87), the Swedish International Development Agency (SIDA), the Norwegian Agency for International Development (NORAD), the German Technical Assistance to Zambia Program (GTZ), the British Volunteer Service Organization (VSO), the Belgian and French group Médecins sans frontières (MSF), the United Nations Development Program (UNDP), the World Health Organization (WHO), international Catholic and Protestant relief agencies, local missionary groups, plus various agencies of the national government each had projects in place. Oxfam America, Cultural Survival Inc., and Africare had also begun operations by 1990.

One of the major projects was an agricultural resettlement scheme funded by the Dutch government and administered by Dutch agricultural experts beginning in the late 1970s. It was their belief that the introduction of improved farming practices in Mwinilunga would be hindered by the local form of social organization. The Lunda generally live in tightly clustered villages with their fields often situated some distance away. Although production is individual, consumption tends to be communal. The Dutch believed that village and kinship ties of reciprocity constrained individual initiative and hindered individual capital formation.[4] The Dutch project thus sought to resettle hundreds of nuclear families on their own individual plots of land within the ten-thousand-acre area allocated to the scheme by the Zambian government. Some local farmers were given financial inducements to leave their villages and join the scheme. There, they were given the necessary materials to construct new homes, along with intensive training in new farming techniques, tools, improved seeds, fertilizers, pesticides, and so forth. The project directors envisioned that with continued instruction and strict supervision they could create a new class of modern farmers who would be relatively self-sufficient and able to generate income through the sale of cash crops. The cash would be reinvested, intensifying and expanding production until farmers reached the stage where economy of scale made the mechanization of labor feasible. It was assumed that the economic advancement of scheme farmers would ultimately entice other farmers to emulate these techniques, resulting in the radical transformation of agriculture in Mwinilunga. The number of participants in the scheme and the acreage brought under cultivation did expand quite rapidly under Dutch supervision. Yields, however, never reached anticipated levels, and when direct Dutch supervision was withdrawn from the project in the mid-1980s, farmers quickly began drifting back to their old villages and resuming old practices.

Numerous other agricultural schemes, locally called *lima* schemes,[5] funded and administered by a variety of national and international agencies, have had more modest aims. Leaving basic social organization and agricultural patterns intact, *lima* schemes sought to convince farmers to plant an acre or two of a particular cash crop in addition to their usual fare. Separate schemes have been developed to increase the local production of maize, rice, groundnuts, sunflowers seeds, and pineapples. Most of these projects possessed similar components: public open-air meetings at which itinerant agricultural extension officers extolled the virtues of a particular crop, dissemination of oral and written information on its mode of cultivation, a plan for extending credit to interested farmers, a newly devised transportation network for distributing the required inputs, and a promise to return at harvest time to collect the crops and make payments. The scope of these schemes, the level of local participation, and the crop yields have all fluctuated wildly from one year to the next. None of these projects, however, has managed to create a core of farmers capable of self-sustained involvement. Even with the best conditions, farmers became trapped in a debt cycle. Some may have generated sufficient revenue to service their old debt, but they invariably required fresh credit facilities for the following year's planting. The majority of farmers defaulted on their loans after a few years of participating in such schemes.

Some international development organizations, such as the German Technical Assistance Program, have focused less on promoting agriculture than on stimulating the growth of microenterprises, such as small-scale rural extractive, productive, and retail ventures. Projects aimed at fostering bee-keeping, wax production, timber cutting, woodworking, furniture building, tailoring, and local craft cooperatives have all been initiated. Despite the millions invested and the years of effort by German technical advisors, the results can only be described as disappointing. Although some projects appeared at times to have reached the stage of local sustainabililty, they usually collapsed once outside assistance was withdrawn.

British efforts in Mwinilunga have involved dispatching volunteers to develop what are called appropriate technology projects. Some projects entailed finding local substitutes for commodities that are frequently in scarce supply and are always expensive even when available, such as soaps and edible oils. Others experimented with new building materials or new ways of harnessing water, wind, and the sun to provide local power sources. Despite the name, many such projects produced curiously inappropriate technologies. The results, far too often, were items whose only worth lay in their amusement value—cute curiosities which people would travel some distance to marvel at. There were, for example, waterwheels that were left high and dry as rivers disappeared during the dry season and were then washed away by the raging torrents of the rainy season. Other projects succeeded in producing the desired commodities but were uneconomic, or were of unacceptable quality by local standards.

Foreign Catholic and Protestant mission groups, which have operated in Mwinilunga for most of the twentieth century, have been notable for their efforts to provide formal education and medical care. Such endeavors have been well received locally. The colonial government paid scant attention to issues of health and education in rural areas, and postcolonial governments have been constrained by lack of resources. In addition to schools and clinics, several mission stations have also managed to build up large farms and to acquire sizeable numbers of domestic stock. These mission stations have become the only significant employers of wage labor outside the government. Mission personnel are, therefore, quite knowledgeable about local affairs, in which they are influential players. Nevertheless, they too have initiated their own string of ineffectual development projects. Expatriate church women in Mwinilunga, for example, are especially fond of securing external funds to organize cooking and hygiene classes for local women. A change in dietary and hygienic habits, they feel, would go a long way toward eradicating some of the diseases that plague Mwinilunga. But although such classes are enthusiastically attended by local women, the information gained is rarely transferred back to the village setting.[6]

The project which has perhaps received the biggest fanfare is the fishpond project, begun by the Catholic mission and heavily financed by the Norwegians. Between 1980 and 1990, hundreds of fishponds were created and stocked all over Mwinilunga with enthusiastic local cooperation. I discuss this project in greater detail below.

Differing Views of the Impediments to Development

If we now tease out the implicit assumptions embedded in the development approaches briefly sketched above, we arrive at the following list of the basic impediments to development in Mwinilunga, as seen by outsiders:

- Lack of skills
- Lack of modern technology (machines, methods, inputs, etc.)
- Poor work habits
- Lack of entrepreneurial impulses
- Adherence to conservative traditions (especially kinship bonds of reciprocity)
- Lack of rural enterprises (to generate and absorb a class of rural wage earners)
- Poor diet and poor health and hygienic practices

The Lunda-Ndembu, however, would passionately disagree with this assessment. The problems, many of them assert in mundane daily conversations as well as in more formal political forums, have little to do with local conditions but are structural in nature, resulting from regional and national shortcomings that set limits on local opportunities. The constraints on development that they most often articulate include,

- Lack of transportation
- Areawide shortage of cash
- Unavailability of capital goods
- Lack of up-to-date information on urban market conditions

The persistence of these problems is locally believed to reflect the relations that developed between Mwinilunga and the central government during the struggle for independence. In the 1960s, as part of the long, organized effort to liberate the colony of Northern Rhodesia from British rule (Mulford 1967; Tordoff 1974), two major political parties, UNIP (United National Independence Party) and ANC (African National Congress), vied for national prominence. Because most Zambians were still firmly rooted in rural areas, both political parties aggressively courted traditional rural chiefs in order to win the votes of their followers. The battle for supporters was intense, often resulting in violence (Wele 1987). UNIP won the early elections, led the nation to independence in 1964, and nine years later declared Zambia a one-party state (Tordoff 1974; Gertzel, Baylies, and Szeftel 1984). The traditional chiefs of Mwinilunga had supported the rival party, the ANC. There is a lingering feeling, not often publicly articulated, that the Lunda receive less than their fair share of national resources as punishment for having supported the wrong side. It is frequently asserted that if the central government would simply ameliorate the major problems listed above, then Mwinilunga would be primed for an economic take-off.

It is not my contention that these economic and political assumptions are necessarily correct; the point is that local people act as if they were. Their individual and collective responses to externally inspired, funded, and administered development projects only become meaningful when viewed through the lens of local postulates about historical causality and appropriate behavior. {Below, I discuss in turn each of the four obstacles identified by the Lunda as hindering development.} We will hear narratives and witness practices informed by local beliefs about the proper relationship among people, land, and other resources. The problem with aid and development workers, according to the Lunda, is not that they tend to be Europeans, but that they have strange notions about a range of things such as land, labor, subsistence, movement, ownership, and productivity.

Transportation is one of the major impediments to development according to the people of Mwinilunga. The general lack of transportation and the unreliability and high cost of commercial transportation, on the rare occasions when it is available, are topics one can hear being discussed virtually every day. There are rarely more than a couple of dozen functioning vehicles in the entire Mwinilunga District. Fewer still are capable of operating during the height of the rainy season. No paved roads service the clusters of villages that dot the countryside, and erosion and washed-out bridges leave some areas cut off from the outside world for months at a time. This situation contrasts greatly with conditions that existed just before colonial conquest, when massive caravans bringing commodities from the coast hustled to be the first to reach Lundaland, the only territory with sufficient population density, surplus food, and commodity availability to absorb such an immense volume of trade.

Central Africa experienced enormous population shifts in the early twentieth century. New enclaves emerged to dominate both the commercial and political landscape. The bulk of Zambia's population now resides either in the tight cluster of cities that sprang up in the 1930s and 1940s around the copper mines or around the capital city, Lusaka, which began as a water stop for the railroad in the early 1900s. Little that the world wants can be found in Mwinilunga. The caravans of the past have been replaced by the occasional itinerant trader on a bicycle laden with cheap cloth and perhaps a bit of salt, sugar, cooking oil, and a few odd trinkets. Trade with old allies in Angola and Congo is now deemed to be smuggling, a punishable offense. Manipulating the terms of trade at the coast is no longer the game of the day. The Lunda-Ndembu are now structurally linked to the urban areas of Zambia that provide only sporadically, at best, the economic opportunities that the caravans used to bring in abundance. In Zambia's copper-dominated economy, the Lunda-Ndembu have few resources with which to strengthen their negotiating position.

Yet, the people of Mwinilunga are well aware that shortages and high food prices periodically plague the cities and larger towns. Indeed, there were food riots in Zambia in the mid-1980s and early 1990s. The Lunda know that they could capitalize on this situation by providing substantial amounts of foodstuffs if only regular, low-cost transportation were available. History does in fact offer some evidence to support this contention; during a brief period in the 1950s, for example, large quantities of cassava were successfully exported from Mwinilunga to feed copper miners. Copper became the mainstay of the Zambian economy in the 1930s. In the early years, European farmers in Northern Rhodesia were given a monopoly on selling food, particularly maize, to the mining companies. From the beginning, mining companies provided food rations to thousands of African mineworkers as part of their compensation. A series of maize control ordinances were implemented starting in 1935 both to insure a steady supply of food for the miners and to protect the nascent European farming community in the colony from African competition (see Vickery 1985). European farmers, however, could not meet the sudden increased demand of the boom economy of the late 1940s and early 1950s. The mine owners, in desperation, sent out trucks to scour the countryside for surplus food to feed their African workers. The ability of the Lunda to produce cassava in huge quantities attracted the attention of the mine owners. In the early 1950s, at least four hundred tons a year of surplus cassava left Mwinilunga, destined for the plates of Copperbelt mineworkers (Turner and Turner 1955). The cash from the sale of cassava gave a great boost to the local economy, and social and cultural transformations accompanied this rapid monetization of the Lunda economy (Turner 1957). But by the late 1950s European farmers closer to urban markets, who received cheap land, loans, subsidies, and technical assistance, were able to increase maize production sufficiently to satisfy the mine owners' needs. The monopoly on the selling of produce to the mining industry was restored to European farmers. The people of Mwinilunga were, once again, pushed out of the cash economy.

In many respects, independent governments have continued the colonial policy of privileging maize over cassava production, even though the majority of Zambia's nine million people were traditionally cassava consumers. Not only is much of the national agricultural apparatus oriented exclusively toward assisting maize farmers, but maize meal itself, until the early 1900s, was further subsidized by the government. Cassava growers with farms located near towns and mines continue to find a ready market, but most such land has been priced out of reach. Those located some distance away find it impossible to pay the high cost of bulk transportation and still effectively compete with the low price of maize meal. The production costs of cassava are lower than those of maize, the yields are better, and there is great demand for this crop (Marter 1978). But many Zambians must forego their meal of preference in favor of the meal they can afford. Thus, one-third to one-half of all the cassava planted in Mwinilunga is never dug up and processed. If low-cost transportation were available, tons of cassava could be shipped immediately to urban markets. The knowledge of earlier boom times is widely known in Mwinilunga, kept alive by the memories of those who participated and prospered in them.

Transportation problems also hinder the export of another crop which the Lunda grow with great success: pineapples. Livingstone noted the availability of pineapples on the upper Zambezi as early as 1854. Interest in the crop revived in the 1920s when the Fisher family, the first European missionaries in Mwinilunga, brought plants from the Belgian Congo to cultivate on their farm in Ikelenge. In usual entrepreneurial fashion, local people obtained cuttings and began their own experiments. The pineapples grew well and fit neatly into the local pattern of labor allocation. Most of the time and energy needed to cultivate pineapples takes place during the dry season, and thus it does not compete with cassava production. The output was initially very low, as they were grown only for private consumption. However, in the 1970s, with international assistance, the Zambian government built a pineapple cannery in Mwinilunga and called upon the local population to increase its production. Local farmers complied only to find the cannery plagued by a succession of problems such as power shortages, unavailability of cans, breakdowns of machinery, and lack of spare parts for the vehicles used to collect pineapples from the farmers. Even though the cannery was the only significant buyer of local pineapples and thus was able to keep the price quite low, it was still continually short of funds with which to pay the farmers. The cannery never operated at more than a fraction of its capacity, and throughout much of the mid-1980s it did not operate at all. By the early 1990s the factory lay rusting, its more useful parts stripped for other purposes. Nevertheless, there remain huge fields of pineapples throughout Mwinilunga District. Pineapples are highly valued in urban areas, fetching up to twenty times the local price. But most of Mwinilunga's pineapples, like much of its cassava, rot in the fields for lack of transportation.

The Lunda economy still contains an extensive extractive sphere. Wild honey, wild fruits and berries, mushrooms, and edible insects are each sufficiently abundant during short periods of the year to saturate the local market. Likewise, at times more vegetables are produced than can be consumed locally. Again, these commodities, although greatly appreciated in urban markets, rarely reach them because of the shortage of transportation.

In the contemporary economic climate of Zambia, private operators find it extremely risky to venture into Mwinilunga because of the high cost of acquiring and maintaining a vehicle, combined with this rural area's treacherous roads. Ample profits can be made from the concentrated populations in the cities and towns, which are themselves still underserved with transport options. Why then would one risk damaging one's vehicle to service the scattered population in Mwinilunga?

The local population long depended for transportation of crops upon the vehicles of the National Agricultural Marketing Board (NAMBOARD), a government-financed parastatal organization designed specially to collect and market the nation's major crops. But NAMBOARD was riddled with problems. Not only was it perpetually short of vehicles, it was authorized to collect only certain crops, principally maize, sometimes rice, beans, and sunflowers, but never cassava, pineapples, or wild produce. Furthermore, it usually paid with vouchers rather than cash. In Zambia's inflationary economy the value of those vouchers would decrease substantially in the months it often took for farmers to cash them in. NAMBOARD vehicles were clearly the least desirable transport option.

Considering these difficulties with transportation, it is not surprising that many in Mwinilunga have long asserted that distribution rather than production is the major problem. The solution is to improve transportation links by consolidating national and international resources rather than to endlessly initiate new agricultural schemes.

The second constraint on development most frequently mentioned by people in Mwinilunga is the areawide shortage of cash. Not only does it limit the ability of local buyers to purchase crops, but it also has other effects. It limits, for example, the extent to which local artisans can practice their crafts. Very few of the individuals skilled in carpentry, brick masonry, basket and mat weaving, and collecting and processing of wild foods can survive by practicing those crafts on a full-time basis. There is a greatly underutilized pool of moderately skilled labor in Mwinilunga, but the cash flow is too small to effectively activate this pool. There are not enough salaried individuals, or even those with predictable access to cash, to keep more than a handful of skilled individuals gainfully active.

The long-distance caravan trade system of the eighteenth and nineteenth centuries promoted increasing commoditization and monetization in Central Africa. Socioeconomic differentiation and occupational diversification thrived as previously separate economies became increasingly interdependent. Copper bars of standardized shapes and weights gained widespread acceptance as convertible currency. Salt and cloth were used as well. During the colonial period, however, Central Africa was carved up into several disarticulated European spheres of influence, and European currencies took precedence over indigenous ones. Specific colonial requirements narrowed the means of acquiring cash, leading to decreased occupational diversity. Concomitantly, acquiring European forms of cash, particularly for paying taxes, became a concern of the utmost importance. Mwinilunga was forcibly integrated into a new monetary union, in a most disadvantageous position. Local economic activities became more oriented toward subsistence. Transactions which had in the past been monetary could be accomplished only through barter or through bonds of reciprocity. Such transactions lack both the flexibility and the multiplier effect of cash transactions. Little changed with independence. The lack of cash in Mwinilunga accentuates an ethos of self-sufficiency, placing a very small premium on specialization. Although the average Lunda man or woman possesses an impressive array of physical, technological, and intellectual skills, most people have much the same array. Yet, large numbers of people in Mwinilunga are continually acquiring new skills and upgrading old ones, both because knowledge is the way of making up for the lack of cash and because value is placed on using leisure time to acquire skills.

Development practitioners who focus on teaching basic skills such as carpentry, bricklaying, furniture building, and bee-keeping seem genuinely unaware of the underutilized skill pool that already exists. They also seem unaware that without a greater inflow of cash, their students will stand little chance of actually earning a living in Mwinilunga from these newly acquired skills.

The scarcity of manufactured or processed commodities is the third factor locally put forward as a major constraint on Mwinilunga's ability to unleash its own economic potential. Even those with cash must often struggle to locate commodities as basic as soap, sugar, and cooking oil. Shovels, wheelbarrows, and fishing nets rarely appear in the district's shops. Many small-scale, locally initiated projects are never fully implemented, or are greatly delayed, for lack of rather simple tools or basic resources. But this is not a problem that can be remedied locally. With periodic shortages and a thriving black market for commodities in the cities, rural areas are simply outbid for their fair share of the national stock of commodities. In spite of government efforts to develop a national marketing strategy which would more equitably distribute scarce goods, city dwellers are virtually vacuuming up all available commodities, blocking the flow to the rural areas. Externally inspired development projects need to be aware of urban-rural dynamics, to recognize that areas like Mwinilunga are not economic islands. The urban-centeredness of Zambia, and of most contemporary African nations, places rural areas at a great competitive disadvantage. Development projects have, at times, managed to temporarily circumvent this problem. Some routinely develop their own networks for channeling scarce resources directly into the hands of rural dwellers, which gives particular projects the aura of being locally sustainable. But once the project has ended and the glare of the public spotlight has faded, Mwinilunga is again invariably outbid in its quest for resources. The struggle for resources between rural and urban areas is by far a greater constraint on entrepreneurial activity than is any adherence of the local people to supposedly conservative traditions.

The fourth major constraint, especially on entrepreneurial activities, is the slow rate at which information flows from the cities and towns into Mwinilunga. There are many accounts of people who managed through Herculean efforts to transport their crops to the city only to find that the item was in surplus that particular week, selling for half of what it had been the week before. In the absence of telephones, televisions, and the latest newspapers, the people of Mwinilunga usually depend on word-of-mouth

for information about the latest pricing trends in the city. Travelers who
have recently returned from the city are quite actively sought out for information on current urban conditions, but much of that information is already at least two or three days old. Speculating on the volatile urban markets is a risky business under any circumstance. It is even more so for those
with only sporadic access to second-hand information.

Projects: (Un)natural (Re)sources for Local Development Initiatives

Most externally inspired and funded projects are met with more than a little skepticism by the people of Mwinilunga. As we have seen, the stated
aims and implicit assumptions of most such projects are incongruent with
local perceptions of basic needs. Why national and international agencies
continue to initiate new projects is a topic often discussed in Mwinilunga.
Some see the projects as vehicles designed to enrich foreign experts and/
or the foreign manufacturers whose products these experts peddle. Others see their own urban-based elite as the driving force, the suggestion
being that the elite regard the projects as opportunities to siphon off resources. Altruistic concern by outsiders for the plight of the rural poor is
a topic I never once heard discussed without solicitation. Even then, it was
usually quickly dismissed as evidence of my naïveté. The constant refrain of
such discussions was that a fraction of the money and energy that had been
directed toward useless projects would have gone a long way toward solving Mwinilunga's real problems: improving the transportation and communication links and increasing the flow of cash and commodities. But
since national and international agencies seem far more interested in solving contrived rather than real problems, people in Mwinilunga have devised their own strategies for widening their access to resources. Development projects are simply considered one more environmental resource to
be harnessed for local aims and incorporated into local strategies. These
perceptions have framed relations with development projects and practitioners over the last several decades; they serve to define the criteria by
which the people of Mwinilunga evaluate the projects and generate plans
for using project resources, including personnel, funds, and equipment, to
solve local problems. Below are a few examples, from personal experience,
of how local perceptions of specific development needs have powerfully in-

fluenced relations with outsiders involved in the development enterprise. These examples provide evidence of the local people's capacity to generate and collectively move forward their own hegemonic ideology about the proper relationship between people and the environment.

The Problem of Transportation

Living in the tropical zone where the sun sets year-round at roughly 6:00 P.M., and lacking electricity or any other cheap source of lighting, the Lunda are accustomed to finishing most essential tasks by sunset. The remainder of the waking hours, which extend to midnight or later, are reserved for large group discussions around the numerous campfires that dot the landscape. Throughout the year most people are engaged in virtually identical productive activities. Thus, the daily routine usually provides little in the way of stimulating conversation. It is to the out-of-the-ordinary event that the conversation turns. If one were to go from village fireside to village fireside on any particular night it would not be at all unusual to hear the same basic topics dominating the discussions. In fact, those who do travel about from village to village serve to cross-fertilize and intensify discussions on specific issues, often resulting in similar interpretations of events and widespread agreement on courses of action relevant to those events.

When word arrives that some new development group will begin operations in Mwinilunga, talk is often first centered not on the stated goals of the project but on the number and types of vehicles that the project will bring to the area. Will it bring in trucks or merely passenger cars? Will local drivers be hired or will project personnel arrive with their own drivers? In either event the first stage of the local response is generally the same. The newcomers must be taught the most inviolable rule of travel in Mwinilunga: never drive anywhere, not even a short distance, without a full load of people. As mentioned earlier, there are scarcely any paved roads in Mwinilunga. During the rainy season some clay roads become as slippery as ice. The weight of a load of people and their possessions is the best way to avoid losing traction. Rain turns other roads into muddy quagmires. Drivers require the assistance of a large number of people to push when they become stuck. During the dry season some roads are covered in loose sand or powder. Again, varying combinations of weight for traction, or people for pushing, may be needed in order to complete even the shortest journey. Furthermore there is the constant danger of washed-out bridges, swollen streams, or large fallen trees blocking the road, obstacles that can only be overcome with the aid of a great deal of human labor. But since villages are scattered, it is undoubtedly best to travel with as many people in one's vehicle as possible. Graphic demonstrations of the perils of driving alone are rather easy to organize, and local people almost invariably subject newcomers to such demonstrations. Drivers may be misdirected toward the most perilous stretches of road and then, when stuck, left unassisted for days. All newcomers quickly learn to ignore any agency rules which proscribe the transport of nonproject personnel. Like all other vehicle operators in the area, they pack in as many people as their land rovers or lorries can accommodate.

Having accomplished their first objective of dictating how vehicles travel, local people turn their attention to acquiring detailed knowledge of when and where those vehicles travel; they then attempt to exert as much control over travel schedules as possible. They quickly ascertain where project personnel must travel to meet their needs. It is not at all unusual to feed project personnel erroneous information in order to extend trips and thereby increase the transportation options. Local goods, for example, may be withheld, forcing more frequent journeys to other areas. Indispensable articles may be misused, forcing trips to the city for repairs. Essential commodities may mysteriously disappear, necessitating travel to replace them. Many in Mwinilunga are quite clever at discovering ways to increase the amount of time project vehicles must spend on the road. Key to this goal is the local individuals who manage to become affiliated with a project and then serve as conduits, channeling detailed information back to the local population, where it is thoroughly dissected, digested, synthesized, and then used to construct new strategies. Most of the local individuals associated with projects become power brokers in their own right. By knowing the schedules of project vehicles they can selectively notify friends, family, or clients early enough to allow them to take advantage of the availability of transportation. It is little wonder that I have frequently heard outsiders who administer projects in Mwinilunga bemoaning their loss of control, or even complaining of feelings of paranoia. Even the most secretly made travel plans somehow quickly become public knowledge, resulting in large numbers of people with their parcels milling around project vehicles waiting for unannounced trips to begin. Travel plans quietly discussed over dinner one night, for example, may be overheard by the cook. Early the following morning some of his family members, friends, or clients may show up with bags packed, pleading for transportation to where they obviously already know the vehicle is heading. Even short trips to a nearby village can turn into all-day excursions with passengers embarking and disembarking at every stop. Inevitably, each project's original estimate of transportation cost has to be revised drastically upward. Since most projects hire numerous local individuals, separate and sometimes competing networks develop, each aimed at manipulating project vehicles for their own benefit. Lines of social cleavage are sometimes crystallized and exacerbated by differential access to transportation resources, straining the capacity for cooperation within this competitive high-stakes game.

An added complication is that there is not a single gas station in the Mwinilunga District. The nearest one is in Solwezi, the capital of the neighboring district, nearly two hundred miles away. Shuttling back and forth between Mwinilunga and Solwezi to keep the gas tank full may represent a tremendous loss of time for project personnel, but it represents a boon for Mwinilunga residents. Solwezi is the largest market town in northwestern Zambia. A trip there provides a precious opportunity to sell local produce while acquiring scarce commodities that rarely reach Mwinilunga. Little wonder, then, that local people have absolutely no incentive to assist project personnel in conserving fuel.

The Problem of Cash

People in Mwinilunga often assess development projects in terms of how much disposable cash they will bring into the area and what must be done to secure some of it. Employment, of course, is the most obvious method of gaining access to project cash. As in the case of transport, those individuals to first associate with a project serve as conduits for directing friends, family, or clients into the available positions. Compromises, however, may be made in labor productivity. It must be maintained at a high enough level for individuals to protect their jobs by appearing to perform adequately, but it is often kept artificially low to force the project to hire as many people as its budget will allow. There is constant experimentation to ascertain the minimum levels of productivity that project leaders will tolerate.

Selling goods and services to project personnel is also a standard method of securing cash. A good deal of attention is focused on learning the habits and preferences of individual members of a project team, such as their favorite foods, beverages, and forms of entertainment; effort is then made to satisfy those needs for a price. At times, conspiratorial compromises are worked out. It is not always most profitable to make the quick sale to project members. Sometimes, after much discussion, it might be agreed that more cash would be generated by transporting a certain commodity to town, where it could be sold on a larger scale, than by a single sale to local project personnel. The best way to force a trip to town may be to convince project members that a shortage of a particular item exists locally. It is one of the more amusing ironies of life in Mwinilunga that people are sometimes seen transporting bags of commodities to town in vehicles that are traveling for the express purpose of acquiring the same items that, unbeknownst to the vehicle owner, are already in the back of the vehicle. The ability to keep secrets on a large scale and to control the flow of certain information to outsiders serves local people well in their attempt to harness project resources.

Other ways to acquire cash from projects are perhaps a bit cruder but often no less effective. Project members are continually assailed with requests for loans, requests for cash to assist in some crisis, requests for investment capital, requests for bribes, requests for protection money, requests for money for sexual services. Outsiders, insecure in their position, may feel that acquiescing to some of these solicitations is simply the price one pays for operating in rural Zambia. It may seem to them impossible to mobilize even the barest semblance of support without regularly dispensing cash.

The Problem of Commodities and Information

An enormous amount of pressure is brought to bear on project personnel in attempts to transform them into petty businesspeople. They are bombarded with appeals to use their influence, their vehicles, and their cash to acquire scarce commodities in the city, or even from overseas, for resale to the rural population. Information, in many respects, is treated as a commodity. Efforts to encourage project personnel to maintain strong communication links with the cities and towns thus parallel efforts at acquiring goods. The scarcity of basic commodities is such a widespread and intense preoccupation that pressure comes not only from the peasantry, but from the elites and representatives of the ruling party and the government as well.

The pressure exerted is extremely subtle and sophisticated, and it gnaws unceasingly on whatever feelings of guilt or inadequacy project personnel may possess. They are constantly reminded of their more privileged economic position and their origins in more developed countries or simply more developed regions of Zambia. People comment on the costliness of their clothes and other material possessions, in contrast to the bleak poverty of those they have supposedly come to assist. Every effort is made to engender a sense of guilt that will compel project personnel to acquiesce to solicitations for help. Their commitment, their sensitivity, even their very humanity may be brought into question. How could they possibly feel comfortable not assisting those around them when they possess such wealth? People also use mercenary incentives. They remind project members of the profit they could reap from trafficking in scarce commodities—profit that any reasonably sane person would not pass up. If project members plead that they do not need those additional sources of income, then they are again challenged to assist the less fortunate rural dweller. The above measures do, in fact, yield results. Even those who initially believed strongly in abiding by project rules soon find themselves yielding. The demands—at times subtle, at times direct—are so relentless that only the strongest, most self-assured or self-centered individuals could resist for long.

People attempt to elicit numerous other benefits from projects. For example, the need of rural dwellers for stimulation, for something to moderate the monotony of daily life, is no less acute for them than it is for urban dwellers. Projects and project personnel are thus viewed as potential sources of entertainment. They may possess radios, taped music, interesting literature, pictures, or, more simply, fascinating stories of life in places that most locals will never see. Second, project personnel are often solicited for medicines. Because of the periodic shortages of drugs in the few clinics in Mwinilunga, no alternative source for medicine is left unexplored. Project members are often asked to secure and make available antimalarials, antiseptics, antibiotics, and pain relievers, and they are openly chastised as lacking compassion if they fail to respond positively. Third, projects are sought out as opportunities to acquire new skills. Mechanics, electrical work, equipment operations, and driving are perhaps the most popular, especially among young men contemplating a move to the city. People who have little interest in the actual aims of a particular project may become associated with it solely in order to acquire skills or commodities.

Project Dilemmas

The people of Mwinilunga have seen projects come and go. They have seen many outsiders conduct their experiments and then move onward and upward in their careers, leaving behind little of lasting value. Because local people are focused on securing items they consider essential for their own plans, a project that assists in that process is highly praised, even if it has not accomplished its own stated objectives. Numerous projects in Mwinilunga operated quite successfully while project members were in the field, primarily because those members spent a good deal of time satisfying local needs and so in return received sufficient levels of cooperation. Nevertheless, many of these projects failed to become self-sustaining. Once project members left, thereby bringing to an end the services they had been providing in the form of facilitating transportation and the flow of cash, commodities, and information, often little remained of the original concept or project design that held much interest for local people.

The Dutch agricultural resettlement scheme, mentioned above, is an excellent case in point. Possessing both land rovers and a large truck, which frequently shuttled between Mwinilunga and Solwezi, the project provided a prime transportation link. Farmers who participated in the scheme had access to a wide range of commodities generally scarce in Mwinilunga, such as cooking oil, soap, sugar, kerosene, flashlights, batteries, used clothing, medicines, and tools, some of which they could pass along to their kin back in the village. They could also pass along up-to-date information about conditions in the Solwezi market and at times managed to transport their kin's commodities there. Not everyone who joined the scheme did so solely in order to channel project resources back to their villages. Some farmers were, indeed, interested in the experiment itself. Others were attracted by its sheer novelty. The young Dutch men who ran the scheme also provided a rather stimulating and interesting environment for local participants. Once the Dutch supervisors and their vehicles left, however, all advantages disappeared. Farmers found themselves isolated; nuclear family units on individual plots of land lacked the dynamic interaction of the typical village cluster, as well as the social safety net that nearby kin provide. Where they had been at the center of an interesting hub of activities, farmers now found themselves on the periphery of the flow of information, goods, and services. The agricultural benefits that may have accrued as a result of dependable access to improved seeds, fertilizers, and pesticides, plus the assurance of timely transport for crops, were now at the mercy of the already over-extended NAMBOARD marketing system. Farmers drifted back to their old villages. The remnants of the project quickly faded away.

Attempts to develop microenterprises generally suffered much the same fate, and for many of the same reasons. Peripheral services offered by project personnel often attracted more participants than did the actual aims of the projects. The strength of the microenterprise approach was supposed to be its dependence on locally available inputs which would insure that people could sustain such projects through their own efforts. But foreign instructors and supervisors, who traveled from village to village to check on progress and then back to their home bases in the city, were marshaled into playing much the same role as the administrators of the resettlement scheme: augmenting transportation and communication links and facilitating the flow of cash and essential commodities.

The *lima* agricultural projects, which urged farmers to add a cash crop in addition to their usual planting, were no more successful. Farmers often decided to participate in the projects because they hoped to acquire preferential access to such scarce equipment as new hoes, axes, and shovels, or perhaps to insure access to transportation. The projects, however, did not take into account the seasonal nature of labor allocation. Cassava is planted almost daily throughout the rainy season, interspersed with periodic breaks to collect wild foods, but the cash crops being touted by outsiders, for example maize, cotton, and sunflowers, must all be planted and harvested within short periods of time. Thus, cultivating most cash crops competes not only with cultivating food crops but also with collecting mushrooms, fruits, berries, and edible insects, which are themselves available only during the briefest of intervals. As a result, cash cropping, which often provides only minimal financial reward, could diminish a farmer's quality of life by limiting his ability to participate in alternative activities at key points in the annual cycle.

Those implementing projects are thus faced with some difficult decisions when they enter Mwinilunga. Acquiescing to demands could easily exhaust much of a project's time and resources, but not responding to them jeopardizes the ability to secure cooperation. It is a dilemma to which most projects have not found an adequate response. Indeed, as a brief digression illustrates, the same dilemma faced those who brought the caravans of the eighteenth and nineteenth centuries into this area.

As noted scholar on pre-colonial Central trade, Achim von Oppen noted, "Before they could engage in any serious negotiations over the purchase of export goods or bulk provisions, European travellers unfamiliar with the customs of the Upper Zambezi and Kasai were faced with what they obviously experienced as rather arbitrary kinds of demands, as innumerable 'extortions, exactions and vexations'[7] by resident chiefs and headmen. As the number of more or less independent local potentates in the area was legion, these demands multiplied, and presented a solid cost factor for any journeys to or through this part of the interior" (1993, 381). Traders could be called upon to pay tribute for the right to meet local chiefs, for hospitality fees for the right to camp overnight, or for transit taxes for passing through particular domains. Entrapment in *mulong'a*, petty legal disputes, was a common occurrence. According to von Oppen, "All travellers' reports contain numerous examples of the most frivolous pretences of crime, for example spitting at someone unintentionally; calling someone by the name of somebody else; unexpected death of the local business partner, his assistant, slave or even dog; passing fields and houses in a hammock; alleged theft by a caravan member, often provoked by placing the 'stolen' object somewhere as bait; injury; failure to pay respect to a headman; placing a gun or spear against a hut; using for camp building a fire-marked tree which was claimed as private property by some bee-hunter or cultivator" (1993, 391). Experienced early traders accepted these tactics as a small price to pay for accessing the lucrative Central African market. The better informed were known to have simply set aside as much as 5 percent of the value of their enterprise to cover these miscellaneous costs (Graca 1890, 368). Yet the record also speaks of the great warmth and friendliness with which many traders were received, and the generous outpouring of gifts bestowed on them. Requests for fees and tribute, thus, were not simply a ruse for extracting commodities from unwary traders. They were mechanisms that served, first, to slow down caravans to allow better scrutiny of their wares. Perhaps most important, however, they were an attempt to establish meaningful relationships between traders and chiefs through material exchange. As LeVine (1976, 121–23) noted, there is a widespread emphasis in Africa on material transactions in interpersonal relations. The relationships between husband and wife, parent and child, and even living and dead are all characterized by standardized forms of material exchange. Thus, involving traders in the giving and receiving of gifts personalized what would otherwise have remained anonymous market-driven encounters. Locally, it was believed that even relationships initially established through *mulong'a* exchanges, legal disputes, stood a better chance of becoming long-lasting ones than did relationships based on no material transaction at all.

The current wave of development practitioners are, in a very real sense, the new caravans. They are subjected to the same scrutiny and enticed into the same relations as were the long-distance caravan members of the eighteenth and nineteenth centuries. This new, unwitting caravan is now the major source for commodities from the outside and the bringer and validator of the only widespread currency. Numerous experiments are underway, new forms of interaction with the environment are emerging, old methods are being reinvigorated in an effort to draw in the truly global caravan of development practitioners.

The fishpond project, alluded to earlier, is an example of a development project that engendered responses to external actors reminiscent of social relations during the caravan era. Its history goes back to the 1970s, when a Franciscan friar stationed at Lwawu began to experiment with man-made fishponds. Using the labor of local young men he had several ponds dug that were connected to a stream by a series of simple dirt channels, with slues to regulate the water level. It soon became evident to all that the wide and quiet ponds were a more productive environment for fish than the narrow, rapid streams that lace Mwinilunga. Despite the arduous nature of digging ponds with little more than hoes and shovels, a growing number of energetic young men began to experiment with their own pond designs, trying different sizes and shapes and different methods of water regulation. The major problem they encountered, however, was the ambiguity of certain local customs surrounding ownership. On the one hand, there is an uncontested rule that anything of value that comes into being as the result of an individual's labor belongs solely to that individual: labor in fact gives a thing its value and confers ownership. Fruit from a tree belongs to the planter, and firewood belongs to the person who chopped down the tree. Yet on the other hand, water, and anything that grows in it, had always been considered a common good, beyond individual ownership. The young entrepreneurs claimed exclusive rights to the fish in their ponds and the right to sell or otherwise dispose of the surplus as they saw fit. Many people not only denied the legitimacy of such claims but would sneak down to the ponds with baskets at night to scoop up fish. Discouraging though this may have been, many young men persisted in their efforts, using the nightly fireside discussions to press home their case for the value of acknowledging the individual ownership of fishponds. They argued that the careful management of ponds through controlled culling would result in a far greater supply of protein food for the area as a whole than would indiscriminate poaching. Again we see the value of "sweet talk," *wuhaku*, the ability to argue a case through impressive oratory skills (see Turner 1957, 16, 103). Fishponds were the subject of many nightly *mulong'a*. As noted earlier, a *mulong'a* is not just a forum for settling legal disputes. The word means "to order," to put things back the way they were, if possible, or, if not, to reorder them in the fashion most acceptable to the greatest number of people. It also connotes order in the sense of understanding where individuals stand on the issue at hand, including who is less than satisfied with the present situation and what he or she might be prepared to do about it. A *mulong'a* is an exercise in bringing to bear the power of persuasion; if not immediately, then over the long haul. No *mulong'a* ever really ends; the participants simply establish the framework for its reopening.

Over a period of years, the tide slowly began to shift toward the position of the young pond builders. By the time the Kanongesha decided to construct his own ponds in 1984, it had become a generally accepted rule that ponds were private property. In smoothing the way toward this local consensus, the new fish farmers had tacitly agreed to be lenient in granting credit to those without cash at the time of culling. The number of ponds being built in Mwinilunga increased rapidly.

The Catholics abandoned their own experiment after building the first set of ponds, but they were fully aware of the new dynamics going on around them. In attempting to assist the young fish farmers, many of whom had attended the Catholic school, the friars sought outside technical and financial assistance. After starts and stops by several international organizations, the Norwegian Agency for International Development (NORAD) agreed to fund and provide technical assistance to a fish-farming project in Mwinilunga. Interestingly enough, this assistance initially served to slow the progress of pond building. Once word leaked out that a new project was coming that would pay people to dig ponds, most digging ceased while people awaited details on how to get paid for doing what they had been prepared to do unassisted. Red tape, pilot studies, and one logistical snafu after another meant that for the better part of two years little aid was forthcoming, and few ponds were built. However, once the project began to function, and the first set of potential fish farmers were signed up, a veritable explosion of ponds occurred. More than two hundred ponds were built in 1986 alone.

One could easily generate a long list of miscalculations and missteps committed by the fishpond project and its personnel. But I, for one, initially assumed that the project would probably succeed because it was doing some very important things right. It was assisting local people with their own development initiatives. It satisfied a locally defined need—the need to complement the activities of hunting, trapping, and the periodic slaughter of domestic stock with an activity that would provide a more stable and predictable source of protein. Furthermore, the digging of ponds can only be undertaken during the dry season, the period when labor requirements for other activities are generally at their lowest. The cropping of the ponds can easily be timed to correspond with the period when the returns from hunting and trapping are at their lowest, which is the height of the rainy season. The fishpond project's prospects for success were further accentuated by the fact that the necessary skills and technologies had been subjected to local experimentation for over a decade, and the results of that experimentation had already been widely disseminated. The cultural conflicts that could arise as a result of incorporating a new productive activity into old patterns, and the ambiguities embedded in long-standing rules that new circumstances tended to bring to light, had likewise been locally debated over a long enough period for a consensus to emerge. Fish farming was already becoming an activity that a significant core of individuals had determined was a worthwhile pursuit, even if undertaken alone. It simply became even more of a good thing when NORAD showed up on the scene willing to assist by providing capital equipment such as good wheelbarrows, shovels, nets for cropping, and fingerlings for stocking. The project also brought personnel who satisfied many of their consumption needs through local cash purchases, who traveled regularly from fish farm to fish farm providing technical services throughout Mwinilunga, and who also had regular need to travel to Solwezi and beyond in order to replenish project supplies. These contributions to local needs were definitely appreciated. But fish farming, I thought, would probably continue in Mwinilunga even when project personnel were removed (Pritchett 1990). It already contained a critical mass of individuals dedicated to the endeavor.

However, on return visits to Mwinilunga in 1993 and 1994 it was apparent that all was not well with the fishpond project. The stability the fishponds had been designed to bring to the Lunda-Ndembu's productive system had been overwhelmed by the fluid matrix of shifting environmental, political, and economic conditions that have long characterized Central Africa. Under NORAD supervision (1984–1990), the terms of engagement had evolved in such a way that greater benefits accrued to those who built new ponds than to those who successfully managed old ones. The distribution of construction materials, fingerlings, fishing nets, training opportunities in the city, and cash stipends was based primarily on the number of new ponds. Mature ponds were to serve as their own reward, attracting few additional inputs of project resources. The project began attracting people who had little commitment to fish farming per se, but who found the economic logic of participation itself enticing. People developed novel methods for minimizing the investment of time and energy required to access project benefits. The result was a proliferation of low-quality ponds, poorly situated with respect to rainy season hydrology, with easily collapsible walls, inadequate water circulation resulting in oxygen-deficient water, and poor fish production. NORAD, disappointed with this turn of events, withdrew from Mwinilunga, pinning the blame for failure on a culture that placed greater value on immediate short-term gains than it did on sustainable long-term rewards.

Africare stepped in immediately to pick up the pieces. Under its auspices there was a shift in focus away from the activity of building ponds. Africare's initial appraisal indicated that fish farmers had not followed established guidelines for maintaining the nutritive level of their ponds. Although this was a substantially accurate assessment, it failed to capture the broader context within which local strategies are situated. Indeed, this approach fit into the now well-established pattern of outside experts attempting to reshape the African landscape in accordance with narrowly defined goals and narrow sets of criteria, measured in isolation from the total eco-environmental context. It paralleled, in most respects, the organized effort to install maize production in Mwinilunga. The focus then had been on yields, on meeting goals for national grain production, on complying with IMF conditions for further loan disbursements. Rather less attention was focused on the narrow range of environmental conditions suitable for optimal maize production. The strength of cassava was its capacity to thrive within extremely wide parameters of environmental conditions, such as soil fertility, rainfall, and pest infestation levels. With maize, particularly the varieties of maize that were being distributed in Mwinilunga, relatively minor environmental shifts can result in nearly total loss of the crop. Maize cultivation also required in-

creased dependence on external inputs such as hybrid seeds, specialty fertilizers and pesticides, transport, and credit and marketing facilities. Delays in
delivery and snafus in distribution occurred frequently. Maize also favored
particular cohort groups. Most of those who currently occupy the culturally
recognized status of junior bigman managed to gain their positions by
squeezing some economic benefit from the maize craze. Many of them had
ties to Lwawu mission that gave them more timely access to mission tractors and haulage equipment for plowing and harvesting.

The fingerlings that were distributed under NORAD were, in many
ways, equivalent to the hybrid maize seeds. The intent had been quite
noble. In a determined effort to boost local fish production, NORAD introduced the fastest-growing kin of the local variety of *Talapia* that it could
regularly obtain. Unfortunately, this particular variety had much greater
nutritional requirements than did the varieties that had populated the original ponds. The indigenous species are top-feeders that thrive on insects attracted to water, as well as their eggs and larvae. The introduced species are
bottom feeders that cannot subsist solely on insects. Their recommended
diet, according to NORAD guidelines, is a mixture of green vegetables and
fish meal. Local experimentation revealed that because of its voracious appetite the introduced species consumed more than it was worth. The prevailing price for the cheapest green vegetable, cabbage, not to mention the
price of fish meal, by far exceeded the prevailing price for dried fish from
any surrounding area. Many people concluded that it was better to eat the
rather large fingerlings and redirect the project's cash, equipment, and
contacts toward more profitable pursuits. The introduced species were also
more susceptible to disease. All the more reason to eat them quickly.

Africare's current thrust is on finding more economical local food
sources for the introduced species. Rather lower levels of support are being
allocated toward the building of new ponds. Should Africare succeed, new
economic equations will no doubt emerge on the local scene; new experiments will follow. But the ground is shifting. A cheap source of protein is
now flowing in from the west.

Going to Cazombo: Back to the Future

War rages in Angola. The section of the border with Zambia, however, particularly that with Mwinilunga District, has for some time been more or less

firmly under the control of UNITA (National Union for the Total Independence of Angola). Peace reigns in that interstitial region. While much of world public opinion portrays Jonas Savimbi and his UNITA movement as primarily Ovimbundu rebels attempting to overthrow the more or less legitimate government of José Eduardo dos Santos's MPLA (Popular Movement for the Liberation of Angola), the Lunda-Ndembu's condemnation of Savimbi is much less severe. His troops allow the Lunda-Ndembu to move freely not only among their own kin on the Angolan side of the border but even as far as the eastern UNITA stronghold of Cazombo, seventy-five miles inside Angola. The troops at Cazombo have not been involved in military action for several years. Their primary struggle is for daily subsistence, obtained mostly through hunting and other extractive enterprises. Although awash in arms and game meat, the soldiers have limited access to meal and manufactured products and are, thus, anxious for trade. Cazombo is a two-day walk from most of Lunda-Ndembu territory. It is located near the site of one of the most famous nineteenth-century caravan markets in Central Africa. That market, which attracted the Lunda-Ndembu to their current location on the upper Zambezi in the eighteenth century, today beckons them once again. At Cazombo, in exchange for the most abundant commodity they possess, cassava, the Lunda can acquire a spectacular variety of game meat, both fresh and dried, as well as guns and ammunition, and even the possibility of participation in the lucrative gem-smuggling trade that finances Savimbi's movement. Just as in the past, the current situation is one in which international trade supports and reinforces local trade. Subsistence production complements production for the market. The current terms of trade with Cazombo are quite advantageous for the Lunda-Ndembu. The long-established relationship with the peoples of Angola also insures good terms of trust.

Fish farming, under the current set of economic equations, exercises little appeal for the vast majority. While a dedicated few may continue to tie their long-term fortunes to pond building and fish farming, the order of the day for many more young men is trekking to Cazombo. The protein needs of Mwinilunga are being well met with cheap meat from Angola. Hunting and fishing is in steep decline, while cassava production is up. The number of people plying the route to Cazombo is reaching caravan proportions. The ultimate settlement of the Angolan crisis, will, no doubt, once again shift the Lunda-Ndembu's relationship with the land and all that affects it. For the moment, however, an old pattern has reasserted itself. Neither government officials nor development practitioners offer appealing alternatives.

Summary

The Lunda-Ndembu complex of beliefs about the environment extends from a deeply ingrained perception of dwelling in a place of unlimited land, of easily traversed space. The environment is alive with mystery, wonder, and untold surprises. Benefits accrue to the courageous seeker, the adventurous traveler. In the rainforest, the ubiquitous presence of navigable rivers had joined distant places and stimulated contact between widely dispersed peoples. On the plateau, only a lack of imagination or ill health constrained movement. Travel is a core metaphor constantly weaving its way through Lunda art and song, medicine and myth, mundane speech and hallowed proverbs. "Knowledge comes with miles, not years." "The man who stays in his own backyard never grows up." The Lunda language contains over twenty individual words denoting different kinds of walking, for example, walking briskly, walking giddily, walking mournfully, walking as if carrying a heavy load, walking about restlessly, and so on. The Lunda are, indeed, great walkers. Covering the seventy-five miles to Cazombo in two days is not considered a particularly taxing feat. With four to five months of dry season each year, few distances are considered insurmountable. The present generation has grown up hearing the tales of old men who, during the era of migrant labor, were forced to walk the five hundred miles to the Northern Rhodesian Copperbelt, or the thousand miles to Southern Rhodesian plantations, or the two thousand miles to South African mines and ports.

The productive relationship with the environment centers around the notions of labor as the primary producer of value and the laborer as the primary owner of any value produced. Land, per se, cannot be owned, but anything of value produced on the land belongs solely to the individual producer. As Turner, von Oppen, Papstein, and others have noted, individual ownership has apparently always been the norm on the upper Zambezi. Tools of production (e.g., hoes, axes, fishing nets, household articles, and guns), rights to resources, and specialized skills and knowledges were all deemed to be individually owned. The matrilineage can in no sense be seen as corporately owning land or other factors of production. It comes into being as a corporate group primarily when an individual dies and it must decide the disposition of the deceased person's items of value.

The focus on individual initiative combined with the perception of endless frontiers produces strong entrepreneurial impulses. Involvement in the environment and the market has long been socially decentralized and involves large numbers of petty producers: men, women, and children. The environment is something to be cleverly used, something to be mastered. There is little evidence in Lunda proverbs or practice to suggest a view of the environment as finite or exhaustible. The international development community's focus on sustainability through the careful long-term management of discrete sets of activities on circumscribed bits of land does not resonate well with Lunda sensibilities. The view from the plateau is one of endless horizons in all directions, of vast interstitial regions between widely scattered population groups. Those regions beckon to be explored, examined, and colonized with meaningful activities. The Lunda world is a world of people in motion, producing many intersecting points. Control over those points, or even the ability to mediate relationships at those points, can provide one with the means of survival, or perhaps eventually with a high position within an old or a newly established hierarchy, or, at the highest level, with the possibility of imprinting one's name and story on the very environment itself. In general, *mpuhu*, fame or remembrance, is the reward bestowed upon those who succeed by local standards. They are the ones who most often acquire a large following and whose names become institutionalized as titles of specific headmanships or become synonymous with particular historical eras. Oftentimes the names of successful individuals saturate the very earth around which they have lived by becoming terms of reference for topographical features. Rivers, plains, hills, and valleys are commonly named after the most powerful individual who resided near them. Yet, movement remains the key to success in any venture.

Generations of cohort groups can be characterized by their differing styles of movement to differing locations: west to the caravan markets, north to the Christian mission station, east and south in search of wage labor, and most recently west again to the market at Cazombo in Angola. Each group of cohorts constructed its separate narrative and its artistic and aesthetic expression of that movement, and each drew its separate lessons and inspiration from the experience. There is, however, collective movement as well. Historical shifts in the terms of trade and the terms of trust with non-Lunda allow the meaningful periodization of more widespread

Lunda-Ndembu experiences. But at the level of tradition remarkably little has changed. Contemporary situations are justified in terms of long-standing agreements about the natural order of things. According to the Lunda, Nzambi, the High God, gave each creature its own unique reper-toire of comparative advantages, for example strength to the lion, stealth to the snake, flight to the bird. Humans were endowed with cleverness, the capacity to endlessly rediscover and reshape the social and physical en-vironment in innovative ways. Movement is the catalyst to human creativ-ity, travel is the font from which new productive knowledge springs. Labor is the only validator of ownership.

The proposed land registration exercise described at the beginning of this chapter provokes a tremendous amount of anxiety. It would mandate a relationship with the land that is, as yet, unjustified by Lunda traditions. It would remove the connection between labor and ownership. It would erect barriers to free movement. The Lunda, who boldly resist having their movements curtailed by nation-state boundaries, are incensed at even the suggestion that they should live their lives in measured squares, pursuing tedious little activities scripted by outsiders. Should land registration be-come the law of the land, however, it is impossible to predict the course of local negotiations. The law may be strongly resisted or subverted for some time, or it may ultimately be reinterpreted and reworked in the local con-sciousness as a logical extension of traditional notions of individual owner-ship of productive resources. Just as in the case of evolving notions of fish-pond ownership, the power of *wuhaku*—the ability of an individual to argue cases, to persuade his cohorts and compatriots of the correctness of particular courses of actions, to justify the new in terms of the old—will be the key to the outcome. The power of individuals, nested in broad arrays of social relations, is the subject of the next chapter.

Chapter Three

The Individual and the Group

Argument at Kamau Village
Dry Season, August 15, 1985

It was late in the dry season, and the elephant grass had long been burnt off. Life was no longer restricted to the narrow, well-worn pathways that linked village to garden, garden to river, and river to neighboring village. The landscape was now covered by a low green carpet of succulent young sprouts. One could see for miles and miles again. In fact, from my village on the Chifunga plateau I could clearly see the chief's capital two miles to the east and the Catholic mission station two miles to the north. West and south I could see into Angola as far as the Lovua ridge, thirty-five miles away, and deep into UNITA-held territory. The rainy season narrows one's range of vision. It narrows one's range of mobility. It narrows the very scale of life itself. Agricultural duties, intense and monotonous, keep everyone close to the homestead. The same old faces are seen each day, the same old arguments are rehashed each night. But the fires that sweep across the landscape when the rains are over burn away the barriers to movement. Life expands. Imaginations soar. The dry season is the time for movement—physically, structurally, emotionally. It is the time for visiting family and friends. It is the time for collecting old debts and making new contacts, for finishing up long-lingering projects and embarking on new enterprises. It is also the time for initiating a new crop of boys into manhood and girls into womanhood. Invariably some new headmen emerge, and long-standing hierarchical relationships have to be adjusted.

Joseph, Richard, and Sebe were inseparable friends. As nineteen-year-old, unmarried, recent school-leavers, still being supported by their parents, they were the very epitome of freedom that dry season. They had walked the ten miles to Sakapoti village hoping for adventure but content just to pass the time. There they visited old classmates, drank copiously, flirted with the young unattached girls, and sang and danced the night away. Staggering toward home the following day, they passed through Chifunga village intent on visiting another old classmate, Alexander Kamau. Alexander had just left that morning to visit some relatives in the city, but the three encountered his young wife Gladys pounding cassava in the shade of the banana grove beside her house. They laughed and joked with her for nearly half an hour. She too had been a classmate of theirs for years at Lwawu primary school. Upon preparing to leave, Richard gave Gladys one of the bars of soap he had purchased at the little shop in Sakapota. Big Kamau, father of Alexander, had been eyeing the transaction from his house next door. He charged the three young men like an elephant defending its calf. Many punches were hurled from all directions. A huge noisy crowd instantly materialized, surrounded the action, and with great effort separated the combatants. Insults of the most vulgar sort, however, continued to fly. Big Kamau accused the three, especially Richard, of having blatant sexual designs on his daughter-in-law. The brazen public displays, the laughing and joking, the slapping of hands were more than ample evidence of their foul intent, he claimed. The presentation of an expensive gift, soap, was additional confirmation. Big Kamau questioned the morals of one who would try to sleep with the wife of a friend, indeed, almost a brother. He was shouting at the top of his lungs about the fate of those who would commit incest. He lambasted the young men for their drunken demeanor. Richard was not passively standing by. He aggressively countered Big Kamau, accusing him of being filthy minded and out of step with the times. At one point he broke away from his handlers and delivered two good punches to Big Kamau's head, causing both of them to fall to the ground. The crowd now forcefully took charge; one group practically carried Big Kamau back to his house, while a separate group of roughly twenty young men of Chifunga village pushed Joseph, Richard, and Sebe the fifty yards to the *chota* (men's talking place) beside my house. I was disturbed and disappointed at the three young men's behavior. They were indeed extremely drunk. While I agreed with them that Big Kamau might have reached some erroneous conclusions and that they perhaps had had a right to defend themselves, I could not understand the vehemence of their verbal and physical attack on Big Kamau. Striking an elder of one of the most well-known and well-respected villages in the area would certainly have its repercussions. When calm prevailed in the *chota*, I was surprised to find that the young men of Chifunga village were far less concerned about the punches than I was. Much of the conversation centered on Big Kamau's audacity in trying to police the behavior of young folks. Even if he had had sufficient cause to be concerned with the actions of Joseph, Richard, and Sebe, he should have politely asked some of the young men of the village to handle it. To attack young people in full view of a half dozen homesteads was clearly unacceptable to them. They agreed that they would try to find a sympathetic elder to approach Big Kamau with their concerns at an appropriate time in the near future. That proved to be unnecessary. When I went to Big Kamau's house later that morning, he was already being counseled by the *akulumpi,* the elders, that he had let down their side, so to speak, with his public display of temper. Young people do indeed have the immediate responsibility for one another's behavior. Elders rule by the power of example. Maintaining decorum is everything. Big Kamau admitted his guilt, revealed that he himself had partaken of drink that morning, and promised to control his temper in the future.

This chapter addresses the tenuous balance between, on the one hand, notions of individual autonomy, freedom of choice, and control over one's own body and, on the other, the collective need to influence, if not regulate, certain facets of the lives of group members. Among the Lunda, powerful expressions of individualism are tempered with equally powerful conceptions of the necessary role played by widespread networks of obligations and claims. Despite the high value placed on individual ownership, personal choice, and autonomous productive activity, embeddedness in multiple social networks is deemed fundamental to human existence. To be human, the Lunda believe, is to be socially connected. Families, kinship groups, village affiliations, neighborhoods, curing societies, and cohort groups create separate, yet overlapping, arenas of incorporation and negotiation. They define the conceptual boundaries within which individual actions are interpreted and given meaning. Social networks set limits on individual behavior, yet at the same time they create spaces that allow individuals the freedom to operate within broad, culturally defined parameters. They also provide forums where individuals can contest prevailing notions and perhaps justify new ones. It is commonly said in Mwinilunga, "to be without social linkages is akin to being lost in the deep forest." Freedom of movement and of choice are meaningless without a sense of direction. Social networks provide direction. They are, in a sense, a road map of the social terrain identifying routes over which the individual is free to navigate. A better comparison, perhaps, is with language. A language is a matrix of rules and interdictions, yet it produces a certain type of freedom. It is only through learning the rules that one can communicate with others and become free to express one's individuality. In fact, the ability to represent oneself is directly related to one's mastery of the rules. Only after mastering the rules can one cleverly manipulate them.

The autonomy and integrity of the individual are evident in many spheres of Lunda social life. From birth an individual is reckoned as a whole person, intrinsically endowed with a set of inalienable rights. Childhood is viewed not so much as a time for molding the child as a time for furnishing the raw material of experience and allowing the child to explore and discover who he or she really is. The process begins with naming. One does not casually bestow a name on a child. Instead, one seeks to discover the name the child wishes, the one that reflects the person the child is already born to be. In the first few weeks and months of life many names are tried. Babies are directly greeted in words and song, using a variety of different names. The one that most consistently draws a smile, or soothes an agitated state, is assumed to be the name a child desires. A person, however, is free to change his or her name at any point in life. A personal transition, religious conversion, or even embarkation on a new enterprise is frequently accompanied by a change in name.

Lunda society is acutely attuned to the tempo of the individual. Babies are fed when they are hungry and allowed to sleep when they are tired, rather than according to a schedule. A child is sent to start formal schooling when he or she appears anxious and ready to learn, rather than at a specific age. Boys are selected for initiation into adulthood when they begin to behave like men. Marriage occurs only after one has reached a certain level of social and productive maturity. Individuals, thus, have wide latitude in dictating the pace of their own lives. This is in no sense viewed as permissiveness. Such freedom is not something that can be given or taken away by the group; it is simply viewed as part of the human condition.

Lexically, parents generally refer to themselves as *wudi na anyana,* being "with" children, rather than "having" or "possessing" children. The phrase connotes sharing experience or existence, rather than owning. In fact, most interpersonal references among the Lunda are expressed in terms that rest on the principle of individual integrity. Harsh talk to children is, thus, strongly criticized. A parent's role is to advise children rather than to command them. Children, in turn, are urged to follow parental advice, rather than being admonished to obey their parents. Instead of being inculcated with a fear of punishment for disobedience, individuals are frequently reminded that unpleasant things happen to those who do not follow advice:

"The one who failed to listen to the elders married his own sister"; "The one who failed to listen to others accidentally drank poison"; "A child who does not listen grew a beard at the back of his head." The authority of parents, elders, leaders, or a social group is like the authority of an encyclopedia: it offers useful advice for those who choose to consult it. It is not, however, an instrument of command or coercion, nor is the acceptance of that authority a challenge to personal integrity.

The emphasis on personal inviolability, however, does not mean that the individual can live in isolation. Social networks are essential for satisfying many individual needs. These include the provision of subsistence while young, the social acknowledgment of one's entry into adulthood, the efficient pursuit of productive activities, the provision of a social safety net to deal with the vagaries of the environment, the efficacy of rituals performed for the individual, and, especially important, the acquisition of *mpuhu*, fame and social remembrance in the afterlife. Social groups differ, however, in the claims made on the individual, the privileges granted, and the degree of choice of association permitted, as well as in how the group may be represented and symbolized by material transactions.

The Lunda's move to the upper Zambezi can be divided into periods: the switch from grains to cassava, the era of caravan trade and roadside services, the rubber boom, the coming of colonialism and the migrant labor era, the cassava boom of the 1940s and 1950s, and finally, the postcolonial era of schemes by the government and NGOs (nongovernmental organizations). This chapter explores the changing context of choices, consequences, and meanings that emerged out of the colonial encounter, the penetration of the newly independent nation-state's bureaucratic network, and the incursions of mercantile and productive capitalist agents. I contend that very little has changed throughout these periods in Lunda social notions of social obligations and practices relating to subsistence while young, entry into adulthood, or ritual efficacy. Change in the efficiency of production, however, varied in accordance with the production options available at particular historical stages, as well as individual propensity within the range of available options. The concomitant impact on meanings and mechanisms of social affiliation has been profound. Comparing data I collected in the 1980s with that collected by Turner in the 1950s, I focus below particularly on analyzing changes in Lunda social organization during this period and suggest some reasons for those changes.

A Nation of Villagers

In the early 1950s, while attempting to reconstruct the Lunda's traditional way of life, Victor Turner detailed many of the social changes that were occurring around him. He furthermore made a number of predictions concerning changes he believed would occur in the near future (Turner 1957). The most forcefully stated and potentially wide ranging of those predictions was that the rapid process of individualization, or atomization, that Lunda society was undergoing at the time would continue. Turner identified several processes that he believed would lead Western-style individualism to take the place of traditional village life, with its focus on communalism and reciprocal ties of kinship obligation: pressure from the colonial government, the frontal assault on Lunda ideological systems by the expatriate-dominated Christian community, and, most important, the Lunda's incorporation into the cash economy. Turner recorded numerous examples of individuals, particularly young males, who were disencumbering themselves from village and kinship social obligations with the aim of accumulating cash for personal use. Such instances, Turner believed, would increase exponentially in the years to come, eroding the foundation on which village unity was based. In other words, the fissioning of villages of the past, which were purported to be constitutive of Lunda unity at higher levels, would be replaced by a new form of schism that would result in nuclear families, rather than lineage-based villages, becoming the dominant form of social organization.

In this chapter I compare quantitative data from the mid-1980s on Lunda social organization, especially village size and social composition, with data of a similar nature collected by Turner in 1952. Such a comparison makes clear that not only did villages remain a major focal point of social organization, but in many respects they changed very little. The first hypothesis I put forth is that Turner misinterpreted the long-term impact that cash would have on village social organization. Rather than necessarily being a disruptive element, cash can actually facilitate and strengthen village bonds. Second, Turner misinterpreted the extent to which the Lunda would be incorporated into the monetary economy. He had no way of foreseeing that rural life in the 1980s would remain virtually as labor intensive, or labor dependent, as it had been in the 1950s. Many essential goods and services are still not available today in rural areas for any amount

of cash and can be secured only through strenuous labor and social connections. As a result, organizations larger than nuclear families are necessary for addressing the complex problems of production, labor distribution, and care for the very young, the aged, and the ailing. Villages remain
an excellent form of social organization for addressing these problems.
Third, Turner did not acknowledge the fact that when people make plans
they often do so with the afterlife in mind. Being comfortable in life is certainly a fundamental objective of productive activity, but being socially remembered in the afterlife by as many people as possible also figures prominently in the strategies adopted by most Lunda individuals. Being an
important member of a large, firmly established village continues to be a
necessary element in achieving this goal.

An important historical event for recontextualizing Turner's suppositions occurred in 1950. In that year the district commissioner of Mwinilunga began to allow new freedom of movement by amending the colonial decrees that had restricted African residence to registered villages. For
nearly three decades the exigencies of taxation and labor control had been
met by requiring individuals to live in a limited number of concentrated
and controllable villages. Perhaps the change in policy extended from the
belated recognition that overcrowding had produced deleterious effects,
but clearly an important colonial aim at that time was to encourage cash
cropping by opening up new areas for cultivation. The change led immediately to a scramble for fertile land along roads, where ambitious individuals could gain cash by growing cassava exclusively for the market.
Trucks began regularly plying those roads looking for surplus food to feed
the exploding number of mineworkers on the Copperbelt. Some farmers
diversified into other crops, with pineapples eventually proving to be the
most profitable. Virtually overnight a new elite class of Lunda farmers
emerged, some of whom were even able to buy trucks to transport their
crops to the city themselves and bring back loads of consumer goods to
sell in their own shops and tearooms, or to exchange for labor in order to
further increase the size of their farms (Turner 1957, 133–35). Their
wealth far exceeded that of any previous group of Lunda. They built larger
homes than even the chiefs did and acquired large followings as well.
These elite African farmers quickly became idols and role models for many
of the young. A new scramble for cash began. This time, however, the
scramble was not just for sufficient cash to pay taxes and return to the village with a few consumer goods, but for enough cash to embark on a

whole new lifestyle. Observing this phenomenon shaped Turner's notions of the three Lunda worlds:

Old men . . . remained obdurately conservative, and deplored the new ways, although they were indulgent towards the young people who practised them. Young men . . . who had worked in Chingola [the Copperbelt], had accepted the new order of things, and wore smart European clothes, owned bicycles and gramophones, played guitars, used Copperbelt slang, and attended traditional rituals only to join rings of young people, who danced the latest dances imported from the Rhodesian or Congo urban areas and sang the latest local or urban "song-hits." Between these two extremes . . . , still belonged . . . a generation which saw success in life as measured by the number of followers a man could acquire, and not by the insignia of conspicuous wealth that could be purchased by money. True, [some] had large houses well equipped with furniture. They had mosquito-nets and oil lamps. But these signs of wealth were rather indices of success in the traditional order than signs of an altered way of life, involving the acceptance of entirely new modes of behaviour and of a new scale of values. [They] continued to work in their gardens, . . . to participate in ritual as cult-members and patients, to exercise their traditional rights and fulfil obligations as kin, and to interact with the older generation in terms of traditional norms. . . . They lamented that so much of [the ancient way of life] had already passed away, and more was passing beneath their very eyes. But they felt that the royal road to eminence within the village way of life now lay through the acquisition of cash. . . . They wanted money to better their position within the traditional system, not as means of loosening their ties with it. (1957, 134)

Turner focused on the first world, the world of the old men whose highest aim in life was to become village headmen. As explained above, however, this world, which Turner continually refers to as "traditional," or "ancient," was in fact a relatively recent response to the limitations imposed on the Lunda by colonial rulers. The *Pax* Britannica had brought an end to the dream of expansionist African states. It brought an end to the long-distance caravan network and the occupational diversity that had thrived in its wake. The slave trade, the ivory trade, and the rubber trade all ground to a halt at the dawn of the colonial era. The generation that constituted the old men of Turner's day was the first to grow to maturity under the constraints of colonial policy. The opportunities of the previously fluid and flexible social and economic environment were not theirs to enjoy. Confined to overpopulated villages, when not being subjected to the vagaries of the migrant labor system, their options for a prosperous and fulfilling life were severely limited. Their only road to eminence lay through the careful manipulation of lineage relationships in order to arrive someday at the position of headman. The early 1950s, however, saw some loosening of constraints. New opportunities arose for those with the capacity for hard work and a basic understanding of the new economic system. Social systems that had been frozen in place for three decades would now have to expand to accommodate a new reality. It was this process which Turner saw as atomization, heralding the death of an ancient way of life. Let us now look in detail at Turner's findings.

Village Life in the 1950s

Village Topography and Demography in the 1950s

The average Lunda village in the early 1950s was a circular arrangement of houses in a cleared space ranging in diameter from thirty to seventy yards (Turner 1957, chapt. 3). The most common type of residential dwelling was a square or rectangular building constructed of clay over a wood and bamboo latticework frame, topped with a grass thatched roof. The houses were generally small, ranging from nine feet by nine feet up to about fifteen feet by twenty-five feet. In the center of the village circle was the *chota*, a circular unwalled structure with a conical thatched roof. The *chota,* the men's palaver hut and mess room, was the place toward which the men of the village gravitated when not otherwise occupied by duties. Outside the village circle and behind the house of each adult woman were smaller structures of varying shapes, which served as cooking and storage places. Typically the houses of the headman and the men of the senior genealogical generation were in one semicircle facing the houses of the adjacent genealogical generation in the opposite semicircle. If there were adult men of the alternate generation present they would build their houses on their grandparents' side of the circle. Men generally built houses for their wives next to their own.

In the mid-1950s there were three classes of villages: registered villages, that is, those listed on the government tax register; unregistered villages, which were newly established villages organized on the same basis as the registered villages but not yet listed on the government tax register; and *mafwami,* farms, which were also newly established villages but tended to consist of a single nuclear family that had detached itself from village affiliation. In the 1950s the average registered village consisted of about thirteen houses containing a total of roughly thirty persons. The average unregistered village contained seven to eight houses and sixteen to seventeen persons, and the average farm, two to three houses and about five to eight persons (table 1).

Villages, however, were not spread evenly across the landscape but were irregularly clustered in certain spots, resulting in complex multi-village units which Turner called vicinages. These vicinages often consisted of several villages with no genealogical connection to one another, each village possessing its own dynamics, moving as it pleased. Villages were, indeed, quite mobile, moving on average every four to six years. The accessibility of land suitable for cassava cultivation, the exigencies of hunting, arguments with neighbors, and deaths all played a role in determining how often and how far a village moved. Some villages tended to move frequently but within a narrow orbit of a few miles. Others moved less frequently but covered great distances when they did move. Not only were vicinages being constantly restructured as a result of village mobility, but individual villages themselves were quite unstable. On the one hand, as Turner showed, tension inherent in the social structure itself often led to village fission. Parts of a village, lineage segments for example, would break away and attach themselves to other villages, or simply declare themselves new independent villages. On the other hand, individuals themselves tended to circulate through numerous villages over the course of a lifetime. A boy born and raised in his father's village might reside with a uterine uncle during his middle years and then establish his own village in later life. A female might reside virilocally with a series of husbands, returning to her father's or a uterine uncle's village upon each divorce, before finally establishing herself in old age at a son's or brother's village.

From census data Turner was able to quantify individual mobility. He established that at the time of his research roughly 85 percent of both males and females were living in villages other than the one in which they had been born (table 2a). Furthermore, 61 percent of the males and 53 percent of the females had been reared in villages other than their natal village (table 3a). And finally, 79 percent of the males and 89 percent of the females had been reared in villages other than the one in which they were residing at the time (table 4a).

Because villages were usually built near one another, changing village affiliation could be accomplished in some cases by simply moving a few hundred yards. In order to add a spatial dimension to mobility, Turner collected data on the movement of individuals through four of the territorially based chiefdoms that served as administrative subunits for the nearly three-thousand-square-mile Lunda territory. The results showed that only around 30 percent of all individuals had been born and reared in the same chiefdom in which they were presently residing (table 5a). At all levels, mobility was a prominent feature of Lunda life.

Social Composition of Villages in the 1950s

With the constant flow of individuals in and out of villages, was there any underlying regularity in the social composition of villages? Although Turner's informants stated that in theory any Lunda was free to live wherever he or she pleased, they also described a generally agreed upon form of the ideal village which individuals strove against all odds to bring into being. This ideal village would have at its core a group of matrilineally related males, their wives, who would be residing virilocally, and their children. The predominance of this pattern can be seen in tables 11a and 11b. Turner suggested that this ideal was consistent with the gendered patterns of labor. Women's work was characterized by productive individualism. Men, however, frequently cooperated in hunting, house-building, and bush-clearing. In the past they had assisted one another in warfare. Turner thus theorized that in the absence of strong central political authority a man's first loyalty was to his village, and cooperation between men was a necessary condition for village maintenance. Because kinship is a major mechanism of social control, the males with the greatest possibility of establishing strong bonds of cooperation would be those linked by consanguineal kinship, especially uterine brothers. For these reasons, matrilineally related males were seen as being the ideal focal point around which stable village life could be organized. But achieving this ideal in one generation leads to structural problems in subsequent generations. Descent among the Lunda is reckoned through the female line. Thus, the children of the village's male core would not belong to the village matrilineage but to their mothers' matrilineage, located elsewhere. These children would in all likelihood eventually choose to reside in a village of their own matrikin. Fathers would endeavor to keep their own children with them as long as possible. Yet ultimately, if the village was to persist with the men's own matrilineal descent group as its basic core, the men would somehow have to attract their matrilineal heirs, that is, their sisters' children, to come reside with them. But according to Turner, despite the affective bond between men and their children, the matricentric bond is the most enduring unit among the Lunda. Young children go wherever their mother goes, and in old age, a woman often goes where her children are. Thus in order for men to bring their sisters' children to their village, they must generally also recruit the sisters themselves. However, while her marriage is strong and her husband is alive, a woman is not likely to leave her husband's village. As Turner noted, "It is to a considerable extent by divorce and widowhood that a village is enabled to persist through time. With a woman come her children, and if she is divorced or widowed after she has passed her menopause she and her sons come back permanently to the village of their matrilineal kin and replace the wives and children of their male kin who have gone out of it. Thus divorce and widowhood act simultaneously as principles of village recruitment and attrition" (1957, 69). Turner's data showed that the majority of marriages ended in divorce (table 6a). Thus, many matricentric families tended to oscillate back and forth between the village of a woman's matrilineal male kin and those of her successive husbands.

After identifying the principles determining village affiliation, Turner went on to show the concrete effects of those principles on the actual composition of the villages he had observed. Using census and genealogical data from sixty-eight villages (both registered and unregistered), he showed that to varying degrees, villages did in fact approach the cultural ideal (table 7a). Headmen and primary matrilineal kin accounted for 37 percent of total house ownership in the villages. The proportion increased to 58 percent when classificatory matrilineal kin were included. These numbers indicate the importance placed on classificatory adelphic coresidence as well as the degree to which men had been successful at attracting sisters and sisters' children to their villages.

The more recently established villages in Turner's survey were more heavily dominated by uterine siblings and their families, whereas the older villages had attracted greater numbers of classificatory matrilineal kin (table 8a): 14 percent of the more recently established villages consisted of classificatory matrikin, versus 30 percent for the longer-established villages. Correspondingly, in the recently established villages the headman, his primary matrikin, and his own descendants represented 56 percent of the village population versus only 36 percent in the long-established villages. Long-established villages also contained a significantly higher percentage of cognatic house owners than did the more recently established villages. The key to enduring villages, Turner thought, was the maintenance of good relations between the men of the matrilineal core, along with their ability, through force of personality or reputation for leadership, to attract their matrilineal heirs. Once a village had overcome the obstacles inherent in the transition from matricentricity to full-fledged matriliny it often gained the kind of widespread renown that made even nonrelated individuals consider it a desirable place to reside.

Matrilineal Descent and Succession

Turner noted that a Lunda village could be viewed as a collocation of matricentric families linked by varying ties of kinship and affinity. As the data show, the majority of individuals residing in a village were matrilineally related to the headman. It was these relationships, in conjunction with the fact that maternal descent was used to regulate succession and inheritance, which gave some measure of continuity to villages. When a mother died, the matricentric family was reduced to a uterine sibling group. The males of this group, particularly those of the senior genealogical generation, were the focal point of village authority. Succession to headmanship was never an automatic process; it required the consensus of all those residing in the village. There were virtually always several possible candidates for the position. The qualifications and personality characteristics of each candidate were usually discussed over an extended period before a consensus emerged. As in the case of village composition, the Lunda had an ideal for how succession should occur. The generally stated preference was for a younger uterine brother to succeed an elder uterine brother. If the village was a long-established one, with deep lineages, then parallel cousins might have succeeded one another in order of age. After the classificatory sibling males of the senior genealogical generation had been exhausted, then succession to headmanship dropped down to the adjacent generation of male siblings. This pattern of succession conforms well with the cultural values the Lunda associate with old age, especially the wisdom, practical experience, and unselfishness that it is believed to embody. This adelphic succession in large villages, in theory at least, would result in a relatively rapid turnover of aged office holders, few of whom would live very long. Such a process contributed to the stability of villages by encouraging ambitious men to remain rather than to break away and form their own villages. If the headmanship is circulating rapidly through the line, then a man need only be patient and his turn will eventually arrive. If younger men became headmen, contenders would realize that they might possibly have no chance for years to come and would have additional incentives to break away and form their own villages.

Every effort was made, however, to protect long-established villages from fission. A long-established village was a source of pride to its members, and headmanship of such a village was the most prized objective of every Lunda male. The name of its founder became institutionalized by becoming both the generally acknowledged name of the village and, through the process of positional succession, the title that each person succeeding to headmanship would inherit. The village's name also served as a geographical point of reference, since nearby rivers, hills, or plains would be renamed after the village. Those who broke away to form their own villages were accused of trying to kill the old village, *jaha mukala*. Thus, the major claim that the village placed on the individual was to keep the village alive.

How well did the concrete reality of village life conform to Lunda cultural notions concerning the transmission of authority? Again, Turner collected information that allowed him to compare notions with actions (table 9a). Headmen were succeeded by younger brothers in 47 percent of the cases he recorded. In 35 percent, the headman was succeeded by his sister's son, his culturally defined matrilineal heir in the adjacent genealogical generation. A sister's daughter's son succeeded in 9 percent of the cases. Thus, cultural notions of adelphic succession and matrilineal descent were strongly reflected in the concrete political reality of Lunda village life. A total of 91 percent of cases conformed to the cultural norm.

Village Fission

Despite the high value placed on membership in a long-established village, the composition of any particular village was rarely stable for long. I have already mentioned that individuals tended to circulate through a number of villages over the course of their lifetime. But the greatest threat to village integrity was fission: the division of villages along lines of structural cleavage or tension. This process entailed segments, rather than individuals, breaking away from an established village and relocating elsewhere. The old village would remain and retain the old name, while the breakaway segment would declare its independence as a new village, usually under the name of its leading member.

Fission occurred for a number of reasons: (1) an ambitious individual unwilling to wait for his turn as headman might organize others to follow him in establishing a new village, (2) a segment of a village might seek out a more peaceful existence elsewhere if the usual juridical mechanisms had been unable to resolve disputes, (3) a segment of a village might decide on economic grounds to move to a less densely populated area if the long-term presence of villages in one location had led to exhausted soils, a short-age of firewood and building materials, and a dearth of game, or (4) a seg-ment of a village might decide to shield itself from witchcraft, accusations of which were often brought on by deaths and illnesses, by placing some distance between itself and the old village, since the power of witches was believed to be effective only over a short distance.

Although in theory any individual who was ambitious, charismatic, and forceful might decide to lead a breakaway faction, Turner noticed that such factions were generally of three types. Uterine sibling groups were the most common unit of fission. Often, finding their rise to the top of the political hierarchy blocked by a large group of males in the ascending generation, they would seize upon any of the reasons listed above as justification for founding their own independent village. Second, if a headman had been successful in keeping both his wife and his sister with him in the village, ul-timately two separate matrilineal segments would have developed. It was not unusual, especially upon the death of the headman, for the entire seg-ment spawned by the wife to vacate the village as a unit. Third, when a headman had a number of fertile sisters residing with him, each was in a sense at the apex of her own matrilineal segment. Matricentric loyalties and disputes over succession made these segments natural units of fission.

Turner collected information on the relationship between the leaders of seceding groups and their previous headmen (table 10a). In 55 percent of the cases of fission he analyzed, the leaders of the breakaway group were the sisters' sons, primary and classificatory, of the headman of the original village. Turner found only one case in which a uterine brother seceded with his followers from the village of his older brother. Sons and cross-cousins of the headmen, however, were each the leaders of seceding groups in 9 percent of the cases. In short, the three categories outlined above, uterine sibling groups, patrilineal descendants of the headman, and matrilineal seg-ments, together accounted for roughly three-quarters of village fissions recorded in the early 1950s.

Village Integrative Mechanisms

Lunda villages were inherently unstable. The two most powerful principles of Lunda organization, matrilineal descent and virilocal marriage, contain built-in contradictions. They bring people together in certain relationships and push them apart in others. They bring together male uterine siblings at the expense of separating them from their sisters and their natural heirs, their sisters' children. They establish a collocation of matricentric families at the expense of separating those families from their matrilineal kin located elsewhere. Matrilineal descent and virilocal marriage generate lines of cleavage between the uterine male sibling groups of adjacent generations, between the descendants of the father's wife and the descendants of the father's sisters, and even between the descendants of uterine sisters.

In order to build enduring villages in spite of these contradictions and cleavages, the Lunda relied on a number of countervailing cultural principles. Succession and inheritance, to the widest degree possible, ran laterally rather than lineally (Turner 1957, 88, 204–5). This process was reinforced by the cultural principle of generational unity. Thus, cross-cutting all principles of kinship, affinity, and friendship were the notions that all village members of a particular generation were linked by ties of reciprocal rights and duties, that they had an obligation to provide one another with material assistance, and that as a collectivity they exercised authority, to a limited degree, over the adjacent descending generation. Thus at one level paternal and maternal kin were partially merged.

The opposition of adjacent generations was counterbalanced to some degree by the alliance of alternate generations (Turner 1957, 80–81). The relationship between grandparents and grandchildren was a particularly special one. Grandparents were expected to advise and instruct their grandchildren on many subjects, including sexual matters. Because many houses contained only one room, when children were considered too old to continue sleeping with their parents they were often sent to sleep with their grandparents. Grandparents and grandchildren were permitted to speak openly to one another about sexual matters and could even witness each other's sexual activities. The type of egalitarian relationship that existed between grandparents and grandchildren was referred to by the Lunda term *wusensi,* or joking relationship. They could tease one another, saying anything they pleased without inciting anger. They could use each other's possessions freely and could call on one another for assistance with the certainty that it would be forthcoming. So strong was this bond that a man wishing to secede from his father's village could not automatically expect his own children's support; if the children were old enough to choose, they might choose to remain with their grandparents. Thus the alliance of alternate generations could serve to counteract the tendency toward fission caused by the opposition of adjacent generations.

Cross-cousin marriage was another mechanism that served to counterbalance opposing forces embedded in Lunda structural principles. When cross-cousin marriage occured within a village, for example, between the children of coresiding siblings of the opposite sex, it mediated against the generally opposing principles of loyalty to one's residential affiliation on the one hand and one's ties to one's matrilineage on the other. In a more general sense cross-cousin marriage was said to help solve the matrilineal puzzle—the divided loyalties experienced by males in matrilineal societies between their own children and those of their sisters.[1] As summarized by Kathleen Gough, "Matrilateral cross-cousin marriage ensures that mother's brother and sister's son have harmonious instead of conflicting marital interests. In particular it gives the wife's father assurance that his daughter and her children will continue to be linked to his own matrilineal group, and so to himself. Patrilateral cross-cousin marriage provides the husband's father with a similar assurance with regard to his son, and in addition ensures that the former's grandchildren will be members of his own matrilineal group" (Gough 1961a, 620).

Finally, when the above mechanisms proved inadequate, when a crisis erupted that led to the crystallization of opposing factions that seemed destined to divide the village, the Lunda called into play the powerful redressive mechanism of public ritual. Turner was the first to note that such episodes generally followed what he called a processional form (Turner 1957, 91–92). First, the breach of a norm governing social relations between persons or groups within the village was made public. Following the breach a phase of mounting crisis supervened. If it could not be resolved quickly or contained within certain limited areas of social interaction, the crisis spread throughout the village, forcing even those not initially involved to become so. As loyalties were called into question by the major antagonists seeking support, opposing positions eventually became conterminous with factions within the village composed of individuals whose primary loyalties to one another transcended their allegiance to the village as a whole. After informal arbitration and formal juridical and legal mechanisms had failed to resolve the crisis, the performance of public ritual was the last hope. Turner saw ritual as primarily a form of communicative behavior. He described its constituent parts, symbols, as storage units containing information that need not be verbalized to be understood but could be comprehended at a preconscious or even unconscious level (Turner 1968, 8). Most Lunda rituals tacitly acknowledged the instability inherent in villages. Thus the dominant symbols in rituals did not reflect major aspects of the social structure but rather focused on the values that all Lunda possessed in common. They animated those values, giving them a compelling authority. Through song and dance, gestures and symbolic manipulation, rituals provoked a high level of emotional intensity and could promote a sense of oneness sometimes strong enough to override previous feelings of intravillage hostility. As the final step, either the breach was healed and the village was reintegrated, or there was a recognition that the breach was irreparable, and village fission occured soon thereafter.

Despite the presence of numerous mechanisms to counteract the cleavages set up by matrilineal descent and virilocal marriage, fission appeared to be the dominant feature of Lunda village life in the 1950s. Lateral succession and inheritance, generational unity, alternate generation alliances, cross-cousin marriages, and public rituals might have retarded the process to a degree, but according to Turner they were being overwhelmed by processes unleashed by colonialism, Christian missions, and especially incorporation into the cash economy. Turner envisioned an evolutionary process leading toward an atomization of Lunda society, a breaking down of traditional structures by the pursuit of cash. Once individuals acquired a certain amount of cash savings, wrote Turner:

It may happen that they wish to invest these in capital equipment, such as a sewing-machine, with the aid of which they make up store cloths into garments for payment, a bicycle, on which they can travel to buy goods cheap and sell them elsewhere at a profit, or a storehouse or tearoom made from sun-dried bricks, to serve as business premises. Once they have taken this step and have invested money to make more money, they find themselves increasingly embarrassed by the demands of their kin for presents in cash and kind. If they wish to become petty capitalists, they must separate themselves from the village sphere and the village way of life. That is why it is usual to find traders and tailors living with their families, in different vicinages, and even chiefdoms, from the village of their close matrilineal kin. To a lesser extent the same set of conditions holds good for petty commodity cultivators, the incipient "kulaks," who grow crops specifically for sale. If the making of money tends to supplant as a major aim in life the acquisition of a following, people try to accumulate money, to be turned into capital and the visible signs of a higher status in terms of European values. A large following then tends to become an embarrassment rather than an asset. (1957, 135)

Turner noted that this process was occurring at such a rapid rate that even in the short interval between his first and second periods of field work, roughly one year, there were enormous increases in the number of *mafwami,* or farms.[2] These farms were usually established by younger men wishing to disencumber themselves from lineage ties so as to maximize profits from raising crops for the market. They broke away from established villages and lived with their own nuclear families. At the same time, more men than ever before were acquiring jobs in the mines on the Copperbelt; many hoped to return to Mwinilunga with sufficient cash to start their own enterprises. Turner acknowledged that there might have been times in the past when Lunda structures had been subjected to pressures that accelerated or retarded the rate of village fission, but he did not believe that these pressures had significantly altered the type of fission that generally occurred, that is, lineage segmentation. The basic unit of fission had historically been a maternal descent group. But since the 1950s, according to Turner, the elementary family had increasingly become the typical unit of fission (Turner 1957, 10). The links among uterine siblings and among matrilineal parallel cousins, which were at the heart of the Lunda village and its system of reckoning headmanship, had worn thin.

Village Life in the 1980s

We will now turn the clock forward by three decades to see how far along the road of atomization the Lunda have proceeded. In this section I revisit Turner's 1950s data on number of houses in settlements, individual mobility rates, relationship of house-owners to headmen, social composition of long-established villages compared to that of recently established villages, lineage depth in genealogies, village size and lineage depth, relationship between headmen and their successors, and relationship between leaders of seceding groups and their previous headmen. My aim is not simply to test Turner's predictions concerning the eventual demise of villages as the focal point of social organization. Rather, I continue the analysis of the interplay between powerful outside forces and local dynamics as the Lunda creatively redefine and reconstruct the relationship between the individual and the group in tandem with shifting political, economic, and environmental contexts. A direct comparison, however, of more recent data with those collected by Turner should be most informative in outlining the degree of change that has occurred in some of the Lunda's most basic systems. Once we are clear about what changes have occurred, we can then endeavor to ascertain why.

In present-day Mwinilunga, villages, per se, continue to exist. The administrative headquarters of the district is a town with a population of approximately three thousand (Central Statistical Office 1990). It contains a hospital, primary and secondary schools, a dozen or so government offices, a few shops, an open-air marketplace, and brick or concrete permanent housing for government officials, a few wealthy merchants, and several long-established missionaries. The overwhelming majority of the town's inhabitants live in clay brick houses with grass thatched roofs outside the commercial sector in what are called townships. But the bulk of the almost thirty-five thousand people in Chief Kanongesha's territory live in identifiable villages, each with a headman. To be without a village is, in a sense, to be without an address, to be without roots. National ID cards, mandatory for all adults in Zambia, list one's village affiliation, as do hospital, school, work, and most government records. However, most villages are no longer circular clearings in the forest but are straight, sometimes double, rows of houses along a road or pathway. Along some major roads the unbroken string of houses makes it difficult for an outsider to know where one village ends and another begins. But the residents have clearly defined notions about the spatial dimensions of their villages and tolerate no encroachment on their boundaries.

Let us first compare the size of villages in the 1980s with that of villages in the 1950s. The distinctions between different types of villages that existed when Turner did his research had disappeared by the later period. Although units called farms continued to exist, and still do today, they are rarely occupied by nuclear families. They usually consist of temporary shelters where people spend the rainy season working tracts of land relatively far from their permanent houses in villages. Because houses are clustered together along roads, many people had to go increasingly far afield to find fresh land to cultivate. At a certain point they found it more convenient to erect temporary shelters near their fields, which family members rotated through during the rainy season, spending a few weeks at a time working the farm. But during the dry season everyone returned to permanent dwellings back in a village. The only exceptions I found to this rule were a few cases where both the farm and the family became so large that permanent dwellings were slowly erected near the fields, and gradually more and more people began to reside there year-round. In these cases the farm began to take on the attributes of a village and was eventually referred to as such. Hence Turner's data are not directly applicable to the situation in the later period, but a comparison is informative nevertheless.

My data from the 1980s show that the breakup of villages that Turner feared had not occurred. But the villages were somewhat smaller than those of the 1950s, with averages of 6.3 versus 10.6 houses per settlement (table 1). The number of people occupying each house stayed about the same, at slightly over two.[3] Hence, the typical village in the 1980s had approximately ten fewer inhabitants than did the typical village in the 1950s. But it should be noted that Turner's sample was dominated by the category of registered villages; these registered villages, with their average of 13.1 houses per settlement, were artificial units forced on the Lunda by colonial policy.[4] After 1950, when the Lunda were given the opportunity to organize themselves as they wished, they chose to settle in somewhat smaller units. If we compare just those settlements of the 1950s that were free of colonial constraints with the settlements of the 1980s, we find the difference in size to be negligible. The combined average for unregistered villages and farms in the earlier period is 5.8 houses per settlement, which is close to the average of 6.3 houses per settlement for the later period. We will return to this point later. But for now it suffices to say that on average the size of villages did decrease from the 1950s to the 1980s if we include all types of villages in the comparison.

Second, we shall look at the question of individual mobility. Turner noted in the 1950s that individuals tended to circulate rapidly through different villages during the course of their lives.

Did the basic underlying dynamics of Lunda villages change? Could it be that the villages of the 1980s had in reality become the *mafwami* of Turner's era, simply absent the name? Farms, as Turner defined them, were essentially stable, nuclear family–based units attempting to maximize their own access to cash by disencumbering themselves from responsibility for the welfare of the wider lineage group. Villages, on the other hand, traditionally belonged not just to their current residents but also to any mem-

ber of the matrilineage who chose to visit, reside temporarily, or stay permanently. Hence, if villages had changed as a result of the reorganization
toward farm life that Turner believed he was witnessing in the 1950s, we
would expect to find a lesser degree of individual residential mobility in the
later period. But when we look at the data from the 1980s (tables 2b, 3b,
4b), we find that 79 percent of the males and 81 percent of the females
were living in villages other than the one in which they were born. Furthermore, 42 percent of the males and 39 percent of the females were actually raised in villages other than their natal village. Seventy-two percent
of the males and 73 percent of the females were raised in villages other than
the one in which were residing. Additionally, table 5b adds a spatial dimension by indicating that much of this movement is between chiefdoms.
This without a doubt represents a relatively high rate of individual mobility; it appears that the Lunda village still exhibited much the same dynamics as it had thirty-five years previously. In other words, villages had not
become simply farms masquerading as villages, but were still fluid, ever-
changing units offering individuals a variety of residential options. But although the rate of mobility was still high, it had decreased slightly. The
small size of both samples may in fact make the observable differences sta-
tistically insignificant. But if the Lunda were in fact moving slightly less
often, how do we account for this? Numerous reasons could be put forward. I propose that the situation may be the result of the odd and unpredictable interplay of three seemingly unrelated features: the necessary
conditions for formal schooling, the declining divorce rate, and changes in
architectural style.

In the mid-1980s only about half the school-age children in Mwinilunga
were enrolled in school, despite the great importance that the Lunda place
on educating their children (see Hoppers 1981; Wilkin 1983). Although
no accurate data exist, it is evident that some families spend over half of all
the cash they can mobilize on school fees and related expenses. But there
are not nearly as many school spaces as there are children wishing to enroll.
Every year on the first day of school one finds long lines of parents pleading with headmasters to find a place for their child or children. If a child
succeeds in being admitted to a particular school, he or she then has a guaranteed spot in that school each succeeding year, as long as academic standards are maintained. But that admission is not transferable to another
school. A child who wishes to stay in school must often remain within walking distance of that school. Unlike in the past, the child may have to forego,

or at least delay, taking up residence with uncles or other relatives elsewhere in the district.

Second, the rate of divorce, which will be discussed in more detail in chapter 6, had dropped precipitously since the 1950s (tables 6a and 6b). Women, with their children, oscillating between the villages of their matrikin and those of their husbands accounted for much of the mobility in Turner's data. A drop in the divorce rate would therefore be expected to reduce women's mobility.

Third, a change in architectural style, much evident in the 1950s, continues today (Turner 1957, 36). Previously, Lunda houses were circular frames of wood and bamboo, covered with clay, topped with a straw thatched roof. They usually lasted about three years, by which time termites would have so weakened the frame that the house needed either substantial repairs or complete rebuilding. Individuals considering moving to a new village would generally do so at this point. But today most houses are built of clay bricks, again topped with a straw thatched roof. Although the roof may need replacing in three to five years, these sturdy buildings can remain functional for ten to fifteen years. This type of house takes much longer to build and requires much more labor, in addition to the assistance of a skilled bricklayer, who generally must be paid in cash. Needless to say, people are reluctant to leave once they have built such a house, or had one built for them. In light of these factors it is remarkable that the Lunda still exhibit such a high rate of individual mobility.

Several questions remain. If villages indeed became somewhat smaller, and people moved slightly less frequently, did the basic composition of villages also change? And should this be the case, what impact would it have on the nature of village affiliation and on notions of rights and duties, claims and responsibilities that link the individual and the group?

A comparison of data from the 1980s with Turner's data sheds some light on the first of these questions. The most striking feature is the preponderance of the headmen's own descendants in villages, nearly 40 percent in the later period versus 11 percent in Turner's era, and the corresponding lack of classificatory matrilineal kin, 4.5 percent versus 21 percent (tables 7a and 7b). It is clear that in the battle between fathers and uncles to attract children to their villages, the tide had shifted firmly in favor of fathers, at least, that is, if the father was a headman. Children, in greatly increased numbers, were remaining longer in their father's village instead of returning to a village of their matrilineal kin. In the past, daughters married and moved to their husband's village. Sons, early in life, moved to a matrilineal uncle's village to claim their position in that hierarchy. Hence, a man was dependent on attracting his sisters' children to form his core of supporters if he wanted to succeed to headman. Had the mode of village recruitment changed? Were men no longer as interested in succeeding to headmanship in a village of their matrikin? Or had the mode of succession changed? Let us first examine several other data sets before we attempt to answer these questions.

Turner had found that long-established villages had a higher percentage of classificatory matrikin than did recently established villages, and that the proportion of the village population composed of the headman, his primary matrikin, and his own descendants was lower in the long-established villages. In other words, in the past a new village was often founded by a man who had seceded from an established village together with perhaps a brother or two, and their wives and children. But if the village persisted it would attract a more diverse array of kin, including classificatory kin. Thus the social composition of villages in the 1980s was quite similar to that of the newly formed villages of Turner's time. Even the long-established villages exhibited this same characteristic of a preponderance of the headman's primary matrikin (table 8b). It does appear that there was a marked diminution in the ability of headmen to recruit members from the larger matrilineal pool. Why was this so?

A comparison of data on age of marriage (tables 13a and 13b) may provide part of the answer. In the 1950s, 71 percent of the males had married by age twenty-nine. Thirty-five years later only 41 percent were married by that age. The corresponding change for females was equally dramatic, with the number of females who had been married before the age of twenty dropping from 61 percent to 27 percent. The divorce rate was also cut by more than half (see tables 6a and 6b). Not only were people waiting longer to get married, but once they had done so they tended to stay married, unlike in the 1950s, when the majority of marriages ended in divorce. As Turner noted, stable marriages tend to retard the growth of villages by keeping men apart from their uterine sisters and their sisters' children (Turner 1957, 69). This insight may go a long way toward explaining the changes that occurred in village composition in Mwinilunga.

Finally if we compare data on succession of headmen (tables 9a and 9b), we find that the traditional pattern of matrilineal succession changed considerably. In the past, succession was adelphic in one generation, passing down a line of brothers from oldest to youngest, then dropping down to the next senior genealogical generation of sisters' sons. Turner's data from the 1950s reflect this pattern. But the more recent data show that the largest category of villages was new villages founded by the present headman. Where an actual succession took place it was more likely that a son, rather than a brother or a sister's son, became the headman.

Clearly the changes in composition of villages revolve around two features: the strengthened marriage bond and the propensity of men to start new villages. Of these two features, the strengthened marriage bond is perhaps the more difficult to explain. The factors involved in the decision of two people to remain together as husband and wife, or to break up, are not only complex but usually inaccessible to outsiders. In fact, individuals themselves often find it difficult to articulate the reasons why their marriage is or is not successful. But understanding this change in the divorce rate is key to understanding changes in village dynamics. At least three major factors have contributed to contemporary concepts of marriage: the emergence of the stable monogamous marriage as a principal symbol of Christian fervor, increased cooperation between husbands and wives in household-based cash acquisition strategies, and the role of national policy in influencing issues of inheritance and heirship. I discuss these factors in more detail in chapter 6.

Elderly mothers tend to gravitate toward the villages of their sons. If sons remain with their fathers, this is an additional force buttressing the parents' marriages, mediating against divorce. I contend that sons are more than ever integrally involved in the cash-generating activities of their fathers first because they are present on a day-to-day basis in their fathers' villages. Whether the father is digging fishponds or clearing fields for cash cropping or hunting, his sons, if not otherwise occupied, are likely to accompany him and provide some additional labor. Hence at a certain point sons often find that even if they did not succeed in school they still have a major financial incentive for remaining in their father's village. Some sons even begin to see themselves as the rightful heirs to their father's enterprise. Their claim would not be based on the traditional rules of inheritance (which would, of course, acknowledge the father's matrikin, not his sons, as his natural heirs). Instead, the claim would be based on principles concerning the inalienable ownership of the fruits of one's own labor. When the father dies, his matrikin would no doubt attempt to claim some portion of his estate. But in cases where the estate was the result of joint endeavors by father and sons it might be difficult, if not impossible, to disentangle the assets of the father from those of the sons. Sons might prevail in the end. In fact, the contemporary design of villages, that is, rows of houses rather than circles, makes possible the creative manipulation of village boundaries in such a way that sons can now remain with their father throughout his lifetime and yet upon his death satisfy the traditional requirement that they leave the father's village without, in, fact, actually going anywhere. Traditional circular villages were impossible to divide without the loss of circularity: separating from an established village meant physically leaving that village and building a new circle of houses elsewhere. But a straight line can be divided into any number of parts, resulting simply in a number of shorter lines. Today it is possible to shift village boundary lines in such a way that smaller segments can declare themselves to be a separate village without physically moving. There have been a number of cases recently where a group of sons deliberately built their and their wives' and children's houses only to one particular side of their father's house. At a certain point they were able to insist that a line existed separating their complex of houses from that of their father. In this way they had become an autonomous village, still located on the land in which they had invested their labor for many years, yet having satisfied the requirement of eventually leaving their father's village.

Returning to an uncle's village because one is entitled to land and a place in the hierarchy that leads to headmanship does not exercise as strong an appeal as it once did. The traditional measures of wealth—large cassava fields, several wives, and many children—are no longer sufficient assets for a headman to do his job properly. One can still derive some economic benefits from being a headman, but first one must be well placed financially to help others. People simply will not allow a person who has not demonstrated superior ability to make money to become a headman, even if he is the eldest member of the senior lineage. On the other hand, if he has this ability, he will attract enough relatives to become a headman wherever he chooses to reside. So today a man exercises his best option for generating cash according to *maplan*, a long-term plan. This may mean starting a new village in an area best suited for the intended economic activity. It may often, as we saw, mean remaining for a long time in his father's village. And wherever sons are doing well, there one will find their mother.

Although Turner's predictions about the rise of individualism and the concomitant demise of the village as the principal agent of action may have appeared well founded in the 1950s, the hindsight of history shows that they were mistaken. The village continues to be a fundamental location for the formulation of individual identity, a necessary element in productive strategies, and a key ingredient in individual plans for the afterlife. Yet, the data suggest there have been changes in the basic composition of villages, the claims they make on the individual, and the degree to which they are malleable to individual initiative. Perhaps Turner underestimated the power of the individual. Perhaps he overestimated the rigidity of the village form of social organization. What is clear, nevertheless, is that the changes that have occurred could not have been predicted a priori as the inevitable outcome of a clash of structures. The changes emanate from a series of choices, hammered out over nightly fireside debates, guided and molded by individuals with *wuhaku*—the ability to persuade others that a move in a particular direction is justified. Contemporary choices (villages built in straight lines, new architectural styles and construction methods, household-based productive strategies, and the adoption of Christian symbolism) were no doubt arrived at peacemeal as the outcome of innumerable discussions, debates, and contestations. Their collective impact, however, is quite comprehensive. As we shall continue to see, each of these outcomes is viewed as being in accordance with tradition. Each may appeal to a different tradition than did its former alternative, but it is a tradition nonetheless.

Extra-Village Linkages or Connections

Turner's perception of the fissioning of Lunda villages was apparently influenced by Max Gluckman's notion that social groups that have an inherent tendency to segment are organized so that conflicts in one set of relationships are absorbed and redressed in countervailing relations. Turner proposed that Lunda unity was maintained not only in spite of fission, but perhaps because of it. Although intravillage hostility is generally at the root of any occurrence of fission, as time passes and tempers cool, the established village and the breakaway faction may reestablish friendly relations. The structural cleavages that led to estrangement can be forgotten, and the continuing bonds of kinship and previous association can be reasserted. The prevalence of village fission means that any individual can usually trace some relationship, whether consanguineal, affinal, or coresidential, to numerous other villages that dot the landscape of the Lunda territory. People can and do travel widely, knowing that wherever they go these intervillage links will guarantee them a warm reception and generous hospitality. Weddings, funerals, and initiations are seized upon as opportunities to reestablish or reinforce links with friends or relatives. Thus the instability of the local residential unit contributes to the widespread links that give the Lunda a sense of unity at a higher level.

Pan-Lunda Linkages

The Kanongesha

The changes noted above in rates of individual mobility and in the social composition of villages have had little impact on the spatial range of contemporary social linkages in Mwinilunga. More important, those changes have done little to diminish the larger notion of Lundahood. The symbolic figure of the Kanongesha, senior chief of all the Lunda-Ndembu, supposedly the direct descendant of the Mwantiyanvwa, leader of the Lunda Empire of old, still plays a profound role in promoting Lunda unity at the highest level. He functions symbolically much as the Shilluk kings studied by Evans-Pritchard: "The King symbolized a whole society and must not be identified with any part of it. He must be in the society and yet stand outside it and this is only possible if his office is raised to a mystical plane" (Evans-Pritchard 1948, 36).

Although all headmen and senior headmen recognize the Kanongesha as their paramount chief, they each remain fiercely autonomous. The major form of collaboration is in national rituals such as the funerary and installation rites of a Kanongesha. Many headmen and senior headmen continue to possess titles that endow them with historically significant ritual functions vis-à-vis the Kanongesha.[5] National rituals serve as opportunities to demonstrate those long-standing connections and as mnemonic devices for animating the continuing pride the Lunda share in their supposedly direct and exalted origins in the empire of the Mwantiyanvwa.

The office of the Kanongesha, thus, symbolizes the unity of all the Lunda first through a sense of common origins. Second, the Kanongesha represents unity as rooted in contemporary notions of shared rights to the use of a clearly defined territory. During much of the Lunda diaspora, a number of equally independent chiefs struggled with indigenous populations and with one another for control over land both for themselves and for the greater glory of their overlord, the Mwantiyanvwa. This period culminated in a series of agreements in which those chiefs pledged to mutually respect the boundaries of each other's territory. To acknowledge the Kanongesha as chief is thus to assert one's unity with all those possessing the rights to occupy and exploit the large region over which the Kanongesha reigns.

Succession to the position of Kanongesha had been patrilineal until 1890, when it was changed to conform to the matrilineal pattern common in the villages. There was, however, a tacit rule that no two successive Kanongeshas should come from the same lineage segment; the office should rotate around to the various segments matrilineally related to past chiefs. The first stage of selection is done by an electoral body consisting of the heads of four particular lineages. Their decision is ratified by a national council composed of all the major headmen of the polity. Royal families have been quite large in the past, and like commoners they have become dispersed over the entire territory. In virtually every village cluster there are individuals who claim some close relationship to the royal family, if not qualification as a potential successor to the Kanongeshaship itself. The chieftainship, thus, does not exist in some separate sphere, isolated from the daily reality of most villagers. It is present, immediate, and sufficiently widespread to involve everyone in the intricacies and intrigues of its functioning.

In theory, headmen should periodically give tribute to senior headmen, and senior headmen to the chief. But the Kanongesha polity is no simple pyramid. Tribute is a moral obligation, a symbolic act reaffirming unity, rather than a compulsory matter. Neither the Kanongesha nor his senior headmen possessed the means to physically enforce their will. Turner frequently spoke of the Lunda as being extremely individualistic, even anarchistic in what he called their "tribal character." History is replete with examples of local headmen not hesitating to fight a senior headman or the Kanongesha himself if they felt either had overstepped his bounds. One nineteenth-century Kanongesha even had his capital village looted and his close relatives enslaved by an angry local headman (Turner 1957, 325). Headmen have been known to unite to protect the autonomy of local village units. Because Lunda political organization at the highest level takes a ritual or symbolic form, any analysis of the day-to-day realities of power necessitates a return to the village level. This subject will be addressed in greater detail in chapter 7.

In-law Relationships

The spatial range of marriage is another powerful feature that both extends from and accentuates a sense of pan-Lunda identity. Turner found that 55 percent of marriages in the 1950s were between individuals who previously had not even been residents of the same chiefdom (table 12a). In many villages one could then find affinal links reaching the length and breadth of Lunda territory, and even into the neighboring countries of Angola and Congo. Villages in the 1980s, likewise, possessed similarly wide-ranging affinal links. Half of the marriages surveyed were between individuals from different chiefdoms (table 12b). Relations of affinity, however, do more than simply contribute to a general, vaguely articulated sense of Lundaness. They form concrete and clearly defined groupings that bestow specific sets of rights and privileges on individuals. They also make claims, enveloping the individual in multiple and at times competing sets of duties and obligations. The Lunda, like most of the peoples of western Central Africa, say that marriages may break up, but the in-law relationship is permanent (von Oppen 1993, 289). Those relationships exist in the rhetorical, symbolic, and proverbial spheres of daily social life. They also have an operational existence in the sphere of material transactions through reciprocal exchanges of goods and services.

There are two varieties of in-law relations: *ishaku*, relation by marriage, of the same generation or age group; and *muku*, father- or mother-in-law and son- or daughter-in-law. In narrative and performance the two types of relationships are expressed as extremes. They are polar opposites on a spectrum of social interaction that runs from fluid informality to rigid formality, and from anarchic egalitarianism to unassailable hierarchy.

The *ishaku* relationship is the very model of equality in social relations. *Ishaku* greet each other loudly with great physical zest. They may shout as they approach each other from a distance. They touch and slap hands frequently. *Ishaku* forsake the use of personal names, preferring to address each other repeatedly as "Ishaku!" It is a happy, carefree relationship, accompanied by lots of laughing, joking, and good-natured teasing. *Ishaku* are like *wusensi*, joking cousins. They may say anything to one another without offense. They may use each other's personal possessions with or without permission. The fluid, free-flowing *ishaku* relationship builds up layers of meanings and consequence over time and is a highly prized social connection. One may go to great lengths to come to the aid of an *ishaku* in need.

The *muku* relationship, however, represents social distance. Social interactions between *muku* are formal, tense, and even anxiety ridden. Greetings are long formulaic exchanges, spoken in solemn tones, with appropriate posture rigidly held. In its most extreme form it may become a relationship of avoidance. Men, in particular, must avoid their mother-in-law. But it must be an elegantly staged avoidance that is noticed by one's *muku*. A son-in-law, for example, upon seeing his mother-in-law approaching on the road, may, in full view, run into the woods rather than cross her path. It is the ultimate sign of respect, his most dramatic demonstration that he is unworthy of even being in her presence.

Women not infrequently come to reside in the village with their husbands' parents. Over time the relationships may grow less rigid, greetings less formulaic. But the same is rarely true of men. For them *muku* relations are modeled on *mandumi-mwiha*, uncle-nephew relations. At their best, they offer the junior male an ally and a source of aid in the ascending generation. They buttress and reinforce the hierarchical position of the elder and offer him or her an ally in the descending generation. A man treats a visit from an elder *muku* with as much pomp and circumstance as he can muster. One treats a visit to *hawuku*, an elder *muku*'s village, as a solemn undertaking, carried out with exaggerated displays of deference and unworthiness.

Turner described the customs of the early marriage years as having changed by the 1950s: "In the past marriage was uxorilocal for the first year, in the course of which the husband had to build a hut for his mother-in-law and clear and hoe up a garden for her with his wife's help. Then he took his wife to his own village and cut, cleared and hoed up the rough ground into a garden for her. . . . Nowadays, the work for the mother-in-law is often commuted into a cash payment, ranging from ten shillings to one pound or more, depending on the wealth and status of the parties involved" (1957, 23).

A husband's initial residence in his wife's village, and the wife and her kin's obligation to accommodate visitors from her husband's village, no doubt provided *ishaku* and *muku* ample opportunities for interaction from the moment their relationship came into being. Today, less than 10 percent of men live uxorilocally for the first years of marriage. The payment for avoiding this task is rarely negotiated as a separate item in the bridewealth package. Thus, neither *muku* nor *ishaku* relations are automatically activated by marriage. They must be sought out, made operational by periodic exchanges of gifts, and carefully nurtured. They cannot be forced or rushed. They are high-maintenance relationships fraught with perils, called upon to mediate some of the slipperiest ground in human relations. In-law relations provoke issues of culturally sanctioned sex between members of different groups. They entail the transfer of physical labor, village affiliation, and perhaps the loyalty of one's kin. They are a necessary element in the procreation of one's heirs, while at the same time physically separating one from those heirs. Yet, with the successful investment of energy and emotions, over time an in-law relationship gains an ontological status that transcends the actual marriage at its base. It may persist beyond divorce, even beyond death.

One is accountable to the in-laws for the health and well-being of one's spouse. Upon the death of either spouse, irrespective of cause, a payment is exacted by the in-laws from the surviving spouse. *Mpepi* must be paid by a woman for her husband's death; *katotafu* by a man for his wife's death. The payment may entail little more than some agricultural produce, and, increasingly, a small amount of cash. Rarely is the amount onerous. But, as emerges time and again in the African context, the initiation, the maintenance, and even the finalizing of a relationship is symbolized by a material transaction. Death is no exception. Death, however, is often accompanied by a divination to ascertain if the surviving spouse played any role in the death. The suspicion embedded in a relationship that carries such social weight frequently bubbles to the surface in the form of accusations of neglect, if not outright witchcraft. Should the surviving spouse be found culpable in any respect, the payment could balloon to devastating proportions.

Paradox and ambiguity abound in in-law relations. Yet they can be a great source of comfort and pride, an aid to productive strategies, a public manifestation of one's skill in managing social relations, a key ingredient in demonstrating one's capacity for leadership, and a step toward gaining *mpuhu* and remembrance in the afterlife.

Curing Societies

The Lunda concept of disease, and the ritual action to which it gives rise, produces another social aggregate into which individuals differentially embed themselves. Rituals, mentioned earlier with respect to the role they play in intravillage unity, also establish intervillage links. Lunda philosophy holds that many forms of illness are caused by the spirits of ancestors

(Turner 1968, 14). A person may be afflicted by a spirit for several reasons. First, one may have failed to fulfill some specific promise made to the spirit while she or he was alive. For example, one may have promised an uncle that one would always remain in his village and would, upon his death, assume the responsibility of caring for his aged dependents. Upon breaking that promise and leaving the uncle's village, one suddenly suffers a debilitating illness. Such would be the classic manifestation of spirit-induced illness. Second, one may be afflicted for the more general reason that family members appear to have forgotten the departed one. Spirits apparently like to be remembered in thought and deed by their relatives. They want future generations to know of their existence and their contribution to the chain of life. The most profound way of remembering a deceased person is by naming a child after him or her. If a good number of children have been born in a village and none has been named after a particular deceased individual, that individual's spirit may afflict someone with illness until the perceived neglect is redressed. Third, individuals may be afflicted because family members are behaving improperly toward one another. Feuding, fighting, or lack of sharing and cooperation among family members are cited as the kinds of activities that most often force a spirit to show its displeasure toward members of the family. In the latter two categories a person is afflicted not for some individual transgression but on behalf of an entire group.

The remedy for a spirit-caused affliction is a rather elaborate and costly ritual that can last several days, or even months. Its aim is to placate the afflicting spirit and entice it to return to the spirit world. The ritual is officiated by a *chimbuki,* head doctor, and his assistants. They are all individuals who, at one time or another, have themselves been afflicted in the same mode, that is, by a spirit who caused the very same sickness in them that the patient is now experiencing. Indeed, if the patient should recover, he or she becomes eligible to join the curing group and serve as an assistant in future rituals for this mode of affliction; with time and careful study, the patient may even become a *chimbuki,* curing others of the illness he or she has miraculously survived. The key point here is that although affliction is thought to be associated with a breach of norms within a specific kinship group, the treatment of the afflicted person is carried out by a collection of ritual specialists who need not necessarily be related to the patient. These groups form what Turner called cults of affliction. There are separate cults for each mode of affliction. Cult membership cuts across all village affiliation and ties of kinship and affinity: "Since most adult members of any village are adepts in at least one cult, and since members of all cults may be found everywhere in the Ndembu and Kosa regions, it follows that the total ritual system provides a set of interconnections which in effect perform a political function" (Turner 1957, 296). By "political," Turner is apparently asserting that ritual performs two very different functions. On the one hand, ritual beliefs and actions underscore, in dramatic fashion, the interrelatedness and interdependence of countless scattered semiautonomous Lunda villages, and thus contribute in a significant way to the creation of a generalized sense of Lundahood. On the other hand, the actualization of ritual requires a structure; the formal structure of the cult of affliction, asserts Turner, plays an essential role in day-to-day governance: "By establishing ties of co-participation in cults which operate independently of kinship and local linkages, the ritual system compensates to some extent for the limited range of effective political control and for the instability of kinship and affinal ties to which political value is attached" (1957, 291). From my observations of intercult relations, it appears that Turner put too much emphasis on formal structures while overlooking the importance of the affective intensity of social bonds created by shared metaphysical experiences. Ritual may provide the opportunity for relations among cult members, but it is the force of emotions rather than containment within a formal structure that defines those continuing relations.

At the organizational level, cult ties come into being when a *chimbuki* is asked to perform his curing ritual for a person deemed by a diviner to be afflicted with an illness curable only by that ritual. After financial arrangements have been made and a date set for the ritual, the *chimbuki* recruits assistants. All individuals who were at one time afflicted and then cured of that illness may assist the *chimbuki* as ritual officiants. Tasks are assigned in accordance with prior ritual experience. Herbal medicines are collected and prepared, and chickens for sacrificing and other ritual paraphernalia are assembled, all under the supervision of the *chimbuki,* who is in complete control of the ritual sequence that follows. During the ritual, the *chimbuki* may ask the assistants to bring him particular articles or to manipulate or anoint the patient's body in certain ways. But generally assistants simply watch and learn, for by doing so they too may someday be sufficiently knowledgeable to serve as a *chimbuki.* Their presence is also deemed pleasing to the aggrieved ancestor and thus brings added efficacy to the ritual. The curing group, which may number no more than a dozen or so individuals, will cease to exist in a few days once the ritual has ended, and it might never be reconstituted again with the same personnel. Months or years may pass between formal encounters of the group, and in the interim, relative positions within the ritual hierarchy may have been modified in accordance with esoteric knowledge acquired by particular cult members. Curing groups hold no regular meetings, and individuals are free to learn as little or as much ritual esoterica as they desire. Some cult members follow a *chimbuki* from performance to performance, rising rapidly in ritual rank and renown. Others pick and choose, participating in relatively few rituals throughout their lives.

Cults of affliction present the individual with an opportunity to participate in the construction and maintenance of a social network. They enable rather than mandate participation. Participation, however, is differentially attractive. Cults are unique social entities. Their mode of composition is unlike any other Lunda social organization in that it is the ancestors who directly recruit one to cult membership. Such a realization can provoke emotions that run from feelings of awesome power to terrifying responsibility to abject horror. Shared metaphysical capacity, however, is a powerful basis on which to further cultivate other multifaceted relations. Cult members may rely upon one another for hospitality when traveling, reliable information about trading prospects, or support in political succession struggles. These relations, just like those with in-laws, must be mutually sought out and delicately managed over time. Ritual may provide the opportunity, but it is the force of emotions rather than containment within a formal structure that defines cult members' ongoing relations.

Friends and Cohorts

The classic anthropological literature has paid insufficient attention to the range of non-kin relations, most especially those based on voluntary friendship, often mediated outside visible social structures. Yet the early literature on western Central Africa is full of examples of the importance of *wubwambu* (friendship) in the conduct of daily social life. Livingstone (1857), Silva Porto (1885), Melland (1923), Baumann (1935), and White (1960) each observed and wrote about the widespread reliance on non-kin-based friendship in facilitating productive activities, giving and receiving assistance, providing hospitality to travelers, and circulating useful information.

Among the Lunda, cohorts are reckoned as *amabwambu* (friends). These friendships, however, are strengthened and given an added dimension by the concept and consequences of age. Because the members are the same age and, thus, share years of common experiences, they form social groupings distinct from those based on kin, in-law, or curing groups. Cohorts may treat one another like *ishaku*, in-laws of the same generation. The relationships can be relaxed and casual at times. They are forged, however, in the furnace of regular and often daily contact. Close constant involvement with another makes visible to cohorts subtle differences in individual competencies and personal preferences, and the points of tension that inevitably arise with intense social interaction. Such relationships take individuals into the core of one another's existence. Cohorts literally witness one another's lives and share one another's transitions and crises. Often they have grown up together, collectively discovering and adjusting to their changing physical state of being, as well as to the changing sets of duties and privileges that attend each stage of life. Cohorts see intimate sides of one another's lives that kin may not even be aware of. As noted earlier, the grandparent-grandchild relation is also based on open friendship, but the age difference sets limits on the degree to which each can participate in the day-to-day life of the other. The gulf of experience between them tempers the relevance and meaning of any advice given. There are few barriers, however, between cohorts. It is, thus, from cohorts that people feel most comfortable soliciting advice about marital relations, child-rearing practices, or other intimate matters.

The act of mutual witnessing is itself laden with symbolic meaning and stocked with utilitarian value. Mutual witnessing serves as a collective mnemonic device in societies based on oral rather than written records. It provides a source of confirmation for agreements reached and promises made. It is the verifier of prices paid and debts due, the validator of duties performed, the reminder of expectations left unfulfilled. It provides the character witness in the slander case, the alibi in the theft case. Mutual witnessing also enables the cohort group to serve as a crucible for refining hierarchical relations. Minor differences in individual rank are worked out at this level. The panoptic nature of cohort interaction makes it a unique arena of both cooperation and contestation.

Each group of cohorts is, in a sense, responsible for policing its members' behavior. Among the Lunda, one is literally one's cohort brothers' or sisters' keeper. There is, thus, a collective sense of equality of the cohort vis-à-vis other older or younger groups. While each group is responsible for its own internal ranking, members collectively strive to raise the rank of the entire group relative to other groups of cohorts. The respect and support of one's cohorts frequently come into play in confrontations with other cohort groups. The result of these interactions is a society of myriad social strata based on age. The Lunda, however, do not possess the elaborate and more formalized age-grade institutions of East Africa. Lunda age groupings are not ceremonially created and recognized, nor are they residentially segregated from the rest of society. Yet, Lunda age layers are nonetheless real and are clearly observable in daily interactions.

At the lowest and most concretely defined level, a set of *amabwambu*, friends, may consist of a dozen or so individuals. Younger people today refer to these groups by the anglicized term *maguys* (the "guys"; female groupings are called *magirlguys*, the "girl guys"). Older groupings still use the term *wubwambu*. Association is purely voluntary, yet membership remains relatively stable. Disputes over hierarchical rank or other issues can lead to estrangement, but the pressures exerted by long-standing bonds of the most intimate nature keep movement to a minimum. It is as difficult to break off relations with old cohorts as it is to develop substantive new ones. Such groups are fundamental to the discovery of one's identity; they are a prime site of the personal experimentation with social roles that accompanies the development of the mature self. Although cohort groups take on a life of their own, individuals retain the power to kill the group, or *jaha*. The loss of a single personality changes the dynamics of group, however slightly, forcing the remaining members to reassess their relationships with one another, both hierarchically and personally. But to kill the group is to kill a part of oneself. Very little of one's identity has its own autonomous existence. One is something only in relation to someone else. It is, thus, only with great forethought, and as a result of extreme circumstances, that a member leaves a long-standing cohort group.

Extending outward from the narrow cohort group is a fuzzier set of connections with other sets of cohorts of similar age. These connections form the basis for reciprocal networks across village boundaries. The carriers of the eighteenth- and nineteenth-century caravans were noted for possessing networks of friendship over hundreds of miles. The migrant workers of the early twentieth century had even more extensive networks. Today, when cohorts travel over long distances, they seek out their counterparts in the villages they pass, initiating informal pacts of mutual assistance sealed by some exchange of goods and services. Itinerant merchants move across the landscape receiving hospitality each night at the villages of friends. Young men travel deep into Angola on trade missions, guided and assisted by counterpart cohorts who advise them on the current status of the war, the safest routes to take, and the prevailing prices for their goods. Traveling by foot to weddings, funerals, and initiation ceremonies through territory where one has no kin or in-laws is much easier if one has friends in the area.

Cohort groups may initially grow out of associations based on kinship, affinity, or ritual association. Increasingly, strong friendships are arising among schoolmates and church members, or through shared participation in government schemes and development projects. A cohort group publicly marks its existence by deliberately developing its own style. Novel slang or other linguistic markers, modes of attire or bodily adornment, handshakes or other methods of touching are subject to elaboration as signifiers of special connections. At a more substantive level, cohort identity may be based on experimentation with novel productive activities. The initial group of fish farmers in Mwinilunga, most of the commercial maize farmers, and the new caravans of youth trekking to Cazombo constitute cohort groups molded by involvement in innovative enterprises. The group provides a forum for sharing technical information as well as emotional support for the anxieties of traveling a less-trodden path. Increasingly, the group is having an impact on village structure. More and more cohorts are deciding to reside together, perhaps to pursue joint ventures more effectively, perhaps simply out of friendship. These villages take on a composite, rather than a strictly matrilineal tone. Friend may even succeed friend as headman. In my 1985 survey of nearly one hundred villages, roughly 10 percent of headmen were unrelated to the previous headman of that village (table 9b). In most cases they were friends. Turner mentions no such cases in his surveys from the 1950s.

Summary

The Lunda are not unique in devising systems that promote wide latitude for individual expression, while also producing a matrix of generally recognized hierarchical structures. Margaret Mead and Gregory Bateson described this combination of autonomy and structure for the Balinese in the 1930s, as did Clyde Kluckhohn for the Navaho in the 1940s. The Lunda represent but one more example of a group possessing the pan-African trait that Vansina brought to our attention, the passionate drive to protect individual autonomy while endeavoring to build up widespread linkages. We return, once again, to the subject of movement—movement according to agricultural cycles, across the landscape for trade, through culturally recognized stages of life, and up and down various hierarchies. The relationship between the individual and the group among the Lunda is ideally suited to cope with and even at times to compel movement.

The household, the village, the kin group, the in-laws, the curing group, and the cohort group provide arenas through which an individual can choose to move, and offer material from which to sculpt a life of connections. The groups vary in the claims they make and the rights and privileges they confer. Their bonds are all, nevertheless, symbolized by material transactions. Physical goods must change hands if a relationship is to endure. The amount and types of goods to be exchanged for particular categories of relations are not prescribed, however; rather, one "talks" with transactions. One states one's desires through the timing and types of exchanges one pursues. Whether one reciprocates quickly or slowly, haphazardly or thoughtfully is a statement about desires. Whether one pursues transactions aggressively or entices them passively is a statement about social position. The plethora of opportunities for developing connections diminishes the need to conform to particular patterns of behavior, thought, or action. The individual is free to develop his or her own unique personal style while simultaneously pursuing productive and comfortable connections. The relationships in which an individual chooses to invest his or her time, emotions, and physical energy may vary over the course of a lifetime as new opportunities emerge and old opportunities take on new meaning.

Understanding the complexities of the relationship between the individual and the group, a theme that will continue to reverberate in the chapters to come, helps to understand the basis of the argument at Kamau village with which this chapter opened. The argument was not really about gifts of soap or suggestions of sex. Nor can the level of rage displayed be attributed solely to sleep deprivation and excessive alcohol consumption. The fight between Big Kamau and Richard that cold and dusty morning on Matonchi plateau encapsulated and publicly dramatized a number of ongoing and emerging struggles. At one level it was a battle about personal integrity and the inviolable autonomy of the individual. Richard's blows carried the weight of all who strike out for freedom, both in thought and deed. The Lunda lay claim to freedom as if it were their own special gift from God, their own unique birthright. When told of the promises and pleasures of life elsewhere, the Lunda reply with the standard refrain, "at least here we are free." When confronted with their own material poverty, again the refrain, "at least here we are free." Yet, freedom is not reckoned as a lofty political ideal, nor as a diffuse set of privileges localized within the collectivity. Instead, notions of freedom are quite particularistic, localized within individuals. Freedom is the right to move across the plateau at will, to control the pace of one's own life, to cultivate relationships, and to map out one's existence with a minimum of hindrances. Big Kamau, at the most visceral level, was an affront to that freedom, the embodiment of restraint. His actions demanded a powerful response.

At another level, Kamau village briefly became a site in the struggle between modernity and tradition. Relaxed and friendly relations between males and females represent a recent and, for some, a reprehensible pattern of behavior. Separation by gender, which I discuss in chapter 5, has long been the primary foundation of Lunda social organization, underpinning the division of labor, the layout of villages, existential status, and even metaphysical relations and interactions between the living and the dead. Uncontrolled contact between males and females is viewed as positively dangerous. Yet, those who have attended school see themselves as a distinct group: the experience of school reduces the distance between classmates, while expanding the distance between the schooled and the unschooled. In fact, casual intergender relations have become the public hallmark of the school educated. The members of *maguys* and *magirlguys* groups are the generation of males and females whose relationships were brewed in the process of mutually witnessing one another's lives in overly crowded rural classrooms and through long walks to and from school together over many years. Theirs is a battle to bring into being a new type of group, indeed, to establish a new basis for generational unity. Yet, many of the older generation, both males and females, find it difficult to disconnect their feelings about intergender contact from notions about illicit sex. The result is a low-level intergenerational struggle that will no doubt persist for some time, flaring into public view ever so rarely, emotions held in check by the overarching principle that each generation holds the primary responsibility for policing itself.

Although it is perhaps unwise to speculate about the motives of inebriated men, it is entirely possible that the fight in Kamau village was given added impetus by poor in-law relations. Some people were aware that Big Kamau was not particularly comfortable with his son's marriage. Young Alexander had been a good student, and there had been much hope that he would somehow continue his education outside the district, and perhaps go on to a government job in the city. For many parents, steady remittance from an urban-based offspring is one of life's most highly sought-after prizes, justifying years of parsimonious existence. Alexander was a handsome and sociable young man who attracted a fair amount of attention from his female cohorts. He had been caught, however, in sexual activities with Gladys, who supposedly became pregnant. A marriage was hurriedly arranged, mostly at the insistence of Gladys's relatives. But when the pregnancy failed to materialize, there was some talk of entrapment, moral laxity, and avariciousness. Kamau may have been striking out indirectly at his in-laws by attempting to cast Gladys in the role of trouble-making trollop. The young men simply provided a convenient context for Kamau to express his frustration at being forced into in-law relations not of his own choosing.

Ultimately, of course, the fight at Matonchi was the classic battle among men, young and old, over prominence and power, influence and ascendancy. The young men, carefree and unencumbered by productive responsibilities, saw the world as their playground. Big Kamau, *Mweni Mukala*, owner of the village, was weighed down with dependents and duties to others. Should not Kamau's position have compelled respect from those too young to have yet built their own houses, let alone a village? Respect, yes, but not necessarily compliance. Public opinion that day suggested that the operative group and the governing set of behavioral principles were other than what Kamau imagined. Subsequent chapters on old and young, males and females expand on other dimensions of these complicated relationships.

Chapter Four

The Old and the Young

He Didn't Respect His Age, So He Lost It!
Dry Season, September 10, 1986

It was my first full day in Ikelenge, a rather densely settled area in the northern part of the Mwinilunga District. I had arrived the night before, with my wife and my eight-month-old baby daughter, to begin a two-month stay. For two and a half years I had been living forty miles to the south in Chifunga village. I had now come to Ikelenge for a number of reasons. First, in the interest of academic thoroughness, I thought it necessary to organize an extended stay in a village some distance from my own in order to gain a sense of the regional diversity of cultural forms, to ponder the degree to which the conclusions that I was beginning to reach as a result of my experiences in Chifunga village could be generalized to other Lunda areas. I must confess, however, that an invitation from a Dutch development officer to look after his extremely modern and well-stocked house in Ikelenge while he went home on leave played a powerful role in site selection. After years of living in a clay house with a leaky grass roof, carrying water from the well, and fighting a never-ending battle against termites, my wife and I were positively giddy at the prospect of staying in a house with hot and cold running water, a stereo, a refrigerator, and a full-time houseboy, all paid up for the next two months. The stay in Ikelenge would clearly serve as a welcome respite from the less comfortable aspects of doing fieldwork in rural Africa. But, as much as I was looking forward to this little vacation, I was nevertheless a bit apprehensive about coming to a new area and having to establish my identity anew. I reflected on the circus-like atmosphere that had accompanied my initial entry into Chifunga village. I remembered the feeling of being watched every waking moment, of having my every movement and utterance endlessly dissected by an entertainment-starved population. I remembered being followed up dusty dirt paths by hordes of children curious as to where I was going and what I would do once I arrived there. I remembered how difficult it had been for people to accept the fact that I was an American—not only was I not white, but perhaps more important I was not rich. And I remembered how it seemed an eternity before the people of Chifunga eventually became sufficiently bored observing me so that I could finally begin observing them under circumstances that were even vaguely normal. As I sat around the new house that first morning in Ikelenge I wondered what would happen when I ventured out into my new world. I knew that living in such splendor in the midst of rural poverty would surely place a barrier between me and the common folk of Ikelenge. Would two months be long enough to break through that barrier and develop meaningful relationships? Or was I destined to remain a quaint curio, an amusing novelty; that black American guy who once stayed in that rich Dutch guy's house. No! That will not be the case, I told myself. I am not a novice at this. I have lived among Lunda people for two and a half years now. I speak their language. I am knowledgeable of the intricacies of their social etiquette. I am intimately familiar with their symbolic systems. Surely the effort I have made to understand something of life among the Lunda will be acknowledged and appreciated. Surely the people of Ikelenge will recognize in me a person of substance worthy of being known and not merely gawked at. At least, I hoped they would.

Before I could muster my courage to leave the house, a welcoming party of young males arrived. They were all employees of the Catholic priest up the road, who, in his more than twenty years in Ikelenge, had built a rather large mission station that offered a wide range of services to the local community. He was, furthermore, one of the few employers of wage laborers in the area. He had apparently informed some of his workers of my arrival and had piqued their curiosity enough to send them scrambling to be the first to try to figure out what manner of being I was. After a few moments of rather stilted conversation they asked if I would be interested in accompanying them to drink *kachayi*, a local millet beer. I leaped at the opportunity. Although I was not particularly interested in drinking alcoholic beverages so early in the morning, I knew that a Kachayi drink would provide me with the perfect forum for demonstrating my local knowledge. Kachayi drinks are always highly ritualized affairs requiring a detailed knowledge of Lunda linguistic, kinesics, and aesthetic forms. Back at Chifunga village I had attended countless Kachayi drinks and was supremely confident of my ability to comport myself well at them. As I accompanied my newfound companions up a dirt road to the drinking spot we passed numerous people, each of whom had to be formally greeted. The formulaic greetings of the Lunda consist of handclaps, handshakes, and several exchanges of questions and answers that must be spoken in a rigidly defined order. As I effortlessly went through the greeting procedure I heard murmurs of approval.

When we arrived at the drinking spot, a grassy place behind a tight collection of houses, the seating arrangement had to be negotiated. Most villages possess a number of goatskin stools, no two of which are exactly the same size, as well as a number of logs, pieces of wood, bricks, rusty buckets, straw mats, and pieces of bark, all of which are used as seats. There is a hierarchy of seats known to all the members of the village. The best seat is always offered to the most senior person present, the second best seat to the second most senior person, and so on down to the most junior person, who must often arrange for his own seating by plucking leaves from a nearby tree and assembling a small cushion on the ground. When a new individual arrives to join an already seated group, all those who are junior to that individual immediately give up their seats and rearrange themselves to reflect the new hierarchical alignment, with the most junior rushing off to pluck more leaves. The situation becomes very complicated, if not outright bewildering, when individuals not well known to one another attempt to sit together, as was indeed the case this day. By my estimate we were all roughly in the same age group. But custom dictates that a hierarchy must be established. The Lunda propensity for exaggerated politeness in uncertain situations can lead to extensive delays before anyone can be seated. No one wants to be seen as aggressively seeking rank. Yet, no one wants to carelessly lose rank either. I asserted my unworthiness for nearly fifteen minutes before finally accepting the large chair that had initially been offered. I heard more murmurs of approval.

Five minutes into the Kachayi drink I spotted an elderly man approaching the group from a distance. I knew that we would have to rearrange our seating pattern to reflect the new hierarchical alignment. I looked around and made a mental note of the seat I would be required to shift down to. I felt that my knowledge of Lunda proxemics was refined to the degree that I would be able to predict at which point in the old man's progression toward us we would all be required to rise up, assume a subservient posture, hands ready to clap, and wait for this senior to utter the first words of greeting. I decided to show my mastery of Lunda social etiquette by rising a half second before everyone else would rise. In a sense I would lead the show of respect for this elderly gentleman. After all, I was sitting in the large chair that would soon be his. At the proper moment I popped out of my chair and assumed the appropriate position of respect. An incredibly awkward moment of silence followed. Everyone looked at me strangely. No murmur of approval this time. The old man was now clearly in our midst and yet no one made a move to acknowledge his presence. All eyes were focused on me, the expression on every face crying out, "Why in the world are you standing there looking silly?" In answer to that presumed question I said loud and clear in my best Lunda, "The elder has arrived!" The seated group replied almost in unison. "Sit down . . . that guy didn't respect his age, so he lost it!" The old man was not offered a chair. Instead, he sat on the ground as would a youngster. When he was finally offered a cup of *kachayi*, he did not accept it in the slow dignified manner of an elder receiving that which is rightfully his, but eagerly reached for it, gesticulating appreciatively as would a kid receiving some unexpected treat from his parents. His weathered and wrinkled features suggested great age, but his comportment was in every respect that of a child.

Reflections on Age

Autonomy and connectedness, egalitarianism and hierarchy are cognate pairs of concepts among the Lunda. Age (*nyaka*) is the dominant idiom for expressing relationships between people. Birthdays, however, are not celebrated and are rarely recognized in any particular fashion. In general, people claim not to know, or are at least reluctant to state publicly, their actual chronological age. Yet relative age is a topic of constant concern, a subject of nightly fireside debates. Arguments over who-is-senior-to-whom seem to lead to more public conflict and produce more long-lasting animosity than any other area of concern. Individuals who have been seen calmly resolving a case of adultery, theft, or other type of offense through eloquently reasoned dialogue may resort to actual fisticuffs over questions of age.

From time to time one encounters individuals in Mwinilunga who, although quite young in appearance, are nevertheless widely acknowledged by the local folks as possessing great age. It is easy to surmise that these are young males who by virtue of wage employment or entrepreneurial skills have far greater access to cash than does the general population (see Weeks 1971; Hoppers 1981). According to the 1990 National Census of Population and Housing, and confirmed by personal observations, young males not only dominate the local job market but are also far more prone than either elderly males or females of any age to migrate to urban areas and return with cash to establish local enterprises. The commonsense explanation— that a wealthy youth is treated with the same respect as an older person— may be sufficient explanation for the periodic emergence of baby-faced elders; but how does one explain the reverse, the occurrence of aged individuals who are reckoned as children?

My encounter with the child-like elder in Ikelenge exemplifies the relationship between two powerful yet seemingly contradictory principles that permeate Lunda society: hierarchy and egalitarianism. Victor Turner made frequent references to the egalitarian nature of Lunda-Ndembu society (see, e.g., Turner 1957, 104, 189). Indeed, from C. M. N. White in the 1940s to Achim von Oppen in the 1990s, nearly every researcher working among upper Zambezi peoples has noted the strong strands of egalitarianism running through various conceptual and applied realms of daily life. Yet notions of hierarchy permeate nearly every aspect of social life as well. For the Lunda, orderly human interaction rests on the foundation of hierarchy or *kavumbi*, respect. *Kavumbi* is a broad concept which entails more than merely being courteous and considerate. It is respect reified, a thing to be given and received in public. *Kavumbi* is the actual performance of specific physical actions, for instance, bows, handclaps, and utterances, which acknowledge and reinforce one's status vis-à-vis another person. These actions must be performed whenever two individuals meet. On one Lunda scale of ideation, no two individuals are equal, with the exception of *ishaku* (in-laws of the same sex and generation) and *wusensi* (joking cousins). Individuals are ranked vertically, and each should occupy a unique position within a hierarchy that starts with the paramount chief and reaches all the way down to the most recently born infant. How then can the Lunda claim to be egalitarian? What, indeed, does the concept mean under such circumstances?

Reflections on the concept of egalitarianism have long been part of Western intellectual discourse.[1] No consensus has emerged, however, on its definition, the conditions under which it flourishes, or the forces that affect its attainment. Because notions of equality can reflect local views of society and human action, the value of a totalizing, essentializing approach to the subject is limited. My aim, therefore, is to discuss notions of egalitarianism embedded in Lunda-Ndembu social action and discourse. As in other areas of social interaction, it is not without contestation. The intensity of contestation, in fact, is the greatest indicator of widespread importance. There is a shared sense that notions of equality and inequality are worth fighting over; that they are perhaps the most justifiable causes for disputes.

Understanding the nuances of the Lunda's conception of egalitarianism necessitates unpacking some generally held beliefs as well as paying greater attention to the multiplicity of meanings subsumed under the broad term egalitarianism. It requires examining egalitarianism along three interrelated but analytically separable axes: wealth, power, and prestige. These axes correspond, more or less, to the three forms of egalitarianism noted in the literature: equality of condition, equality of opportunity, and moral or legal equivalency of individuals or social groups. Although many authors restrict their comments and analyses to just one of these forms of egalitarianism, the three forms can occur in a single analytical space as interrelated phenomena linked by a range of processes from economic to intellectual. Such is the Lunda case. Hierarchy in the domain of prestige facilitates and mediates between the ideology and the perception of equality in the domains of wealth and power. In other words, the Lunda mandate inequality in the prestige sphere through actions that produce equality in the other two spheres. Ideally no two individuals are equal in prestige, and individuals are encouraged to compete with one another in the pursuit of high status. The mechanisms used to gain position within the prestige sphere not only are inextricably linked to processes in the spheres of wealth and power but are mechanisms that actually advance the production of equality in those two spheres. Furthermore, this type of egalitarianism is not an artifact of the Lunda's low level of political and economic development, as many theorists would suggest, but is instead an active and continually reconstructed device which assists in the creation and maintenance of group ties that are larger than those required by economic imperatives. I discuss the three axes of wealth, power, and prestige in turn before moving on to a discussion of egalitarianism, group formation, and the uses of age.

The Nature of Wealth and the Structure of Conditions

What constitutes material wealth among the Lunda? How is it acquired? To what degree is it distributed evenly or equitably? Most Lunda today subsist primarily on agriculture, supplemented by hunting, fishing, collecting wild foods, and raising domestic stock. Yet, they have long been dependent on external trade to supply many basic necessities. In the precolonial period the Central African caravan trade network linked the local economy to that of Europe and Asia. (I discuss the creation and meaning of wealth during that period in chapter 6.) Today the Lunda are dependent, for the most part, on the industrial centers of the Copperbelt and the capital city, Lusaka, to provide them with such basic commodities as salt, sugar, cooking oil, soap, clothing, and a range of manufactured goods. These goods must be acquired with cash, which is obtained mostly through the sale of foodstuffs, but also through the limited opportunities for wage employment. Cash is also needed for school fees, the greatest single item of expenditure by parents on children. Because land is quite abundant, with a population density of roughly six persons per square mile, the subject of land rarely arises in the local discourse over wealth.

The Lunda divide *yuma*, things, into two main types: *ibomba*, common property, commonwealth, things shared by all; and *maheta*, things belonging to an individual, individual riches or wealth. Items of value that result from collective effort could belong to either category, depending on the form of organization that brought that value into being. One could also talk about "wealth-in-people," or "wealth-in-relationships," such as children, relatives, and friends who are willing to assist an individual and who enrich his or her life. But these relationships have more to do with the production of opportunities than with the structure of material conditions, a feature which will be discussed below.

Individuals possess differing amounts of *maheta*. *Mukwakuheta* are the rich, those who possess many things. There is a fair amount of difference in the sizes of people's houses and fields, the number of animals they possess, their access to the inputs of cash cropping, and their access to cash itself and the things it can purchase. Likewise there are differences in the ownership of things such as tools, household articles, clothes, jewelry, and other bodily adornments. These items are individually, not collectively owned. Ownership among the Lunda confers upon one the right to use one's possessions as one wishes. The fruits of a person's labor also belong unambiguously to that person.

The theory of ownership of things, however, can be contrasted with day-to-day social practices related to things. Unlike actual ownership, access to and use of *maheta* in Mwinilunga is relatively evenly distributed. This reflects the widespread tendency of individuals to convert items of material wealth into prestige by utilizing them in culturally acceptable ways, primarily through *ambula*, which denotes both sharing and loaning. The principle of reciprocity is strongly embedded in both of these meanings. The failure to share is not a passive act but a socially aggressive one. It is rarely expressed as the simple negative of *ambula* (*hiambulaku* or *ambula wanyi*), but instead by a separate verb, *didinda*, willfully refusing to share or loan.

Wealth is something that should be shared, at least with one's kin, if not with needy strangers as well. The desire to share is stimulated by several factors. First, with the exception of cash, the inelasticity of individual demand for, or capacity to consume, items of wealth encourages sharing. One can eat only so much food, use only so many tools, sleep in only so many rooms. Second, sharing places an obligation on those with whom one shares. The receiver is obligated to repay in kind, and more often than not is expected to provide some service for the giver as well. The receiver may be asked to assist in agricultural work, to accompany the giver on hunting or fishing trips, or to assist in the keeping of domestic stock. With a little ingenuity the labor of the receiver can be put to use in ways that will enable the giver to continue to be prosperous and, consequently, generous. By sharing one can, in a sense, transfer perishable surplus through time, converting this year's surplus into labor which will most likely result in a surplus next year as well. The philosophical underpinning for this claim on the labor of receivers is summed up in the Lunda notion of *paseta*, a tip or bonus. The extra handful of beans, rice, or onions that market women add to the purchases of their regular customers is called *paseta*, as is the extra splash the bartender adds to the drinks of his regulars. Likewise, it is said that those who help others are entitled not only to the fair return of what they have given, but also to a little something extra for their generosity.[2] *Paseta* in this case may take the form of a few extra commodities, a little extra labor, a little extra political or moral support at crucial moments. Thus, greater benefits accrue to those who share or loan than to those who hoard. Third, social pressures are placed on those with a surplus to share or loan. They are persistently sought out by borrowers and continually urged to enter into reciprocal relationships. If they do not comply they may be accused of not acting in accordance with their social position, their age, and may thereby lose some of it by popular consensus. In other words, the image of an ideal elder is that of a person who through long years of hard work has managed to build up his estate to the point where he can now serve as *mukwakwashi*, one who helps others. Not all *mukwakuheta* (those with *maheta*, wealth) are necessarily *mukwakwashi*. The inability to live up to the image of *mukwakwashi* calls into question one's status and can possibly constrain one's ability, in the long term, to stay *mukwakuheta*.

The possession of wealth tends to attract a large following which, in turn, consumes that wealth. Those in need of a place to stay gravitate toward those with large houses. Those with productive gardens always seem to attract guests for dinner. An individual's capacity to serve as *mukwakwashi* is constantly evaluated, and any underutilized capacity is quickly seized upon. Sharers or borrowers of wealth self-consciously recognize their own value. As dependents they are, in a sense, the score points on the tally sheet of hierarchical reckoning. They possess the capacity to augment or depress rank, not just through intellectual discourse, but through repositioning themselves vis-à-vis those aspiring to the status of *mukwakwashi*. Prestige is not just made manifest in performances, but is actually created through performances. People do not just do things for you because you have prestige; rather, you have prestige because people do things for you. Position is the essence of life. Those who would rise in rank must continually *diisha antu yakudya*, feed the people, that is, spend wealth on social prestige, transform *maheta* (things) into *kavumbi* (respect). This feature of Lunda social life has thus far prevented the accumulation and intergenerational transfer of great wealth, and its corollary, the formation of rigid class structures.

The Nature of Power and the Production of Opportunities

The local semantics of power revolve around three conceptual markers: *wanta, wudumi,* and *ngovu.* In casual conversation these words are used interchangeably to signify power, strength, or capacities in a general sense, covering a wide range of contexts. Etymologically, however, they reflect and make possible interesting and often intense debates over the forms and natures of power. *Wanta* is the conditional nominal form of *mwanta* (chief). *Wudumi* shares its root with *mandumi* (uncle). *Ngovu*'s root is *-ovu*, the category of things that are powerful and useful because they are pliant, malleable, flexible, or adaptable. At one level the three types of power constitute a hierarchy extending downward from chiefly power to the power of the matrilineage to the power of the individual. On another level, however, they form three equal spheres of juxtaposed power: power acquired through a consensus of the people, power acquired by effective utilization of birth position, and the power of the individual to bend with, or mold and manipulate, the other forms of power. The three might even be meaningfully viewed as representing culture, nature, and the individual. Much effort is expended to make sure that the three check and balance one another. The drive to maintain individual autonomy while simultaneously building up widespread networks keeps power from being concentrated in one of the spheres. Debates continually rage over what degree of cooperation or competition among the spheres is mandated by particular circumstances. Sides shift and coalesce with the passage of time and the unfolding of events. Debate is accentuated by the fact that questions about forms of power provide ample fodder for those aspiring to *wuhaku*, that is, those who gain their own power and supporters through a demonstrated command of tradition as embedded in fables and proverbs, presented persuasively through an especially engaging style of oral performance. Tradition provides ample ammunition for all sides of the debate, however. There are, for example, many fables and proverbs glorifying each of the three forms of power.[3] Likewise, an extensive stockpile of oral admonitions warns against the dangerous potential of all forms of power.

Ultimately, power remains an extremely polymorphous concept in its application. For the sake of clarity, power can be divided into two analytically separable elements: control (or coercion) and influence (or persuasion).[4] Control is a physical matter, influence a psychological one. In both cases, the only real proof of the existence of power is its actualization. In the first instance, power is the ability to exercise coercion in obtaining what is sought and to punish those who fail to comply; in a sense, it involves control over bodies, both one's own and others'. How is this form of power distributed across the social landscape of Mwinilunga? While acknowledging plenty of room for debate, it would appear that the right of day-to-day control over one's own body is well ensconced in Lunda tradition. The integrity of the individual is reflected in many conceptual and pragmatic applications. The lack of well-developed coercive measures—structurally, operationally, ideologically, or even proverbially—is perhaps most responsible for the egalitarian aura of Lunda society noted by Turner and other scholars of Central Africa.

A brief look at the domestic sphere serves to illustrate some of the ways that notions of age and authority interact within that domain. Although parents can exercise a measure of control over young children, that control is quite tenuous at best. In theory, at least, young children assist their mother in her daily round of chores. Upon completion of *mukanda*, the male initiation ritual, a boy increasingly joins his father, assisting him in the male activities of hunting, housebuilding, horticulture, animal husbandry, and so forth. A girl, even after completing her puberty ritual, generally continues to work side-by-side with her mother until she marries and moves to the village of her husband. Children are rarely punished or forced to do things against their will. There is a demonstrated, often articulated, self-conscious awareness on the part of older children, in particular, that their labor makes a valuable contribution to their family's subsistence needs. Even while quite young, children independently collect whatever wild foods grow near their village, construct and manage small bird and rodent traps, carry water up from the springs, collect firewood, and provide a range of much-needed services. The awareness of their productive utility accentuates children's sense of independence and autonomy. Older children, especially, enjoy a great deal of flexibility in selecting a place to reside. If for any reason they are not satisfied with life in their parents' village, they are always welcome to stay with grandparents or other matrilineal kin, particularly their mother's brothers.

Although the nature of male-female power relations within the privacy of the domestic sphere is always elusive, publicly neither husbands nor wives possess the right, or even the ability, to coerce one another in a sustained fashion.[5] Among the Lunda nearly all production is individual. Men and women each plant their own gardens. Thus, on the one hand, men's and women's activities reinforce a sense of independence and autonomy. Yet, on the other hand, the major division of labor, based on gender, results in a situation where men's and women's contributions are deemed equally essential to the maintenance of an acceptable lifestyle. Schematically speaking, women are responsible for food processing and childcare, while men are responsible for construction and for providing the family with meat. Each is free to pursue whatever cash-earning strategies he or she desires, and cash obtained is under the exclusive control of the individual who earned it. As Turner noted in the 1950s, and as is still true today, husbands and wives are frequently unaware of each other's cash holdings, and it is considered inappropriate even to inquire. They may request loans from each other, but these loans must be repaid, with *paseta*.

The degree of coercion that can be exerted by a *mukwakwashi* is debatable. Some theorists would assert that sharing and patronage, which are part of most hierarchical systems, necessarily create unequal power relations. The fact that such relations are encased in an egalitarian ideology does not necessarily deny the possible existence of coercive elements. Theorists from Machiavelli to Foucault have noted that power is more effective when masked. However, the reverse is true as well. Power becomes weaker, less oppressive, and more diffuse when its mechanisms are made explicit. As noted above, relationships between a *mukwakwashi* and a client are locally constructed and articulated as negotiated relationships. They are publicly said to be mutually and equally beneficial to both parties. Such relations create structures of opportunity on both vertical and horizontal axes. Hierarchically, they address the issue of the intergenerational transfer of power. They create a gerontocratic ladder that allows for movement up the hierarchy. Today's children are tomorrow's parents and grandparents. Today's clients are tomorrow's patrons. Time mediates any momentary vertical inequalities. On the other hand, opportunities for lateral movement are ubiquitous. The social landscape is saturated with possibilities for defining and redefining one's relationship with others. The multiple networks noted earlier—kin, curing groups, village-mates, and cohorts—represent a kaleidoscope of power positions, shifting, changing, and distributing opportunities in ways that permit the perception of equality of opportunity. This constant shifting limits the extent of control that anyone can exert over another.

The second element of power—influence, or persuasion—is extremely difficult to bring into sharp focus. Power not only influences the actions of individuals, but it also influences how individuals interpret those actions. The notion that giver-receiver and lender-borrower relations are governed by rules of reciprocity must be maintained if those relations are to proceed smoothly over time. Each party in such relationships sees himself or herself as making a valuable contribution to that relationship, as being capable of exerting some influence over the other party, as being entitled to renegotiate or question the terms of the relationship, or as being able to simply dissolve the relationship if dissatisfied for any reason. The power to withdraw is an inalienable right. As noted in the preceding chapter, the ability to kill a relationship confers power on the individual. Thus, power, when defined as persuasion, is relatively evenly distributed in Mwinilunga—at least, this is so at the level of local perception.

Moving from interpersonal and domestic power to power of a larger political nature, the important positions are headmen of villages, chiefs who preside over larger territorial units, and the senior chief, the Kanongesha, who is acknowledged as the ruler of all the Ndembu-Lunda in Zambia. None of these figures, however, can impose his will on his subjects. The primary role of headmen and chiefs is to serve as arbiters for the settlement of disputes. Though they may quietly negotiate behind the scenes to resolve problems before they reach crisis proportions, they in fact have no official function until the disputants call upon them to intervene. Even when approached, headmen and chiefs have no coercive powers; they simply lead the search for a consensus. If disputants are not satisfied with the results of their discussion with a particular headman, they may take their dispute to another headman, or to a senior headman, and then on to a chief.[6] They may ignore, if they wish, the advice of each in turn. Friends and relatives may attempt to pressure disputants into accepting a solution to their problems. They may even threaten to withhold friendship or to completely ostracize the disputants. But they will not, or cannot, threaten the economic survival or the physical person of another. Thus, ultimately, each individual is given a remarkable degree of latitude to think and behave as he or she wishes. Freedom from physical coercion is put forward as a fundamental right of all Lunda. Even the most disruptive individuals are shown a great deal of tolerance.

Prestige as Moral Scorecard

Prestige here refers to an individual's social or moral ranking vis-à-vis others. On first appearance, prestige among the Lunda seems to be a function of relative age. The Lunda themselves often state that in the past a person's position in the prestige hierarchy depended almost entirely on his or her relative age. With age came not only wisdom, but also access to the labor of children and other young dependents. The more labor one had access to, generally, the more agricultural surplus one could generate. This surplus could be converted into social capital when used to sustain relatives, friends, or neighbors in times of need. Whatever the truth of these statements, it is clear that in the contemporary world cash can now serve as a shortcut to what once might have taken a lifetime to acquire. With cash even a young person can hire laborers to build a large, comfortable house,

clear and plant extensive fields, tend many animals, found a village and acquire lots of clients, and hence be in a position similar to that of an elder.
Indeed, those best placed to earn cash today tend to be younger people
who have had some formal education and hence have increased employment opportunities, or those who have traveled sufficiently to pick up new
ideas about manufacturing or marketing nontraditional items and have embarked on some entrepreneurial pursuit. Today, one's position in the prestige hierarchy is reckoned as a composite of age, acquired wealth, formal
education, travel experience, industriousness, and, perhaps most important, how one uses the opportunities and powers at one's disposal for the
benefit of others. Age may be weighed more heavily than other factors, but
because certain acquired traits also affect prestige, individuals of the same
chronological age may often occupy very different positions in the local
prestige hierarchy.

Evidence of the prestige hierarchy is omnipresent in daily life. It manifests itself in the greetings and linguistic forms used between individuals; it
is expressed in kinesics, seating arrangements, and even the walking order
of people passing on the roads. The Lunda lifestyle requires the constant
running of small errands—collecting kindling to restart the fire, fetching
drinking water for a thirsty guest, taking a quick trip to the garden for
condiments to accompany supper, searching for paper for an individual
who wishes to smoke, tracking down rumors about meat or vegetables that
may be for sale. The daily list is endless. A senior may request any of his juniors to fulfill such tasks, who may in turn pass the request on to one of his
juniors and so on. The hierarchical relations between any interacting group
of individuals are constantly being dramatized by the perpetual passing
down of requests to run errands.

Although few people know their absolute chronological age, relative age
is very important; nearly everyone can confidently state his or her time of
birth vis-à-vis other individuals in the vicinity. This is because birth order is
a frequent topic of conversation, especially among mothers. Whenever
women with babies meet they discuss which baby is *mukulumpi* to which,
that is, which was born first, which was born second, and so on. They relate the times of birth not to any absolute calendrical date, but rather to
seasonal or other productive activities they were involved in, or incidents
that occurred on or near the time of birth. Furthermore, when women
with young children meet they force their children to greet one another,
instructing each child how to adopt his or her prescribed role as senior or

junior with respect to the other children present. Even before children have learned to speak, their mothers take them by the hand and demonstrate the proper physical movements of greeting, and then on each child's behalf speak the words appropriate to his or her hierarchical position relative to the person being greeted. Because the Lunda tend to live in tight village clusters, it is not at all unusual for each individual to greet a hundred or more other individuals each day of his or her life. Thus the hierarchy is more than an invisible framework linking everyone from youngest to oldest within a unitary structure.[7] It is, in fact, so omnipresent that it takes on a life of its own. People live and die, but the hierarchy is everlasting. It is believed, for example, that relations established during life continue into the afterlife. Hierarchy, thus, cuts across villages, across lineages, across territories, and across worlds, permeating all of Lundaland with a sense of order, place, and appropriate behavior.

Hierarchy, Equality, and the Maintenance of Group Ties

In Lunda discourse the concept of hierarchy is expressed as central to all human interaction. The reasons cited are rather consistent and unambiguous. Without a clearly defined hierarchy there would be chaos, confusion, and conflict. The overwhelming majority of disputes that lead to actual physical confrontations occur between individuals whose relative hierarchical positions are roughly similar or are uncertain or suspended. Everything from Lunda ideology to metaphysical notions to the mode of production to child-rearing practices appears to combine to produce persons who are extremely protective of their individual prerogatives. Although consumption may be communal, production is generally individual; no one has any inherent rights to the fruits of another's labor. Land is abundant, and the simple tools of production are virtually within the reach of all. Those who wish to can strike out on their own and produce, to a large degree, the means of their own survival.[8] Individuals may do so when they feel that the seniors in their village are making excessive demands on their time and labor without reciprocating properly. Among the Lunda, *mukulumpi-kansi*, senior-junior, relations, are akin to the patron-client or lender-borrower relations discussed earlier. They are based upon exchange and are reflected in material transactions. With respect to any senior, a junior must adopt the correct greetings and forms of speech, give the senior the larger chair, and take care of any small errands that may be required. But if the relationship is to be ongoing, then the senior is obligated to reciprocate by assisting the junior in his or her time of need. A senior male, for example, may be called upon to help assemble bridewealth if one of his junior males wishes to marry. He may be asked to assist in providing meat and beer for an important gathering, or he may be asked to contribute his wisdom and experience toward solving a problem. It must be understood that the constraints on each party in a senior-junior relationship are equally binding. A senior who is reluctant to share his resources receives overt reminders of the unacceptability of such behavior, reinforced by the disinclination of others to assist him. A senior who flaunts his position and allows questions of inequality of power to rise to the surface will, likewise, find himself censured. One of the sadder sights in Mwinilunga today is that of the dejected old senior, living alone in a once grand but now dilapidated village, abandoned for his lack of competency in fulfilling his role as *mukwakwashi*. A senior male who is particularly generous and genteel, however, attracts lots of followers who usually provide him with the assistance needed to reproduce the means for his continued generosity. The salient point is that although from one point of view the system forms a giant pyramid of social ranking, from another point of view it is can be seen as a dense matrix of dyadic relationships in which the privileges of each senior are counterbalanced by his responsibilities to each of his juniors. A breach of this social contract by either party can lead to public accusations, which often result in a general discussion and reassessment of the hierarchical position of the individuals in question.

Although individuals readily acknowledge that they derive material benefits from living in large village groups and developing junior-senior relations, they generally state that it is a matter of enjoyment, rather than of economic imperative.[9] The hubbub of a crowded village, with children running everywhere and lots of people to converse and share experiences with, is a setting in which most people take great pleasure. But if they feel that they are not being treated properly, they will not hesitate either to argue the point or to leave that village. Although there is general agreement on rights and privileges, passive individuals who do not actually assert their rights and privileges may lose them. They will find their more aggressive age-mates, by public consensus, rapidly rising above them in the hierarchy. An individual who allows those who are clearly his junior to disregard the rules of linguistic or kinesic etiquette in his presence or to refuse to run his requested errands is deemed, in a sense, to be defiling his position within the hierarchy and weakening the importance of the prestige hierarchy itself. His reduction in ranking becomes necessary to protect the integrity of the system, as in the case of the old man at Ikelenge. Thus from childhood, individuals, most especially males, are taught that it is one's responsibility to protect one's rights and that one must react quickly and firmly to transgressions from others.

Embedded in the Lunda complex of ideas and ideals are extremely strong notions concerning the rights of individuals to express themselves verbally, whatever their position in the prestige hierarchy. The frequent mixture of alcohol and vigorous fireside debates at times challenges the restraint and self-control of some individuals, and Lunda debates often degenerate into shouting matches. But the mere mention of *kavumbi* (respect) from the *mukulumpi* (the eldest one present) can quickly calm the situation. The behavior of those present changes as suddenly as that of soldiers being called to attention by their drill sergeant. There is much clapping and bowing as individuals, through physical acts, acknowledge the hierarchical alignment of the group, regreet one another individually, and then restart the conversation on a much calmer note. There is always the potential of violent explosion between individuals whose relationship is uncertain or reckoned as nearly equal, if one of them even inadvertently slights the other by assuming a posture which implies that he is the senior of the two. Such individuals can only maintain social relations by being overly cautious and polite or by explicitly agreeing to treat each other as *wusensi* (joking cousins), a relationship in which all the rules of accepted behavior are suspended by mutual consent.[10] *Wusensi* relations can be fun, socially valuable, and refreshing in contrast to more formal relationships. Still, these relationships are unstable, and one misstep can result in violent consequences. The most stable and enduring social groups are those that contain individuals whose relative hierarchical positions are unambiguously clear and who confine their behavior to what is appropriate to their category.

Thus are notions of hierarchy and equality interwoven to produce a Lunda social reality. Deep respect for the prestige hierarchy and the performance of the physical acts that such respect implies make orderly social life possible in the absence of physically coercive measures. The inequality of prestige is produced through processes that tend to equalize wealth: those who are generous with their belongings rise in prestige. Differential ownership of wealth is based on differential access to labor, which is expressed as a negotiated, rather than a coercive process. The reciprocity embedded in such labor relations gives them the aura, if not the substance, of equality. Thus, to Lunda sensibilities, hierarchy and egalitarianism support rather than contradict one another. Together they constitute a framework over which all other notions of Lundahood are draped. They underpin the claims to unity of a people scattered over thousands of square miles.

Perhaps one of the more telling arenas of social interaction is the large group meeting such as the *mulong'a*, a villagewide forum to resolve a dispute; the intervillage gathering for a marriage or an initiation ceremony; or the gathering of local party members to discuss the latest directive for the capital. With people of myriad statuses present a plethora of relational terminologies could be employed, but these merge instead into a dyad: *nkaka* and *mwizukulu*, grandparent and grandchild. *"Mwani vude! Ankaka namwizukul!"* ("Greeting to the grandparent with the grandchildren!") is the prescribed and generally adhered-to preface to any remarks made before a large crowd, and it is the concluding phrase to every speech. Grandparent-grandchild relations, as noted earlier, epitomize the merger of hierarchy and egalitarianism. The age and experiential gap between them is so great as to make hierarchy undeniable. Yet the mutual dependence of each on the other, economically, socially, and metaphysically, blurs the lines of power, creating the friendliest and most open of relationships.

The prestige hierarchies that the Lunda so diligently construct are vastly larger social units than the economic groupings on which individuals depend. Clearly this hierarchy-constructing behavior is given impetus by more than just economic considerations; economic security, complete with a safety net for the occasional hard times, can usually be obtained at the village level. Men, in particular, however, endeavor to create and rise to the top of prestige hierarchies that span the widest possible area. Many layers of cultural meaning could be uncovered in explaining their reasons for doing so. One insufficiently examined reason revolves around philosophical notions of the purpose and meaning of human life.[11] In the Lunda context, two concepts concerning the ultimate goal of human existence stand out as deserving special attention: *iyala muneni* and *mumbanda muneni*, bigmanship and bigwomanship. Their meanings have altered over time with changes in resource availability, economic opportunities, and cultural constructions. For example, during the era of the Central African long-distance trade caravans of the eighteenth and nineteenth centuries, notions of bigmanship and bigwomanship no doubt revolved around the quality and quantity of one's involvement in trade.[12] During the early colonial regime, only those who served colonial needs either as participants in the government or as migrant laborers prospered.[13] But two components of the concepts of bigmanship and bigwomanship have remained relatively constant: the demonstrated capacity to secure comfort for one's self and others in life, and its concomitant reward, remembrance in the afterlife. In order to discern the difference between attaining the status of bigwoman and bigman, we need to understand something about the Lunda concept of afterlife.

The Lunda, like many other African peoples, believe in levels of death. For example, the birth of a child represents the death of a fetus, and the attainment of adult status is symbolized as the death of a child. When a person dies, an ancestral spirit is born; the final death does not occur until all those who remember an individual spirit have themselves died. At that point one's existence ceases, even in the spirit world. The spirit of the dead person is peaceful and content as long as it is remembered by anyone alive. Lack of remembrance produces a dreadful transformation, a breaking of long-established bonds, and a closing of the door between two worlds. Socially recognized acts of remembrance can take many forms. The three most common are, (1) casually mentioning the names of the deceased in daily conversation—commenting on their exploits in life and referring to their contributions to the group; (2) symbolically offering food and drink to the deceased at communal meals—in a sense, recognizing their continued membership in the social group; and (3) formally naming a child after the deceased.

The matrilineal nature of Lunda society supports women's efforts to become bigwomen. In theory, at least, any able-bodied woman capable of producing lots of able-bodied offspring can, with their support, live relatively comfortably in life and have a reasonable guarantee that those offspring and their descendants will perform acts of remembrance for her in her afterlife. They will do so both because of their appreciation of that woman's biological role in the unending chain of life and because of her apical position in social reckoning. Furthermore, to forget her is to invite supernatural sanctions in the form of life-threatening physical disorders, the only recourse for spirits sensing neglect (see Turner 1968). Bigwomanship, then, is a status open to the vast majority of women. But few men obtain bigmanship. Although there are no absolute limits to the number of men who can live comfortably, there are constraints on how many will

be long remembered after their deaths. Because men are not used for social reckoning, only those few who distinguish themselves in life will be
long remembered in the afterlife.[14] In general, remembrance is the reward
bestowed upon those men who reach a high level on the prestige hierarchy.
They are the ones who have acquired a large following and whose names
have been applied to the titles of headmanships, to geographical features,
or to historical eras. The large groupings mapped out by the prestige hierarchy exist for the purpose of providing males with a larger playing field and
a larger audience in their competition for prestige. This competition is not
just for wealth to convert into social capital, for deferred payment to be
used in old age, or for seeing who can make whom run the most errands.
It is a battle for the honor of being remembered in the afterlife, indeed, to
extend life itself. The ideology of egalitarianism keeps the game civil, as-
suring that no one has any inherent advantage and that those who reach
the top genuinely deserve to have done so. They are the ones who have
used their wealth to improve the conditions of others and their power to
provide opportunities, and who have done so in a manner that did not provoke jealousy or animosity. They brought dignity, grace, and a sense of
morality to the game.

But why is the battle for prestige clothed in an idiom of age? At one level,
age is conflated with a mixture of innate, acquired, and socially bestowed
qualities including wealth, knowledge, experience, power, and prestige. But
it was the traditional metaphor for encapsulating an ideal, naturally occurring
mix of these elements. Age maintains its status as the dominant metaphor
today even as the factors in the mix are being recalculated, reappraised, and
reapportioned. At another level, this conflation of chronological age and
prestige is clearly an example of what Bloch (1989, 61–78) describes as the
"ritualization of power," where the fluid outcome of purposive human behavior is enveloped in a widely shared rhetoric of morally sanctioned constancy. An achievement-based system of prestige, with its elements of con-
tingency, instability, and unpredictability, is transformed into something
which more closely conforms with nature, something which seems timeless
and therefore more sacred and deserving of respect. In the case of the Lunda,
the unpredictability of individual accomplishment is fused with the natural
element of the orderly passage of time. In an area where life can be difficult
and uncertain, reaching old age is considered virtual proof positive of supernatural favor. It is no wonder, then, that age becomes a shorthand for talking about respect. The young men who become reckoned as elders must do

more than merely possess cash and *maheta*; they must also possess the experience and skill to take on the style of an elder. They must use their wealth in goods and knowledge in socially ordained ways that make them worthy of respect and raise them from simply being *mukwakuheta* (those who possess things) to being true bigmen, *mukwakwashi*.

Ritually Reconstructing Hierarchy and Equality

The relationships between young and old and between the notions of equality and hierarchy are deeply embedded in the quotidian rhythm of life. They are, however, most dramatically expressed in ritual. Two rituals in particular exemplify the all-encompassing nature of the focus on equality and hierarchy. In *mukanda* and *nkanga* (respectively, boys' and girls' puberty rites) the notions of equality and hierarchy are raised beyond the level of mundane social practices; they are cloaked in an aura of metaphysical necessity, sanctioned by the power of the ancestors and by the inviolable laws of nature itself. Victor Turner's treatment of the *mukanda* rites in *The Forest of Symbols* (1967, chapt. 7) remains one of the most powerful descriptive and analytical pieces in the anthropological literature on the ritual process. Most of what Turner had to say about *mukanda* in the 1950s remains true today. Thus, the following description is meant to serve as a schematic overview for those unfamiliar with Turner's work and to bring into relief those features of the ritual that relate to the topic at hand.

Mukanda: *A Male Rite of Passage*

Mukanda is perhaps the most powerful, the most awe-inspiring experience of every Lunda man's life. The locally articulated objective of the ceremony is to turn boys into men, quite literally. Three separate but interrelated processes are involved in this usually month-long ritual. First, the boys are circumcised. The uncircumcised are considered *anabulakutooka*, those who lack purity. They are restricted from participating in certain activities and from contact with certain persons. In theory, at least, they may not even eat food cooked on the same fire used to prepare food for a circumcised male. In fact, they are not considered members of the male community at all. Their labor is controlled by, and generally performed for the benefit of, their mothers. The knife that removes a boy's foreskin is said to sever the residual female part of his anatomy. *Muvumbu*, the foreskin, is compared to *nyisunda*, the labia majora. The knife severs a boy's attachment to his mother, and thus to the female world. It welcomes him into the fraternity of males and gives him the full complement of every Lunda man's rights and responsibilities.

Second, *mukanda* is an educational camp, a sort of finishing school. Although lessons in history, customs, and etiquette, as well as the practical skills of hunting, fishing, and trapping are an informal part of daily life, *mukanda* represents a time of strict formal instruction and testing to insure that every participant possesses the basic minimum corpus of knowledge expected of an adult Lunda male.

Third, *mukanda* is a time for emphasizing and animating the basic concept of respect for hierarchy. It is a time for demonstrating to the younger generation, in a very dramatic fashion, the physical, intellectual, and even metaphysical power of the *akulumpi*, the elders.

Boys are circumcised in groups of ten, twenty, or more each year during the cold dry season (July and August). Their ages range from eight to the mid-teens. The senior headman of each village cluster makes an annual assessment to decide if the villages in his area have a sufficient number of boys ready to be circumcised to warrant organizing his own *mukanda* camp. If not, the few boys in his area who are ready may be sent to a camp in another area. Circumcision groups do not become age-sets as they often do elsewhere in Africa. Hence, where and with whom one has been circumcised is not nearly as important as the mere fact that the circumcision has been successfully completed. Ultimately, the decision of where and when the rite occurs rests with a boy's father and uncles.

Once the decision to hold a *mukanda* has been made, the first step is to secure the services of an *mbimbi*, head circumciser. While the *mbimbi* is busy organizing his *yifukaminu*, assistants, and preparing his *nfunda*, the medicines necessary to speed the healing process and protect the boys from supernatural harm, others spread the word concerning when and where the *mukanda* will take place. Those interested in sending a boy as an initiate must assemble both sufficient food to support that boy during the month-long ceremony and ample alcoholic beverages to animate the associated celebrations. The evening before the *mukanda* proper begins, boys and parents assemble at the village of the sponsoring headman for prayers to the ancestors, the lighting of a sacred fire that will burn throughout the duration of the *mukanda*, and an all-night dance.

The *kwing'ija*, a ceremony of separation, takes place the following morning. While mothers weep loudly, the *mbimbi* and his assistants appear suddenly out of the bush, quickly build a *mukuleku*, a sacred doorway out of branches, at the very edge of the village, and then loudly and aggressively lead the frightened and sleep-deprived boys through the doorway and out into the deep woods, miles from the nearest village. No women or uncircumcised males may follow them through that doorway, which serves as the symbolic portal between the physical and metaphysical realms. The initiates spend the remainder of that day constructing out of branches and leaves an *ng'ula*, a circumcision lodge, where the ritual officiants sleep. A fence of brushwood extended in a circle from the lodge encloses an open space in which the boys sleep for the duration of the camp.

The actual circumcision takes place the next morning in an area designated as *ifwila danyadi*, place of death for uncircumcised boys. The newly circumcised boys rest for the next couple of days, after which they are taken to the nearest stream to wash off the bloodstains. Thereafter herbal medicines are frequently applied to their wounds. The rest of the month consists of formal lessons. Any adult male known to be well versed in a particular subject or proficient in a particular skill might be invited to spend a few days instructing and testing the initiates. In addition, each initiate has a *chilombola*, guardian, a young adult male assigned by the parents to collect their son's daily food rations from the *kaweji*, a sacred trestle built on the pathway to the lodge, where parents place food each day. The *chilombola* also serves as the initiate's personal tutor throughout the *mukanda*. Lessons are punctuated by frequent beatings for responding too slowly to an instruction or command from a ritual officiant or even for a defiant or disrespectful demeanor. Should an initiate ever behave disrespectfully after the *mukanda*, the ritual officiants, especially those serving as *chilombola*, are chastised severely for not having beaten the initiate sufficiently during his stay in the camp. This harsh physical treatment contrasts mightily with notions of the inviolability of individual bodies in every other social context.

In the past, a number of *makishi*, masked dancers, would make an appearance at the camp. Today, these appearances are less frequent. *Makishi* are locally believed to be physical manifestations of powerful demigods or nature spirits. These figures, wearing strange costumes and large gruesome masks, would appear suddenly in the dead of night to terrorize the initiates, sometimes chasing them in panic into the bush. The main purpose of the *makishi* seems to have been to emphasize the power of the elders, who appeared to control the *makishi*. Elders often humble wayward youngsters by threatening to call forth *makishi*.

The end of seclusion is preceded by a final cleansing ceremony at the stream and followed by a festive all-day coming-out ceremony, *kwidisha*, during which time the initiates receive new clothes from their parents and gifts from friends and family. The ritual officiants receive their pay in cash and kind. Feasting, singing, and dancing proceed until everyone is exhausted. The camp itself is set ablaze, with some of the ashes being saved by the *mbimbi* to concoct medicine for use in a future *mukanda*.

The ritual of *mukanda* is said to have been brought by the Lunda-Ndembu from the central Lunda Empire. It is present among most other peoples of the upper Zambezi River, including the Luvale, Luchazi, and Chokwe, who also trace their origins to the empire. In the past, *mukanda* rituals may have lasted up to two years. In the imperial age, the age of Lunda military expansion, each *mukanda* group became a military regiment, with the *Kambanji*, the most highly rated boy in the group, becoming the war leader. At that time boys were initiated at or just after puberty. Today, boys are initiated at a younger age and for a shorter period of time. Such a change provokes questions about *mukanda*'s continued status as a puberty rite. Reasons have been put forward for the change. Turner, in agreement with C. M. N. White, asserted that schooling and the need for young men to earn money was the factor determining age and duration of initiation. These may, indeed, have, played some role. But few teenagers in this area of Zambia would have had access to schooling, and there was, and still is, little work in town for someone of that age. An alternative explanation emerges from a view of *mukanda* not just in terms of what it does or means to young boys, but rather in terms of the opportunities it provides for a society to talk to itself about itself. *Mukanda*, in many respects, is a series of contestations. It is not simply a mechanically acted-out ritual of primeval origins; it is about the construction of a physical and social space where people and principles reorient themselves. *Mukanda* is a large public event composed of multiple, overlapping layers of meaning. At one level it is about labor relations, about male versus female control over a valuable young labor pool. The initiation of a dozen or so boys into the male community represents a dramatic local shift in the balance of labor between males and females, especially in a society dominated by a gender-based division of labor. It is bound to be contested at some level. Yet, *mukanda* cannot take place without the active support and strenuous effort of women. One likely reason that males and females would have cooperated to lower the age of initiation arises from the contingencies of the migrant labor era, beginning in the early 1900s. During that time, an average of 30 to 40 percent of the adult male labor was absent from the village at any point. There was no doubt a need to redress this labor imbalance by rushing more young boys into the adult male category. This topic will be taken up more extensively in the following chapter.

Mukanda also provides a space for males to reconsider or reconfirm their status vis-à-vis one another. Men compete for the positions within the enactment of *mukanda*, especially for the three major positions of more or less equal importance. The first, *Chijika Mukanda*, "he who stops up *mukanda*," is the establisher, or organizer; receiving this position is momentary acknowledgement of one's moral, if not political, leadership. The second, *Mbimbi Wuneni*, is the senior circumciser. Any number of skilled individuals may actually operate on the boys, but to become the senior one must have demonstrated power. One must be able to produce medicine that can protect the boys from supernatural enmity, especially during the liminal phase when they are most vulnerable. One must be an acceptable conduit to the ancestors, able to interpret their wishes and appease their expectations. The third position, *Mfumwa Tubwiku*, husband of the novices, is the senior instructor. This position, which may fall to an individual who has more than one son in the camp, recognizes the fullness of one's knowledge and capacity to supervise the intellectual development of boys. Intrigue runs rife before each *mukanda*. Men caucus in small groups to debate the relative merits of possible candidates for the titled positions. Potential candidates lobby friends and relatives to mobilize support and recognition of their status within the group. The jockeying for position may, in fact, continue throughout the year, reaching a fever pitch as *mukanda* time approaches.

Beneath these three positions are perhaps dozens of individuals serving in one of two categories. *Yifukaminu*, assistants to the camp, must have attended at least three *mukanda*. They are the logistical support staff, assisting each of the three titleholders in his duties. *Ayilombola*, guardians, who are generally older siblings, cousins, or friends, are personally responsible for individual initiates and may have previously attended only their own *mukanda*.

The boys themselves compete for rank within the *mukanda*. *Kambanji*, war leader, is the title awarded the oldest, ablest, or most developed boy. This appellation will follow him throughout his life. The second-ranking boy is called *Mwanta waMukanda*, the third *Kaselantanda*, and the fourth

Mulopu. The last boy to physically arrive, the least developed, the slowest in answering questions, or the one who cries out the loudest when cut is called *Kajika kaMukanda,* he who closes the *mukanda*. Although these titles are awarded on a provisional basis at the beginning of the *mukanda*, the positions shift back and forth, almost daily, reflecting the individual behavior and performance of each boy throughout the various phases of the *mukanda* camp.

There is an obvious focus on hierarchy. The existence of ranked titles, and the use of those titles as forms of address, stresses hierarchy. Boys in the camp are circumcised, fed, and constantly paraded about in order of rank. A major purpose of the camp is clearly to teach the *ayilombola*, the junior guardians, as well as the boys being initiated, to respect and obey their elders. They are required to maintain a modest demeanor throughout, to speak only when spoken to, to fetch and carry anything required quickly, and to run errands. Yet, much of the semantics of *mukanda* stresses egalitarianism. The ritual is full of prayers and proverbs, music and messages that assert the equality of the participants. An often articulated theme of *mukanda* is *Mwana kamwanta wafwana musuka*, "The son of a chief is like a slave." In the *mukanda* camp there is a reduction to equality, not the reversal of status that characterizes other rituals. Equality is asserted at four levels: (1) the equality of all circumcised men vis-à-vis uncircumcised boys, (2) the equality of all men vis-à-vis women, (3) the equality of the living vis-à-vis the dead, and (4) the equality of all Lunda-Ndembu vis-à-vis other groups. Older men, particularly fathers, exercise some leverage over youth in controlling their access to the status of adulthood. Yet elders can move up in ranking themselves only by pulling up the youth behind them. Thus, in a sense, all are equal in constructing and maintaining a ritual system that facilitates the orderly passage of individuals through the successive stages of life. This feature is perhaps most powerfully symbolized by the eating of the *nfunda*, medicine. Eating it is akin to incorporating the very nature of *mukanda* into one's person. Each lot of medicine putatively contains substances from performances going back to the beginning of time. Each new set of initiated males adds its own essence (blood, burnt foreskins, ashes from the camp) to the medicine, which will be used in future *mukanda*. It symbolizes the death of initiates, yet the immortality of the Lunda.

Beyond the domestic level, *mukanda* was, and perhaps still is, an arena of contestations of a suprapolitical nature. *Mukanda* is a time for powerfully presenting a particular worldview. Colonial and missionary ideologies have been encroaching from the turn of the nineteenth century onward, and the assault on Lunda precepts continues today via the political and educational apparatus of postcolonial governments. The lowered age of initiation might reflect a perceived need to counteract the impact of those ideologies on the young at increasingly earlier stages of their life. *Mukanda* is a major salvo in the battle for ideological primacy. It offers the youth a place in a hierarchy that can provide them with opportunities for prestige, a social safety net in time of need, and a sense of autonomy and equality. The missionary, colonial, and independent government hierarchies offer the youth only the bottom rung of a ladder that leads neither to prominence nor to equality.

Nkanga: *A Female Rite of Transition*

The girls' initiation ceremony differs in many major respects from that of the boys. Whereas boys are initiated in groups in the bush, girls are initiated individually in the village. Whereas boys are subjected to hard labor and harsh discipline, girls are pampered, groomed, sung to, and relieved from doing most daily chores. Boys are circumcised, but girls do not undergo clitoridectomy. Whereas the physical actions of the male community are thought to turn boys into men (by removing their female aspect, i.e., the foreskin), nature is understood to turn girls into women. The *nkanga* begins shortly after a girl experiences her first menstrual period. The purpose of the ceremony is not to enact any physical change but, for the most part, to remove the girl from secular life—to give her a period of time in seclusion to reflect on her newly acquired capacity to reproduce.

Nkanga does parallel *mukanda*, as do all Lunda ceremonies, in its conformity with Van Gennep's three-stage ritual scheme (Van Gennep 1960). There is a ceremony of ritual removal from secular life, *kwing'isha*; a liminal period, *kukunka*; and a ceremony of reintegration, *kwidyisha*. The *nkanga* ceremony begins quietly at night with the initiate, her mother, and the *kasonsweli*, a young girl selected to be the attendant, offering prayers to the ancestors. The next morning the initiate is carried to *ifwilu dakankanga*, a place of dying, a spot where she remains motionless under a blanket all day while women dance around her in a circle, singing songs extolling female virtues and ridiculing male vices. Many of the songs have provocative lyrics, discussing female sexual appetite while taunting and teasing the men, who organize their own circle of dancers nearby. Meanwhile, a group of males is busy constructing an *nkunka,* a small grass hut in the village to which the initiate is carried at sunset. This hut serves as her place of seclusion for up to two or three months.[15] During this period the initiate must not speak except in soft whispers and must not go out unless she is covered by a blanket from head to toe. Her attendant remains with her throughout to attend to her personal needs, and a daily procession of older women visit and instruct the initiate in matters concerning sex and childbirth. These lessons are often animated affairs accompanied by alcoholic beverages, much laughter, and graphic demonstrations of sexual positions and techniques. The initiate is also subject to a number of food taboos while in seclusion.[16] She is periodically given herbal medicines to make her strong, to ensure her fertility, and to enhance her milk production in the future when she has children.

The coming-out ceremony begins with *ng'oma,* an all-night sing and dance attended primarily by close family members and friends of the initiate. A grand public affair begins the next morning. The initiate makes her reentrance into society by performing *hang'ana nkanga,* a special dance she learned while in seclusion. She then sits quietly for the rest of the morning receiving presents of cloth, cash, and utilitarian goods. Both men and women dance in a circle around the initiate, singing songs encouraging her to be fertile and produce lots of children. Drinking and feasting continue for the rest of the day or until supplies are exhausted. The initiate, along with the rest of the village, returns to normal life the following day.

As in *mukanda,* the basic themes, texts, and subtexts of *nkanga* conflate notions of hierarchy and equality. Hierarchy is reflected in organizational positions and the differential allocation of privileges to bigwomen who have produced many children and to those possessing esoteric knowledge of the set of rituals related to women's illnesses. Equality, as in the case of *mukanda,* is expressed on four levels: (1) the equality of all women with reproductive capacity vis-à-vis young girls, (2) the equality of all women vis-à-vis men, (3) the equality of the living vis-à-vis the dead, and (4) the equality of all Lunda-Ndembu vis-à-vis others.

Summary: Orality and Order

This chapter has addressed the cultural underpinnings of traditional gerontocratic forms of local power, the means by which the differential distribution of privileges and duties is explained and given force, and the subsequent renegotiation of the relationship between young and old in light of new external forces and internal desires. Much changed during the twentieth century in Mwinilunga. The Lunda are no longer an autonomous political entity, having been more or less implanted within a new nation-state. The institutions and ideologies of that nation-state reach into Mwinilunga in a comprehensive attempt to define the relations between citizens and the state, as well as the relations of citizens to one another. The government's message is brought by bureaucratic functionaries, broadcast via newspapers and radio, and taught as part of the public school curriculum. But the Lunda, for the most part, remain largely embedded in an oral society.

Orality dictates its own set of relationships between the young and the old. The anthropological literature is rich in examples of local ideologies of wisdom, associated with the elderly, in systems primarily dependent on the physical labor of the young. Most of that literature focuses of the esoteric body of knowledge that the elderly are assumed to possess. Each individual is a positioned subject, positioned to know certain things and not others. In an oral society the elderly serve as exemplars of social etiquette, encyclopedias of historical facts, repositories of juridical precedence, and custodians of the ritual repertoire. Furthermore, having lived through many of life's inevitable crises, the elderly can provide emotional guidance during times of despair. In fact, the presence of elders adds a certain emotional stability to life, instilling in the youth a sense of confidence that life's many challenges can be overcome.

The importance of such exoteric knowledge, however, should not be overlooked. Every day a new generation is born, another comes of age, another passes away. In an oral society even the mundane and utilitarian must be continually rewritten on the consciousness of the living. People are quite literally texts, and the elderly have been more fully inscribed. The newly established trade link with Cazombo, Angola, for example, brings the value of elderly memory into bold relief. From these memories young men extract logistical information, such as the location of friendly villages, dangerous forest regions, and river crossings. Young men, likewise, gain encouragement and confidence that the broad expanse between the two areas can be mastered now as it was in the past.

The exoteric and esoteric knowledge of the elderly is activated by the physical strength of the young. The Lunda system glorifies hard work and individual initiative in the creation of surplus and yet also encourages the widest distribution of that surplus by providing tangible rewards to those who do so. That reward comes in the form of daily references to one's contributions to the moral and material base of society (expressed through forms of greetings, seating arrangements, and the ready availability of those willing to do one's bidding). If young men are fortunate enough, and clever enough, to make contributions comparable to those of an elderly *mukwakwashi*, the Lunda believe that they deserve to be regarded in the same fashion. To the outsider this may appear to be a simple pragmatic quid pro quo arrangement. To the Lunda, however, there is much more. Accomplishments act more to confirm than to generate one's position within the hierarchy. As in Calvinism, the degree of success obtained in this world is viewed as merely a sign of the far more important measure of grace awaiting one in the next world. To many Lunda, notions of hierarchy and egalitarianism resonate with metaphysical significance. But they devote little time to pontificating about the reasons why. To them, their system not only makes good intuitive sense but also has the mystical aura of having been ordained and continually sustained by the actions of ancestors. Such notions will take center stage in chapter 8.

Whatever the intellectual framework one uses to explain how the Lunda conceptualize their system, the artifact of their way of thinking is clear: a social environment in which some young men, by virtue of their access to knowledge and cash, become elders. And some elders without the material and personal wherewithal to live up to the image of *mukwakwashi* find themselves sliding down the hierarchy. Some, such as the old man in Ikelenge, attach themselves to young men of wealth in a dependent fashion that results in a boost to the young men's status and a reduction of the elder's status to that of a child. In a very real sense this elder has bartered away his age, receiving some measure of financial security in return. The young man to whom the elder is particularly attached has taken on the financial risks of caring for an elder who is not a kinsman, in return for a huge boost in his prestige ranking. This is Lunda entrepreneurship in action. Increasingly one finds such young entrepreneurs who, by investing in prestige, are also distributing the wealth to which they have differential access.

Thus, in contradistinction to evolutionist paradigms, egalitarianism among the Lunda is not an artifact of a low stage of political and economic development. Nor is it disappearing with the Lunda's incorporation into a global economy that emphasizes cash and individual transactions. It is instead a mechanism which, in its most elaborated form, stimulates the development of a polity that is deeper and broader than economic and political concerns would necessitate.

Age is a condensation of a bundle of socially significant achieved statuses. The composition of the bundle changes over time, as does the significance ascribed to individual components within the bundle. But the logic of those ascriptions of significance remains firmly rooted in plans for both life and the afterlife.

The King and His Court
Senior Lunda Chief Kanongesha Silas *(sitting)* with his sister, guard, councillor, and youthful retinue. Silas spent a good part of his life on the Zambian Copperbelt, where he was active in party politics and owned a fleet of taxis. In 1966 the Lunda customary council of electors, in a strange last-minute reversal of an earlier consensus, surprised the local population by proclaiming Silas the new senior chief. Hence, he was affectionately nicknamed Chief Oops! He died under mysterious circumstances in 1994.

Heir Apparent?
Kanongesha Silas's favorite nephew, Vincent Chiteka, with his wife and children. Vincent regularly professed his intention to succeed his uncle. But at the time of Silas's death, Vincent was himself suffering from lingering and at times violent bouts of illness. It was widely believed that he was bewitched by other pretenders to the throne. His seeming inability to counter that witchcraft with a power of his own seriously diminished the viability of his candidacy. Yet, he is perhaps still young enough and smart enough to position himself better the next time.

Akulumpi: The Elders
Senior Headman Isaac Nkemba *(second from left)* with his brothers of the ruling senior genealogical generation. Isaac is the reigning Chifunga, a title that was said to have nearly
equaled in rank that of the Kanongesha in precolonial times. However, neither the colonial
nor the postcolonial government officially recognized the title. Local people, nevertheless, ac-
cord the Chifunga the highest level of respect, calling on him frequently to solve disputes and
mediate conflicts.

Maguys: The Guys

Joking around at the end of the day, trying to cajole one another into buying the next bottle of *lituku*, a high-proof cassava liquor distilled by local women. This thirty-something crowd was the first group to benefit from increased opportunities in formal education during the 1960s. On average they are highly literate, well traveled, and far more ambitious than the preceding generation. Most are married with children and have well-managed farms and cash-generating enterprises.

Generation X?
Cool clothes and hot music on the radio. These teens are highly educated and acutely attuned to national and international trends. Farm-based lifestyles are not in their plans; the big city beckons.

Children of the Great Decline
Virtual collapse of the national copper mining industry and massive foreign debt, combined with international pressure on Zambia's government to slash spending on education and health care, reverberate throughout society in the form of shortages of teachers, places in school, clinical staff, and essential medicines. These children represent the first generation in fifty years to experience declining literacy rates, economic opportunities, and lifespans.

The *Mukanda* Camp
Participants in the major male rite of passage. Newly circumcised youths kneel in front; their guardian angels hover behind. As the age of initiation becomes lower and lower, the notion of *mukanda* as a puberty rite is in need of reinterpretation.

Bigwoman Ifezia
The matriarch of Josayi village, grandma Ifezia *(center)*, sits contentedly at the end of the day surrounded by daughters, daughters-in-law, and grandchildren. Such groupings are social worlds unto themselves; they design their own economic strategies, share and allocate labor as they deem best, and assist one another in times of need, sharing moments both simple and sublime, in life and in death.

Bigwoman Nyampasa
The matriarch of Kamau village, Nyampasa *(center left)*, pounding cassava with her daughter-in-law *(center right)*. The name Nyampasa means mother of twins, an exalted status among the Lunda for all it symbolizes about female fertility.

162

A Small *Chenda*

Many male productive activities, such as house building, require cooperative action. Brothers, cousins, fathers, and sons are the most common groupings. But labor can also be mobilized through holding a *chenda*, a work party. Alcoholic beverages and prepared meats are assembled and displayed at a work site. Volunteers give their labor in exchange for the feast that follows. The more copious the liquor and the more succulent the meat, the more energetically people will work, it is said.

Racing against the Elements
Newly framed roofs of bamboo, wood poles, and bark fiber affixed to the top of clay brick walls. Massive amounts of thatching grass need to be secured and lashed into position before the rainy season begins. The products of five different ecological zones are needed to complete the typical Lunda house.

The Daily Grind
One of the most ubiquitous sights of daily life in Mwinilunga is women pounding cassava. After maturing for eighteen months, cassava roots must be peeled and soaked for a couple of weeks, pounded with a mortar and pestle, sun bleached for a few days, pounded again, and finally sifted into flour before they are suitable for cooking. These laborious and time-consuming steps are needed to rid the roots of poisonous hydrocyanic acid. Young Kangasa demonstrates picture-perfect form and the good upper-body strength characteristic of most Lunda women.

To Buy or Not to Buy?
Stone Mafulo and *maguys* bargain with an itinerant trader over the prices of new dresses for their wives. Energetic young men with large straw baskets attached to bicycles crisscross the landscape peddling the latest wares from the city.

Kid Power
Young labor has historically been a key ingredient in the maintenance of the Lunda lifestyle.
These kids will move over two thousand clay bricks to the site of house construction for the
sheer fun of hanging out together and doing something different.

The Witch and the Night Warrior?
The stuff of legend. Daniel *(right)*, the head bricklayer at Lwawu Catholic mission station, one of the highest paid workers in the area, has on more than one occasion been accused of manipulating forces and beings in the metaphysical world to his personal benefit. The Chifunga *(left)* is also believed to know much about that world but has a widespread reputation for using his powers only for good.

Chapter Five

Females and Males

Katoka Beats the Wife
Dry Season, July 1992

Katoka was painfully limping up the path on his way home to Chifunga village. He had just come from the clinic at the Catholic mission station, two miles away. His left knee and right hand were heavily bandaged. Both arms were covered with scratches. His right eye was nearly swollen shut. He had a huge bump on his forehead and bite marks on his neck. Horrified at the condition of my friend, I dispensed with the usual formulaic greeting ("Mwakola, are you strong?") and shouted out instead, "Good heavens, what happened!" In a weak voice he replied, "I had to beat the wife last night." "Looks like she put up a pretty good fight," I said, stifling a chuckle. "Oh yeah! But we men always win, somehow, in the end," said Katoka. "Even if only in the retelling?" I offered. "Yeah," he laughed.

I followed Katoka, knowing that in his condition he would not be doing any serious work that day. He would, no doubt, head straight for a drinking spot, where he would receive the sympathy of other idle men and perhaps a few bottles of local brew to ease his pain. There, the whole story, with all the steamy details, would be dragged out of his inebriated consciousness.

"You have to stay away from their upper body," someone would be shouting later. "Women are stronger up top—all that pounding, ya know!" "Bob and weave, punch and kick. Don't let them get their hands on you."

Meanwhile, Edith, Katoka's wife, was surrounded by her own sympathetic supporters. "I got him good!" she was heard to say. "I pounded his skinny ass like I was pounding meal in the mortar. And not that soft soaked cassava meal. I worked him over like *kabaka kachinana* [the exceptionally hard-kerneled yellow American maize that the United Nations High Commissioner for Refugees gives to Angolan refugees]."

The *mulong'a*, the local gathering to resolve the case, was an especially short one. Edith accused Katoka of letting the village structures fall into disrepair and of not providing the family with meat. He denied it and accused her of failing to cook for him. The assembled masses agreed that both had behaved shamefully, that their union was without hope, and that they should be considered divorced from that moment on. However, since they were cross-cousins, they were still obligated to look out for one another's welfare and especially for that of their children. Katoka continued to reside in his old house. Edith, with the children, moved two hundred yards away to her elder brother's village, where her mother also resided. Katoka and Edith continued to see and formally greet each other virtually every day. Within two years each had married again.

Talking about Matriliny

[T]he study of matrilineal society represents the promise of a complicated social organization, rich in strange institutions, imbued with an atmosphere of the dramatic. . . . it is no coincidence that almost all monographs which have had wide repercussions have been about matrilineal societies.

Lévi-Strauss 1969, 117

Matrilineal societies have long been sources of amazement for and speculation by scholars of human social organization. J. J. Bachofen was one of the first to attempt to explain why some societies reckoned descent solely through females. In his 1861 book *Das Mutterrecht* (*The Mother-right*), he proposed that the dawn of human social life was characterized by widespread sexual promiscuity. Motherhood was the only parental relationship that could be determined with certainty. Women were initially at the mercy of more powerful men, but, at some point, they overcame their precarious position by entering into relationships of exclusivity with one man in return for his protection against other men. Through this action, women, in effect, established the institution of the family, with matriliny as its central feature. In addition to women's position being crucial for reckoning descent and interfamily alliances, women, Bachofen claimed, invented agriculture and were the most productive element of society. Furthermore, they controlled important religious activities. Female deities, earth mothers, and fertility goddesses dominated the transcendental world. High priestesses interpreted and influenced the impact of supernatural forces on the world of the living.

Eventually, according to Bachofen, men grew to resent their inferior position in society, began to assert fatherhood as a higher religious principle, and ultimately seized social and symbolic control from women. Patriliny thus evolved out of matrilineality. Societies that remain matrilineal, according to Bachofen's line of reasoning, are anachronistic entities in which men have yet to organize themselves to gain power.

Friedrich Engels, writing thirty years later, agreed with the basic evolutionary theme of Bachofen's argument but asserted that materialist forces had caused the shift from matrilineal to patrilineal descent. In *Origins of the Family, Private Property and the State*, Engels wrote: "In proportion as wealth increased, it made the man's position in the family more important than the woman's, and on the other hand created an impulse to exploit this strengthened position in order to overthrow in favor of his children the traditional order of inheritance. This, however, was impossible so long as descent was reckoned according to mother-right. Mother-right, therefore, had to be overthrown, and overthrown it was. As to how and when this revolution took place among civilised peoples, we have no knowledge. It falls entirely within prehistoric times" (1892, 58). The theses put forward by Engels and Bachofen are similar in their use of an evolutionary perspective, their reliance on assertions rather than evidence of the world-historical defeat of the female sex, and their assumption that matriliny necessarily implies matriarchy (Engels 1892, 59).

As social theorists moved from the armchair to the field in the early part of the twentieth century, they began to accumulate evidence that refuted the notion that matrilineal descent implied female rule. In fact, the new dogma became that leadership everywhere was part of the male domain. How then are we to explain the cultural notion of reckoning descent solely through females while political power flows through males? Malinowski, writing on the matrilineal Trobriand Islanders, provided one line of reasoning, claiming that "knowledge of impregnation, of the man's share in creating the new life in the mother's womb, is a fact of which the natives have not even the slightest glimpse" (cited in Leach 1969, 90). From the beginning, Malinowski's assertions were greeted with a great deal of suspicion in some quarters. Edmund Leach, however, was perhaps most instrumental in finally putting to rest this "denial of physiological paternity" thesis, in what became known as the virgin birth controversy (Leach 1969). Meanwhile, others continued to rely on theories that used notions of female promiscuity or of female vulnerability to male sexual advances to explain the original emergence of matriliny.

When the functionalist paradigm rose to prominence in anthropology during the 1950s, the focus shifted from explanations of origins and development to explanations of the internal workings of matrilineal societies. Of particular concern was identifying the ways in which matrilineal societies differed from patrilineal ones. From an analysis of G. P. Murdock's "World Ethnographic Sample" (1957), David Aberle noted that most matrilineal societies tended to fall within the narrow ecological niche of economies with a horticultural base. Rarely were they found in association with the plow and animal husbandry or among predominantly pastoral societies. Murdock himself had asserted in the late 1940s that power, property, and prestige spelled doom to matrilocal principles of residence, and by extension to matrilineal modes of descent reckoning. Jack Goody, arguing along the same lines in the 1950s, proposed that balanced reciprocity with distant uterine kin was an essential feature of matriliny. Large inequalities of wealth would mitigate against equal exchanges, ultimately rendering the system unworkable. Hence, matriliny was incompatible with economic advancement, which tended to generate, or at least exacerbate, socioeconomic differentiation.

The massive volume *Matrilineal Kinship* (1961), edited by David Schneider and Kathleen Gough, provides perhaps the most rigorous examination of the diversity of early functionalist-inspired theories of matrilineal societies. Schneider (1961) noted that the fundamental difference between patrilineal and matrilineal systems is that in the latter, descent and authority run through different lines, whereas in the former they are traced through the same line. Continuity in matrilineal groups depends on the behavior of both its male and female members. Women in patrilineal groups, however, transmit neither authority nor group affiliation. Patrilineal groups, therefore, in theory at least, can more easily relinquish a female member to the control of other groups. Furthermore, the relationship between the descent group and in-marrying affines differs in patrilineal and matrilineal systems. In patrilineal groups, the key in-marrying affines, the ones whose offspring would inherit lineage membership, would all be females. Since females generally lack power, so the argument goes, they can more easily be ignored. By contrast, in matrilineal groups, the key in-marrying affines would be males, and these males represent a potential threat to the ability of the lineage to exercise control over the female members who become their wives.

In summary, Schneider and Gough (Schneider 1961, 8–28) asserted that the system of matrilineal descent had embedded in it three major lines of tension: (1) *Between brothers and sisters.* This relationship is strongly binding yet highly ambivalent. On the one hand, a brother must be interested in his sister's sexual activity, for it is she who will produce his heirs. But on the other hand, a sister is sexually taboo to her brother; it is generally forbidden for them even to discuss sex in each other's presence. (2) *Between proximal generations.* A great source of tension exists between a woman's husband and her brother—between the role of father and that of mother's brother. The affective bond between men and their children stands in opposition to the bond linking the children to their mother's brother. Matrilineal societies must, therefore, place limits on the authority of men over their wives and their own offspring. (3) *Between the nuclear family and the descent group.* Because the nuclear family contains members of different matrilineages, its bonds of unity must be weakened if the bonds of the descent group are to be strengthened.

Schneider and Gough concluded that matrilineal descent groups are inherently unstable and prone to segmentation, but that matrilineal societies could persist if they possessed balancing mechanisms to counteract embedded contradictions. When confronted by the capitalist market system, the common standard of value, the unitary market, and the commoditization of private labor, however, matrilineal societies are no longer able to resolve their contradictions in favor of the descent group, and they gradually disintegrate: "In their place, the elementary family eventually emerges as the key kinship group with respect to residence, economic cooperation, legal responsibility, and socialization, with a narrow range of interpersonal kinship relationships spreading outward from it bilaterally and linking it with other elementary families" (Gough 1961b, 631).

Since the 1960s, numerous scholars have contested the model of matrilineal societies delineated by Schneider and Gough. First and foremost, Mary Douglas, in her brilliantly succinct classic "Is Matriliny Doomed in Africa?" (1969) turns her seasoned analytical eye on the distribution and continued viability of matrilineal societies in Africa. Douglas unravels the earlier arguments on matriliny, bringing to light two rarely articulated but often implicit aspects of the debate. First, she points to the operational belief that the nuclear family is really the basic unit of social organization, regardless of whether the society in question is patrilineal, matrilineal, bilateral, or what have you. Anything that weakens the bonds of the nuclear family is seen as threatening the stability of society as a whole. Ipso facto, matriliny is an inherently unstable state of being. Second, Douglas again calls attention to the less than systematic use of the term matriliny and the confusion wrought by conflating aspects of matriliny with those of matrilocality and matriarchy. Using Schneider's "Introduction: Distinctive Features of Matrilineal Descent Groups" (1961) as her point of departure, Douglas lays out her own version of the eight essential features of matriliny. Her list differs from Schneider's mainly in the positive value placed on particular features. Whereas Schneider and others saw shallow lineage depth, weakly ascribed status, and the difficulty of recruiting by birth as major disadvantages of matrilineal systems, Douglas gives these features special value inasmuch as they tend to lead to open recruitment of talent and labor power, strong intergroup alliances that override local loyalties, and a broad scope for individual achievement. Matrilineal societies, she claims, possess their own form of flexibility and adaptability that could serve them well even under modern market conditions: "Matriliny should be capable of flourishing in modern market economies wherever the demand for men is higher than the demand for things. Because of the scope it gives for personal, unascribed achievement of leadership, matrilineal kinship could have advantages in an expanding market economy. On my view the enemy of matriliny is not the cow as such, not wealth as such, not economic development as such, but economic restrictions" (Douglas 1969, 131).

C. J. Fuller (1976, 144) also takes Schneider and Gough to task for what he calls conceptual and definitional muddles relating to terms like "family," "household," and "kin group." Analytically distinct aspects of the family—for example, kinship group, residential group, property-owning group, and consumption group—had not been separated. Unidirectional, reductionistic arguments proposing that matrilineal family organization is incompatible with economic progress are overly simplistic, he argues. According to Fuller, the ethnographic literature is unclear concerning the decline of matrilineal systems. He points to evidence that clearly shows the persistence of particular matrilineal systems long after their immersion into the capitalist market economy. Concomitantly, there is rather persuasive evidence indicating that where change has occurred, it has occurred for reasons not necessarily related to the internal organization of matrilineal systems.

For some social theorists, such as Wendy James, the problem with Schneider and Gough's approach runs much deeper than ambiguous definitions and bias in the selection of ethnographic cases (James 1978). The more disturbing issue is the primacy given to jural authority and power in defining essential forms of social life: "This 'jural model' of society, being founded in Radcliffe-Brown's writing, for example those dealing with the structure of men's rights over things and rights over persons (including women), tend to leave women out of the picture even in matrilineal systems. The ideal of descent itself came to be equated with the transmission of power and authority, though the ethnographic evidence surely shows that there may be many other components in the idea" (James 1978, 145). Society is too often seen as a system of rules defining rights and duties and powers, according to James, and women are always seen as being under the authority of men. The problems supposedly inherent in matrilineal systems are only problems for males. It is they who must resolve the conundrum of how to keep control and exercise authority when continuity and recruitment are reckoned through females. In James's view, society consists of numerous, overlapping links between individuals, and the most obvious links—those most accessible to anthropologists—may not necessarily be the most meaningful. James advocates an emic approach to identifying and defining the essential elements of particular societies. She asks, "Do the people who practice matriliny see it foundering on contradictory principles? Do they see it as a structural power game more puzzling for men than other modes of organisation? Or is it possible that they may see the system in a different perspective? Perhaps their ideas of citizenship and identity, and of authority, their definitions of status and ties of loyalty are far more complex and subtle than those of the average structural anthropologist" (1978, 148). In James's alternative view of matriliny, women do not serve as passive intermediate links for the transmission of authority from male to male but rather occupy nodal positions in the logical, formal ordering of wider relationships. James is able to show that some societies which previously had seemed riddled with organizational contradictions in fact make perfect sense once one takes a matrifocal point of view and ceases to see the social structure as a system for the maintenance and transmission of male authority. James likewise disputes the notion that matrilineal systems are doomed to disappear in a confrontation with modern global economic forces. She argues that matriliny can often contain features that are advantageous in an expanding modern economy, and that in one or two cases matriliny has actually emerged in recent historical time (James 1978, 158).

Karla Poewe (1981), working along the same lines as Wendy James, has been particularly effective at exposing the fiction of universal male dominance. Poewe's research in Luapula, Zambia, focused precisely on seeing how society is organized from the point of view of women. In the course of her fieldwork she was able to isolate submerged social structures which hold important implications for our understanding of gender relations and notions of power. True enough, Poewe acknowledges, men in general possess more brute strength than women and are particularly prone to making public pronouncements about the nature of society—pronouncements which find their way into the anthropological literature more often than do women's views. Nevertheless, Poewe was able to show that women create their own ideologies concerning gender relations and the nature of society and can generate their own structures to bring society into conformity with those ideologies. Some of these structures can be uncovered only through ongoing, intimate relations with women involved in the process of pursuing their own interests and re-creating and refining the networks and mechanisms that facilitate that pursuit and give it meaning. Poewe (1981, 52) proposed that some societies are better understood not from the perspective of dominance but in terms of sexual parallelism, where males and females control predominantly different spheres of society.

For Poewe, the question of matriliny's decline in the face of modern developments is far more complex than had previously been realized and cannot be predicted with any degree of certainty. It can be addressed only in relation to the concrete reality of the dialectics involved in local gender politics. According to Poewe, "Matriliny consists analytically of three ideational phenomena: (1) kinship and descent principles, (2) kin categories, and (3) associated norms and values. It is a 'total system' and consists of the combination of matrilineal ideology and the social actions and relations which are meaningfully informed by it" (1981, 53–55).

Poewe thus concurs with James, Fuller, and others who assert that matriliny cannot be said to be in decline merely because the associated norms and values have changed; it can be said to be in decline only if the ideology of matrilineal descent itself is in decline. Most who have hypothesized about the decline of matriliny have focused primarily on inheritance. The productive individualism inherent in capitalism is said to run counter to the distributive communalism generally associated with matrilineal systems. As men accumulate wealth privately, they seek more and more to consolidate that wealth and transmit it directly to their own offspring. But productive individualism was and still is the norm in many matrilineal societies. It therefore does not logically follow that productive individualism of a capitalist nature need necessarily lead to the emergence of a patrilineal inheritance mode. The proposition's only analytical weight lies in the assumption that an increase in personal wealth strengthens the affective bond between a man and his own offspring at the expense of his bond to his sisters' children. Yet this position could be criticized as a form of psychological reductionism.

From Poewe's perspective, we can see that most theories of matriliny discuss the transmission of male-held positions of authority and male-controlled resources while saying little about how females transmit their resources or how they reconstruct their cultural categories from generation to generation. Nor do they address the question of why men cannot inherit from their fathers and still consider themselves part of a matrilineal descent group. In truth there is no reason.

Poewe's data are particularly interesting for our purposes. The people of Luapula among whom she did her research, although separated from the Kanongesha Lunda by five hundred miles and numerous other ethnolinguistic groups, are nevertheless people of the Lunda diaspora. The founders of the Luapula and Kanongesha polities, according to both oral traditions, left the Lunda Center together in the early 1700s. After a period of coresidency southeast of the empire's capital, they went their separate ways in the mid-1700s (Schecter 1976, 98–110). The Lunda who went east to the Luapula now speak a different language (Bemba) and have adopted many of the cultural traits of the people among whom they have settled. Nevertheless, over two centuries later, their gender politics, as outlined by Poewe, are similar in many respects to those of the Kanongesha Lunda today. The Luapula matrilineal ideology encourages separate but parallel participation of the sexes in the economic and political affairs of society, as does the dominant ideology of the Kanongesha Lunda (Poewe 1981, 55). The notion of sexual parallelism may indeed have heuristic value in understanding Lunda gender politics. One need not be a woman focusing upon the women's view of society to arrive at this conclusion. Even an outsider totally absorbed in the male world would have to recognize the limited points of contact between that world and the world of females.

Gender Relations among the Lunda-Ndembu

Relations between males and females among the matrilineal Lunda-Ndembu are heavily infused with the notion of *chaambu*, separation. As LeVine noted, the focus on social distance between persons differing in age and sex is ubiquitous in Africa. There is widespread and pervasive institutional emphasis throughout Africa on avoidance, segregated activities, and formality of interaction, even between members of the same household. As we saw in the last chapter, separation based on age tends to be reckoned vertically. In this chapter we note how separation by gender, at least among the Lunda-Ndembu, tends to be reckoned laterally. Here I lay out localized notions of gender by examining three areas in which separation is made visible and declared important by the Lunda : (1) the division of labor, (2) philosophical notions about existential status and/or metaphysical relations, and (3) strategic planning for life and the afterlife. From these three areas one can begin to tease out sets of abstract notions that can be said to form grand traditions. These traditions frame debates and serve as the most public means for either justifying continuity or embracing change. Concepts of gender separation evolve and unfold in an environment saturated with long-standing debates, emergent modern notions, and the myriad disagreements that come up in quotidian struggles between men and women.

Matriliny and the Division of Labor

Niyala wubinda, namumbanda lusemu. *(For the man, huntsmanship; for the woman, procreation.)*

Lunda-Ndembu proverb

The division of labor among the Lunda is such that there is little observable overlap in male and female activities. In many senses each is autonomous. Any competent adult woman can grow and process more than sufficient food to feed herself and her children. Women also control the labor power of young boys until they reach the age of circumcision, and young girls until they marry. The Lunda population is quite young, with nearly 50 percent under the age of fifteen (Central Statistical Office 1980, 2). There is, thus, a great deal of youthful labor at the disposal of adult women. Each woman, as head of her own little economic corporate group, designs strategies for the effective utilization of the child labor under her control and the natural resources within her reach. Some children may assist her regularly in the fields, while others collect firewood, haul water from the stream, and care for younger siblings. Women organize gathering parties to collect wild foods such as mushrooms, wild fruits and vegetables, and edible insects. Many of these items, although seasonal, can be collected in prodigious quantities, dried, stored, and consumed throughout the year. Their contribution to the local diet is quite substantial.

Women also use child labor to assist them in processing cassava flour for the marketplace. At various points in history, food shortages elsewhere have enabled Lunda women to reap considerable cash profits from their surplus production. On a more regular basis, women earn cash from the sale of alcoholic beverages. The production of distilled spirits is usually done only by women and large numbers of children. Well-coordinated personnel are required to undertake such a laborious enterprise. Some must chop wood to keep a roaring fire going all day, while others keep a vigilant eye on the hissing and sometimes dangerous distillery equipment; still others carry out the daily chores of cooking, cleaning, and childcare. Some women also earn cash from craft production. Children assist by gathering and preparing reeds for weaving mats and baskets or by preparing clay for molding pots.

Women also use children as their primary communication network. Although women may be isolated from one another throughout much of the day, there is a continual stream of children moving among them collecting and disseminating socially and economically relevant information, such as who has surplus commodities for sale, who is seeking to purchase particular items, where mushrooms have sprung up recently, or where wild berries are ripe. At the end of each day, when the tasks are completed, women gather together to pool their information and evaluate and refine their economic strategies.

A man, regardless of his relationship, has nothing to say about how a woman organizes her time. She is an autonomous entity, going and coming as she pleases, raising cash and using it as she will. Husbands, for example, tend to have little idea how much cash their wives possess, and it is not considered proper for them even to inquire. Truly, the universality of male dominance has been exaggerated. Furthermore, male brute strength seems to play a minimal role in gender relations. Women do not seem the least in awe of it. Nor do women depend either on husbands to protect them from other men or on brothers to protect them from husbands. Indeed, women have been known to assemble and confront head-on any male who physically threatens a member of their group.

Women also develop networks to assist one another in the event of illness and to work out disputes that may arise among them. Males have a hierarchy based on notions of age and position in the descent system. But because the Lunda more often than not adhere to a virilocal postmarriage residence pattern, most adult women in a village are unrelated. Thus, the quotidian networks within which women operate are usually unrelated to the descent system, and their linkages cannot be identified from a study of genealogies. Their relationships tend to grow out of daily personal interactions that lead to friendship and mutual respect. These networks are fluid and ever changing, as new women marry into the village and other women marry out; nevertheless, they are arranged hierarchically. Age is perhaps the most important component in determining a woman's position in the hierarchy, but factors such as numbers of children, managerial skills, industriousness, and personality are also factored in. This hierarchy is acted out daily. When women greet one another, titles such as *kansi* and *mukulumpi* (junior and senior) are embedded in the language of the greeting. When women sit together, just as in the case of men, a determination must be made as to who is honored with the best seats. For reasons discussed earlier, relations between women do appear to be a bit more egalitarian than those among men. Women, particularly those with control over children, are more autonomous and self-sufficient than men as individuals. The salient point, however, is that women are linked to one another in relationships that contain structure and function, that persist through time, and that have very little to do with kinship. That structure is underpinned by an ideology that maintains the importance of the autonomy of individual females at one level and the unity of all women vis-à-vis men at another level.

The men's world is difficult to comprehend from the village perspective. Indeed, men often seem out of place in the village. While women are busy rushing to and fro, producing, processing, and preparing food, shouting orders to their young workforce, men are usually casually sitting together in the *chota*, the men's talking house, whiling away the hours in seemingly idle chatter.[1] One needs to follow men into the bush to grasp the essence of their world. Lunda males tend to conceive of themselves as hunters, regardless of how much or how little time they actually spend hunting. Some men do indeed devote a good portion of their time to seeking game in the bush. Others, however, may make only a few trips to the bush during the dry season. Some who hold salaried employment may have been on only a few hunting trips in their entire lives. But the concept of "man the hunter" permeates and defines men's relationship with women. As noted earlier, hunting involves more than merely tracking game. Hunting parties also spend time fishing, setting traps for birds and mammals, gathering honey, insects, and other wild foods; collecting bamboo, reeds, bark fibers, thatching grass, and other construction materials; and securing medicinal plants. The cooperation and comradeship of men in the bush contrasts markedly with the aggressive individualism and self-centered arrogance they display in the village. In the bush, men, in a sense, mold themselves into single-sex families, well-oiled productive units every bit as effective, autonomous, and self-sufficient as the village-based economic units that women create.

Parallel conceptual worlds thus exist: men in the bush, women and their children in the village. Where, then, are the points of overlap between these two worlds? When groups of males who have been surviving quite adequately in the bush—indeed, feasting and enjoying themselves—begin to break camp in preparation for the return to village life, more often than not they joke lightheartedly about their urge for *shimba*, sex, and *nshima,* the soft paste made from cassava flour. They comment on how the women might refuse them if their catch of meat is inadequate. In truth, the relationship between men and women is neither as simple nor as crude as meat in exchange for sex and *nshima*. Jokes to that effect are humorous precisely because they are exaggerations; but they are exaggerations which nevertheless contain a kernel of truth. Between men and women there is much evidence of love, affection, and concern for the well-being of each other and of their offspring. But at the conceptual level, each group, male and female, conceives of itself as autonomous, independent, self-sufficient, and not really in need of the productive capacity of the other group. All of the public posturing is to that effect. People are segregated by gender in nearly every activity; even husbands and wives are rarely seen interacting in public. The relationship between men and women is conceived as a voluntary association for the attainment of mutual benefits, rather than as a bond of mutual dependency. Of course it is obvious that men and women need one another in order to produce the children whom parents hope will take care of them in their old age and ensure the survival of their memory after they have gone. But the mutual desire for children is a given that seems to play a very small role in determining the dynamics of political posturing between men and women. Women, as a collectivity, assert that they do not need men. Neither meat from the bush, nor male labor to keep the village in repair and to clear fresh garden land is an absolute necessity. Women could survive adequately without these services. But these services can make a woman's life more pleasurable and contribute indirectly to her own productive efforts. Conversely, men, as a collectivity, assert that they do not need women. Sex and *nshima* may be pleasurable, and in their own way contribute to a man's productive efforts, but men could survive without either. In a sense, then, Lunda gender politics is about negotiating for benefits in a way that does not threaten that which is most important to either side: autonomy and independence.

The interaction between males and females is far more complex than the abstract model outlined above. But the model does say something important about the basic ideology which gives form and meaning to gender relations among the Lunda. For example, disputes between husband and wife that become public concerns almost always take the same form. He accuses her of refusing to prepare *nshima* for him or of refusing him sex. She accuses him of failing to bring meat regularly or to keep her house in repair. It would be absurd to believe that these are the only problems that Lunda couples ever experience. But it is easy to comprehend that regardless of the true nature of the underlying conflict, public appeals are always made in an idiom that reflects those limited, culturally acknowledged areas where the male and female worlds overlap. The concerns and activities of each sex are postulated as being so separate that for arguments to occur over anything other than sex and *nshima,* meat and building repairs, would indicate an encroachment on the autonomy and independence of one of the parties involved.

Contemporary public posturing, however, belies the historical complexities of male-female relations among the Lunda. Those relations have been constantly evolving over the centuries. For example, the seventeenth-century switch to cassava from millet and sorghum no doubt brought about a fundamental rethinking and reordering of the division of labor. Because cassava production does not require mass mobilization of labor, it played a key role in freeing male labor from the production of food and facilitating men's participation in the caravan economy of the eighteenth and nineteenth centuries. As noted in chapter 2, the impact of cassava on women is still very much in debate. On the one hand, women became less dependent on men for critical inputs in agricultural production; but on the other hand, women's workload increased tremendously. Some see cassava as having primarily increased the productive burden placed on women. Von Oppen, for example, argues that "cassava cultivation marks the beginning of a history of women's subordination as subsistence producers, at most as unpaid family labor to subsidize male export production" (1993, 261). Many dispute this view, however, and see cassava as having had a more liberating effect.

The rapid nature of its adoption suggests that it was attractive to women. Cassava became the standard caravan food for all who entered Central Africa. Von Oppen estimated that upper Zambezi producers were capable of supplying over fourteen thousand tons of surplus cassava annually to foreign travelers throughout the 1800s (1993, 96). Women's increased labor in processing cassava perhaps gave them additional power in controlling the crop, selling it to caravans, and turning the profit into ornamentation and other items of value that they would not lose in the event of divorce or widowhood. Livingstone, Silva Porto, Capello and Ivens, and other early travelers to this region noted the decentralized nature of the food trade and women's active participation in it. Women even incorporated cassava as an element of their social identity. Cassava, especially *wun'ga,* the pure white cassava flour, is a dominant symbol in every female ritual.

Women also clearly benefited from men's involvement in long-distance trade. It has been estimated that 50 percent of the goods flowing into Central Africa via that trade were cloth, 20 percent alcohol, 10 percent guns, and 20 percent an assortment of household utensils, beads, necklaces, bracelets, and other items of bodily adornment (Miller 1988, 73–78). This ratio no doubt reflects women's purchasing power at the time. However, a large quantity of these items were also purchased by men for women: "Men often felt obliged to pass on to their wives a share of what they obtained through their better external links, and such obligations may have been one of the stimuli for them to establish such links" (von Oppen 1993, 268). Was this simply a new way for men to discharge their old obligations, or did women acquire additional bargaining power vis-à-vis men during this period?

During the height of the caravan trade, it is estimated that over fifty thousand Ovimbundu traveled to or through the upper Zambezi region every year. Untold numbers of traders and carriers from other ethnic groups flowed through the area as well, nearly all of whom were males. Evidence indicates that sexual services were at a premium. An extremely lucrative market opened up for those women willing to provide such services either on a short-term or long-term basis. Additionally, within the region males competed with one another for wives across ethnic boundaries. The Chokwe, the Lunda's neighbors to the northwest, were known at one point to have acquired 80 percent of their wives from neighboring groups. Travelers' reports and oral traditions claim that most of those wives were slaves. But reports also repeatedly single out the Chokwe as being particularly generous to their wives, especially in providing them with foreign luxuries from external trade (Miller 1969).

Foreign goods increasingly found their way into bridewealth negotiations, as well. Beads, necklaces, bracelets, white stones, cowries, enamel plates, and especially cloth are remembered as important forms of bridewealth. These items, whose quality and quantity varied depending on the overall wealth in an area, were traditionally distributed widely to members of a woman's family, both male and female. The bridewealth negotiation provided a forum for discussing and assigning relative values to things. It was also a time and place to negotiate and emphasize the material transaction that would characterize the ongoing relationship between husbands and wives, between consanguineal and affinal kin. Although it would be difficult to generalize about the relative strength of male and female bargaining positions, one can speculate that the balance may have tipped in favor of women during the early caravan period. Their position, however, no doubt fell when the slaving frontier reached the upper Zambezi and then rose once again with its passing.

The migrant labor system of the early twentieth century siphoned off much male labor, impoverishing village life and necessitating, once again, a reformulation of the division of labor. Women were forced to take on increasing responsibility for village maintenance, in an economic climate which severely circumscribed their own trade and cash-earning opportunities. The early colonial period brought an end to the caravan traffic, placed limits on physical movement, and saw the deliberate destruction of local craft production that might compete with migrant labor as an alternative source of cash. Women were trapped in a world of arbitrary demands and random brutality, and they became dependent on male workers to provide them with the commodities they had previously been able to acquire with their own resources. Yet history rarely leaves its victims completely powerless. During their long absences, men became increasingly dependent on women to maintain the legitimacy of their positions within the village world. Migrant work provided little in the way of long-term security. It was the fate of all but a few migrant workers to spend their waning years back in the village, cash depleted, dependent for their survival on the estates built up over the years by women. Women were thus well placed to make claims on the cash men earned during their productive years. The basis of those claims is clear. Absence could not absolve men of their traditional responsibilities, if they later wished to use those same traditions as a basis for reclaiming their positions in the village. The social relations which established rights to residence and to support had to be continually nurtured and symbolized through material transactions.

As mentioned earlier, some women in Mwinilunga managed to reap respectable profits by providing cassava for the rapidly expanding body of mineworkers on the Zambian Copperbelt. The mid-twentieth century also saw the first generation of females moving to the cities and mine compounds to make a living. As Parpart (1986) notes, "Colonial policy pushed men into migrant labor, leaving women stranded in the rural areas with an increasingly onerous work load. The cities began to look attractive as rural conditions deteriorated. Moreover, while women had little chance for wage employment in town, other opportunities to earn money existed. Beer-brewing, gardening, selling food and services (including sexual services), and above all, partnerships with men, offered women the means to survive in town" (1986, 3). Parpart richly illustrates the protracted nature of negotiations between men and women in town, as well as the collusion between colonial officials and village elders in an effort to control women's sexuality. Yet women were not mere pawns in a male-dominated game. They countered all attempts to control their movements and proscribe their activities, and they developed strategies and networks of mutual assistance to wrest a living from the often hostile urban environment.[2]

Despite women's commercial acumen during the caravan era, their personal agency in the early urban context, and their contemporary assertions of sexual parallelism, men still have control over one key social position: the headmanship. How do we explain the absence of a female as the focal point of village unity? In truth we cannot, although we can suggest some possibilities. It must first be clearly understood that the position of headman is not a position of authority in any real sense. Headmen cannot command, they can only persuade. As will be outlined in chapter 7, charm and economic cleverness are the prerequisites of headmanship. Yet since women can also be charming, and many are quite astute at generating cash, we can only assume that the prevalence of male headmen is the result of a historical struggle or a negotiated process sufficiently submerged to have left few ripples on the current political surface. Women, for some reason or another, have been persuaded to allow men to control the position of headmanship. Perhaps men were able to negotiate control over the headmanship by reference to their responsibility for building and maintaining village structures from materials which primarily derive from the male domain, the bush. Perhaps the negotiations revolved around the differences between men and women in the organization of labor. Lunda males would perhaps assert that there is simply a better fit between the duties of a headman and the male work pattern. Women's work is characterized by a steady, constant effort that tends to fill the entire working day, day in and day out. Men's work, however, is characterized by spectacular bursts of energy during which they may work virtually around the clock, alternating with periods of extended leisure. It is during these periods of leisure that a man can concentrate on his duties as a headman. Even heated disputes between villagers need not necessarily be resolved immediately. A headman can often successfully appeal to disputants for a period of calm, a cooling-off period, during which time he can complete whatever tasks he is undertaking at the moment. Afterward he may spend several days addressing the situations that have arisen since his last period of leisure. Senior Headman Chifunga, for example, virtually always operates in his fashion. In fact, one senses a profound reluctance on his part to become too quickly involved in others people's problems, hoping that they will eventually work out their differences themselves. But once a month or so, he sets aside his own work in the fields or around the village for a few days, convenes a series of meetings, and attempts to resolve a half dozen or more lingering disputes, one after the other.

Whatever the nature of the gender politics that led to the contemporary control by men over the position of headman, it should be noted that political leadership has not always and everywhere resided exclusively in the male domain. Periods of political centralization, in particular, have spawned female leaders of the highest order both at the Lunda Center and in the Lunda diaspora (see White 1949; Miller 1969; Papstein 1978; and Birmingham and Martin 1983, vol. 1). A woman, Lueji, was responsible for the first pan-Lunda capital city and the political reorganization that allowed for rapid expansion during the imperial era. Nyakatolo, the Lunda diaspora chieftainess of Nana Candundo, for years controlled the largest of the market towns on the long-distance caravan network. The Nyakaseya, the beer pourer of the Kanongesha, and one of the most powerful chiefs among the Zambian Lunda, was originally a woman. Central African oral traditions are replete with the exploits of famous female chiefs. But in most of those cases, the positions occupied by females exempted them from performing daily tasks such as planting, processing, and preparing food. They were positions to which tribute flowed, allowing the occupant to focus full-time on administrative duties. No such positions currently exist. All able-bodied Lunda are expected to toil. Neither headmen, nor senior headmen, nor even the Kanongesha himself are exempt from physical labor. Thus, perhaps the flexibility of the male work schedule was indeed a significant factor in the gender dynamics which led to the current male control over the position of headman. On the other hand, one could argue that the reverse might equally well be true. Perhaps men fight to monopolize the tasks which require only sporadic inputs in order to free themselves up for leadership positions. The genderization of occupational status remains one of those human universals that has thus far eluded universal explanations. The male strength hypothesis, the fertility maintenance hypothesis, and the child-care compatibility hypothesis are standard explanatory frameworks presented even in introductory anthropology texts. Although they may possess some heuristic value in globalizing the issue, however, each has been shown to possess limitations in addressing specific local contexts. What we do know is that once a particular task becomes assigned to a particular gender sphere it also becomes enmeshed in webs of gender-specific symbolism that further embed and naturalize that assignment. The original logic of the assignment itself need not be revisited often.

Life Givers and Life Takers: The Colors of Ritual

The three colors white-red-black for the simpler societies are not merely differences in the visual perception of parts of the spectrum: they are abridgments or condensations of whole realms of psycho-biological experience involving reason and all the senses and concerned with primary group relationships. It is only by subsequent abstraction from these configurations that the other modes of social classification employed by mankind arose.

Turner 1967, 91

For the Lunda, notions of *chaambu*, separation between males and females, flow through several abstract and philosophical realms, including that of color symbolism. Whatever the veracity of Turner's theory of color classification, he is most assuredly correct about its abridging and condensing function. Lunda musings about color weave together disparate notions of how things ought to be and how the various elements of society ought to relate to one another. Colors also link quotidian social practices with the realm of ritual experience. The symbolism associated with white and red,

in particular, enables one to glimpse some of the metaphysical underpinnings of Lunda discourse about gender relations. The following account
and exegesis is of necessity synthetic. The relevant components and their
interrelations are as limitless as the human imagination and as ever changing as social circumstances.

When asked to reflect on the symbolism of the color white, Lunda informants invariably mention its association with goodness, health, strength,
the absence of death, and chieftainship or authority. It is generally a positive
color, standing in opposition to both black, which represents the entire domain of things hidden, unknown, or unknowable and therefore negative,
and red, which can be either positive or negative depending on the context.
The physical referents that most powerfully convey the notion of whiteness
are semen, milk, and cassava flour. Not only is each a white substance, but
each is associated with nourishment. Collectively, they represent the maintenance of life, and indeed, the very flow of life itself. The role of milk and
cassava in nurturing life is obvious. But semen also plays a most important
role. Biological conception for the Lunda is often expressed as a process
rather than an event. Semen is the glue which congeals female blood to form
the body of a baby. A man must continue to have sexual intercourse with his
wife even after she is known to be pregnant. The glue must be repeatedly
applied lest the baby form incompletely, resulting in a miscarriage. Thus,
conceptually, it is the man's task to nourish the unborn with semen, the
woman's task to nourish the newly born with milk, and the task of all adults
to nourish themselves by planting cassava. Semen, milk, and cassava are
often associated with rivers in parables and riddles: semen, the river that
grows restless at night; milk, the river that flows when babies cry; cassava,
the river that drowns *nzala*, hunger. Semen, milk, and cassava are the three
tributaries of the white river of life. Such formulations genderize the ecol-
ogy of social existence. Men and women are represented as separate yet
commingling metaphysical streams splashing along the banks of life.

The white realm also includes both the male and female initiation ceremonies, *mukanda* and *nkanga*. The dominant symbols in each are white/
whiteness. Much of the activity of the girls' *nkanga* ceremony, for example, takes place around a *mudyi* tree. When cut, the *mudyi* tree exudes a
thick white latex, which in this context is said to symbolize milk, motherhood, femaleness, and matriliny. Boys are also circumcised under the *mudyi*
tree, but in this context whiteness is said to represent semen, fatherhood,
and maleness. Despite the multiplicity of themes weaving through both

ceremonies, notions of hierarchy and separation by gender are given the most forceful and dramatic treatment, as we have seen, and leave perhaps the most long-lasting impression. *Mukanda* and *nkanga* stand alone as the only rituals that every Lunda interviewed still claims to have undergone. The riddle of the rivers, with its metaphorical prescription for gender relations, is thus firmly ensconced in the psyche of each member of society.

If white can best be described as the continual flow of orderly life, then red is best visualized as two end points, or moments of profound transition—birth and death, a beginning and an end. Red is the blood of parturition, as well as the blood of killing (human or animal). It is neither absolutely good nor absolutely bad. As the blood of childbirth it is good. As the blood of miscarriage it is bad. As the blood of animals to feed the people it is welcomed. As the blood of murder it is positively dangerous. Its only constant symbolic association throughout all contexts is that of power—raw, unyielding, natural power which humans can never control but only moderate.

Redness, at one level, symbolizes the idea of the opposition of maleness and femaleness. The ideal woman is a life-giver. The ideal man is a life-taker. Women give life to children, to crops in the field, and to the village as a whole through processing and preparing food. Men bring death to the animals, death to the trees of the forest by clearing garden spaces for women, and, if necessary, death to the enemies of the group through warfare. This formulation clearly submerges part of each identity, but such submersions may be necessary in order to bring complementarities and oppositions within a single philosophical framework. They may allow differences to be dichotomized in a way that facilitates particular strategies. Lunda philosophy holds that every type of living entity possesses a unique vital force which interacts with the vital forces of other living entities in deterministic ways. The vital force of a woman is like a mantle of life, an aura extending from her body, which reaches out to all she comes near, accentuating, stimulating, and expanding the capacity for life. The aura of a man is death. Men and women are thus at one level dangerous to each other, and their contact must be highly regulated. During childbirth, for instance, no men, or even their articles of daily use, may be present. Vital force has a way of extending itself beyond the physical being of a person, of lingering in the places he or she habituates, of clinging to frequently used articles. The vital force of men, that aura of death, can be especially harmful to women and their babies at that critical liminal phase of parturition. Men, on the other hand, must refrain from contact with women before setting out for the bush on hunting expeditions. If they should happen to carry with them any remnant of the female aura, it might reach out to the animals to give them life. The animals would flee, the hunter would be blind to their presence, or his aim would be unsure.

At the level of ritual, the red realm contains the ceremonies of the female fertility complex and the male hunting complex. The three major rituals of the female complex, *nkula*, *isoma*, and *wubwangu*, are each performed for menstrual disorders, barrenness, miscarriage, and the ill health of infants. The dominant symbolic actions of *nkula* include dressing the patient in red hunter's attire and carving a sacred *mukula* tree (a tree with red sap) into the figure of an infant. *Isoma* rituals feature washing a husband and wife with red medicines while they are seated in holes dug at the base of termite mounds (usually red clay), and sacrificing chickens. The *wubwangu* ritual is dominated by symbols of duality, along with ribald cross-sexual joking; "red words" that are considered especially dangerous and spiritually polluting in other contexts.

The male hunting complex is composed of a hierarchical sequence of rituals: *mukaala*, *chitampakasa*, *kalombu*, *mundeli*, and *ntambu*. Each is performed for poor hunting luck, believed to be caused when a spirit either chases game away, makes animals invisible to a hunter, or causes a hunter to miss his aim through trembling. The main ritual features of each include blood sacrifices, anthills of red clay, and effigies of animals carved out of red wood. Each step up the sequence is believed to bring both greater hunting acumen and greater spiritual power over the forces of nature.

Midwives and hunters are both said to be red leaders. Most of the polities of Central Africa, according to myriad oral traditions, were established by hunters. Thus, at one level, the power of the hunter stands in opposition to the power of the chiefs or the headmen. The latter are often associated with whiteness in a fashion that feminizes village social life and contrasts it with the masculine forest existence. On some formal occasions, the chief and the headman are referred to, respectively, as "mother of the nation" and "mother of the village." In theory, at least, they are the direct descendants of the original owners of the land, the senior members of the oldest lineages, and are thus the living embodiments of continuity and respect for hierarchy. White power is related to the maintenance of life, the orderly progression of time, the slow steady movement up the hierarchy. Red power is associated with one who overthrows and reestablishes a political order through access to the forces of violence and death. In general it is said that hunters make poor leaders. The characteristics of a good hunter are the antithesis of those desired in a good headman or chief. Wrote Turner, "The professional hunter . . . is a man of the bush who spends much of his life alone, pitting his wits against the fleetness or ferocity of animals, fierce himself, boastful, dreaded as a sorcerer, by character and mode of living unable to stomach the authority of another, patriarchal in his family life in a matrilineal society. . . . It is clear that such a personality type is diametrically opposed to that thought proper for a headman" (1957, 202–3). Headmen are sociable characters. Great hunters are solitary figures, separated much of the time from the village and from women. In some sense they are seen as maleness in the extreme—red maleness unencumbered by the constraints of white social unity. But according to historical accounts, hunters apparently do make good conquerors and good founders of royal lineages. Conquering hunters, however, always formalize their rule by marrying into the oldest lineage of the conquered people, thereby becoming the fathers of new lines of kings or chiefs. Such scenarios are pregnant with symbolism. The red realm can momentarily conquer the white realm but cannot rule it. Instead, it gives birth to and strengthens a new line of leaders within the white realm. White is the flow of life, and red is the end points. White is continuity. Red is the momentary.

According to some Lunda, white represents the healthy and complementary aspects of gender separation—the independent unions of men and women that collectively maintain and nourish life. It is the rite of passage, the orderly flow of events. Red, however, represents the dangerous aspects of gender relations. It is the rite of affliction, adversity to be overcome, and potential destruction. Men and women are metaphysically equipped and existentially destined to face different challenges. And they must face those challenges on behalf of one another. Lunda philosophies about gender separation are fraught with inconsistencies and submersions, fine lines and flexibilities. But they provide a rich body of images and feelings with which to think about and debate, contest and construct deeply gendered social and metaphysical worlds.

Strategies for Life, Strategies for Death

Gender relations entail far more than struggling over the assignment of subsistence tasks, jockeying for rights and privileges, and battling symbolically over ontological status. Notions of *chaambu*, separation, reveal themselves in strategic plans that bridge the physical and metaphysical, life and the afterlife. They are reflected in daily thoughts and actions that transform the necessary into the desirable. The struggle for the positions of *iyala muneni* and *mumbanda muneni*, bigman and bigwoman, provide a vantage point from which to witness some of the most important dimensions of gender relations. Bigmanship and bigwomanship are widely pursued with a quasi-religious zeal, and often with meticulously thought out and pragmatically executed plans. Their social dimensions were laid out in chapter 4. Here I examine the strategic dimensions of planning by both sexes to maintain productive autonomy, to control their own and their heirs' bodies, and to secure a particular status in the afterlife. Husbands and wives figure prominently in each others' plans in ways that have changed in recent decades; the justification for these plans is the subject of much contestation. The most dramatic quantitative evidence of the changing relationship between men and women is the declining divorce rate, which dropped from 61 percent in the 1950s to 28 percent in the 1980s (discussed in chapter 3). An analysis of this change brings the issue of gender relations down to the level of lived experiences in contemporary Mwinilunga. At least three major factors can be put forward as powerfully influencing concepts of marriage and the acceptability of divorce: Christianity, household-based cash acquisition strategies, and the national policy on the issue of inheritance. I discuss each in turn.

In 1986 nearly 60 percent of individuals surveyed identified themselves as staunch Christians who regularly attended one of the local churches.[3] Many others attended Christian churches more sporadically for a wide range of personal and professional reasons. Christianity was seized upon as a mechanism for community formation, as a source of new social networks, and as an opportunity to obtain goods and services provided by expatriate missionaries. Evangelical Protestants, who arrived in 1906, were the first Christian missionaries in Mwinilunga District. Today, their churches are well established in even the most isolated villages. The Protestants teach that the monogamous Christian family is the most fundamental manifestation of Christian faith. Divorce is, therefore, an anathema, an affront to God himself. The first Catholic church was established in Mwinilunga in 1947. Presently there are large Catholic cathedrals in the areas of highest population density, and perhaps fifty major outstations, that is, village congregations, which are attended to daily by a local catechist and visited regularly by expatriate itinerant priests. Marriage is viewed as an indissoluble bond between two Catholics, undertaken with the permission of a priest. Although annulments are possible under exceptional circumstances, they are severely discouraged. The third most populous denomination in Mwinilunga is a loose confederation of congregations calling themselves the New Apostolics, whose teachings are primarily based on the Old Testament. It differs from the others in its belief that a man may have as many wives as he can properly maintain. But the local Apostolics also believe that adultery is the only legitimate grounds for divorce, and that adultery must be witnessed by at least two persons to be substantiated. Thus, accepting Christianity in Mwinilunga has always been virtually synonymous with accepting the notion that marriage is a permanent bond.

The particular collection of expatriate missionaries who brought Christianity to Mwinilunga tended to place less emphasis on issues of philosophy or theology than on observable symbols and social practices. Their aim was, so to speak, to present the new religion in a fashion the "natives" could understand. Complex beliefs were pared down to a few simple themes. Christianity required a conversion to a new lifestyle, a new way of acting. One had to demonstratively manifest one's transformed state. Just as elsewhere on the African continent, the construction of square rather than round houses, the adoption of Western attire, the speaking of a European language, the use of eating utensils, and most often, the acceptance of monogamy became powerful symbolic markers of conversion to the new religion.

There is now, however, a new generation for which the acceptance of Christianity requires a far less dramatic transformation. Expatriate churches have become an accepted part of the social and economic landscape. The young have no memory of the time before the missionaries and their churches arrived—the social and physical world of the Christians is an intrinsic part of their personal strategies. Expatriate missionary Christians may be outsiders in certain contexts, but they have been around long enough to have become indigenized in some respects. Missions and missionaries are shaped and molded by local forces and oriented toward serving local needs. They are continually draped and redraped with local symbolism.

The second proposed major influence on the divorce rate is the increased importance of cash. In Turner's era, the sale of crops, especially surplus cassava, was the greatest generator of cash in Mwinilunga (Turner and Turner 1955). During the mid-1950s, however, European commercial farmers situated on transport lines near the major urban areas were gaining the capacity to produce sufficient maize to satisfy the needs of mineworkers (e.g., Vickery 1985, 232). Mwinilunga cassava was no longer needed in commercial food markets, and many people were, in effect, kicked out of the cash economy. The impact was especially hard on women. Men could still sell their labor, hunt and sell game meat, gather honey in the forest, or perhaps even acquire a government loan and embark on raising some marketable crop. But women had been heavily dependent on the sale of surplus cassava to earn cash. Traditions which dictate that women are primarily responsible for child care limited their cash-earning options. Government policies which discriminated against women in the granting of loans or the provision of training further limited women's options.

The intense struggle among men to attract women—sisters and wives—to their villages in the early 1950s, a struggle that was the subject of much of Victor Turner's early theorizing, may have been accentuated by women's capacity to earn cash during that period. Although Lunda individuals rarely pool their earnings, not even married couples, a women with cash would be a welcome addition to any village in which she chose to reside. Today, however, the competition for women could hardly be described as intense. Although it is still generally acknowledged that everyone has the responsibility to assist kin in need, it would be difficult to imagine a brother plotting to undermine his sister's marriage solely for the purpose of enticing her back to his village, as was said to have occurred in the past. Followers today are not automatically an economic asset. Extra labor power cannot always be made to generate cash. Although any able-bodied woman should be capable of producing more than enough food to feed herself and her children, she still needs cash for clothes, soap, meat, cooking oil, salt, and other commodities deemed essential. Hence, men are a bit more selective today as to the point in their lives when they desire followers, and as to the physical makeup of those followers. Increasingly the creation of a following must be done according to *maplan*, a master plan.

Men still dream of arriving at old age as the headman of a large village, but they realize that without a substantial amount of cash this is an unlikely outcome. Thus, everywhere in Mwinilunga today one finds young men involved in long-range plans to acquire cash. Some are cutting down trees and painstakingly digging up the roots so that at some point in the future they will have fields that can be plowed and seeded with a cash crop. Others are clearing land along river banks to embark on intensive horticulture of green vegetables that are generally scarce during the dry season. Some are digging fishponds with picks and shovels and slowly rerouting streams to insure an adequate supply of fresh water, hoping someday to capitalize on the perpetual shortage of protein foods in Mwinilunga. Some are working as wage laborers in the government center or mission stations and using their salaries to buy a few domestic animals each year, hoping someday to engage in full-time mixed farming. Some spend virtually all their time in the deep bush, hunting, trapping, and fishing, drying their catch, and then transporting it to areas where it will fetch a high price. Some young men spend years serving as apprentices to skilled carpenters or bricklayers, slowly learning the trade and saving money to buy tools so that someday they will be able to earn even more cash as independent craftsmen. At the end of every day when men sit around the village fires, they always discuss ways to make money and ways to use that money to make even more money. No evening would be complete without at least one story joking about some person who gained a lot of money and then lost it because of managing it improperly or yielding too easily to the demands of relatives.

A common Lunda proverb states, *Chazenzama kumona maheta kumona hadi babala* (When a stupid person finds wealth, he finds it for those with brains). Yet, on the other hand, it is widely accepted that people are obligated to assist relatives in need. Selfishness is still considered one of the greatest sins.[4] But the more cash one is known to possess, the more needy relatives one will undoubtedly attract. So to avoid conflicts, men have developed an array of tactics to camouflage their wealth in cash and kind. If a man is attempting to build up a large flock of domestic animals, for example, he might scatter them around, asking friends or relatives in different parts of the district each to care for a few animals. In exchange they would be given every second or third offspring of those animals. The man might say that the animals were causing a problem in his home village by eating his neighbors' gardens, hence the need to move them. Yet this same man might himself be caring for the animals of friends or relatives from another part of the district. A survey of the domestic stock of any particular village usually reveals that many or most of the animals present actually belong to people in other villages. At the point when a man feels he is ready, perhaps in old age, he gathers together all his stock. If relatives, suddenly aware of his newly revealed wealth, come to join him at this point, he can now make effective use of their labor to herd, build fences, or gather manure to fertilize vegetable gardens. His dream of bigmanship, or headmanship of a profitable village, will have been realized.

Many men go barefooted and wear ragged clothes for years while qui-etly storing away money in old tin cans before their ultimate plans unfold. Few men of the older generation embarked on plans as sophisticated as those being devised by today's young men. The idea of simply returning to an uncle's village and waiting one's turn to become headman no longer holds much appeal, unless the uncle's village is a well-functioning eco-nomic unit generating surplus cash. In many cases an uncle's village is sim-ply not ideally located for cash cropping or fish farming or herding animals. Hence, a large number of men prefer to start their own villages and then invite relatives to join them at the point when they can most profitably use additional labor or most easily absorb the losses that would result from sup-porting nonproductive relatives. But young men are far more likely to enter into economic alliances with friends or old schoolmates who have shared interests or complementary skills than they are to align themselves simply on the basis of kin relationships. One of these friends that increas-ingly plays an integral role in the long-term economic plans of a man is his wife, just as he himself is figuring increasingly prominently in her plans.

One of the major sources of cash for women is brewing alcholic bever-ages. This was virtually the only economic avenue open to women after Mwinilunga suddenly ceased to be a source for surplus cassava for the na-tional market in the mid-1950s. As men found increasingly ingenious methods for reentering the cash economy, they had more money to spend on recreational activities. And the most common recreational activities of Lunda men are drinking alcohol, singing, and dancing. The Lunda pri-marily drink three kinds of alcohol: *kachayi*, a fermented millet beer, *kasolu*, a fermented honey beer, and *lituku*, a high-proof distilled spirit made from cassava. Traditionally women had brewed beer, which was an integral part of all Lunda ceremonies. But increasing beer production to satisfy the recreational consumption of men presented an entirely new set of prob-lems, the solution to which had the effect of more firmly linking a woman both to her village-mates and to her husband. First, brewing beer is time consuming. It takes women away from the daily routine of planting, weed-ing, pounding, cooking, and cleaning. Distilling *lituku* is an especially de-manding undertaking. Such an allocation of time is possible only if some-one else attends to some of a woman's daily chores. Women with mature daughters are ideally placed to brew lots of beer. But some groups of women have developed relationships whereby certain daily chores are col-lectively done on a rotating basis. Each woman's cash receipts are her own, but the sharing of labor is a significant development. Most of the mature women in any particular village tend to be unrelated, since they have moved there to be with their husbands. Turner contrasted the lives of men, who cooperated in hunting, housebuilding, and other activities, and generally ate together, with the isolated lives that women led. He painted the image of a woman as a solitary adult working in her own fields or kitchen, surrounded by her children, jealous and suspicious of other women. Her closest emotional attachments remained to her own kin in her matrilineal village, to which she frequently returned (Turner 1968, intro.). But today there are clearly observable networks of women who are bonded by friendship and share responsibilities to the economic benefit of all.

The production of beer must be carefully controlled so as not to exceed the consumption capacity of the area. Both honey beer and millet beer ferment so fast that even a few hours can make a radical difference in taste. If these beers are not sold on the day they peak, they will be undrinkable, and hence unsalable, the following day. So women have developed not only strong intravillage cooperation, but widespread intervillage communication links as well. Women who brew regularly are generally well apprised of the intended brewing schedules of women in all the neighboring villages.

Men can assist their wives' brewing activity in three important ways. First, if his wife wishes to specialize in brewing honey beer, a man may provide the initial capital. Honey is gathered only by men who sell it for cash and is always in great demand. Since men's activities tend to carry them farther from the village than do women's activities, men are better placed to follow leads concerning who went to the bush looking for honey and when they might return. Men can then assist their wives by making spot purchases when the opportunity arises, knowing that they will be reimbursed later. Second, a man can serve as an additional set of eyes and ears, keeping his wife informed of activity in the area that might result in men buying more beer: which day the mission workers will be paid, when the grain marketing board will release funds to the maize farmers, or when an important ceremony will take place or an important visitor will arrive. Third, and equally important, a man can actively assist his wife's business by spreading the word among friends and associates on days when she brews, and he can passively assist by maintaining a large, comfortable *chota*, men's talking house, and developing a reputation for his village as a pleasant and peaceful place to drink.

Many women do make a great deal of money brewing beer. But, as has been shown, such success reflects not a woman's individual skill at brewing, but rather the ability to organize chores to allow the necessary amount of free time, strong bonds of reciprocity with other women, and sound ties of cooperation with her husband. These are not the kinds of ties that one can develop quickly or easily; they can only be cultivated slowly, in an atmosphere of trust and mutual economic interest. It is not unreasonable therefore to suggest that women's economic activities have contributed significantly to the drop in the divorce rate. On the one hand, they strengthen and add new dimensions to a woman's bond with her husband; on the other hand, they loosen her bonds to her matrilineal village by placing her economic interests more fully in the relationships she develops with women in or near her husband's village.

Another aspect of long-term financial planning that affects gender relations is the hope of almost every parent that at least one of their children will receive enough education to get a good job as a government worker, a teacher, or an agricultural officer. The Lunda are not at all naïve about long-term economic trends in the nation as a whole. Prices will inevitably rise, and money will be worth less and less. There is no shortage of old men in every village to remind people of the time, not so long ago, when the average pay for a worker was a penny a day, and a pair of pants could be bought for six cents. Likewise there is no shortage of visitors to keep everyone informed of the latest round of price hikes in the distant cities. Everyone is well aware that in order to maintain their current level of existence they will need increasing amounts of cash each year. Only those with stable, secure, well-paying jobs that have a built-in annual cost of living adjustment (as do many government jobs) have some immunity to inflation. It is such positions that parents desire for their children. Furthermore, the options available to the average Lunda for earning cash nearly all involve hard physical labor and are suitable only for the young and strong. Old men do not make good hunters or honey gatherers. They cannot clear fields and dig out tree stumps as well as the young. Old women have difficulty chopping enough wood to keep a distillery going all day. It is evident to all that the young have a decided advantage in the rush to earn cash. Although everyone hopes that their youthful investment of labor will result in dividends that can be drawn on in old age, it is also evident to all that a gainfully employed child sending regular remittances back to the village is the best hedge against both inflation and waning physical strength. Toward that end both men and women spend a large portion of their cash on school-related fees for their children. For most individuals today it is the single greatest item of expenditure.

In a truly matrilineal society one would expect that because a man's heirs are his sisters' children, they rather than his own children would be the principal focus of his cash investments. But this is not the case. One can only speculate about why this is so. First, in the past most boys did not return to an uncle's village until they were in their teens (assuming their parents had not divorced earlier). But school places are difficult to find, and if a teenage boy is in school it is highly unlikely that he would jeopardize his education by changing residences at that point solely to satisfy tradition. Furthermore, it is likely that his mother and father, not his uncle, had been his principal benefactors up to that point. Thus he has additional incentive to remain where he is. But why then do uncles not make prior claim on their traditional heirs by paying their school fees from the beginning? Perhaps it is because most men have more than one sister. Should a man take on the responsibility of educating all of his sisters' children? This would be unlikely. Even most parents cannot afford to educate all of their own children. A selection is usually made based on demonstrated desire on the part of the child and the parents' estimate of the child's likelihood of success, within the framework of available household resources. This is an agonizing process for most parents, who at least have the benefit of daily and intimate interaction with their children before deciding how to invest their scarce cash. It would be a very risky proposition for a distant uncle to try to choose which of his many likely heirs had the best chance of success in school. In the 1980s, only one in ten youths scored high enough on standardized competitive entrance exams to earn a place in secondary school. Only nine boys per thousand and two girls per thousand were entering university. Although uncles might be the first ones approached by a child if parents were unable to pay school fees, a somewhat vicious cycle has come into effect. As men increasingly focus on their own children, they are less able to assist their nieces and nephews.

Furthermore, the greater economic interdependence of husbands and wives, as outlined above, would clearly equip women to put unprecedented pressure on their husbands to keep cash within the household by supporting their own children. Although women traditionally depended heavily on their brothers throughout their early years, in later life it had always been their sons (and secondarily their daughters) they sought out. This has not changed. To the degree that a woman can succeed in getting her husband to support her children's education, she is correspondingly enhancing her own options for later years. This joint investment on the part of husbands and wives in the education of their children has the reciprocal effect of further binding the nuclear family unit. In no way should this imply that Lunda couples see children principally as objects of investment. The love of children for their own sake is abundantly evident in the intimacy of day-to-day interactions. But the amount of money dedicated to education is staggering; the amount of labor, overwhelming. Surely such an outpouring of effort has the ability to reshape attitudes. Children are well aware of the magnitude of the sacrifices made on their behalf. Being able to assist parents in living a more comfortable life is one of the most often articulated objectives of today's youth (e.g., Hoppers 1981, 84–88). Those who have actually done so are venerated as local heroes, pointed out as models for others to emulate.

Finally, we must address the role of national policies in shaping the contemporary notion of marriage and their impact on the meaning of divorce. Although most of the ethnic groups in Zambia are part of what anthropologists commonly refer to as the matrilineal belt, there is a decided bias in government policies away from what are understood as matrilineal patterns of inheritance. This is perhaps most evident in the handling of government pension funds. All employers in Zambia, whether government or private, urban or rural, are required by law to deduct a small sum from each employee's wages and forward it along with a matching sum from the employer to be deposited with the National Provident Fund. Upon reaching the age of retirement a worker receives the totality of these lifetime contributions to the fund, plus interest, all in one lump sum. Should he die before reaching the age of retirement, as is often the case, his benefits are paid to this next-of-kin, again in one lump sum. If a person has been employed for many years, his Provident Fund benefits can add up to a considerable sum. For that reason, one reads in the newspaper and hears rumors almost daily of this or that family fighting and sometimes killing over the control of a deceased person's National Provident Fund. Especially common are cases where a man's matrikin, upon his death, evict his wife and children and manage to obtain his benefits. Many woman have been beaten or worse for not handing over a man's assets to his matrikin. The magnitude of the problem is so great that the government has been forced to issue clear, legally enforceable guidelines as to who constitutes the "next-of-kin," that is, who, in what order, and in what amount may share in a man's benefits.[5] The government periodically launches publicity campaigns informing people of this policy, even in the most remote regions (*Working Paper on Customary Law of Succession* 1976). For it is in remote areas, where money is most scarce, that conflicts over benefits tend to be the most vicious. It is widely known throughout Mwinilunga and elsewhere that the government favors wives and children as heirs rather than brothers and nephews. Increasingly, the names of wives and children of employees are required to be kept on file at the National Provident Fund headquarters, and, in the event of death before the age of retirement, only wives and children can apply for benefits. Furthermore, forceful attempts by matrikin to claim a portion of this money directly from wives and children are now viewed as extortion and can lead to criminal prosecution. On the other hand, should a young unmarried worker die, most of his National Provident Fund benefits are paid jointly to his mother and father if they are still alive.

It is unclear why the national government has designed a policy so contrary to the prevailing tradition of matrilineal inheritance. One can only speculate. National policy-making in Zambia is very much concentrated in the hands of the upper echelon of the ruling political party, and the lack of public debate makes it difficult to assess motives. However, it should be noted that the present generation of leaders was raised in an era when the only schools in the nation were run by European- and American-based missionary organizations. Virtually all of today's leaders were mission educated. The first president was the son of the first African missionaries in Zambia, and the second president formally enshrined in the federal constitution the nomenclature of Zambia as a Christian nation. One might suspect, therefore, that an internalized notion of the primacy of the Christian nuclear family is revealing itself in the policy arena. This cannot, however, be stated as fact, for in numerous other areas of social life the government has indeed been a strong advocate for maintaining traditional values and structures (e.g., Kaunda 1967, 1974). But the government could have shown its concern for widows and children by pressuring matrilineages to provide support for their own widowed kin, rather than by constructing and enforcing a concept of "next-of-kin" that runs contrary to prevailing norms. Perhaps the government adopted this policy in an attempt to reduce the number of claimants, thus facilitating capital accumulation and stimulating entrepreneurial activity. If Provident Fund benefits were divided among all of a man's matrikin, the individual sums would be too small for investment purposes. But such a policy would seem to be a contradiction in a nation where socialist development was for long the stated objective.[6]

Although the reasons behind the policy are unclear, the impact is quite obvious. A new element has been added to an already complex matrix of relationships. A man with a job now knows that he is accumulating assets first for his mother and father, and later for his wife and children. The law does not take into account his personal preferences: it is the new national custom which supersedes all local customs. Only by living long enough to reach the age of retirement can a man regain control over his assets. But in the meantime, wives and children have strong incentives to keep a marriage together if the man of the house is employed. Fathers have a strong incentive to assist their own children with education so that they may later find jobs. Thus, government policy, in conjunction with the economic factors mentioned above, has powerfully altered the old competition between fathers and uncles, heavily tipping the scales toward fathers. In the past, a father's main weapon in the competition had been his close personal relationship with his sons. But only uncles could offer a man the key to headmanship. Today, however, cash is a necessary ingredient of leadership, and maintaining a close personal and economic relationship with one's father may be more advantageous than following the tradition of returning to an uncle's village during one's teens.

Government policy, although perhaps not strong enough, in and of itself, to change traditional concepts, does open up a debate where none existed previously. Mwinilunga is part of the modern nation-state of Zambia. The Lundaland of old no longer exists. People realize that in the future they will be increasingly integrated into the mainstream of the political, economic, and social life of the nation as a whole. In debates concerning the role of various local beliefs in relation to national laws, it is not uncommon to hear many people, especially young people, declare that they are Zambian first and Lunda second, and that the laws of the land take precedence over traditional rules. Some now use government policy to lend ideological support to the contention that a person is equally related to both mother and father; hence, there is nothing wrong in choosing to remain in their father's village, especially if their mother is also residing there.

Summary

Male-female separation is a model, a metaphor that most dramatically manifests a host of cultural ideas and ideals about separation. *Chota* and *chin-*

sambu (palaver hut and kitchen) separate men and women, traditional village layouts separate older from younger generations, *mukanda* separates the circumcised from the uncircumcised, and *nkanga* separates the fertile from the prefertile. Whereas differences in age are most often reckoned in terms of vertical distance, gender differences are most often reckoned in terms of horizontal distance. The gendered division of labor sends males and females trekking across the landscape in different directions. It subjects them to lives of differing physical demands, ultimately sculpting fundamentally different types of bodies. Lunda men are hunters whose most trusted weapon is endurance, whose most reliable technique is simply to chase animals until they drop from sheer exhaustion. Most Lunda men are built like marathon runners, lean and sinewy. The life of a Lunda woman, however, is one of endless lifting and pounding: lifting calabashes of water from the stream, lifting enormous baskets of food from the garden, lifting firewood, lifting young children, but most especially lifting a heavy six-foot-long wooden pestle and pounding it down in a mortar hundreds, if not thousands, of times each day, pulverizing cassava roots into the pure white flour that is eaten with virtually every meal. Lunda women have powerfully built upper bodies, indeed, an overall portly, rounded appearance.

The very tone and rhythm of men's and women's lives vary in fundamental ways. They have differing residential patterns, differing options for support and assistance, differing relations to their children, and differing bases for planning existential and metaphysical life. Lunda symbols and representations sharpen gender distinctions. Men and women are made to stand for every opposition. Yet in doing so, they are also made to exemplify every complementarity. They are ritually dangerous to one another, and thus must be kept apart. Yet, their coming together is necessary for the creation, nurturance, and continuation of life. It takes powerful symbols to mediate such potent and elemental forces—powerfully ambiguous and elegantly crafted. The delicate balance is not easy to maintain. Symbols and representations cannot always be relied upon to smooth the messy terrain of daily male-female interactions. As in the case of the fight between Katoka and Judith, explosions of anger can occur. The subtleties of the case may have been a topic for discussion with their closest group of friends, but public appeals needed to be couched in precise language that protected the always precarious equilibrium between separation and unity, opposition and complementarity, danger and nurturance.

Change is in the air, however, and is causing some uneasiness. The enthusiasm for formal education, for example, is tempered by the social anxiety that it produces, particularly among the older cohort groups. School might provide the key to the resources of the contemporary nation-state, but it also presents a challenge to some long-standing notions of gender separation by bringing males and females together for large parts of the day. In school, boys and girls study the same subjects in the same room with the same teacher. They have vastly more shared experiences than did the youth of even a couple of generations ago. In addition to the experience of formal schooling, the joint long-term planning of some married couples, along with the financial, social, and emotional interdependence that it fosters, also serves to mediate the distance between the sexes.

For some Lunda, these trends are reprehensible; for others, spiritually polluting; and for still others, simply aesthetically unpleasing. Some people blame the relaxation of the rules of separation for nearly every social and economic problem in Mwinilunga, most especially the outbreaks of HIV/AIDS. This area of social discussion represents the next dynamic stage of the historical development of gender relations. It is one to keep an eye on. Its parameters, however, are too inchoate for analysis at this time; its outcome is beyond our predictive capacity. The evolving structure of the government policy apparatus, the oscillating fortunes of the war in Angola, the ebb and flow of externally inspired development initiatives, and the differing strategies of generations of cohorts seeking their own best interests will continue to affect gender relations.

The younger cohort groups, it must be noted, are not simply spoken about and spoken to. They are active players in the current dialogue. Many, while aligning themselves with the forces of modernity, still find value in mastering the powerful rhetoric of riddles and proverbs. One hears them nightly during the fireside debates playing with and empowering the traditional components of contrast and complementary between maleness and femalenesss, adding their own dimensions to the symbolism of red, black, and white. From such discussions a future both similar and dissimilar to the past will no doubt emerge.

Chapter Six

The Rich and the Poor

Chifunga's Walking Stick
Dry Season, August 1984

Huge calabashes of *kasolu* kept arriving in the *chota* from out of the darkness. As soon as we finished off one batch of the sweet but strong liquor, another would appear in the midst of our circle. From the howls of laughter all around I assumed that other circles of imbibers were receiving equally generous treatment. Most were drinking out of sheer elation that the long electoral process was finally over—and that the outcome had provoked no open hostility from any quarter. Kapala, however, was drinking out of deep despair. This should have been his moment of glory. After all, he had been the first to predict that Isaac Nkemba would be the next Chifunga. When Kankinza had passed away back in March, seven names had immediately begun to circulate throughout the village cluster as candidates to replace him as senior headman. Each was a classificatory nephew. Yet, to me at least, Nkemba had seemed the rank outsider. I had never heard of him. Apparently he had left the area thirty, forty, or perhaps even fifty years ago. No one was quite sure. He had spent the majority of his life in South Africa, married and raised a family there, and for the last few years had been living forty miles away, outside the Boma. The other six candidates had spent months making the rounds, lobbying hard for votes, cashing in old debts. Nkemba was nowhere to be seen. Yet from the beginning, Kapala was certain that Nkemba would prevail and had begun preparing a gift. Each night around the fire he passed the time carving a walking stick that he hoped would become part of Nkemba's regalia. It would be a gift not just from himself, but from his entire cohort, who would be the structural grandchildren of the next Chifunga. That Kapala would take the initiative to construct the gift was interesting, but not particularly surprising. He was a unique and energetic individual. On the one hand he was part of the mission elite. Like others of his clique, he had been educated by American Catholics at Lwawu. Yet, he had followed a different path than most. He loved to immerse himself in the symbols of Lunda tradition. He had three wives. And he took far greater interest than any of his friends in traditional herbalism and spiritualism. He rarely attended mass, yet he somehow managed to hold on to the well-respected and well-paid position of tractor driver for the mission. He was a slim, baby-faced man who looked to be in his twenties, perhaps thirty at most, yet he had hordes of faithful dependents who claimed that he was a big man of at least fifty.

Kapala had carefully selected a piece of *mubanga*, a wood so dense that it does not float and is impervious to the ravages of time or termites. He had had to stop and resharpen his carving knife every few strokes. It was a slow and tedious task. The design that emerged after months of work was a study in simple elegance. The walking stick was further embellished with a sheen from a lacquer that Kapala had concocted from local plants. But the simple exterior hid a secret. Tug on the handle, and out popped a blade. Kapala had heated and endlessly hammered the blade to make it razor sharp. The Chifunga would no doubt anoint that blade with his own supernatural medicines later, but Kapala's effort symbolized the gift of protection to the grandfather from his grandchildren.

It wasn't clear to me when or how the actual election would take place. But one day the word went out that Nkemba and his family had arrived. Everyone rushed to see them. There before us stood an extremely handsome elderly gentleman with a large handlebar mustache, impeccably dressed in a three-piece tweed suit, homburg hat with feather, and wing tips. Beside him stood his wife, a large, light brown skinned South African woman of the type generally referred to as Cape Coloured. With them was an elder son, introduced as a major in the Zambian army, and his gorgeous wife from unknown parts. Also present were a younger son and daughter, strikingly fit and fashionable, looking as if they had just stepped out of the pages of *GQ* and *Vogue,* respectively. The next thing I knew Nkemba had been declared the new Chifunga, and the liquor began to flow freely.

In retrospect, I now remember one of the missionaries also saying that Nkemba might win the election. The Lunda are prone to vicious gossip and incessant jealousy, he had said. Nkemba, by having been away for so long, might simply have fewer detractors and defamers than the others. I don't think that was the case, however. I was there. I felt the power. Nkemba definitely had a seductive aura of worldliness about him that the other candidates lacked. In his presence the dusty village grounds seemed momentarily transformed into a royal plaza. Everything about Nkemba exuded a confident power. The way he walked and talked, the way he shifted his weight back and forth while leaning on his brass duckbill cane, the way he lifted that cane in the air at just the right moments to forcefully punctuate his remarks, all mesmerized the crowd. He was so perfect in his appearance and performance that Kapala felt embarrassed to even think that Nkemba might want to trade in his British-made brass cane for a crude locally made wooden one. He never marshalled the courage to bring up the subject.

Victor Turner, Max Gluckman, C. M. N. White, and most of the other early scholars writing about social processes on the upper Zambezi during the 1940s and 1950s saw egalitarianism as the prevailing economic condition. They frequently stated that the low levels of production and of available commodities mediated against the formation of economic classes. Prestige was determined more by the number of dependents or subjects a person had than by the number of material possessions. While this may have been true of that particular period, evidence from an older literature suggests the need for a less static model and for a more complex discussion of the role and meaning of wealth, of how the gap between rich and poor was mediated, and of the ideological and symbolic components of that mediation. The history of Central Africa can be characterized by stages of differential access to historically specific items of wealth and continual redefinitions of notions of wealth in tandem with radically shifting economic blocs. At different times, the constellation of Lunda polities have been incorporated into the Indian Ocean trade network, the Atlantic trade world, a colonial bloc that linked them primarily with southern African, and the globalized economy of independent nation-states whose impact is filtered through capital city politics. This synthetic periodization, although oversimplified, will nevertheless serve to temporalize the discussion of wealth.

The history of commercial incursions into the interior of Africa is an unfolding tale filled with temporal and geographical gaps (see Birmingham 1966; Vansina 1966; Alpers 1975; Schecter 1976; Papstein 1978; Clarence-Smith 1979; Thornton 1983; Harms 1981; Reefe 1981; Hilton 1985; Miller 1988). The aim of this chapter is not to fill in those gaps but to turn the reader's attention to issues of placement and participation in global processes. In many respects, the Lunda and their neighbors, located in the very center of Africa, represented the point of overlap between east-coast and west-coast trading systems. This feature initially presented the Lunda with a unique range of opportunities for participating in both systems, and at times to play one against the other in the pursuit of better terms of trade. Ultimately, the forces unleashed by those two trading systems tore apart the far-flung Lunda Empire, resulting in long trains of Lunda people being marched off to both coasts as slaves. Between those two historical points much transpired: (1) the portion of Central Africa bound in tributary relations with the Lunda Empire more than quadrupled in size, (2) new occupations and new economic strategies emerged, (3) new symbols of wealth arose, and (4) multiethnic, multilingual communities whose unity was based on shared economic activity and shared relations to the means of production appeared.

All of these changes, however, were underlain by an older tradition of converting wealth into followers, dependents, and clients and its corollary, the search for patrons and protectors. Igor Kopytoff may have identified this tradition as a central feature of his pan-African ecumene, yet it was J. C. Miller who breathed life into the concept. Miller's interpretation of the traditional value of material goods and people in African political economies in *Way of Death* (1988) contains perhaps the most astute observations to date on the nature of capital in precolonial Africa and on the logic of the slave trade in local capital accumulation strategies. Capital, everywhere, is simply that which can produce future wealth. In the low-energy-technology economies of Africa, people were the only reliable capital, and authority over people was mediated through the control of necessary and scarce material goods (Miller 1988, 41). Thus the often-mentioned unquenchable African thirst for foreign goods was not necessarily for either their prestige or use-value, but rather for their value in the quest for dependents. Ultimately, access to foreign goods would not only be a major determinant of the quality of one's life but would hold important implications for the quality of one's afterlife as well.

Whereas chapter 4 took a more analytical approach to the relationships among wealth, power, and prestige, this chapter examines more descriptively the historical dimensions of wealth and the dynamic interaction between rich and poor. I should remind the reader that documents linking the Lunda-Ndembu on the upper Zambezi to each and every event described herein do not exist; but I firmly believe that the available evidence points to a free flow of objects and ideas across the Central African plateau and that it would be a great mistake to imagine that Lunda-Ndembu discourse about commodities and capital, prestige and persons took place outside of and unaffected by regionwide processes.

Central African Trade: The Pre-Atlantic Era

Travelers who visited Central Africa before the grand era of coastal trade described it as being traversed by long-distance trade routes running north-south, linking the peoples and commodities of the rainforest with those of the savanna, down to the Zambezi River.[1] From the Kasai River in the west to the Rift Valley in the east, goods flowed up and down parallel routes. This trading zone, over six hundred miles square, was one of the largest to develop in Central Africa without being directly affected by the international economy in slaves and ivory. The basic commodities of that trade are believed to have been iron, cord, baskets, pottery, musical instruments, beads, ornamental feathers, copper, raffia-cloth strips, salt blocks, iron hoes, and food products such as vegetable oils, salt, and smoked fish. Unflanged copper crosses of a uniform shape, cast into four or five standard sizes, have been found throughout the area. The smallest and most numerous are one quarter to one half inch long, and the largest and least numerous are over four inches long. Some crosses were tied together in packets of varying quantities. Uniform shape, standardized sizes, and packaging are evidence that these crosses were an extremely widespread unit of exchange, or currency, throughout Central Africa. This trade dates back to the early centuries of the second millennium but reached unprecedented heights between the fifteenth and eighteenth centuries.

Archaeological evidence indicates that by the fourteenth and fifteenth centuries the Katanga mines along the Zambia and Congo Copperbelts were in full production (Bisson 1975, 276–92; Phillipson 1977). In Phillipson's opinion, "It is surely not coincidence that the development of copper mining and trading is indicated at the same general time as the local rise of centralised states, and that the chiefly dynasties of surrounding areas trace their origin to south-eastern Zaire, which saw the greatest development of the copper trade" (1985, 201). The kingdoms of the savanna, from the Kongo to the Lunda, had many structural similarities with those of the Sudanic kingdoms of West Africa. Although situated on the savanna, their development as states owed much to their control over a variety of ecological zones, particularly control over commerce between those zones. Such trading systems fostered occupational specialization and its concomitant, economic differentiation. As noted in chapter 1, evidence from the few early grave sites that have been excavated indicates that tremendous differences in wealth existed, even among members of the same community (Nenquin

1963; de Maret 1975; Phillipson 1977). Fish merchants of fourteenth-century Kisale were buried with a wide array of prestige goods including commodities from the Indian Ocean, over a thousand miles away. Perhaps then, as now, the belief existed that relationships established in life persist even after death. The rich, in that case, would have been buried with the means of continued wealth in the afterlife. Wealth, however, was measured less by the quantity of commodities amassed than by the quantity and quality of social relationships secured through those commodities. The articles with which one was buried represented not so much exchange value accumulated in life as it dstatus achieved.

The Central African regional commercial zone was in indirect contact with the Indian Ocean before A.D. 1100. It would appear that copper, salt, iron, fish, raffia cloth, palm oil, mbafu oil, and red dyewood flowed to the east coast in exchange for cloth, beads, shells, and other Indian Ocean goods. Central African commodities contributed substantially to the development of the Swahili city-states along the East African coast that prospered from the mid-thirteenth century until the end of the fifteenth century: "All the way down the coastline of Somalia, Kenya and Tanzania, there sprouted urbanized Islamic communities, building in stone or coral rag and wealthy enough, for example, to import such luxury goods as Thai stoneware and the porcelain of late Sung and early Ming China. The Kilwa sultans of this period even minted their own silver and copper coinage" (Oliver and Fage 1962, 81–82). Kilwa, like its coastal predecessors, is known to have become wealthy as a result of its middle position between Indian Ocean and African commerce. African goods arrived in Kilwa from as far afield as Zimbabwe and the Katanga region of southern Congo. The early involvement of Central Africa in this trade was no doubt indirect. Goods flowed in and out in stages, passing from group to group, gaining added value with each change of hands. The desirability of goods from Central Africa, however, is attested to by the continual pioneering of new routes to its markets, the emergence of new states that struggled for control over those routes, and the longevity of the trade itself.

Central African copper was one source for the coinage of the Indian Ocean trade bloc, coinage which led to increased investment in new productive activities such as plantations of cinnamon, cloves, and sugar cane. Changing terms of trade would later lead to the drawing off of labor from Central Africa, as well as copper and specialty items such as exotic skins, ivory, copal, and nutmeg. Many extended battles occurred among Arabs,

Swahilis, and coastal Africans for the control of routes to the interior of Africa. The English explorer Richard Burton noted in his diary that as late as the 1850s he was advised to avoid the neighborhood of Kilwa: "The burghers of that proud old settlement had, only a year before my arrival murdered an Arab merchant who ventured to lay open the interior" (1860, vol. 1, 5).

African polities, which had long sought expansion in a north-south direction in order to access the goods of differing ecological niches, increasingly sent out tentacles to the east. According to Thomas Q. Reefe, "The path of eastward expansion of the Lunda in the early eighteenth century and the related growth of the Kingdom of Kazembe at that time were determined, in part, by the availability of salt and copper between the Upper Zaire and Luapula Rivers. The penetration of long-distance trade routes carrying non-African commodities from the Indian Ocean has long been recognized as having served as a catalyst for the expansion of states in central Africa" (1981, 200). The Kazembe, the king of the easternmost Lunda state on the Luapula River, reached the zenith of his power by about 1800. His capital grew wealthy from the flow of tribute and the influx of traders from Tete in the lower Zambezi valley. Trade reached new heights in the 1830s when Swahili traders opened up a route from coastal Tanzania, with Kazembe's capital becoming the major way station on a route that went on to the capital of the Mwantiyanvwa, the Lunda emperor. Direct contact lowered the cost of doing business for both ends of the trade by cutting out some of the levies previously imposed by middlemen. Middlemen, however, swiftly countered any attempt to isolate them from the flow of goods moving across their territories. Tremendous demographic shifts occurred as some groups moved eastward to situate themselves closer to the east-coast market, others assembled armed caravans to carry their commodities directly to the coast, and still others resettled along the caravan routes to siphon off its resources through whatever means possible.

By the late 1700s, Nyamwezi traders from Tanzania were regularly crossing Lake Tanganyika and venturing as far south as the copper mines of Katanga. During the mid-1800s at least one Nyamwezi caravan traveled west, establishing direct contact with the Lunda Center. The famous Nyamwezi caravan leader Msiri (also called Mushidi in some accounts) settled in Katanga around 1860, made contacts with the Portuguese to the west, obtained guns, and built up a formidable empire based on trade just to the east of the central Lunda cluster of polities. Violent competition with the Lunda ensued. As Cameron noted on his journey from the east coast, "Mshiri has collected around him large numbers of Wanyamwesi and malcontents from amongst the lower order of traders from the East Coast, and obtains supplies of powder and guns by trading both to Benguella [Angola] and Unyanyembe. Caravans commanded by half-caste Portuguese and slaves of Portuguese traders have visited him for over twenty years and furnish numerous recruits to his ranks. Ivory being scarce, his principal trade is in slaves and copper" (1877, 2:140). Dan Crawford, upon reaching the same locale in 1890, wrote the following about the ethnic composition of Msiri's empire: "Lubans from the North, Lamba people from the South, Lunda from the East, Ushi and Vemba from the South-East. The flotsam of negro humanity, here they are, so to speak, washed up on the shores of the capital, all jabbering out their own patois, and all daily taking on more local colour and simulating a sort of black cockneyism" (1912, 192).

Msiri's success demonstrates the role that crude force could play in the furtherance of trade. Well armed, he violently took control over the most productive copper and salt mines in Central Africa. He demanded that all surplus commodities from surrounding areas flow into his trade bazaar or run the risk of confiscation. Traders from the east traveled under his protection and had to visit his court to do business, under the threat of being plundered. What may have begun as a relatively small, ruthless band of malcontents from various ethnic groups grew by leaps and bounds into a full-fledged state that brought the surrounding peoples under a unified economic framework through the force of the gun. Ultimately it developed its own language, cultural and symbolic forms, and relatively stable political institutions. Yet it remained a fluid, constantly changing polity throughout its existence. Many of Msiri's followers established themselves on the east coast—some with his permission, some without. As Crawford noted: "There is a constant stream of Mushidi caravans worming their way out to all the Coast settlements. There they gorge themselves with so-called civilisation. All along the East Coast you can find a Mushidite who, when he first sighted the Ocean, resolved never to leave it. And there he is to-day, a prosperous trader or the like" (1912, 189). For those who absconded with merchandise, Msiri would claim 100 percent compensation from the defaulter's own family, or would enslave them if they were unable to pay. Msiri was well known, however, for his success at enticing those from the east to remain in his polity, with their wares:

. . . many an Arab arriving at Mushidi's capital never again to leave it. Mere pack-men as such often are, Mushidi politely plunders the trader—with the man's own permission, the bargain being a dark affair in which the new-comer is presented with a wife and fields in exchange for the trade goods of some defrauded Coast merchant. . . . Thus Mushidi squares accounts with his commercial foes. (Crawford 1912, 190)

For when this Mushidi leapt into the light of history in the interior, the good news spread, and many a young man out East, catching the spirit of the thing, re-solved to go West and win to wealth and lands of his own. (Crawford 1912, 197)

Msiri's fame, indeed, spread throughout Central Africa, where it had a major impact. His success led to a scramble to acquire advanced guns at all cost and the formation of numerous armed bands that made a living through plunder. The lavishness of his court, and his ability to bring in pre-viously unknown or unaffordable imports, set new standards of wealth which others would aspire to emulate. His capital was reckoned to be the largest and wealthiest city in Central Africa at the time, perhaps reaching twenty thousand residents. Vernon Cameron heard both horrific and hon-orific legends of Msiri all along his cross-continental trek, particularly among the Lunda. He wrote in his diary, "I have no doubt that many of Mshiri's men have visited both coasts, and that a message might be sent by means of these people from Benguella to Zanzibar" (1877, 2:208).

Second only to tales of Msiri's violent nature were the stories surround-ing his style. Crawford, who was present during one grand occasion, wrote the following description:

The great Mushidi, who is bent on besting his imaginary rival, is in the hands of his satraps, who are dressing him up for the show, the distinctive feature of his purple and fine linen being a vesture, twenty or thirty yards long, to which they finally add his regalia of Omande shells. Certainly he takes the shine out of every-body, for hanging around his neck, like a walking Christmas tree, they have dan-gled scissors, looking-glasses, and curious sundries. Mushidi is borne aloft on a zebra-skin palanquin by more than a hundred men, and a far-off war-song tells of the approaching general and his army. (1912, 222–23)

Msiri passionately sought out the new and different, combining a love for novelty with an insatiable desire to symbolically demonstrate his powerful connections with the outside world. Crawford was present at the court when, after years of machination, Msiri successfully contracted for a "white wife" in order to link himself more firmly with the European elite of the west coast and to demonstrate this connectedness. Maria de Fonseca was her name; she was the daughter of a Portuguese officer and the sister of Lourenço da Souza Coimbra. "Arriving in the Interior [Maria de Fonseca], not by any means in the first blush of maidenhood, here she is frivolling about the capital, and hating the whole harem of rivals. Many an envenomed glance she shoots at an enemy, and many a plot she hatches for the downfall of some poor harmless soul. Talking Chiluba with a fierce flippancy, she it is who, Lady Macbeth-like, urges Mushidi on to his deeds of blood" (Crawford 1912, 191). Not to be outdone, the east coast countered with its own proposition. Msiri was sent a bride from among their ranks: "Here was a lady of lineage [Queen Matayu], brought in from the Far East by the Arabs as an offset to the Maria de Fonseca marriage of the Portuguese, the two Oceans bidding for Mushidi's commerce with the debasing bribe of rival queens" (Crawford 1912, 295).

The sordid details of Msiri's reign have been well cataloged by Crawford. It suffices here to note that Msiri's empire was underpinned by his ability to gain access to immense quantities of guns and powder from both coasts. However, one major consequence of that empire was increased interaction and cultural exchange among African societies that owed little to European influences:

An increased pace of culture change had indeed begun during the heyday of the Kazembe state, but Msiri carried it much further with the introduction of new types of copper mining and especially with a flood of new orders and laws designed to reconcile Nyamwezi customs with those of the local people. Earlier Lundaization had no doubt prepared the way for further change, but the new regulations covered the whole gamut of social relations from bridewealth to the proper composition of social groups. Political ideology, kingship, and symbols of office were imported wholesale from Nyamwezi country, but they also accepted some cultural features from the conquered people. (Curtin et al. 1978, 434)

The Indian Ocean trade, thus, spread Lunda cultural production east, at least to the Rift Valley, but also resulted in the Lunda taking on, manipulating, playing with, and transforming economic and cultural forms originating in the east. For nearly four hundred years (from the twelfth to the sixteenth century), the east had reigned uncontested in Central African consciousness as the source of wealth and cultural innovation. However, by the beginning of the seventeenth century a new set of players had arrived on the scene from the west. New languages, new commodities, new exchange values, and new cultural forms led to another round of Central African growth and innovation.

Advent of the Atlantic World: Cassava, Capital, and Credit

The Lunda involvement in the Atlantic trade world represented neither a sudden nor a complete shift from the Indian Ocean trade network. Despite four centuries of immersion in the aesthetic traditions and the transitions of Indian Ocean commodities, the Lunda had remained strongly connected to westerly peoples. They had common origins, they spoke related branches of a common protolanguage, they possessed similarities in ecological adaptation and technological development, and they shared aesthetic forms and cultural expressions. Phillipson, in assessing the archaeological evidence, noted the long-standing and widespread continuities in the material culture of western Central Africa, including the Upper Zambezi region of western Zambia that reached back to the first millennium A.D. (1985, 200).

The Atlantic world perhaps first signaled its presence in Central Africa when new food crops arrived from the west. The American assemblage of cassava, maize, citrus fruits, new varieties of legumes, cucurbits, and leaf vegetables, introduced along the west coast by the Portuguese in the late sixteenth and early seventeenth centuries, rapidly spread to the interior. The adoption of cassava occurred simultaneously with a series of droughts which devastated the millet and sorghum crops of Central Africa but barely affected the new cassava gardens (Miller 1988; von Oppen 1993). Thus cassava won its place in Lunda life under fire, through direct trial with the indigenous crops. Its origins in the west gave cassava a certain cachet, a certain ease of acceptance; its adoption was also no doubt facilitated by its high-yielding properties in comparison with sorghum and millet. The Lunda were acutely aware of the value of surplus food from their experience with caravans from the east. This was an experience that more westerly people would not have for years to come.

New foods were followed very quickly by new commodities that initially gained acceptance in small quantities, if for no other reason than their novelty value. These first sets of goods were often deemed inferior in quality and elegance to comparable Indian Ocean wares. Yet, there is evidence that newness, rareness, and distinctiveness were long-standing symbols and generators of wealth and rank in Central Africa. Individuals and groups repositioned themselves geographically, structurally, and even ideologically vis-à-vis the ebb and flow of new goods.

Central Africa became, in a sense, both a linchpin and a point of intense competition between two trade blocs, east and west. Products from the east continued to arrive, but increasingly large caravans laden with western goods began to appear in the Lunda capital as well. Portuguese goods were transported principally from the port city of Benguela up to the Bihe plateau in Angola by mbailunda merchants and porters. But the people around Bihe initially exercised a monopoly on the transport of goods beyond that point. Crawford noted that the Biheans came to be known as the Unyanyembe or Munyamwesi of the west, in reference to the African middlemen of the East African trade network. The Biheans' relationship with their Portuguese suppliers, however, was said to differ substantially from the Munyamwesi's relationship with their Arab partners: "For unlike the Bihean's Portuguese master, the fastidious and aggressive Arab kept commerce in his own hands, disdaining a delegate. On the other hand, the lethargic Portuguese threw all the initiative on the bold Bihean, of course throwing at him at the same time a few hundred pounds' worth of guns, powder, and calico. . . . Thus it came to pass that in a quarter of a century the Bihean legend spread far over the Interior, and these 'black Portuguese' became the great knights of industry in the land" (Crawford 1912, 32).

Many Bihean Africans who successfully pioneered new trade routes to the interior became fabulously wealthy, amassed tremendous followings, and surrounded themselves with the accoutrements of the European world of their new business partners. Many became fluent in Portuguese, even taking on Portuguese names, Portuguese dress, and at times, exaggerated Portuguese manners and social etiquette. This style ultimately became their social marker in the interior. It symbolized the closeness of their connections to the Portuguese and therefore the continued likelihood of their remaining in the business of bringing the west into the interior. A certain flair, a touch of the exotic, was clearly a business asset. Much of the trade with the west was done on credit and required new levels of trust between individuals. The successful caravan leader was one who had the appearance of a man worthy of trust, and one whose trust one dared not betray. Serpa Pinto commented on one such African trader: "José António Alves is a negro *pur sang*, born in Pungo Andongo [on the plateau], who, like many others trading from that place and from Ambaca, knows how to read and write. In the Bihé they call him a white, because they bestow that name upon every man of color who wears trousers and sandalled shoes and carries an umbrella. He is about fifty-eight years of age, somewhat grizzled, thin in body, and suffering from a lung complaint. He lives like any other black, and has all the customs and beliefs of the natives" (1881, 99).

As trade with the west expanded, so too did the boundaries of the Lunda Empire under the Mwantiyanvwa. In addition to steadily incorporating previously unrelated peoples on the margins into the tributary system that provided the Center with its trade commodities, it also periodically spawned émigrés, real or putative, who conquered people beyond its margins and established a series of semiautonomous polities loyal to the Lunda Center. As noted earlier, the Kanongesha was one such individual, who arrived on the upper Zambezi around 1740.

Over time, Central Africa experienced diminishing terms of trade and declining profit margins, in tandem with the accelerated flow of commodities to the coast. The Lunda also began experiencing difficulties keeping the trade routes west open to their caravans. Groups to the west were becoming better armed owing to the willingness of many European traders, particularly Portuguese, to sell guns and powder to their coastal African partners, despite official sanctions to the contrary. After the official ban on the sale of guns to Africans was lifted in 1767, the Lunda found it virtually impossible to push through the territories of either their northwestern neighbors, the Chokwe, or their southwestern neighbors, the Ovimbundu. Yet even with greater access to guns, those groups remained far too small to pose a serious direct threat to the Lunda polity with its massive, well-fortified population centers. Furthermore, the Lunda were one of the few polities in Central Africa capable of producing commodities in sufficient quantities to attract the largest of the caravans from the coast. During the eighteenth century the Lunda capital increasingly became the final destination of numerous trade caravans, some with up to two thousand merchants and porters, laden with European goods from the Congo and Angolan coasts, seeking to acquire tropical products at first, then slaves and ivory, and later rubber and wax as well. The Lunda Center continually repositioned itself as a prime producer of export commodities, embarking on extended military campaigns against all that might rival its preeminent position.

The Lunda-Ndembu moved south and west, forcefully taking control of the territory astride the trade route to the capital, and thrived by selling food and other services to the passing caravans. The emergence of the trade system from the west created a spasm of demographic shifts in Lunda territory, followed by a period of relative stability until the slave frontier reached the upper Zambezi in the mid- to late eighteenth century. European goods, values, and cultural expressions circulated widely, even while coastal peoples successfully blocked the inward movement of the Europeans themselves. Even in the nineteenth century, Cameron noted in his journal that he was discouraged from visiting the Lunda capital and was refused assistance: "Even if I reached the capital I was warned that I should never return, as the last white man known to have visited his sable majesty was forcibly detained to instruct the people in the art of European warfare, and after four years of dreary captivity died there, having had no opportunity of escaping" (1877, 2:59).

The Chokwe and Ovimbundu fiercely protected their position not only as the filter through which western commodities flowed to the Lunda but also as the interpreters of western culture to the interior. While extolling the virtues of their European wares, they nevertheless discouraged the Lunda from attempting to make direct contact with Europeans by portraying them as uniquely dangerous creatures. Europeans were said to possess the power to turn African bodies into oil, flesh into meat, brains into cheese, bone ash into gun powder, and blood into wine. One particularly fanciful yet widespread story about Europeans, collected by Burton in eastern Central Africa, stated:

They had one eye each and four arms; they were full of "knowledge," which in these lands means magic; they caused rain to fall in advance and left droughts in their rear; they cooked water melons and threw away the seeds, thereby generating small-pox; they heated and hardened milk, thus breeding a murrain amongst cattle; and their wire, cloth, and beads caused a variety of misfortunes; they were kings of the sea, and therefore white-skinned and straight-haired—a standing mystery to these curly-pated people—as are all men who live in salt water; and next year they would return and seize the country. (1860, 1:262)

Stories circulated in Central Africa about the need for special metaphysical protection when dealing with the white man. The adoption of elements of Portuguese style was thus an indicator of the mastery of powerful alien forces. A set of spiritual/magical practitioners arose who specialized in charms and rituals to fortify those engaging in business with Europeans. Indeed, no trade caravan was complete without its own traveling *nganga*, medicine man, charged with taming the dangerous forces inherent in the process of bringing the African and European worlds in contact with one another. These medicine men traveled throughout Central Africa dispensing their highly sought out secrets, for a dear price.

While "whiteness," in the form of people, was still a new phenomenon, all early travelers noted that European products were well ensconced in local African economies. Cameron noted the general lack of familiarity with whites when writing about his encounter with the wife of the Lunda tributary chief Kasongo: "She [Kasongo's wife] enquired whence I had come, where I was going, put a variety of questions to me, and then became curious as to whether I was white all over. With much laughter she insisted on my boots and stockings being taken off in order that she might examine my feet" (1877, 2:60). Yet Cameron's personal articles were familiar to people as far east as the Lualaba River:

A number of his [a Portuguese agent's] people came over and were a wild rough-looking set of nearly naked savages, carrying old Portuguese flint-lock guns with inordinately long barrels ornamented with an immense number of brass rings. They were very inquisitive and wanted to see everything I possessed, and expressed much delight on recognising any object similar to what they had seen near the West Coast, such as cups, books, or anything European. These they pointed out to the Warua, who had joined them in staring at me and my belongings, as being quite common in their country, and claimed superiority on that account. (1877, 2:56)

During the 1800s the number of well-organized caravans crisscrossing Central Africa reached phenomenal proportions. Only the immense potential for profits could explain the vast numbers willing to weave their way two thousand miles from coast to coast through a maze of small well-armed predatory groups. Waves of fear and anxiety mixed with expectation pulsed across the landscape. Trades routes shifted with the wind. All of the nineteenth-century European travelers attested to the reign of instability that ensued as the trade of the two coasts collided with and bypassed each other in Central Africa. Even while trade from the west was growing in Central Africa, the basic mechanisms for dealing with the east coast remained intact. Later, the reduction of slaving on the west coast would result in the massive redirection of slaves for export to the east coast. Domestic slaves, however, were still sought for transporting the ivory, rubber, and other forest products that flowed to the west. Bihean traders from Angola regularly crossed the continent and did business at Zanzibar. At the same time, Zanzibaris were known to make visits to Benguela. Beads from both coasts gained widespread currency. The more powerful Lunda chiefs were regularly approached by sets of traders coming from both coasts.

Slave Trade: The Debt Comes Due

The slave trade, perhaps more so than the production of primary products, dominated the economic, political, and cultural life of the nineteenth-century Lunda. As Cameron wrote in his journal in 1874, "Innumerable old camps along the road bore testimony to the large traffic, principally in slaves, which now exists between Bihe and the centre of the continent" (1877, 2:168). Rarely a week went by during Cameron's trek across Central Africa without word of another caravan passing nearby. Cameron reported that "On the lines occupied by the Portuguese, especially that from Bihe to Urua [the Lunda] and Katanga, there is a vast amount of internal slave-trade; but the greater portion of those captured—for they are nearly all obtained by rapine and violence—are not taken to the coast, but to Kaffir countries where they are exchanged for ivory" (1877, 2:323). Indeed, one caravan that Cameron joined for the protection of his small party, instead of engaging in trading, unexpectedly turned to slaving: "At starting the whole caravan may have numbered seven hundred, and before leaving Urua (the Lunda) they had collected over fifteen hundred slaves, principally by force and robbery" (1877, 2:107).

By the mid-1800s, Central Africa was increasingly characterized by small fortified villages. The larger polities, such as that of central Lunda, were being rent asunder by indiscriminate slaving. More modern guns were flooding into Central Africa. The era of the small well-armed group was in full swing. Such groups could move across the landscape far faster than heavily laden caravans. They needed to carry little except their weapons, since they subsisted primarily by pillaging villages for food. They were more flexible in their itineraries and could shift their economic focus quickly. They might hunt for ivory should elephants be present, or perhaps plunder an unarmed village of all its valuables and sell the occupants to the next passing caravan for food and powder. Sometimes they acquired carriers by force: "In the countries where ivory is cheapest and most plentiful none of the inhabitants willingly engage themselves as carriers, and traders are obliged to buy slaves to enable them to transport their ivory to a profitable market" (Cameron 1877, 2:322). Or small armed groups might, instead, plunder a caravan and sell its wares cheaply to nearby villages. Lunda lore is rich in stories of colorful bandits, rough and ready individuals making a living by taking for themselves any wealth within their reach. Their ultimate desire usually remained to legitimize that wealth, however ill-gotten, by founding a village, acquiring followers, living out their days in the style of a chief, and presumably being long remembered in the afterlife.

The wholesale removal of human beings from the productive sphere to serve as beasts of burden in the long-distance trade network must inevitably have affected the general level of food production in Central Africa. Little has been written on this point. It is evident, however, that the Lunda-Ndembu fared quite well throughout most of the 1800s as food producers. The territory immediately to their west was consistently referred to by travelers as the hungry country. The massive involvement of the Chokwe and Ovimbundu in trading activities meant that insufficient food was produced in their territories to outfit large caravans. Those arriving in Lunda territory from the coast were invariably hungry and prepared to pay top price for food. The security and stability of this trade in surplus food appears to have dissuaded most of the Lunda-Ndembu from more active participation in the slave trade. For the Lunda-Ndembu, food was an effective entrée into the world of Western commodities. Land where cassava could thrive was abundant. The simple inputs required were readily available to all. Although few Lunda-Ndembu acquired the levels of wealth associated with famous caravan leaders, the successful producer enacted his best imitation of that lifestyle. At times the food situation to the west so deteriorated that the Lunda-Ndembu were able to reap an incredible windfall. Some even acquired a few slaves during these times. Crawford (1912, 30), for example, mentions that 1889 and 1890 were particularly hungry years in western Central Africa. He noted that young slaves were acquired for as little as a truss of calico, a few colored handkerchiefs, or an old waterproof coat. More commonly, however, the bargain struck was a bag of corn or cassava meal for each human being. Along the west coast, slaves were periodically available at greatly reduced cost during times of drought, famine, and disease (Miller 1982). During normal times ivory or guns might be the only items acceptable in exchange for a slave.

Early accounts also show that many in the interior, the Lunda included, endeavored to hold on to their slaves, buying more whenever possible and selling only when in dire straits. Slaves became the quintessential symbol of wealth in Central Africa. They were a tangible, visible, self-reproducing form of wealth. They were a fully convertible currency, easily disposed of should the need arise. They were also an extremely utilitarian form of wealth; not simply working capital, but a form of capital that could actually work. They could be used as field hands or domestic servants, as skilled craftsmen producing for the market, as trusted partners in a business venture, or as loyal supporters in a local struggle for political primacy. Furthermore, because social relations in life were believed to continue in the afterlife, slaves could be a useful asset in one's later metaphysical existence. Indeed, there are tales of slaves being buried alive with their masters in order that they might immediately accompany that master to the other world and continue to serve him there as well.[2]

Long after slavery ceased to be the focus of the Atlantic world, slaves remained a valuable commodity in the interior, as well as the dominant commodity funneled to the Indian Ocean trade world from Central Africa. The longevity of this latter trade is indicated in the following passage: "On 15 October 1893 the White Fathers decided to abandon Old Mambwe mission [in Zambia's Northern Province] because the heavy traffic of caravans carrying slaves which use to pass through the station from Lunda and Bemba country to the east coast made missionary work difficult. They felt that if they were to make any progress in evangelising the people they would have to move away from the distractions and interference of what was not only an international highway but also a busy slave trade route" (Meebelo 1971, 35).

Not every Lunda was content to live out his or her life as a cassava producer. Myriad other strategies were devised to make a living during the turbulent times in Central Africa. Small-scale robbery of, or with, caravans became an option that many pursued. At the end of one caravan trip, Cameron observed that "the porter were . . . paid from eight to twelve yards of cloth each, and a few charges of powder. This, together with the twelve yards every man had received before starting, made in all about twenty yards of cloth as pay, and a few charges of powder as a gift, for upwards of two years of service. Of course men would not engage for such ridiculous rates of pay were it not that they profited by rapine and robbery in passing through countries where the people did not possess guns"

(1877, 2:202). The Portuguese explorer Serpa Pinto, operating in the same time and place, was forced to pay his carriers half a yard of striped cloth a day, over fifteen times the above rate, presumably because he permitted no plunder or pillage by members of his caravan.

Theft from caravans by their own carriers was also common. Richard Burton (1860, 1:10), for example, was advised to carry over ten thousand rounds of ammunition on his expedition into Central Africa, not because of the external dangers he would face but because of the high rate of theft he would no doubt experience from his own carriers. Livingstone noted in his journal the insecurity of the trader, far from home, dependent on his carriers to see him safely through: "The uneasiness of the trader is perpetually shewing itself, and upon the whole he has reason be on the alert day and night. His carriers are of the Songo tribe, and of course partake of all the vices of heathenism, thieving perpetually the goods entrusted to their care and thereby causing a great diminution of the trader's gain. He cannot openly accuse them, for they might plunder and leave him in the lurch in revenge" (1863, 240).

Caravans were often quite porous entities, with carriers absconding with merchandise at every juncture and new carriers joining along the way, more to assess the potential pickings than because of any long-term commitment to the venture. A common tactic was to sign up for a trip, receive as much advance pay as possible, and then flee back to the village at the first opportunity. Dan Crawford offered the following reflections on recruiting carriers: "Be sure you write in pencil, though, not ink, for generally a few negro wags lead off by making counterfeit overtures to join your caravan, the false names being eagerly recorded by the impatient white man" (1912, 68). He noted, further, that "this compact is generally signed, sealed, and delivered by a sort of 'taking the shilling' on his part—calico, not cash, being the currency. It must be white and not dark in colour this fabric, otherwise you will have symbolised sorrow and not joy" (1912, 66).

Central Africa is striped with numerous rivers that caravans had to negotiate carefully, lest they lose merchandise and perhaps even carriers to the many torrents. Local entrepreneurs capitalized on this need by establishing toll bridges and canoe ferries at specially good crossing points. Seeking up-to-date information on river crossings was a constant preoccupation of caravan leaders as they sought to avoid those ferrymen who were known for charging inflated fees for their services or for otherwise preying on caravans. A particularly colorful, though not altogether unique, character was described by Crawford: "It is a remarkable fact that old Kasonkomona, on the Lufira, used regularly to capsize his canoe at the precise point where, on the morrow, he would dive for the lost treasure—of course, after his half-drowned passenger was well on his way to the next camp. A strong swimmer, he always dramatically saved the sinking voyager, the greedy glitter in his eyes bespeaking salvage operations on the morrow—guns, spears, beads, all harvested from the river bottom" (1912, 35).

All of the early writers noted delays as the most constant source of aggravation for caravans in Central Africa. Local inhabitants had absolutely no incentive to assist caravans in speeding along their way. Every day that a caravan could be delayed in one's area was one more day to devise plans for accessing its stockpile of goods. Livingstone's journal, for example, is rich in descriptions of efforts to delay his progress. In one instance, "we were conducted to another village, and as usual they made every effort to induce us to remain and trade in food . . . the people refused to shew the path unless we should remain and buy food for a day" (1963, 246). "They are terribly . . . keen traders, and every art is tried to detain us for a single night at their villages in order that they may have the pleasure of trading in meal, manioc roots, & ground nuts. Some few specimens of copper are offered" (1963, 249).

Sometimes delays were aimed at enticing caravan members to purchase local products or to sell their own commodities at a cheaper price. At other times the tactic was to entrap caravan members into violating some local law, real or imagined, whereby they could then be fined. As Cameron noted, "they invent many claims as a means of extorting goods from those passing through their villages. Everything in their mode of living is regulated by the magicians or fetish men, and they cleverly lay traps for the unwary traveller. Thus, should a stranger chance to rest his gun or spear against a hut in their villages, it is instantly seized and not returned unless a heavy fine is paid, the excuse being that it is an act of magic intended to cause the death of the owner of the hut. If a tree which has been marked with fire should be cut down for building in camp, similar demands are made; and so on through an unlimited category" (1887, 2:164). Crawford, writing in a similar vein about his experiences just south of Lunda-Ndembu territory, noted: "Here you have a whole tribe spreading its nets and lurking by the roadside for loot. Legal loot, though, this claims to be; for when the word is passed along the path that a caravan is advancing, there is a tribal flutter, and this news draws them like a magnet. Each person looking for an excuse to put forward a lawsuit for some infraction touching a person the wrong way, stepping in the wrong place, calling a person by the wrong name, spitting in the wrong place, etc. . . . Be sure of it, from the Atlantic to the Indian Ocean, these lawsuits in Africa are legion, the be-all and end-all of their lazy lives. From prince to beggar they have resolved to trade on the local sanctions and punishments of society" (1912, 139, 141). Caravans were evidently seen as being outside the local moral community and were therefore fair game for any clever, or not so clever, deception: "The art of cheating is very well understood by the native fishmongers, for in the centre of some of the baskets I found earth, stones, broken pottery, and gourds so stowed as to make up the proper weight and bulk. Indeed, as far as my experience goes, the noble savage is not one whit behind his civilised brethren in adulterating food and giving short measure, the only difference being in the clumsiness of his method" (Cameron 1877, 2:175).

Serpa Pinto noted in his journal that even the loneliness of the virtually all-male caravan crews could be exploited as a source of revenue:

I was much struck with the type of many of these girls, which was perfectly European, and I saw several whose forms, as they undulated in the dance, would have raised envy in the hearts of many European ladies, whom they equalled in beauty and surpassed in grace of motion. . . . It would appear that these Ambuellas, on the arrival in the country of a caravan are accustomed to flock into the camp, to sing and dance; and, as night advances the men retire, and leave their women-folks behind them. It is their hospitable custom thus to furnish the stranger wayfarers with a few hours of female society. On the following morning, at daybreak, the visitors steal away to their villages, and rarely fail to return to bring gifts to their friends. (1881, 148)

Despite the prevalence of theft and deception as methods for quickly separating caravans from some of their wares, many in Central Africa sought to establish long-term relationships with outsiders based on friendship, trust, and honesty in commercial exchanges. Most travelers noted encountering some chiefs or other individuals who provided lavish hospitality, dispensed useful information, and sometimes protected the interests of caravans from the malevolent designs even of their own countrymen. Livingstone commented on one such individual whom he visited on several occasions:

(June 14, 1855) We came to Katema's town. . . . He is out hunting skins for his paramount lord Matiamvo [the Lunda king], but his domestics sent five large baskets of manioc meal, a fowl, fifteen eggs, and some beer.

(June 15th) Katema came home today, having heard of our arrival. He desires me
to rest myself today. . . . This is in order that he himself may have a rest and prepare for our reception in style. His wife sent three baskets more of meal, some
fish, and a fowl, with earth nuts and compliments. The Balonda [Lunda] of these
parts are very kind. May God look on them in mercy.
(June17th) . . . he (Katema) presented 6 baskets of meal, a basket of putrid buf-
falo meat, 3 fowls, & sweet potatoes. . . . I [Livingstone] presented a red cloak
ornamented with lace which cost 30/- at Loanda, a large piece of broad striped
calico for a mantle, beads large & small, 1/4 lb of gunpowder, and an iron spoon.
(1963, 259)

As noted above, the availability of easy credit, particularly from Portuguese merchants on the Congo and Angolan coast, played a profound
role in shifting Central African trade toward the west. Enterprising African
traders competed with one another for market shares by further extending credit to clients in the interior. Virtually all of Central Africa was ad-
dicted to the trade system long before the declining terms of trade compelled them to switch the form of payment from ivory and other tropical
goods to human beings. Chronic indebtedness and machinations to collect or avoid debts are constant themes in the literature on Central Africa.
According to J. C. Miller, "To judge from the widespread and persistent
indebtedness of African importers throughout the history of their trading
with Europeans, most developed techniques of delayed payment to a high
art" (1988, 123).

New systems evidently arose to keep track of and manage the unprecedented amount of outstanding debt. Cameron noted one such system in a
village house he visited in the late nineteenth century: "Looking up to the
beehive roof I spied a number of tiny white flags flying, mere ribbons of calico these, some grimed with soot, and one quite new. 'Oh!' said the owner
thereof, 'these are receipts of debts I have paid.' Commoner still is it to find
little packets of twigs scrupulously tied together, the varying sizes all elo-
quent of some transaction represented by these vouchers—a long tusk of
ivory, for instance, being memorised by a longish twig, and so on in ratio
right round the various sorts and sizes of tusks" (1877, 2:177).

Cloth, perhaps even more than guns, was the major commodity changing hands on credit. Roughly 50 percent of the goods, by value, brought
into Central Africa consisted of cloth. This seemingly insatiable appetite for
cloth extends from several factors. The political centralizing wars of the
1740s and 1750s among the western Lunda, just east of the Kwango River,

resulted in massive numbers of people fleeing from the river valleys up to the previously lightly populated plateau. The Lunda-Ndembu and others also increasingly recognized the agricultural potential of the plateau. Although poorly suited for the traditional crops of sorghum and millet, plateau soils were ideal for cassava and required less tree clearing than the more densely wooded river valleys. Supplies of skins and raffia, however, were inadequate for clothing the rapidly expanding population at this colder elevation. Livingstone noted on reaching a Lunda area far off the usual trade routes: "The sensation of cold after the heat of the day is very severe. The Balunda don't leave their fires till near midday. They don't clothe better, from absolute want of the materials" (1963, 265). Travelers frequently mentioned nakedness, particularly of Lunda women. As Livingstone wrote, "The effect is painfully visible in the appearance of the inhabitants who are situated far from markets. The women at Kawawa's and many other parts of Lunda are nearly quite naked. A patch of cloth or skin about three inches broad is esteemed apparel, and nothing could exceed the eagerness with which they offered to purchase strips of calico. They were delighted with about two feet for a fowl and basket of meal, and, when we could no longer purchase, with true maternal feelings they held their little naked babies before me, entreating me to sell only a rag for them" (1963, 255). As late as 1875, Cameron noted the difficulty of obtaining supplies for his party after his stock of cloth ran low: "For a piece of salt I obtained a fowl; but the people would not even look at my remaining beads, being very eager for cloth, of which I had none for trading" (1877, 2:162). His party frequently went hungry, "the people only consenting to sell provisions for slaves, cloth, and gunpowder, none of which I could give them" (1877, 2:167). Yet while traveling among people closer to the coast, he noted, "Being satiated with cloth owing to their constant intercourse with the coast, the people would sell us nothing, or asked higher prices than we could afford" (1877, 2:198).

The historical importance of cloth owes much to the need for bodily covering on the plateau, but cloth was also a mode of payment, a medium of exchange, and a store of wealth. Along with beads and wire bracelets it became a major multipurpose currency in the Central African region. Imported cloth was hoarded, and it was also used as a display of rank—a truly pan-African, if not global phenomenon. Early travelers' accounts frequently mention attempts by chiefs to monopolize new styles, or at least to have first choice from new supplies of cloth entering their territories. The wealthy were often buried in rolls and rolls of cloth. Many an early traveler remarked on the fact that on grand ceremonial occasions, chiefs were often wrapped in so much cloth they could hardly move. Although locally produced cloth continued to be used out of necessity, local dyes could not match the brilliant colors of European, Indian, or Asian cloth. In the areas astride the caravan routes, imported cloth became indigenized by being incorporated as a standard part of bridewealth negotiations. Burton (1860, 1:118) noted, for example, that during the mid-1800s six to twelve yards of imported cloth was the minimum acceptable quantity.

Thus, in the era of long-distance trade that preceded the colonial period, we find the Lunda living under a wide range of economic conditions. Some experienced oscillating fortunes as raiders, traders, entrepreneurs, or scoundrels preying on caravans. Others subsisted as wealthy or poor cassava producers. Still others were reduced to slaves, held locally or exported to either coast. The myriad caravans snaking their way across the Central African plateau brought with them new occupations whose benefits waxed and waned with the ever-shifting terms and conditions of trade. Yet, there was a certain measure of continuity in the meaning of wealth, even as the symbols of wealth changed. Simply put, wealth could ultimately be measured in the number of followers one possessed, be they kin, slaves, or hangers-on. Wealth-in-things became particularly meaningful if it could be converted into wealth-in-rememberers, that is, those who would mourn one's death and keep the memory of one's existence alive.

The British or the Portuguese: The Rock or the Hard Place?

In contrast to the era of long-distance coastal trade, the colonial period for the Lunda-Ndembu is perhaps best characterized as a time of economic dediversification, a time of decreasing economic options. The turn of the twentieth century saw the decline of mercantile capitalism, driven by the slave and ivory trades, and its gradual replacement by industrial capitalism, led by the mining revolution of southern Africa. Agents of Cecil Rhodes's British South Africa Corporation (BSAC) arrived to take control of Mwinilunga in 1906. The BSAC immediately set about terrorizing the population—destroying crops, burning huts, and raping women—all in the name of pacifying the territory. Without a large and effective administrative structure in place, the BSAC tended to rely on random and arbitrary violence to compel the population to comply with its demands. The cruelty of the BSAC has been well documented. One account, for example, tells of an incident when a man named Smith "came to a village Kasanga, and demanded food and men to porter. He was given food and people. The Capitao caught a girl and slept with her and gave Ngoza to Smith to sleep with. Then they tied up the headman of Kanyanga village and burned it. The two girls were from this village. The men fled to the bush and other girls were raped. There were 17 huts destroyed at Toteras, the next village" (Luchembe 1992, 37).

The initial demand was for labor, primarily to prop up more established British enterprises to the south, that is, European plantations in Southern Rhodesia and mining operations in South Africa. The company discouraged or destroyed most of the traditional means of subsistence, enforcing migrant labor as the only option. This included taking over salt pans, banning metal working, and outlawing all craft production. The BSAC did employ some local people for porterage, domestic work, and station maintenance. Its major focus, however, was on stimulating the flow of labor out of Mwinilunga. Using recruitment agencies, such as the Rhodesia Native Labour Bureau (RNLB), the BSAC directed labor south to Zimbabwe and beyond. The contribution of RNLB to the labor force of Zimbabwe rose from 29 percent in 1906 to 42 percent by 1910 (Macpherson 1981; Luchembe 1992). From 1910 onward, the company also served as the local representative of the Robert Williams Company, which recruited labor for the Katanga Coppermines in the Congo. There, workers from Mwinilunga would earn a minimum wage of 15 shillings a month, free rations, medical care, and compensation for accidents while on duty. Nevertheless, the Lunda-Ndembu strongly resisted BSAC objectives, according to both written and oral sources. Villagers fled en masse to either Angola or Congo, only to return upon experiencing the even harsher realities of Portuguese and Belgian colonialism. Still, the Lunda were noted for their exceptionally high rates of tax default and high frequency of desertion when pressed into forced labor gangs. The introduction of taxes in 1913, combined with the ongoing application of violence, ultimately succeeded in converting much of Mwinilunga's male population into migrant workers.

In addition to the removal of labor, the BSAC profoundly transformed daily life in Mwinilunga in other ways. Virtually from the beginning it attacked *chitemene*, the traditional system of slash-and-burn agriculture, regarding it as a wasteful method of cultivation (BSAC, 423). Furthermore, the BSAC was concerned that the dispersal of people and villages over wide areas constrained its ability to implement an orderly system of administration. The collection of taxes, the enumeration of population censuses, and the maintenance of law and order could be more effectively pursued if people were concentrated in larger villages. Toward that end, the BSAC undertook a colony-wide forced villagization program. As one native commissioner described it: "A good deal of work has been done in gathering scattered villages and individuals together under their headman. Practically every native in the district must be now aware that he can no longer move about to build and cut timber from land he chooses with impunity and has been warned that prosecution will be commended during the year of damage to the trees" (National Archives of Zambia 2AZ/2/3: Annual Report for Batoka for the year ending 31 March 1914).

The entire colony of Northern Rhodesia was eventually divided into a series of Native Reserves, where Africans were forced to live in large overcrowded villages, while most of the more fertile land was set aside as European or Crown land, to which African access was severely restricted. The impact on daily life of taxation, labor recruitment, migration, urbanization, legislation aimed at conservation, village concentration, anti-hunting laws, and the attack on *chitemene* is becoming increasingly well documented by a new generation of historians at the University of Zambia.[3] These historians have shown that during the early colonial period there was a drastic decrease in the amount of land at the disposal of Africans, as well as a decrease in the number of things that Africans could do with the land. The draconian measures of the BSAC reduced economic opportunities essentially to two choices: subsistence crop production or migrant labor. Although the Lunda-Ndembu could have made significant contributions to the food needs of the new colony, they were prevented from doing so.

Increased publicity in Britain about the violent excesses of the BSAC precipitated a scandal that forced the Colonial Office to revoke the BSAC's mandate and assume direct control of Northern Rhodesia in 1924. Immediately the focus of new policies shifted toward developing the territory as something other than a vast labor reserve for the development of other southern African colonies. The new emphasis centered around the expansion of mining operations, innovations in public management, and the increased involvement of foreign missionaries in local affairs. Mining, management, and missionaries, thus, became the nodes of economic activity which local Africans seized upon as three pathways to economic liberation.

Mining had actually begun with the extraction of lead and zinc at Kabwe, in central Zambia, as early as 1904. The discovery of vast new deposits and the expansion of copper mining during the 1930s, however, transformed Zambia from a labor reservoir for Zimbabwe, South Africa, and Katanga into a major regional labor market in its own right. New possibilities opened up for the Lunda-Ndembu. By 1930, thirty thousand African and four thousand white mineworkers annually required three hundred thousand bags of maize as well as other foodstuffs. As Yona Seleti noted: "The huge work-force and increased urbanisation generated a rising market and the demand for foodstuffs to feed them. The sustained expansion of the mining industry in the postwar period provided steady and profitable market conditions. By 1941 the demand for maize outstripped the supply by 400,000 bags. Consequently, the state abandoned its policy of protecting European farmers and adopted one which encourage both peasant and white settler production" (Seleti 1992, 167).

New markets for African produce led to increased social differentiation in rural areas. The Lunda-Ndembu's capacity to generate surplus cassava in abundance was rediscovered. The impact, as noted in chapter 3, was the social transformation so carefully detailed by Victor Turner in the early 1950s. The roads connecting Mwinilunga to the new Copperbelt were greatly improved. The frequency of truck traffic between the two increased. With the lifting of regulations confining the population to overcrowded registered villages, ambitious individuals rushed to establish commercial farms along the roadways. Many grew wealthy exporting surplus food east to feed the new Copperbelt towns, whose population had exploded to over a million people during the 1950s. A group of elite farmers emerged virtually overnight who managed to amass sufficient capital to buy their own trucks; they transported their surplus east and returned with consumer goods to sell locally. They opened their own shops, tearooms, bars, and restaurants. They set up tailoring establishments, butcheries, and beauty salons. They built large houses and stocked them with the latest accoutrements of the Western world: store-bought furniture, gramophones, mosquito nets, oil lamps, and expensive chinaware. They wore smartly tailored suits, bowler hats, and shiny leather shoes. They carried flashy timepieces and umbrellas, and littered their speech with the latest Copperbelt slang, usually in an Anglicized Bemba patois.

Turner believed that he was witnessing a new phenomenon among the Lunda-Ndembu in the 1950s: the breaking down of a long-standing communal way of life. He saw the emergence of a self-centered petty capitalist class attempting to disencumber itself from the reciprocal bonds of obligations that characterized the village world—a group of petty kulaks, he called them, who measured success in life by the insignia of conspicuous wealth that could be purchased by money. Yet, in many ways this period was remarkably similar to the earlier era of long-distance coastal trade. In contrast to the period of limited economic options under BSAC rule, the 1940s and 1950s were decades when long-constrained entrepreneurial creativity reemerged. Individual movements were not designed primarily to avoid obligations to family and friends but were rather bold attempts on the part of individuals to take advantage of new currents of economic activity. The heady pursuit of novel foreign items was in no way a rejection of local cultural production; it was instead the latest manifestation of the long-standing tradition of symbolically demonstrating one's connection with and mastery of the outside world. Material transactions are the most public and powerful symbol of personal relations among the Lunda-Ndembu. The possession of imported commodities, in a sense, personalizes one's connections with the world that produced those commodities. The business reputation of those who seek to make a living by serving as facilitators of exchange between two worlds is enhanced by the appearance of thorough immersion in both worlds. Those called petty kulaks by Turner were not attempting to cleanse themselves of the traditional world but were for the most part endeavoring to expand their public personae with the addition of a layer of foreignness. Turner, perhaps, extrapolated too heavily from the seemingly self-centered actions of youths, who, in the early stages of their long-term economic plans, focused most heavily on personal accumulation. Yet, buried in Turner's own rich ethnographic data are the bits and pieces of life histories that show that more mature wealthy individuals sought to surround themselves with followers: family or friends, needy or otherwise. They actively participated in local rituals as cult members and patients, exercised their traditional rights, fulfilled obligations as kin, and interacted with the older generation according to traditional norms. They sought out chieftaincies or headmanships of established villages or became de facto headmen of villages of their own construction. Ultimately they used their wealth to better their positions within the traditional system rather than as a means of loosening ties with it. For many, the route to local eminence was a circuitous one that led through commercial farming, trading with the Copperbelt, and providing local services to arrive finally at the status of *akwakwashi* (patron, one who helps others), and perhaps headman as well.

The second economic node during the later colonial period, after mining, was the pursuit of innovative new strategies in public management. These strategies led to the development of what Samuel Chipungu called the Boma class. "Boma" has been a widely used term in Zambia since the colonial era to denote a local administrative center. The Boma class, thus, refers to the group of local Africans paid, mostly from local funds, to serve in administrative capacities. The structure of colonial administration was formalized with the Native Authority Ordinance and the Native Courts Ordinance of 1929. These ordinances mandated the selection of a senior chief and some subordinate chiefs for each ethnic group and the creation of a Native Authority staff of Africans responsible for much of the day-to-day administration of rural districts. Throughout the 1930s, the paid Native Authority staff of a district generally consisted of a chief, a court clerk, an assessor, and a number of *bakapasu* (messengers or guards). Unpaid headmen, however, were shouldering much responsibility. In 1937, Native Treasuries were created to encourage development by offering Native Authorities control over a percentage of funds from poll taxes, court fines, dog and firearm licenses, permits (for beer brewing, travel to urban areas, hunting, and fishing), levies on properties, slaughter and market fees, and livestock dipping charges. In the 1940s, with the continuing focus on rural development, Native Authority staff were expanded to include skilled councillors in the areas of education, health, agriculture, veterinary care, fisheries, and public works. Some employed administration and bursary councillors as well. By the 1960s, with independence approaching, each Native Authority employed twenty to fifty people. Nationwide, there were at least three thousand salaried staff and more than twenty-three thousand headmen in the Native Authorities system. Although in theory Native Authorities were autonomous units, colonial control was maintained through the power to dismiss individuals or even to restructure or amalgamate whole units.

Although the salaries of Native Authority personnel were ridiculously low in comparison with those of their European counterparts in the colonial administration, they constituted a significant sum for rural Africans starved for cash to pay the ubiquitous taxes and levies. By the mid-1940s a senior chief could receive as much as eight pounds annually, but lesser chiefs were paid as little as one pound, and the *bakapasu* generally received less than two pounds. Skilled councillors and treasury clerks were the highest paid, averaging about fifteen pounds annually. By comparison, the average African miner on the Copperbelt at that time was paid eleven pounds annually. Furthermore, as Chipungu points out, members of the Boma class could invest a disproportionate amount of their salary into productive activities because, unlike mineworkers, they usually could provide for their own subsistence without using cash: "The Native Authority employees produced much of their own food in the village fields as they were predominantly local. Nor did these employees, unlike some of the urban workers, have to pay rent or similar costs as they lived in their villages or in structures near the chief's palace as part of their public ties. With such reduced expenditure, therefore, Native Authority personnel could purchase equipment after several months of saving from their salaries. For instance, a single-mould plough which cost between 7 and 15 pounds in the 1950s could be bought by an assessor or clerk out of some three months' savings" (Chipungu 1992, 83). The pattern of investment among Native Authority employees tended to follow regional economic specializations, such as cattle rearing in the south of Zambia, fishing in the west, and so forth. In Mwinilunga, the Native Authority employees generally followed the trail blazed by the elite farmers mentioned above. Many used their positions to secure estates along the roadways and invested their salaries in labor to produce surplus cassava and other foodstuffs for the Copperbelt market. They likewise branched into trade and services.

Although salaries were an important source of investment capital, it was the Native Authority Treasuries that provided the real material base for the emergent Boma class. Even the smallest Native Authority Treasury offered modest development loans, and employees were far more likely than non-employees to have their applications for loans approved. The record shows, however, that loans were rarely repaid in full. Employees would endeavor to pay the minimum installment allowable, stretching out repayment as long as possible, taking out new loans whenever the opportunity arose, and often retiring from service before settling the debt in full. Some Native Authority employees took a bolder and more direct route to capital accumulation: embezzling treasury funds. Theft and fraud increased as the size of treasuries grew. The annual reports of the auditor-general of the colony noted that cases of embezzlement more than doubled between 1940 and 1950. The sums embezzled also increased, from a few pounds in the early years to thousands of pounds at a time in the later period. Chiefs' clerks and treasury clerks, who were responsible for collecting, recording, and forwarding monies, were those most often accused and prosecuted for embezzlement. By the 1940s and 1950s, it became increasingly common for returning labor migrants to campaign for Native Authority jobs. Previously, the educated had shunned such positions in preference to higher-paying jobs in urban areas. But the exploding producer price for rural commodities and the burgeoning size of Native Treasuries presented an enticing package. A range of strategies emerged reflecting personal propensity and differential positions within the Native Authority system. "The Boma class was far from being monolithic: it was a collection of Native Authority employees with unequal access to the Native Treasury. The wages were differentiated between various positions. The educated ranks were more likely to receive higher salaries and 'perks' in the form of loans and advances than the bakapasu and other underlings. The educated were better placed to misappropriate larger sums of the Native Treasury by virtue of their position. However, the Treasury was an avenue for accumulation for all strata of the Boma class" (Chipungu 1992, 91).

The third node of economic activity that arose with the passing of the BSAC era centered on the increasing involvement of foreign missionaries in local affairs. The impact of missionaries on religious life in Mwinilunga will be explored more fully in chapter 8. Their impact on economic life, however, was quite profound, paralleling and underpinning the strategies of both elite farmers and the Boma class. Waves of evangelical Protestants, known as the Plymouth Brethren or the Christian Mission in Many Lands (CMML), settled in Mwinilunga beginning with the founding of Kalene mission by Dr. Walter Fisher in 1906.[4] Lacking a wealthy home organization capable of funding overseas activities, each mission station was individually responsible for its own economic viability. The Brethren, from the beginning, pursued a wide range of economic strategies, including cash cropping, cattle rearing, exporting honey, wax, and other tropical commodities, craft production, and trade in local consumer goods. The Franciscan Order of Roman Catholics, which began to operate in Mwinilunga during the late 1940s, in many ways followed the Brethren's economic example.[5] Each group, Catholic and Protestant, developed the capacity to hire far more labor, often at better wages, than could the Native Authority system. Employees invested these wages in the same way as did the elite African farmers and the Boma class. Foreign missionaries were also a font of innovation, often experimenting with novel crops, new technologies, and the marketing of nontraditional commodities. Hordes of people settled around the half dozen or so major mission stations seeking jobs that would allow them to avoid the vagaries of the migrant labor system.

A mission elite emerged whose history is less well documented than that of the Boma class but whose impact was no less significant. The mission elite consisted of those who managed to secure the full-time positions that mission stations offered: cooks, houseboys, launderers, gardeners, truck and tractor drivers, carpenters, mechanics, bricklayers, supervisors of casual laborers, and lay religious leaders on whom the missionaries depended heavily. The mission elite built their homes near the mission stations; they developed large farms with family labor to provide their subsistence needs and invested most of their salaries. They tended to pursue economic strategies that would capitalize on their access to mission resources. Missions generally maintained regular transportation and communication links with town and could, thus, provide their workers both with information on current marketing trends and prices and with a ready outlet for their surplus production. Many mission stations possessed fully stocked machine shops with electric generators and power tools. Favored employees might gain additional income in their spare time by producing furniture, tools, and other household articles, or by offering repair services locally. Most missions also possessed a tractor or two and made them available for hire when not needed at the mission. A few larger missions established hammer mills and seed presses, where local Africans, for a fee, could have raw commodities processed into flour and oil. As noted earlier, missionaries, with lots of time on their hands, were fervent experimenters. Those employees who worked most closely with missionaries gained invaluable insights into the viability of novel productive practices. With knowledge gained from the missions they popularized, for example, the production of pineapples, sunflower seeds, and new fruits and vegetables, as well as the construction of fishponds. Close contact with missionaries, thus, facilitated a wealth of economic options.

The mission elite developed their own unique personal style characterized by duality of presentation—showing one face to the missionaries and another in their villages. No matter how wealthy, they eschewed the flashier style of the elite farmer-cum-trader, presenting themselves to the missionaries as poor humble servants, barely eking out a living, continually overwhelmed by the burden of supporting destitute kin. They "dressed down," wearing their most threadbare clothing on the job. Their demeanor was usually profusely deferential, expressing exaggerated appreciation for the smallest courtesy from their missionary patrons. Stories abound to this day of missionaries abhorring Africans who presented themselves as the equals of Europeans. It was said that one could be fired for simply having the temerity to stand tall and look a European in the eye. One European who lived in Mwinilunga in the 1920s is infamous for having beaten Africans for daring to wear shoes in his presence, or even on his property, which extended over several square miles.[6] One local African was derisively given the name Katoloshi, (*ka*, a diminutive + *toloshi*, trousers) by missionaries for being the first in his area to proudly wear long European-style trousers rather than the short pants expected of African males.

The mission elite were known for littering their speech with Christianisms, managing to infuse God, Jesus, or biblical themes into the most mundane of conversations with missionaries. They seized every opportunity to demonstrate their mastery of religious teachings and the earnestness with which they accepted those teachings. They attended church regularly, sang the loudest in the choir, wept most profoundly at funerals, and railed most publicly against those who had yet to accept Christianity.

At home, in the village, however, the mission elite often presented very different personae. There, they were the doyens and custodians of tradition. They demanded and received respect paralleling that of a chief. They were given the most elaborate public greetings, the largest chairs, the positions of honor in local gatherings. They supervised *mukanda* and *nkanga* ceremonies and were frequently practitioners in traditional pan-village healing cults. They spoke longest and most eloquently at *mulong'a*, the traditional gatherings to resolve local disputes. They were *akwakwashi,* generous benefactors, the conduits through which flowed the goods and services of the missionary world. They were sought out for jobs, information, technical skills, and assistance in assembling bridewealth for younger kin and clients alike. Most eventually attracted large followings and finished out their days as respected headmen of well-established villages.

Individual missions not only produced their own clusters of elite Africans but were central to the formation and maintenance of the Boma class and the wealthy farmers-cum-traders as well. Education was the key to obtaining jobs in the Native Authority system, and education was the domain of missionaries. Missionaries were, in fact, invited to Mwinilunga and assisted in settling there precisely to provide the structures of formal education that the British Colonial Office felt it could not afford. In 1924, the Brethren opened Sakeji, a boarding school at Kalene Hill in northern Mwinilunga, designed initially to educate the children of European missionaries. Later, promising young Africans were admitted as well. The Brethren also established a lower school in the capital village of each Native Authority chief in their area and gradually built up a network of village schools, or out-schools, some up to one hundred miles from Kalene. These schools were staffed by African Christians, most of whom had been trained at Sakeji. The best students from these out-schools were themselves channeled to Sakeji, where they continued their education with European instructors. The curriculum at out-schools was extremely elementary, focused primarily on preparing Africans for Christianity rather than for skilled positions. As described by two Europeans present at the time: "These lessons cover the elements of the three R's, and the majority of the pupils have learned enough after eighteen months of school to read the Lunda New Testament and to write a fair letter. In this part of the mission field, this is regarded as sufficient head knowledge for an average boy or girl who will never be anything more than a manual labourer or field worker. For those above the average intelligence there is the central boarding school at Kalene" (Fisher and Hoyte 1948, 187).

Few African students progressed beyond the third grade. Even Sakeji did not meet the minimum academic standards required to receive government grants-in-aid until 1936. By 1958 the Brethren ran nineteen registered schools in Mwinilunga, with only Sakeji offering classes beyond the sixth grade. The Africans who completed their coursework at Sakeji were, for the most part, expected to become teachers at a village school, where they would recruit a new generation to Christianity. These teachers' wages were extremely low. The honor of educating one's own countrymen and spreading Christianity was supposed to be its own reward. The Brethren often paid African teachers less than they paid African mechanics, carpenters, drivers, cooks, and other skilled personnel around the mission station. As a result, many African students from Sakeji left the mission field, choosing instead to seek positions at the Boma under the Native Authority or mining jobs on the Copperbelt.

Fifty miles to the south of Kalene mission, the Franciscan Catholics later set up a similar network of village schools, channeling the best students to their boarding school at Lwawu mission, St. Kizito. Students from St. Kizito likewise went on to fill the ranks of the Boma class or to secure jobs in the mines.

The wave of elite farmers who emerged with the expanding market in agricultural produce during the 1940s and 1950s also owed much to the presence of missionaries. They did not have to feign interest in Christianity, however, for their relationship with missions was based on mutually beneficial economic exchange. Wealthy farmers could afford to pay cash for services that only missions could offer. It was within their means to rent mission tractors for plowing and land clearing. They were able to pay top prices for the use of mission machine shops to repair their vehicles and other equipment. They could, at times, gain additional income by hiring out their own vehicles should a mission require temporary additional haulage. Missions and wealthy farmers could coordinate their buying excursions to town, saving one another the added expense of unnecessary travel. They even coordinated the placement of their trading establishments so as to reduce direct competition for the limited disposable cash in the area.

In summary, the late colonial period was a time of flourishing African entrepreneurship. After an era of brutal constraints under BSAC rule, new economic pathways were opened by the expansion of mining operations, local public administration, and missionary activities. Separate but overlapping elite groups developed who grew wealthy by penetrating those new economic worlds, but who, in general, legitimized and indigenized their newfound wealth by becoming *akwakwashi*—headmen, chiefs, and prominent participants in the traditional world.

Political Economy on the Periphery

Few new routes to wealth have emerged for the citizens of Mwinilunga since Zambia became independent, in 1964. Despite rhetoric to the contrary, the country's economic direction has changed little, especially not in ways that would benefit the area. The national economy is still dominated by copper mining. During the early years of independence, the world market price for copper remained relatively high and government coffers filled with surplus revenue, much of which was dedicated to extending social services to the long-neglected poor. The government embarked on ambitious programs of road, school, and clinic building. The number of teachers, medical clinicians, and agricultural and veterinary officers on the government payroll expanded. These programs sputtered when copper prices leveled off, however, and they began to decline after the mid-1970s. For much of the time since then, mines on the Copperbelt have operated at a loss. The number of workers employed has steadily declined, as has the mining sector's contribution to government revenue. The quality of town life has deteriorated drastically. Rising prices, exploding crime rates, and discrimination in employment practice have made towns decreasingly attractive for many Lunda. Indeed, census figures indicate that Mwinilunga has one of the lowest rates of out-migration of any district in the nation. Commercial maize farmers, situated primarily along the rail line that links most of Zambia's urban centers, monopolize much of the government resources allocated to the agricultural sector. There is little demand for Mwinilunga cassava. In some parts of the district, groups of young cohorts have combined to form cooperatives specializing in the production of maize. But maize is an extremely destructive crop for the generally thin soils of Mwinilunga. Local cooperatives have for the most part experienced sharply declining yields after an initial period of moderate success. Problems such unreliable transportation, lack of timely arrival of seeds and fertilizer, and limited availability of credit facilities have also severely constrained the growth of local maize production. The era of the wealthy farmer-cum-trader, reaping tremendous windfalls from the urban need for food, is now only a fading memory.

The expansion of the new national administration into Mwinilunga since the 1960s has had significantly different economic effects than did the establishment of the Native Authority system in the 1930s. The British system of indirect rule was philosophically underpinned by the notion that people are best ruled by members of their own ethnic group. Members of the Boma class were firmly ensconced in the political, social, and economic dynamics of their assigned areas. The new independent government, however, feared the potentially divisive effects of ethnically based governance. Access to administrative jobs was therefore based on performance on standardized exams, without regard to ethnicity; as a result, quality education increasingly became the major prerequisite for government service. Yet the Lunda were disadvantaged in this respect. As Paul Wilkin (1983) noted in his dissertation on education in northwest Zambia, the general quality of educational facilities set up in Mwinilunga by both Catholics and Protestants lagged far behind contemporaneous missionary facilities in other parts of the country. Today it is the children of the urban-based elite, with access to libraries and other educational materials, and often with the advantage of private tutoring, who dominate the ranks of the academic achievers. The new teachers, nurses, agricultural and veterinary officers, and general administrators who have flooded into Mwinilunga since independence are far more likely to be from other areas and from other ethnic groups. No doubt far more important than their ethnic classification, however, is the short time that most of them stay. Transfers are a frequent occurrence in government service. The new administrative elite, unlike the old Boma class, have been reluctant to make long-term investments in nonmovable enterprises. They tend to live as nuclear families in enclaves of government housing rather than surrounded by extended kin in large villages of their own construction. Although they may seek to build up a network of supporters within the administration, they rarely seek to become *akwakwashi*, headmen, or chiefs to the local people. They show little interest in building up clientage through providing bridewealth, mastering ritual specialties, or contributing to local ceremonial life. Some may dabble in local trade to augment their earnings, but the major focus of their investment is usually elsewhere. Financial irregularities, including embezzlements, continue unabated in the new administrative order. Today, however, the money is far less likely to remain in Mwinilunga, far less likely to be invested in augmenting local productive capacity. A few exceptional Lunda have managed to work their way up the administrative ladder, and a few have excelled in electoral politics. But the pipeline that once ran directly from mission schools to Boma or town jobs has long disappeared.

Today, the Brethren continue to support Sakeji school, which remains one of the better primary schools in the district. The Catholics, however, closed their premier school, St. Kizito, in the late 1970s in a dispute with the government over curricular requirements. All the other former mission schools in Mwinilunga are now under direct government management. In many respects, the great age of missionary expansion and experimentation is over. The smaller European mission stations have been closed. The spiritual needs of small village congregations are generally attended to by African lay religious leaders, visited and assisted periodically by European missionaries. The larger mission stations have settled on their particular economic specialties, such as farming, ranching, trading, or transport, and generally direct their profits toward maintaining mission-run hospitals and clinics. The first generation of missionaries was quite successful in recruiting other expatriates to join them in the field. The current generation, however, is aging rapidly, and few replacements from overseas are in sight. The missionaries, now more than ever, seem determined to generate an African clergy capable of maintaining the numerous churches that have been built up over the years. Mission stations continue to hire a wide range of skilled and casual labor, but new options are opening for those willing to undergo formal ecumenical training. With declining Boma and urban-based opportunities, missions loom larger than ever in the economic strategies of many. The contemporary Lunda elite is largely a mission elite. It has matured and is perhaps more diversified and stratified now than at any time in the past. But it is still characterized by its ability to channel mission resources into the local economy and to convert mission-derived wealth into social prestige. It remains an elite connected to and created by the local poor. Its wealth might derive from the mission, but the meaning and uses of that wealth are uniquely local cultural constructions.

After independence, Native Authority chiefs became government-recognized chiefs, with only minor changes in form or function. They continue to receive salaries and the services of retainers in exchange for facilitating local compliance with national directives. Chiefs in Mwinilunga were paid an average of 20,000 kwacha per month in 1994 (roughly U.S.$30). At that time Lwawu mission paid its most casual laborers a minimum of 1,000 kwacha per day. Top-level workers received two to three times that amount. Thus, government remuneration alone is insufficient to propel chiefs to the top of the local economic hierarchy. They are forced, in most cases, to enter into various sorts of economic partnerships with mission stations in order to augment their earnings, buttress their status, and keep pace with the innovative productive activities of the mission elite. In many respects, the chiefs of Mwinilunga have become yet another stratum of the mission elite.

The nongovernmental organizations (NGOs) managing development projects in Mwinilunga, as described in chapter 2, provide another important arena for economic strategizing, with potentially profound implications for future economic stratification. The parameters of participation in these projects are still far too inchoate to allow one to draw firm analytical conclusions about long-term effects. Yet, as long as projects remain entities capable of channeling cash and commodities from the outside into this area starved for resources, projects will remain the targets of entrepreneurial impulses.

Finally, as also noted in chapter 2, "going to Cazombo" is a new economic strategy being pioneered by a younger generation of cohorts in Mwinilunga. It is a venture as risky as the civil war that spawned its development. The antigovernment military machine in eastern Angola is desperate for supplies, particularly foodstuffs. The trade-induced hungry country of the eighteenth and nineteenth centuries resurfaced as the war-ravaged hungry country of the late twentieth and early twenty-first century. Now, as then, the Lunda-Ndembu are responding with enthusiasm. Predicting the long-range outcome of this economic activity, however, is an exercise as precarious as forecasting the outcome of this decades-long civil war.

Summary

Entrepreneurship is the ability to assemble or reassemble a new kind of activity from what is available, and the ability to reinterpret the meaning of things and fit them together in new ways. This conception of entrepreneurship is not restricted to the western variety of entrepreneur, the industrial type. In non-industrial societies, trade, transport and services are important outlets for entrepreneurial responsiveness.

Seleti 1992, 150

The Central African archaeological record informs us that trade, transport, and services have long been prominent features of Lunda economic strategies. Productive individualism, constant innovation, and decentralized involvement in a multiplicity of shifting markets dominate Lunda economic history. Chiefs may have had some advantages but were seldom able to exercise total control over any facet of economic life. To a large degree, success is perceived locally as the reflection and the just dessert of individual, rather than collective, effort. Enterprises requiring the participation of numerous people are most often carried out under the sponsorship and for the ultimate benefit of particular individuals. In a way reminiscent of Calvinism, success in life is believed to signal the state of glory in which one will rest in the afterlife. Wealth equals success, however, only after it is converted into social capital. One must use wealth to become *akwakwashi*, amassing sufficient supporters and dependents to make the memory of one's existence an enduring feature of the social landscape.

For centuries the Lunda economy has been inextricably linked to long-distance trade. The commodities most responsible for the generation of local wealth, such as ivory, slaves, rubber, and food, were commodities for which the local demand was rather inelastic. Expansions and contractions in foreign markets, therefore, precipitated local ebbs and flows in the generation of wealth. Concomitantly, foreign markets provided the very commodities which served locally as symbols of wealth. Foreign cloth, beads, utensils, and a wide variety of seemingly useless trinkets were highly prized and proudly displayed symbols of wealth.

The type of entrepreneurship that most flourished among the Lunda was one aimed at pioneering new methods for accelerating extraction and production for export rather than one aimed at controlling the means by which local societies reproduced themselves. Subsistence production and residential construction remained substantially unaffected by the export sector. There has historically been a good deal of complementarity between the activities men undertake for subsistence and those aimed at securing items for export. The relationship between rich and poor was thus characterized not by great differences in consumption levels of local commodities but by differential access to imported luxury goods. Unlike today's urban-based elite, who tend to segregate themselves in affluent enclaves, the rich were not separated residentially from the poor. Quite the contrary—the rich were the focal points around which the poor gravitated and were at the very center of village life, physically and socially. They were the initiators, the officiants, and most likely the sustainers of local ceremonial life. The rich provided the stylistic identity of an area, expanding the pool of aesthetic choices available. But they needed the poor. Only the poor had the power to transform the wealthy into the socially successful and famous. Rich and poor, as well as the varying shades in between, were necessary distinctions in a single but multifaceted social construction.

The love of novelty and the drive for individual style are features rarely highlighted in the literature on Africa, where life is often said to be ruled by blind adherence to long-standing traditions. Crawford claimed to have heard the following refrain in 1889, sung by a line of caravan carriers plodding across the Central African plateau:

A well-worn trail is a very good thing
It must lead up to a very great King;
and so with customs of days of yore,
we do what millions have done before. (1912, 8)

For Crawford, the tendency of Africans to walk in straight lines, single file, carving deep but narrow paths into the terrain, was the perfect metaphor for the African worldview. Africans plod through life, he said, without thought, without imagination, fearing innovation or deviation, unnaturally adhering to narrow traditions: "The negro's way of doing a thing is merely to do it as the man who went before him did it. The slaves of precedent, they dog the steps of a thousand ancestors, and such is the tenacity of the negro type that to this day their whole outfit of the twentieth century A.D. can be found perfectly reproduced on Egyptian monuments of the same century B.C." (1912, 9).

Such a conceptualization leaves out key elements of the African personality, if one could so generalize. Clearly there exist certain traditions that could be compared to a well-worn path. But individuality and creativity can be expressed ever so well by the way one walks that path. Traditions such as the quest for dependents and patrons, the maintenance of social distance between persons differing in age and sex, the emphasis on material transactions in interpersonal relations, the functional diffuseness of authority relations, and respect for hierarchy perhaps etch deep grooves on the African psyche. But methods for influencing the outcome of life lived within these grooves are subject to stylistic variations. Hierarchies, on one level, are functional social constructs that enable deeply felt desires to be fulfilled. An individual occupying the highest position in a hierarchy is the one most likely to be remembered, at least in the short term. The longer term prospects for being remembered improve if one is capable of leaving behind a bit of oneself as a social mnemosyne. Unlike women, men are not the nodal points for reckoning descent and therefore must constantly construct new and different arenas within which to compete with one another for prominence while endeavoring to keep alive the old hierarchies. The new may even be reshaped and recast as the old. Those who reach the top and become *chimbuki* (ritual doctor), *mbimbi* (head circumciser), or *katepa* (diviner) leave behind knowledge. Those who continue to live with and benefit from that knowledge are likely to remember their benefactors for some time. Those who become chiefs and headmen leave behind their names, perhaps on the village itself or the surrounding landscape. Those who reach the top of the wealth hierarchy are able to help the most people and will be long remembered as *akwakwashi*. Reaching the top of a hierarchy is, thus, the well-trodden path. Individuality is expressed through the selection of the particular hierarchy within which one feels most capable of succeeding, the manner in which one strives to reach the top, or the construction of a new hierarchy.

Most of the ways of obtaining wealth require the bold use of youthful energy. Slaving, ivory collecting, rubber gathering, surplus cassava production, and now, going to Cazombo, are all activities best pursued by the young. The positions obtained from succeeding in such activities are difficult to transmit through time. The wealth acquired has a temporary quality. Second-hand luxury items have no power. Imported goods are symbols of connectedness to a larger or different world. The power of these symbols lies in their acquisition. It is the demonstrated ability to acquire the object, to have access to the new and different, to establish powerful connections that evokes respect and prestige. To simply inherit items upon the death of another merits little respect. Such items might become the source of envy, but never of power. This feature places limitations on the ability to transmit status intergenerationally. High status must be individually acquired through deeds, which constrains the formation of enduring classes in the traditional world. Each generation must work out its own game, devise its own rules, and produce its own hierarchy, embellished with its own style.

Chapter Seven

Us and Them

We Are All Lunda Now!
August 1986

An extraordinary meeting was held at Chief Kanongesha's capital village toward the end of the dry season of 1986. The meeting was called *Musolu Ndeki da Lunda*. The term *musolu* generally refers to a special, sacred place in the bush where invocations or prayers are made to the High God Nzambi for rain, success in hunting, guidance, or assistance in matters directly affecting all Lunda-Ndembu. *Ndeki* in contemporary parlance most commonly refers to airplanes. Debates raged, however, over the prior meaning(s) of *ndeki* in the context of a traditional *musolu*. Some insisted that *ndeki* meant anything that was "of" the people, yet rose "above" the people. Unifying beliefs that all look up to were, thus, said to be an intrinsic part of the meaning of *ndeki*. Others insisted that the term *ndeki* was more properly glossed as "modern thing," the most recent, the most sensational. *Musolu ndeki* was said to be a transformative event that moves the people onward and upward. Nevertheless, all agreed that the event taking place was an extraordinary convocation of all the Lunda-Ndembu chiefs in Zambia. It was said that such grand meetings used to be annual affairs in the old days. One had not been held, however, since the death of Chief Kanongesha Mulumbi in 1939. The meeting was billed as a return to tradition—a redefining, reaffirming intensification of what it meant to be Lunda-Ndembu. Chief Kanongesha's *kapasu* (messengers) spent weeks walking the length and breadth of Lunda-Ndembu territory, spreading word of the upcoming meeting. Preparations were in full swing several months in advance of the announced date. Men were called upon to donate materials and labor for the construction of temporary shelters to house the hundreds of headmen who would accompany their chiefs to the meeting. Women were called upon to pound and store extra cassava flour to feed the guests. Prosperous individuals were asked to make donations of meat and beer. There was a great deal of excitement in the air as village people sat around their fires, night after night, discussing what would happen when all the chiefs met and what would be discussed, enacted, or enabled at the meeting. The majority of the population had not even been born when the last *musolu* was held. Elderly people, thus, suddenly became extremely popular as everyone yearned for information concerning the format and outcome of past meetings of the chiefs. Intimate details about the personalities and life histories of contemporary chiefs were exhaustively discussed, compared, and contrasted with those of famous Lunda chiefs of the past. All across Lunda territory, old men and women were retelling, reconstructing, and repositioning the oral histories of individual lineages, their connections with the Kanongeshaship, and thus their positions within the wider Lunda-Ndembu sociopolitical matrix. And for the first time in a long while, youths were listening intently to the elders, filling in the gaps in their fragmented knowledge of local history, and debating among themselves the meaning and significance of it all.

Early morning on the opening day of the *musolu* found approximately five hundred men from all over the territory seated in the courtyard at the Kanongesha's capital, anxiously awaiting the start of what promised to be a historic meeting. Approximately a hundred women were present, seated in small groups a short distance away from the men. While all were waiting for the chiefs to make their appearance, the senior assistant of Chief Kanongesha stood before the masses and announced in a hyper-formalistic speech that the purpose of the meeting was to discuss Lunda traditions and, thus, it was expected that everyone would behave in accordance with said traditions while attending the meeting. The speaker then reminded the crowd that Lunda tradition held that no person was allowed to sit in a chair in the presence of a chief. The chairs were collected and taken away, and grass mats were brought out from nearby houses. Much discussion ensued concerning which individuals should receive mats. A crude hierarchy had to be worked out in order to determine who were the most senior headmen from each area of the polity. After each senior headman had received his mat, it was then his task to decide which dozen or so individuals from his area held the highest rank and thus merited seats on his mat. After two hours of grumbling, gesticulating, arranging, and rearranging, during which the crowd had to be reminded several times that arguing in the presence of chiefs was also forbidden, a crude hierarchy of the chiefdom was finally worked out and made visible for all to see in the seating arrangement. The women, only slightly less noisy than the men, had likewise arranged their own hierarchical alignment. Approximately two-thirds of the people present were left to sit on the bare earth. Many complained loudly; a few stormed off angrily. When calm prevailed, seven royal stools were brought out and placed on animal skins. One straight-backed chair was brought out as well. The largest stool, placed on a leopard skin, was for the Kanongesha. The people then rose to their feet and clapped in rhythmical fashion as seven chiefs in full regalia and the district executive secretary (DES) of the ruling political party paraded in and took their seats; the straight-backed chair was for the DES. Two of the chiefs, the Ntambu and the Mukang'ala, were considered by the Lunda to be the equals of the Kanongesha's four subchiefs, the Ikelenge, the Mwiniyilamba, the Nyakaseya, and the Chibwika. They had not been recognized, however, as Native Authority chiefs by the British administration during the colonial period, nor were they now officially recognized as chiefs by the independent government. The DES, a non-Lunda, officially opened the meeting by speaking at length about how the party had taken power from the British and given it back to the chiefs. He expressed the party's faith in the ability of chiefs to rule and exhorted those present to obey and cooperate with their chiefs. He talked of the urgent need for Zambian peoples to return to and strengthen their traditional beliefs in order to counteract the destructive effects of colonial ideas. The speech was followed by polite but less than enthusiastic applause. One individual, an in-law of the Kanongesha, quickly rose and asked the DES why, if the chiefs did indeed have power, it had been necessary for them to gain permission from the party and its government before the *musolu* could be held. The DES, noticeably embarrassed by the question, denied that permission, per se, had been necessary. He stated that he had merely intervened to coordinate the meeting date with a time when government vehicles would be available to transport the chiefs. After all, he noted, only one Lunda chief had his own vehicle. The DES then nervously apologized to the crowd for scheduling problems that would prevent him from remaining at the meeting any longer and said that he needed to return immediately to the Boma. The crowd remained silent until his motorcade sped away up the dusty road. Then, seemingly spontaneously, they began to roar, over and over, in unison, "*Ejima wetu waLunda hohu*" ("We are all Lunda now!")

Primordialism, Instrumentalism, and Constructionism

Who are these people who felt so compelled to shout out their shared sense of "usness" to the swirling clouds of dust that August morning? As individuals they were each encased in multiple levels of "usness": nuclear family, village, village cluster, district, chiefdom, nation, humanity. The form of "usness" salient at any particular moment depends largely on the objective of the moment. Feelings of "usness," in fact, reflect and are constructed in tandem with equally heartfelt notions of "otherness." What were the objectives relevant to that historical moment and what was the place of the "other" within those objectives that informed and made meaningful the above events?

This chapter focuses not so much on individual constructions of self within the group as on notions of "groupness" as constructed by collections of individuals. Who are the Lunda-Ndembu, or, as they are more commonly known today, the Kanongesha Lunda? How did they come to be what they are? What does it mean to be Lunda-Ndembu? Such questions nest more or less within wider discussions of ethnicity in Africa. They are questions which have stimulated four decades of anthropological research, have spawned powerful yet competing paradigms, and have, at times, provoked much heat and animosity.

The relation of ethnic identity to the twin processes of migration and urbanization in Central Africa has been popularized especially by the works of A. L. Epstein, J. C. Mitchell, and others of the Rhodes-Livingstone Institute. Mitchell, particularly in *African Urbanization in Ndola and Luanshya* (1954), and Epstein, in *Politics in an Urban African Community* (1958), gave disproportionate weight to urban dynamics in the formation of social identity. In short, they argued that in the congested confines of the newly emerging urban world of Africa, disparate groups became intimately familiar, often for the first time, with the cultural differences which set them apart from one another. They often exaggerated, amplified, reified, and seized upon those differences as unifying agents in the intense urban competitions for jobs and residential space. Newly created stereotypes were then exported back to the rural areas where they were further elaborated, thereby establishing the ethnoregional character of the struggle for place within the colonial world. Since the 1960s, several dozen theses have been written on the subject of ethnicity in Zambia (see Mwanza 1990). While many acknowledge the value of earlier studies in highlighting the power of colonial economic forces to produce ethnic stereotypes, many also note the inability of such studies to explain either the origins or reasons for persistence of identities based on ethnicity. The contours of the anthropological discussion of ethnicity in Africa have become more sharply focused of late. The concepts of primordialism, instrumentalism, and constructionism make up the dominant framework within which current investigations of ethnicity are most often situated. At the risk of oversimplifying, let me briefly review these three positions.[1]

Primordialists can be said to view ethnicity as a set of long-shared values through which people conceptualize their world and give meaning to their place within it. They see ethnicity as an innate part of the human condition, a naturally occurring phenomenon requiring little in the way of sophisticated explanation. The heightened sense of ethnicity that swept through twentieth-century Africa was a direct response to the disruptive events of the eighteenth and nineteenth centuries. Africa was, in a sense, psychologically traumatized; it was socially, economically, and politically dismembered with overwhelming brutality. Africans' invocations of a golden age, a lost past of firm values, are attempts to counteract social fragmentation and to regain psychological security through the reestablishment of cultural integrity. Appeals stated in terms of common language, religion, history, and heroes emphasize, naturalize, and give power to supposedly primordial attachments.

The quintessence of the second approach, the instrumentalist view of ethnicity, can be seen in Abner Cohen's *Custom and Politics in Urban Africa: A Study of Hausa Migrants in Yoruba Towns* (1969). Ethnic attachment is viewed as a resource that is rationally chosen in order to pursue or defend individual and group interests. Cohen describes how the Hausa in Yoruba towns enhanced and intensified their "Hausa-ness" as a functional device to maintain control over the lucrative long-distance trade in kola and cattle. They adopted the strict tenets of the Tijaniyya Muslim sect in order to more clearly distinguish themselves from their Yoruba hosts, and they gave added powers to their Malams (Muslim priests) to impose sanctions on individual behavior, thereby strengthening social cohesion and the capacity to act as a unified body. Ethnicity, Cohen would argue, is more an economic and political phenomenon than a cultural one. The process of ethnic intensification in postindependence Africa is not simply a revival of old customs. Rather, as the Hausa case shows, old values are given new social significance in the context of changing political and economic structures of opportunity. Ethnic groups are essentially interest groups, competing for social resources along ethnically constituted lines.

The constructionists approach, by contrast, tends to view ethnicity as something actively formed and fashioned by social actors rather than something that simply arises through the instrumental selection of momentarily useful elements from a primordial assemblage of shared cultural material. Ethnicity is constructed through a process in which people comprehend the differential distribution of social and material resources and attempt to exercise power by virtue of group affiliation. Ethnicity is, thus, a historical force embedded in social relations, an opposition marker that explains and manages asymmetrical power relations in terms of "us" versus "them."

It would be unfair, perhaps, to accuse instrumentalists of analyzing ethnicity in a historical vacuum. Cohen, for example, provides a good deal of historical background in his investigation of Hausa identity. Yet, the specific components of ethnicity in his account appear rather atemporal; they already exist before anyone selects them. Cohen does not propose a mechanism by which shared cultural material is kept ready and available for situational use. Constructionists such as Leroy Vail and Jean Comaroff, however, assert the pivotal role of social actors in creating ethnic sentiments (see esp. Comaroff 1985). "Culture brokers" or "culture entrepreneurs" are necessary for forging the symbolic links between past and present, for interpreting current needs in terms of previous associations, and for legitimizing contemporary modes of collective action as natural extensions of ancient practices.

Debates about the relative explanatory force of primordialism versus instrumentalism versus constructionism may continue for some time. I agree with Keyes (1981), however, that a useful theory of ethnicity must consider the strategic uses as well as the cultural formulations of ethnic identity. Likewise, I believe that Vail is correct in arguing that ethnicity is protean, with different appeals on different levels and in different situations. No one explanation suffices to explain it wholly and in every instance. Yet, Vail's own treatment of the primordialist and instrumentalist approaches combined with his positioning of the constructionist perspective suggest a new synthesis. Rather than delineating the three as competing approaches, we might perhaps best view them as simply addressing different levels or explaining different aspects of the broad phenomenon of ethnicity. Collectively, the three constitute, in a sense, the what, why, and how of ethnicity. Primordialism focuses primarily on "what" ethnicity is. It is naturalizing a social unit by endowing it with the legitimizing aura of longevity, the sanctity of age. Assertions of shared etiological myths and common language, religion, and historical experiences are its standard stock in trade. Instrumentalism, in turn, focuses on the "why" of ethnicity—demonstrating its usefulness in compelling, justifying, and understanding collective action under historically specific conditions. Constructionism can be said to deal with the "how" of ethnicity because it explores when and under what circumstances certain social actors are both motivated and able to impress upon a group of people an ethnic interpretation of extant social processes. This expanded thesis will serve as the framework for a historical overview of the shifting meaning of ethnicity among the Lunda-Ndembu.

Instrumental Constructions of Primordial Connections

The earliest explorers who mentioned the people living along the upper Zambezi referred to them collectively as the Ngangela (or Ganguela) (Silva Porto 1885). It was said to be a widely used term, probably of Ovimbundu origin, that simply meant "easterners"; those who lived on the escarpments east of the Congo divide. The so-called Ngangela lived in rather small autonomous polities, some no more than a few large villages. The groups were differentiated more by their habitats or adaptations to the environment, such as plateau versus valley dwellers or cultivators versus hunters and fishers, than by other cultural features. The mutual intelligibility of languages diminished gradually as one moved across the landscape, giving each group a large linguistic area within which it could comfortably operate. For some time after the emergence of the highly centralized Lunda polity to the north, those along the Zambezi to the south continued to identity themselves to outsiders either by lineage names or by referents to geographic markers. The first reference for dating the development of the Kanongesha polity is contained in the journal kept by Correia Letão in 1756 (Dias 1938). He mentions the death of the Lunda emperor, Mwantiyanvwa Mukanza, the previous year in a conflict with the Amalas. According to the oral traditions of numerous peoples along the upper Zambezi and the Luapula, the Kanongesha and others departed the central Lunda capital during the reign of Mukanza. The weight of evidence suggests that the Kanongesha polity was established around 1740, or shortly thereafter (Schecter 1976, chapt. 4). The polity was well ensconced by the early 1800s, as indicated by Burton: "On his journey from Angola to Mocambique, [the trader] Baptista reported meeting a party not far due south of Musumba (the Lunda capital) carrying tribute from Canonguesa (Kanongesha) to the Mwaant Yaav. This was in 1806" (1873, 170).

As noted earlier, the development of the Kanongesha polity on the upper Zambezi was but one facet of the strategic repositioning sweeping through all of Central Africa. The upsurge in long-distance trade during the eighteenth century precipitated a complete reformulation of the political map of Central Africa. Small groups developed linkages and alliances, often under the forceful hand of new power brokers, in an attempt to maximize trade opportunities by establishing monopolies over large territories and the marketable resources contained therein. Larger units were clearly seen as more effective at influencing the terms of trade. New names emerged as the identity markers for more or less inclusive units of people with shared relations to productive and mercantile processes. To be a Kanongesha Lunda meant that one accepted the Kanongesha as one's overlord, one had productive rights within his territory, one was entitled to protection from the encroachment of "others," and one acknowledged one's responsibility for helping to protect or even expand the polity. It also meant that one was most likely a producer of cassava for the caravan market at Nana Candundo, one acknowledged *mukanda* or *nkanga* as the only acceptable mark of maturity, and one shared in a lineage history that through either migration or marriage linked one with the Kanongesha's tradition.

The Kanongesha oral tradition consists primarily of genealogies that include praise names and descriptive narratives. Robert Schecter, who has spent more time than any other researcher collecting the numerous variants of this tradition, observes that "the genealogy operates as a framework and repository for especially important precedents, an outline of past personal and intergroup relations which can be cited in present day situations" (1976, 10). The Kanongesha oral tradition gives the polity its overarching structure, its dominant symbols of unity and integrity. It provides the mnemonic devices and the historical motifs used in justifying the polity's claim to longevity and stability. It naturalizes the existential status of the polity.

The Kanongesha's assertion of seniority rests on two features: the title's original link to the central Lunda Empire, and the claim of having legitimately defeated and subsumed the original inhabitants of the area, the Mbwela. The legitimacy of subordinate titles is contingent upon their connections to the same processes. Titleholders' power flows to them solely through the Kanongesha. The history told by each segment of the polity begins, therefore, with the same narrative, outlining the origins of the senior title before moving on to establish its own particular links. Local histories are political texts that serve to support declarations of political status within the wider polity. For this reason, each lineage has some incentive for keeping alive its own segment, its own version of the oral tradition. Some titleholders have special reason to remember the widest range of genealogical connections: the Kasungami, the deputy who must perform the duties of the titleholder when the latter is absent or ill; the Mulopu, the designated but by no means certain heir; and the Mwambayilunga, the one who presides over the often extended interregnal period. Other lineage-owned titles acknowledge especially close association with the Kanongesha: Kambanji, the war leader; Kalula, the royal councillor; Chivwikankanu, the ritual installer; Kanampumba, the head of court; and so forth. Yet, there are no trained historians among the Lunda-Ndembu. There are no individuals whose specific social function is to learn about the past and then hold that knowledge ready for others to use, no perpetually inherited grave-keepers, professional court orators, minstrels, or griots. Oral traditions may, in fact, remain silent and submerged for years under the sea of activities that constitute day-to-day life. Yet these traditions rise to the fore during the period between the death of a titleholder and the installation of his successor. Elders of the relevant groups meet to discuss potential heirs, genealogical connections, and historical precedents, in an atmosphere often filled with contention and contestation. The process may drag on for years before any semblance of consensus or compromise is reached.

Below are five synthetic accounts of local oral traditions that illustrate widely acknowledged stages of historical development. Variants of the first four form part of nearly every lineage history among the Kanongesha Lunda. The fifth is uniquely associated with the senior headman, the Chifunga. The oral traditions of other senior headmen also tell of significant connections with the Kanongesha, and those of lineage heads link them with particular senior headmen. And so it goes: from chiefs to subchiefs to senior headmen to headmen to individual members, a group called the Kanongesha Lunda asserts and justifies its existence through myths of primordial attachments.

As Schecter noted, published oral traditions from people throughout Central Africa share with the Kanongesha texts the claim of Lunda origins, expressed with many of the same themes, episodes, characters, and locales. These traditions are not identical in every respect. However, the peculiar way in which each of the accounts deals with the common body of data (stages one to three) to spin a virtually seamless web of concordance strongly suggests that each version of the tale alludes to the same realities. The testimony of each tradition projects a more or less different point of view. These neither contradict, nor absolutely mirror, but complement one another. Each provides some evidence which fills in the gaps or clarifies the allusions in others (Schecter 1976, 83).

The accounts are told here in rather minimalist form simply to establish some of the themes that are still drawn upon to construct primordial connections between individuals and groups who identify themselves as Lunda-Ndembu. Schecter presents more multifaceted and problematized accounts of the Kanongesha oral tradition in "History and Historiography on a Frontier of Lunda Expansion" (1976).

Stage One: Creation

In the beginning Nzambi (God) created Samuntu and Nyamuntu. They were two identical sexless beings living identical lives, but having little contact with one another. One day Samuntu made the long, arduous trek to the place in the deep forest where Nzambi dwelled. He asked Nzambi, "Why have you made two of us? We have nothing to do with one another." Nzambi, after some thought, handed Samuntu two sex organs, instructing him to choose one for himself and to carry the other back to Nyamuntu. Samuntu was perplexed by the instructions. He could not imagine the purpose of the two organs, or how they might serve as the answer to his question. Nevertheless, he eventually selected the long protruding member, attached it between his legs, and began the journey home. After walking for several days in the hot sun, Samuntu noticed that the organ he was carrying for Nyamuntu had begun to smell. He discarded it in the fork of a tree. Upon Samuntu's return Nyamuntu saw his new appendage. She went to visit Nzambi herself and asked why she had not also received one. Nzambi informed her of the instructions he had given Samuntu, but he gave her another organ. Upon Nyamuntu's return, Samuntu saw her new organ. His own began to swell. He now understood its purpose. But Nyamuntu was angry and refused to have anything to do with him. Samuntu returned to Nzambi. He begged for forgiveness and for help. After scolding Samuntu for his original disobedience, Nzambi gave him a fox and a plan. Late one night, Samuntu released the fox. It entered Nyamuntu's house and growled. She ran terrified to Samuntu's house. That night they slept together. The next morning, fearing the fox might return, Nyamuntu asked if she might stay with Samuntu again the following night. She promised to prepare food for him in exchange.

Stage Two: The Tower of Kaposhi

Samuntu and Nyamuntu had many children. Generations passed, and the land was filled with people. Everyone in the world lived in a single kingdom in those days, and their king, the Mwantiyanvwa, was thus the most powerful individual on earth. Possessing all the riches of the land, he sought to gain, as well, the richest jewel of the heavens, the moon. He ordered the construction of a tower tall enough to enable him to pluck the pearly orb from the sky. All the people on earth were set to work building the tower of Kaposhi. They toiled day and night, nonstop, for many years, and a tower of bamboo rose ever closer to the moon. As the tower neared completion, termites weakened the bottom poles and it fell over. People working near the top fell to their deaths. But others were flung far and wide about the earth. They landed dazed and confused, speaking different languages in accordance with how far they had fallen. Thus, they became the Lunda, Bemba, Lwena, Chokwe, Mbunda, Luchazi, and so forth. It was the Mbwela who landed on the upper Zambezi.

Stage Three: The Early Lunda

Many generations after Kaposhi, Iyala Mwaku Nkondi was chief of the Bungos at Musumba. He lived with his wife, Mumbanda Nkondi, two sons, Chinguli and Chinyama, and one daughter, Lueji. One day Iyala Mwaku was making a mat in the courtyard. He was softening the reeds with water from a calabash. His two sons observed his actions, and, believing that he was using beer instead of water, became infuriated and beat him for his supposed stupidity. Lueji, the daughter, came to her father's rescue and treated his wounds. Iyala Mwaku cursed his two sons and declared that upon his death Lueji would succeed him as chief. And so it came to pass. The two brothers rejected the decision, mobilized their followers, and fought a long war with Lueji. She managed to fight them to a standstill and ultimately drove them to the margins of her kingdom.

One day Lueji's servants found a weary Luba hunter collapsed at the royal well. Lueji took him in, and the handsome hunter, Chibinda Ilunga, rapidly regained his health. Lueji married him. The next month, when her menstrual period began, she gave the *lukanu* (a bracelet that served as the highest symbol of her authority) to her new husband for safekeeping. Lueji's children were appalled when they discovered the Luba hunter wearing the *lukanu*. But Lueji demanded that they respect Chibinda as if he were their father. Some of the children, including the Kanongesha, left Musumba and moved south to Katukangonyi. Kazembe was the leader there until one day he cooked food and put the hands of a person who had tried to commit adultery with his wife at the bottom of the pot. When it was discovered, the others became disgusted and left him. Each came to the area that they now control.

Stage Four: The Kanongesha

The Kanongesha and his followers from twelve royal lineages came to the upper Zambezi after a sojourn on the Ndembu stream. On the Zambezi they discovered the Mbwela, who were as numerous as termites. The Mbwela had no proper villages; they simply moved from place to place in the forest. They had no proper chiefs and paid no tribute to anyone. They had no proper manners, but ate like animals. After a long series of battles, the Kanongesha succeeded in defeating the Mbwela. He made the highest among them his ritual installer and gave him the title of Chivwikankanu. He married one woman from each of the Mbwela lineages and taught all of the Mbwela how to live properly, how to give tribute to chiefs, how to be Lunda. And so we are all Lunda now.

Stage Five: The Chifunga Tradition

The Kanongesha had been fighting the Mbwela for fifty years. Things were not going well. He would no sooner scatter the Mbwela like termites than they would regroup and attack from another direction. Their superior knowledge of the terrain and their skill at surviving in the forest made them formidable opponents. They were a small but hardy people, with inexhaustible stamina. They could hide in the smallest of places and attack without warning at any moment. The Kanongesha's men were hungry, tired, and discouraged. The Kanongesha sent word back to Musumba, begging for Ipepa to assist him in the battle. Ipepa was one who had power. After Ipepa joined the Kanongesha, things began to change. When the men were hungry, Ipepa would plant a single seed in the ground and immediately a tree would sprout with ripe, delectable fruit to eat. When they encountered a large river, Ipepa would wave his cane and the river would part. At night he could become invisible, sneak into the enemy's camp, and steal all their weapons. At other times he would hurl such terrifying images into the minds of the Mbwela that they would drop their weapons and run in fright. After the Mbwela surrendered, Ipepa was given the sister of the Kanongesha as his wife, a large territory of his own, and the title of Chifunga. And, thus, the Kanongesha and the Chifunga are *ishaku* (in-laws).

Making Meaning

The stage one tradition has much in common with tales of origin told elsewhere in Africa. A High God creates the earth and the first couple. The original state of existence, however, is modified in some way with input from the first humans. In the Lunda version, the original couple is genderless, performing identical tasks. Samuntu's pondering which sex to select represents something of the degree of arbitrariness in the original division by gender. The tale is rich in material for fireside musing. One can interpret its meaning about the basic nature of males and females in various ways. For example, are males inherently selfish creatures whose primary interest in females is sexual? In giving Samuntu the fox, did Nzambi ordain a special covenant between males and the forest domain? Did females seal their own destiny by offering to prepare food in return for male protection? Why was Samuntu, rather than Nyamuntu, the first to express dissatisfaction with the human lot? Why did he leave Nyamuntu's organ in the fork of a tree? The elements of the tale may be akin to a canon, but rather than being a canon beyond dispute, it is a canon specifically for dispute. To be Lunda is to accept this particular canon rather than any other as the framework for debate, as the assemblage of social artifacts out of which meaning should be constructed.

The stage two tradition begins by asserting the original unity of all humankind, divided only by gender, and ends with the development of distinct ethnic groups. Its similarity to the Tower of Babel myth in Christianity has been duly noted in the literature. The theme of the smallest of God's creations foiling the plans of the mightiest also has universal resonance. The earliest versions tend to list only Central African peoples such as Lunda, Luvale, Chokwe, and Bemba as having been spawned by the events at Kaposhi, but later versions include the Nyamwezi, Zulu, Ngoni, and others. As Schecter notes, the continual incorporation of new peoples into the original tale illustrates the propensity to bring history up to date so that it conforms to current perceptions of the order of things. The most recently collected versions of the Kaposhi tale even include Europeans, with the commentary that they were the people highest up on the tower who managed to survive. They fell so far, hitting the ground with such an impact, that they lost their color. Their language and customs are, correspondingly, the strangest. At a certain level Europeans can be said to represent the farthest point on a scale of closeness according to which Kaposhi is the central starting point for reckoning connections. Nearness to the beginning of things is said to confer its own form of power. Yet, there is still debate among the Lunda over why those who happened to be working higher up on the tower should now be considered less closely related to those who were working lower down and so fell closer to the original home of humankind.

The stage three tradition marks the beginning of a distinct Lunda history. The universal Samuntu and Nyamuntu of stage one, whose names quite literally mean Mr. and Mrs. Person (*sa* or *nya* + *muntu*), have now become a particular Iyala and Mumbanda (man and woman) of a particular lineage (Nkondi). The Kanongesha people refer to themselves as Eni Kondi, the family of Nkondi, a narrower grouping than that of the people spawned at Kaposhi. We also find the beginning of the Central African tradition of powerful female chiefs whose reigns often brought major transformative moments in the history of their people. Under the reign of Lueji the Lunda were confronted with an intrusive element from their neighbors to the east, the Luba. New titles and new forms of social organization arrived with Chibinda Ilunga. It is unclear whether Luba influence was invited or imposed. Nevertheless, that influence in some way precipitated Lunda expansion on the southern frontier under the leadership of Kazembe Mutanda. At some point the behavior of that leader, remembered as his cannibalism of a rival, led to his loss of rank. A constellation of Lundaized polities developed, all of which stand in perpetual relation to one another as "brothers." They included, at minimum, Kanongesha and Ishindi to the south, Musokantanda to the east, Kazembe Mutanda to the north, and Kazembe Luapula far to the east. Some traditions tell of the development of other Lundaized polities whom the Kanongesha Lunda recognize as joking cousins, principally the Luvale, Kaonde, and Chokwe.

The stage four tradition deals specifically with the development of the

Kanongesha polity on the Zambezi. Here we note that conquest was legitimized by the giving and accepting of titles which served to link the indigenous Mbwela to the Kanongesha, and through him to the central Lunda polity itself. The fundamental genealogical nature of the Kanongesha tradition—positional succession and perpetual kinship—casts political relationships between groups of people in terms of biological links between titled personalities in a number of descendant and parallel lines. This creative manipulation of a system of ritual and administrative titles, developed earlier in the Lunda Center, has long been acknowledged as the signal feature in the development of the Lunda diaspora.

The stage five tradition is a somewhat typical senior headman tale. When retold in a formal context it would be prefaced with its own version of stages one through four. But the teller would expand in unique ways the Kanongesha tradition of each stage and would insert the founding ancestor of that lineage at the center of some important historical development. In the case of the Chifunga tradition, the founding ancestor is said to actually surpass in importance the founding ancestors of those currently acknowledged as the Kanongesha's subchiefs. More elaborate versions of the Chifunga tradition address the role of colonialism in redefining relationships within the Kanongesha polity. The border established between Portuguese Angola and British Northern Rhodesia in 1906 bisected the territory of the Kanongesha, running right through the middle of the Chifunga's territory. People on each side of the line had their own Kanongesha, who received recognition from each colonial power as the senior traditional authority of the Lunda-Ndembu within its borders. The Chifunga, however, was viewed by both the Portuguese and the British as a rather insignificant village chief, quite peripheral to the mainstream of events in Lundaland. When the Chifunga and his supporters finally moved fully within the borders of Northern Rhodesia in the 1930s, it was too late for him to receive a Native Authority position. The Native Authority Ordinance of 1929 had frozen in place a system of chiefs and subchiefs that remains in force to this day. Although the Chifunga formally acknowledged the Kanongesha residing in Northern Rhodesia as sole legitimate heir to the Lueji tradition and in return received validation as the sole legitimate heir to the Ipepa/Chifunga tradition, there was little else that could be done. The Chifunga is treated locally with the respect of a chief, but the title has never been granted nationwide recognition. Numerous other senior headmen make similar claims.

Oral traditions cast the history of Central Africa in terms of changing relationships between groups of people. They say little about the changing relationship between people and environment, and they say even less about the dynamic interaction between trade and social usages of the environment. The debate over the numbers of people who moved about during the expansion of the Lunda Empire in the seventeenth and eighteenth centuries is inconsequential to the more certain reality of Lunda titles moving across the landscape, in tandem with changing notions of "usness" and "otherness." A set of "brother" polities developed that had brotherly squabbles and fought the occasional war but for the most part recognized each other's borders and got on with the business of constructing new identities within those boundaries.

A broadly utilized Central African style developed: find or create an "other" to conquer, develop new social linkages by awarding titles to preexisting social units in exchange for tribute and recognition of suzerainty, and consecrate the whole with a grand unifying etiological tale that grows more sacred with the passage of time.

What accounts for the value of a prestigious title? What was the value of being connected with the Lunda Empire? Why, furthermore, did this phenomenon of polity formation through dispensation of titles occur only during certain periods? Some evidence suggests that the Lundaization of Central Africa took place in energetic bursts rather than through gradual accretion. The first Lunda diaspora was perhaps forged during the seventeenth century, most notably by Lueji's so-called brothers Chinguli and Chinyama, who developed the respective polities of the Imbangala and the Lwena (Luvale). They attempted to control the early pipeline of goods to Musumba, the central Lunda capital. Yet, we also know that at least two others from the central Lunda Empire, Saluseki and Dyulu in particular, further Lundaized the south during this same period. The development of another Lunda diaspora occurred in the early eighteenth century, when Kazembe Mutanda, Kanongesha, Ishindi, Musokantanda, Luapula Kazembe, and perhaps others forged polities among groups of peoples variously called Mbwela, Ndembu, Kosa, Sanga, Humbu, and so forth. Although the Kanongesha and his "brothers" were at least several generations removed from the earlier Lunda initiatives to the south, they were in some sense a part of it. These polities played a key role in developing the enormous breadbasket needed to provision the caravans that were to crisscross the Central African plateau. Differential relations to the increase in long-distance trade and expanded production became increasingly important components in the new identities being constructed.

The role of military initiatives cannot be minimized. A join-us-or-fight ethos prevailed. Titles were an alternative to war, or, in case of war, part of the peace treaty. The use of entitlement to effect political integration found special expression in early Kanongesha-Mbwela relations on the Zambezi. The Mbwela were recognized as necessary participants in rituals designed to ensure the fertility of the land. They were formally acknowledged as conduits best able to mediate between the living and the spirits of ancestors residing on the land. Yet over time, the spirits of those reckoned as Kanongesha Lunda would so populate the landscape that the Mbwela's original status as "owners of the land" or "first citizens" came to be de-emphasized. References to them in the oral tradition often consist of just a few formulaic comments about their crudeness and the noble effort of the Lunda to domesticate or civilize them. There is little inclination to elaborate on their pre-Kanongesha existence.

The element of style, indeed, the power of style should not be overshadowed by tales of military thrusts and parries or of strategic and technological improvements in the capacity to wage war. The "brother" polities of the Lunda diaspora experienced parallel dynamics that produced outcomes remarkably similar to those that emerged under the Kanongesha. For a thousand miles on the Central African plateau one finds striking parallels in social forms, symbolic expressions, and justifying traditions. The ritual installers of the Musokantanda and of the Luapula Kazembe, for example, have for long been considered the lineal descendants of the pre-Lunda inhabitants, just as the Kanongesha's own Chivwikankanu is of Mbwela origins. *Mukanda* and *nkanga*, the major ceremonies of maturity, are put forward as ethnic identity markers throughout the region. There are similarities in the physical arrangement and collegial responsibilities of many of the titleholders resident at widely separated Lunda capitals. Most capitals are laid out in an anthropomorphic shape. The king constructs his residential cluster in the heart, the middle of the capital; a favorite set of relatives, known as *mesu* (eyes), build in the very front; military personnel build at the rear; and councillors build in what are called the right and left arms of the capital.

According to Schecter, of all the diaspora polities, the Kazembe Luapula polity was best able to replicate the central polity in density of population and complexity of titled positions:

The Kazembe had a capital of thousands during some periods, among whom resided for greater or lesser intervals the most important officials of the kingdom. . . . Compared to the Central Lunda and Kazembe kingdoms, the Kanongesha polity, save perhaps during the formative era, never seems to have functioned as a state at all, even though the structure implied by the Lunda-styled title system might have suggested otherwise. The titled lineage heads immediately subordinate to the Kanongesha did not live at the capital. And there is no evidence that they even visited it frequently. Thus, they did not form permanent councils, although it is said that they often and even regularly sent youthful representatives to perform on a day to day basis the functions which their titles implied. (1976, 213–15)

It was said that the Kanongesha did not dismiss titleholders. Each managed his own affairs, and successions and funeral rites for the Kanongesha were virtually the only occasions for them to come together formally. The Kanongesha did not so much rule through his great titleholders as exercise influence through them. He was the primus inter pares in a largely ritual kingdom made up of otherwise independent lineages. The relation of the Kanongesha to most of his subjects was "father" to "child," in contrast to the greater diversity of relationships found at the Lunda Center and among the Luapula Lunda. This difference owed much to the disparate environments within which the polities were situated. Because the Kanongesha adopted cassava production rather than relying on the grain production and fishing that sustained the Lunda Center and the Luapula, the Kanongesha's area has always been less densely populated. Fewer political positions were needed, particularly within any confined area. Although the absolute number of title holders was smaller, the Kanongesha did manage to dispense virtually the entire range of titles that were present at both the Lunda Center and the Luapula capital. And the holders of those titles stood in identical kinship or functional relations to the Kanongesha as did their counterparts to their chiefdoms.

Central Africa has a rich history of state formation that no doubt predates the rise of the Lunda Empire. Titling systems are ubiquitous. As Schecter noted, "The ancient and elaborately comparisoned [*sic*] gravesites on the Lualaba [twelfth to sixteenth centuries] are one of the best arguments that state organization in the region long predated the present polities among the Luba and Lunda peoples who divide this belt in the savanna. In this view, any group in the region would have had many of the titles at hand to use in elaborating a political system" (1976, 223). Yet, neither the Kanongesha nor the leaders of his brother polities drew on the wider repertoire of titles. Instead, they faithfully replicated, to the best they could within ecological constraints, the system extant in the Lunda capital during a particular epoch. This fact buttresses the contention of local oral traditions that state formation and the emergence of new identities occurred in spectacular bursts of political and military activity. Far less uniformity would be expected if social formation had been the result of slow diffusion or the haphazard spread of cultural elements. The gradual accretion and amalgamation of social features would probably have introduced more diverging elements. The evidence, thus, strongly suggests that the titles came to the upper Zambezi more or less in a block.

Subordinate chiefs sent tribute to the Kanongesha from time to time in accordance with productive windfalls, and at least once a year under any circumstances. During the twentieth century each newly appointed Kanongesha was sent gifts to the central Lunda king only at the point of the former's succession to the throne. Yet it has always been an impressive array of gifts that has fulfilled an invaluable function: to validate and reinforce the link between the Kanongesha and the Lunda Center in a fashion that also recognized local autonomy of operation. The key value in being a Kanongesha Lunda was that it offered protection from the Center. There is no evidence that the famous roving tribute collectors of the Lunda Center, the *kakwata,* ever came into the upper Zambezi area, or that its slaving parties did. Even as the Center increasingly turned to slaving as its major economic activity, the "son" polities on the upper Zambezi were extended an umbrella of protection that lasted for centuries. The phenomenon of slavery accentuates the need for more precise definitions of "us" and "them." Many of those forced to become slaves in Central Africa were not people who had been captured in war, but those who had been stripped of their identity as "us" for some reason or other. Much of the struggle sweeping Central Africa from the seventeenth to the nineteenth centuries was, in fact, over the right to be the definer of "usness" and "otherness," indeed to become the new focal point around which identity was reckoned. The harsh reality of slavery required unambiguous identities. Equivocating could be dangerous. Being firmly embedded in a protective social unit was, no doubt, an ongoing preoccupation, a necessary part of individual survival strategies. The developers of the Lunda diaspora thus benefited from the widespread and urgent need for clarity of identity.

The analysis of cultural traits does not get us very far in distinguishing one so-called ethnic group from another throughout much of Central Africa. Most groups possess similar forms of social organization, aesthetic expression, and ritual life. It is, rather, the adoption of particular notions of origins and corresponding sets of rights and duties, along with recognition of shared position within regional productive processes, that stands at the center of notions of "usness." Identity has been and remains largely leader-centered. War and conquest were key elements in identity formation, but they represented only half the equation. Bringing a new group into being and forging a collective identity meant integrating a plethora of local stories, offering an attractive, easily adoptable cultural style, and demonstrating strength and connections in high places. One had to be a skillful culture broker if one was to become a regional power broker. Those from the Lunda Empire had advantages that others lacked. Independent would-be state builders would have had great difficulty competing against the powerful Lunda economic monopoly and its attractive cultural package. The Lunda advantage, however, was specific to particular historical phases of Central African development. Certain entrepreneurial uses of culture, in conjunction with specific economic conditions and environmental responses, were necessary to produce the flurry of state building and people formation that brought the Kanongeshaship into existence.

Badmen, Books, and Bibles

The impact of colonizing forces, in the form of military campaigns, missionary proselytization, and administrative formation, on the construction of ethnicity among the Kanongesha Lunda is a story yet to be told with any degree of specificity. It differs little in its generalities, however, from those of the Lunda's neighbors, which have been more adequately examined. Papstein on the Luvale, Gluckman on the Lozi, Crehan on the Kaonde, Reefe on the Luba, Miller on the Chokwe, Geisler on the Toka, van Binsbergen on the Nkoya, as well as von Oppen on the entire region of the upper Zambezi all tell remarkably similar stories of the impact of colonialism on ethnic formation in Central Africa. The Kanongesha Lunda's initial response to British incursions was a military one. But they resisted, evidently, as Kanongesha Lunda rather than in coordinated fashion with their brother polities. The military forces of the British South Africa Company (BSAC) were able to engage and defeat each Lundaized polity independently, without fear of rearguard actions from another. The BSAC military campaigns, in fact, became an additional force for intensifying local constructions of ethnicity (see Meebelo 1971; Macpherson 1981; Chipungu 1992). The campaigns themselves were organized on the basis of British knowledge of preexisting social formations. Each was aimed at pacifying a specific people that was widely known enough to be acknowledged as such by the invading forces. Each military encounter became the stuff of legend, generating its own oral traditions concerning not only the tactics and strategies employed by the parties involved, but also more totalizing notions about the psychosocial makeup of the "other." These notions continued to be elaborated and acted upon in the postpacification period. Chipasha Luchembe (1992) has outlined how thirty-four years of BSAC rule led to the entrenchment of racial and ethnic or tribal stereotypes. The following hierarchical generalities about the various peoples of Zambia evolved from British oral tradition:

- Bemba: Finest and most warlike.
- Ngoni: Second in quality; although of Zulu stock, have mixed with inferior races.
- Southern races (Batoka, Tonga Ila): Self-reliant, self-confident, more friendly and more advanced in knowledge and ideas than others.
- Lozi: Friendly and amenable to law and order.
- Kaonde: Good physique, good for mining.
- Lunda: Inborn distaste for work, very poor physique, bones, and stamina. Inferior to southern races.
- Lamba: Criminal tendencies (drugs, prostitution, beer brewing, petty trading, hawking).

One would expect that Europeans participating in the so-called pacification of Central Africa, particularly those on the front line, would have preferred quick capitulations to extended, lethal encounters. Yet, the groups that resisted most forcefully ultimately received the most detailed and honorific treatment in British oral traditions. "Stronger" groups that put up more formidable defenses, that protected their interests with bloodshed, were reckoned by the colonial forces to be more "superior" peoples; they were believed to be more noble, more like the British themselves. Peace with them could be an honorable affair in which each party would be expected to dutifully carry out the terms of an agreement. Those groups that appeared to acquiesce to British overlordship too quickly were deemed weak. Those that responded by retreating from military confrontation altogether were deemed weak and sneaky. Such groups were seen as less honorable, less likely to abide by the terms of any agreement, and, therefore, in need of more direct and intrusive management.

This oral tradition moved into colonial reports and early surveys of local peoples and ultimately into the arena of applied policy. The "superior" groups were trusted to manage their own affairs and were given more autonomy. They were models of, and for, indirect rule. Individuals from these groups were seen as having a more acutely attuned sense of the value of law and order. They were thought more likely to make good police officers or other supervisory personnel. Inferior groups could not be trusted and, thus, merited less autonomy. Members of such groups, it was believed, served best as domestics or as chain labor on highly supervised projects. The Rhodesian Native Labour Bureau, which was formed in 1906, further codified ethnic stereotypes through its recruiting practices. Specific peoples were actively sought after for specific kinds of work. Stereotyping was used to rationalize the state use of violence in tax collection, labor recruitment, and the assignment of productive tasks within the newly emerging economic framework.

The Kanongesha Lunda had barely managed to repel an all-out assault on their territory by the Chokwe when British forces arrived at the turn of the twentieth century. Unprepared materially, and perhaps psychologically, for another major military encounter, they waged sporadic hit-and-run campaigns. They even fled en masse several times back and forth across the Angolan–Northern Rhodesian border before some finally acknowledged British overlordship. They were, thus, relegated to the status of an "inferior" group in the minds of the British—inferior, and, indeed, quite marginal to mainstream British interests in Central Africa. Their territory had neither exploitable mineral resources nor land sufficiently fertile to attract the attention of European settlers. Only two groups of missionaries deemed it worth their while to compete for local souls. The Lunda themselves were said to be less capable mentally and physically than other groups, not even suitable as domestic workers. They were among the least desirable part of the Northern Rhodesia migrant labor stream, having to travel the farthest from home for the lowest paying jobs. It was not at all uncommon during the 1920s and 1930s for Lunda males to work as plantation hands in Southern Rhodesia or dock workers in South Africa because they could not find employment closer to home. And even in those locales success might have been related to the propensity of the Lunda to conceal their ethnic identity. Their place within the Northern Rhodesian urban division of labor was usually restricted to garbage collectors and graveyard workers.

With acknowledgment to the contributions of Mitchell, Epstein, and others in pointing out the role of urban interaction in solidifying African ethnic identities, it must be noted that the treatment of African individuals in the newly emerging urban context was often based on preexisting notions of the physical and moral worth of their group. Notions that emerged during preurban contact between Africans and Europeans greatly influenced the structure of opportunities and constraints awaiting migrants in the cities and mines and on the plantations. For the Kanongesha Lunda, shared tales of misery and mistreatment and shared occupational experiences in the colonial order of things formed an additional layer buttressing their construction of "usness."

As many have noted, the migrant worker system everywhere in southern Africa was a force for both the intensification and the transcendence of ethnic identity. One's identity as a worker might supersede all other notions of "usness"; yet migrant workers lived in at least two worlds, and in the rural world ethnic identity legitimized one's access to land and other resources and defined one's rights, privileges, and duties. The fact that most migrant workers were male emphasized in their own minds, at least, the need to constrain women's ability to make decisions or take actions that might curtail men's access to land and socially valued positions in the village in spite of their extended absences from their rural homelands. Ethnic, or tribal, identification would evidently appeal to migrant workers, who were some of the greatest supporters of local chieftaincies and the Native Authority system during the early colonial period. For the migrant workers, a good chief was a necessary and reliable proxy who would protect their interests while they were away. Without a heightened sense of ethnicity, the migrants would have been less secure in their ability to influence the flow of events and to maintain their positions in the rural societies to which they would eventually retire. The "other" was constructed, more broadly than in precolonial times, as the other officially recognized groups with whom the Kanongesha Lunda had to compete for positions within the colonial order.

The administrative structures that emerged with colonialism intensified the territorial component of ethnic identity. Tribes, as spatially defined sets of people, were the basic conceptual units of the British system of indirect rule. The people of Kanongesha were further confronted with the problem of having their territory split between Portuguese and British colonial spheres. Every dilemma, however, is accompanied by its own set of opportunities. Each of the two Kanongeshas who claimed chieftaincy of all the Lunda-Ndembu, one on each side of the colonial divide, was able to reach back into lineage history to justify the legitimacy of his claim to sovereignty. One widespread oral tradition states that after the death of Nkuba, the first Kanongesha on the upper Zambezi, his brother Sakapenda succeeded to the throne. Another asserts that his son, Kabanda, was the second Kanongesha. All acknowledge that the succession was contested and that a split occurred in the late 1700s. Most note that two Kanongeshas existed for a time, and some assert that the two factions were rejoined into a single polity when Njonga, the third successor of the Sakapenda group, gave important subordinate positions to the pretenders and supporters of the Kabanda faction. The Kanongesha of Northern Rhodesia claimed to be the heir of the Sakapenda tradition, while that of Angola claimed Kabanda origins. A debate that seemingly had been resolved for one hundred and fifty years was suddenly reopened. The central argument in each case revolved around who had received the *lukanu* (bracelet of authority) and the blessings of legitimacy directly from the Mwantiyanvwa of Musumba. Each Kanongesha evidently had a *lukanu* in his possession, along with a story of its receipt that challenged the authenticity of the other's claim. Thus, even in the 1900s, connection with the central Lunda polity, then located in the Belgian Congo, was considered proof positive of the right to rule. Although the Kanongesha Lunda of Northern Rhodesia had begun constructing an identity that was territorially specific, primordial relations with the central Lunda Empire remained an essential component. The Northern Rhodesian Native Authority Ordinance of 1929 cemented that identity into law. The Kanongesha Lunda became an officially recognized unit of the colonial state, ruled most directly by a European district commissioner and his military attachment, with the assistance of the Kanongesha and four of his subchiefs. The Kanongesha was said to have had twelve subchiefs, but the British had their own ideas concerning the number of local chiefs needed per number of subjects; eight Lunda-Ndembu subchiefs were thus decommissioned.

Labor recruitment and tax collection were channeled through chiefs, and each individual was seen as unambiguously under the day-to-day authority of a particular chief. As noted in the previous chapter, the establishment of Native Treasuries in the 1930s gave added meaning, relevance, and power to the system of local chiefs. In the early years, a kinship link with a chief was the most valuable asset in securing one of the prized positions within the Native Authority system. Subsequently, greater attention was given to the level of literacy and numeracy of job applicants. Yet, even in the late colonial period membership in the correct ethnic group was a prerequisite for working within any particular Native Authority unit. Colonial administration at the local level, thus, worked in tandem with larger economic processes to produce heightened sensitivity to ethnic affiliation.

Expatriate missionaries also played a powerful role in ethnicizing the people among whom they worked. Each mission conceived of its task as bringing the gospel to a particular ethnic group. The peripheral goods and services they offered, likewise, were most often restricted in a similar way. Yet the primary influence of missionaries was to create, through language and literacy, local elites who became a force for both modernity and tradition. The first generation of missionaries among the Kanongesha Lunda, Dr. Walter Fisher at Kalene mission in the north, George Suckling at Chitokoloki mission in the south, and Fr. Adrian Peck at Lwawu mission in the central region, with the indispensable assistance of the initial converts, began the process of translating the Scriptures into the local language. The language spoken by the Kanongesha Lunda, however, was characterized by many subtle regional variations. Consonant use varied, for example, with the "L" of certain areas being replaced by "D" in others. The patterns of vowel coalescence and elision shifted slightly from place to place, and stress and tonality varied among speakers. Local vocabularies reflected different amounts of lingering linguistic influence of Mbwela and other pre-Lunda peoples. Thus, the process of rendering the Kanongesha language into written form entailed many arbitrary choices. The collection of choices that finally emerged was popularized by missionaries in the sermons they preached, the Bible classes they taught and, later, the schools they established. The mission version of the language increasingly became the standard which rebounded back into village vernaculars. Its effect of standardizing local languages paralleled the process that occurred after vernacular translations of the Bible appeared in Europe during the sixteenth and seventeenth centuries. The increasing value of literacy for navigating the colonial world gave the new standard widespread appeal among the Kanongesha Lunda.

The missions' part in standardizing local languages was seminal to their role in producing the locally, and, later, nationally educated elite. As Vail and others have noted, language stands as the central item in the assemblage of any cultural package. Community and communications are inseparable concepts. African youth socialized in the new language at mission schools adopted it as part of their ethnic identity. Its adoption, in fact, became their badge of membership in the modern world as well as an affirmation of their ethnic identity. The new elite that were forged in the mission fire would go on, in many cases, to become the heirs and authenticators of local traditions. Literacy provided them with a new set of tools for validating oral tradition by connecting it with other more widespread and seemingly universal traditions. Literacy makes more information available. The new elite among the Kanongesha and other groups set about assembling written local histories which gained added force, in some cases, simply because they were written down. Their texts entered into mission journals and personal diaries as quickly as they entered into the field reports of colonial officers. It was the new elite who served the British as consultants for the process of codifying local laws, and it was their interpretation of local jurisprudence that most often found its way into colonial accounts, along with those of anthropologists.

The struggle leading up to independence presented new opportunities and new usages for heightened sensitivity to ethnic affiliation. The whole colonial pie was up for grabs. Which piece would go to "us" and which to "them" was the major question of the day. The use of ethnic intensification as a mobilizing tool to bring about the end of colonialism in Zambia has been well addressed elsewhere (Mulford 1967). The first political parties each developed a national reach in the 1950s and 1960s. Yet the origins of those parties lie in the amalgamation of Native Welfare Societies that arose in the 1940s. Each society had begun as an ethnically based social safety net to provide help to its members as they alternated between rural and urban existences. The organized efforts to bring about independence that have been most studied are those of the mine workers, clerks, teachers, and other urban-based young intellectuals. The mixing and mingling of people from a multitude of different ethnic backgrounds in the urban setting gave the drive for independence its nationalistic tone. Two major political parties, UNIP (United National Independence Party) and ANC (African National Congress), vied for national dominance in those early years. As it became increasingly clear that independence was within reach, the battle between the two parties for supporters grew intense, often leading to violence. With few exceptions, the nationalist leaders tended to view chiefs as conservative old men who, at best, were concerned only with tribal politics, or, at worst, were collaborators with colonialism. Nevertheless, the majority of Zambia's population was still firmly rooted in rural areas where chiefs exercised considerable influence. Furthermore, few of the leaders of the independence movement possessed a genuinely national constituency or were even widely known in rural areas. So, although most of the anticolonial confrontational politics that led to independence took place in urban areas, the political parties contesting the first elections found it necessary to court rural chiefs aggressively in order to win the votes of their followers. Both parties wrapped themselves in cloaks of traditionalism, portraying their struggles as efforts both to return the nation to its rightful leaders and to forge ahead in developing new national structures capable of bringing about rapid economic development. In doing so, they promised to acknowledge the right of chiefs to continue to rule in the rural areas, even after an independent government had been established. The dynamic process that led to independence, thus, resulted in a number of modifications in the role of chiefs in national political life. In short, the power of the chiefs increased greatly in postcolonial Zambia. This increase in power was the outgrowth of at least four distinct processes: (1) advancing the House of Chiefs as an advisory group to the government; (2) granting more autonomy to chiefs' courts; (3) providing increased economic opportunities to chiefs; and (4) increasing the focus on "tradition" as a contemporary legitimizing force.

UNIP, after winning the early elections, eventually eliminated all opposition by declaring Zambia a one-party state in 1973. But the party held true to its earlier campaign promise by installing in the new constitution a proviso institutionalizing the House of Chiefs. Lunda chiefs were active participants and, at times, held leadership positions within this body, which until 1992 met several times a year in Lusaka to discuss a wide range of issues. Their participation, of course, lent a sense of legitimacy to the ruling party by acknowledging its apical position in a system of neotraditional rule. But in return, the House of Chiefs provided the traditional chiefs with a forum unlike any they had possessed in the past. They were able to make appeals, push for policies, and in general make their influence felt at a national level. Although the constitution did not provide them with a mechanism for actually deciding national policy or implementing laws, their collective weight as representatives of the rural masses meant that their positions on issues at least had to be heard and somehow attended to.

The senior chief and his subordinates had always been central to the Lunda-Ndembu's construction of identity. The emergence of an independent government did little to change that fact. The chiefs became, and for the most part remain, the local extension of the national government. Even today they are the primary disseminators of information for the government. The most effective way to notify every Zambian citizen of a particular piece of information or a change in national policy is by notifying the chiefs. The chiefs can then call for meetings of all the senior headmen in their areas, and the latter can, in turn, pass on the information to even the remotest village. In a nation where newspapers have limited circulation and numerous languages are spoken, this system has time and again proven its effectiveness. Most contemporary chiefs are able to understand the national lingua franca, English. The chiefs' *kapasu*, messengers, are all aware of the location of important headmen in their areas and can transmit messages relatively quickly. And all headmen know that a summons from the chief takes priority over any other business. Through this system, information can flow from the capital city to the most isolated villages in a matter of a few days.

A second action of the postcolonial government that strengthened the chiefs' power was to reestablish the so-called traditional chiefs' courts. In Mwinilunga the court's function is modeled on the role chiefs played in the period following the pacification of the indigenous Mbwela people, that is, chiefs as the "objective outsiders." Any litigating parties, by mutual consent, can have their case heard by the chief, providing they agree beforehand to abide by his decision. Before the hearing, both parties are required to give the chief tribute, for example, a chicken, a basket of food, or a piece of game meat. This is viewed both as symbolic acknowledgment of his role as chief and as compensation for infringement on his time. In the 1950s, under British rule, chiefs were permitted to try minor offenses, but they were required to be assisted by government-paid assessors. All cases heard had to be recorded and forwarded to the district commissioner for review, along with all fines collected. Now, however, chiefs operate independently. Any fines levied are usually paid to the winner of the case, and if actual punishment is thought to be required it usually consists of laboring in the chief's fields for a certain number of days. No report need be filed with any government authority.

Chiefs are the final authorities on all land issues in their areas. None of the villagers in Mwinilunga possess freehold rights to land. A generally agreed upon system of use-rights is still in existence. Land near any village is considered to be part of that village, and anyone who wishes to use it for any purpose is supposed to first ask permission from the nearest headman or senior headman. Seeking permission from the headman is principally a mode of informing him of one's intentions and of finding out if any prior claims exist on that land. In the past, the most common problem to arise was when two villages both wanted to expand into a piece of land that lay either between or equidistant from them. A chief would invariably be called upon to decide the disposition of such cases. Thus, while the national government was actively constructing new symbols of a Zambian identity, such as a flag, an anthem, a unified legal framework, standardized school curricula, national sports teams, a synthetic history of the past, and a vision of a common future, its day-to-day practices of governance accentuated notions of local ethnic affiliation. Ethnic appeals ran rampant in local political campaigns, and local politicians were evaluated on their capacity to channel national resources to their home group. All politics is ultimately local. And as the account below will show, Lunda chiefs are as skilled as any other political actors at manipulating local symbols and structures for their own benefit.

The Musolu

The *musolu* described at the beginning of this chapter was a multipurpose attempt at ethnic intensification. After the party secretary had departed the subchiefs spoke, each giving a brief history of his respective chiefdom. The Kanongesha next spoke at length about the reason he had called this particular meeting, which was to discuss the applicability of traditional laws in contemporary social life. The format followed involved dividing the crowd into seven discussion groups, each chaired by a senior headman. These groups met all day, discussing which traditional laws they felt were still applicable in light of contemporary circumstances and which they felt to be obsolete. Each group then presented the highlights of its deliberations at a plenary session in the evening and listened to the thoughts of other groups. In subsequent meetings they attempted to resolve differences among the groups. The meetings lasted for three days, by which time a general consensus emerged. On the final day the following list of twelve resolutions received the approval of all present:

- The *musolu* must be held each year.
- Chiefs Ntambu and Mukang'ala should receive their chieftainships back.
- The chiefs' palaces should be enlarged.
- Chiefs should wear their traditional garb at all meetings or ceremonies.
- Drums should be beaten when a chief is going away from his area or returning.
- A special person should be appointed to greet chiefs on ceremonial occasions, in a traditional manner.
- Chiefs are not to be greeted by hand, that is, no one should touch the person of a chief.
- A chief should not sleep in another chief's palace.
- When a chief is away, his head wife must remain near the palace.
- Christians should conduct their *nkanga* ceremonies without singing church songs.
- Tribute given to chiefs should be given through one's local headman and senior headman.
- Tributary wives may not be given to chiefs.

During the course of the meeting several other resolutions had been presented and discussed, but lack of time prevented the group from reaching a consensus on those points. It was decided that these points would be the primary focus of a meeting the following year:

- Juniors cannot greet elders first.
- Uncircumcised boys may not eat with adults.
- Men and women may not walk together.
- During their menstrual periods women may not pass through the middle of the village, may not cook, and may not sleep in the main house.

The chiefs did not take a visibly active part in the discussion groups; instead, they held their own private caucus throughout the day while the groups were in session. Thus it would appear that any resolutions agreed upon were based on a consensus of the people rather than having been orchestrated by the chiefs. However, unbeknownst to most people present at the *musolu*, the chiefs were kept fully informed of the deliberations through a number of intermediaries and were able, to some degree, to direct the course of individual group discussions. Thus, the points discussed during the three-day *musolu* offer us a great deal of insight into the reasons the chiefs decided to hold this meeting. They were attempting, first, to regain the traditional basis of their authority and power through the reinforcement of specific principles of social organization. Second, they were attempting to check the potentially divisive effects of Christian religions, which had been modifying key aspects of Lunda ceremonial life—aspects whose purpose included reinforcing basic principles of social organization. As I have described earlier, separation by gender and hierarchy is the very foundation on which Lunda social organization rests. But the exigencies of the modern world are rapidly eroding distinctions based on gender or age. Cash, and the methods for obtaining it, have led to the increased interdependence of males and females and also to the breaking down of the relationship between age and wealth. Respect for the concept of hierarchy remains generally strong, but it is much more difficult to reckon hierarchical position in today's complex world than it was in the time when all women raised cassava, all men were hunters, and differences in accumulated wealth were closely correlated with age. Some elders are very concerned that this state of affairs is producing a socially unhealthy environment for the younger generation; they fear that the young are being taught to respect cash rather than the concept of elderhood. Increasingly, young people are refraining from giving the public signs of respect traditionally due anyone their senior. Instead, they reserve such displays for those seniors whose wealth is known to exceed their own. Poor elders are sometimes, in a sense, reckoned as children. The chiefs are especially concerned because the increasing emphasis on cash accumulation has paralleled the declining tendency for their subjects to give them gifts. Thus, the interests of the chiefs and of the headmen merged on the issue of tribute. Through tribute some of the wealth of the area could be siphoned off and funneled upward through the network of headmen, senior headmen, and finally chiefs. Each of these leaders would keep a portion for himself before passing the rest up the hierarchy.

It remains to be seen if chiefs and headmen can indeed gain the support of the general population for the reinstitution of a tribute system. Should they succeed however, it would revolutionize the nature of rural politics. It would, in effect, revitalize the financially rewarding nature of traditional positions by reestablishing the link between age and power. The duties of headmanship require a certain degree of wealth. Yet today, young men are better placed than elders to acquire that wealth. If, however, the position of headman entitled one to tribute, then simply acquiring the position would in itself give one the wealth to fulfill the concomitant functions. This could lead to a reversal of the trend toward younger headmen by creating a new pool of resources to which elderly men would have disproportionately greater access. In a sense the resolution to restore the tribute system was an attempt to turn back the clock, to reestablish the correlation not only between age and wealth but also between chiefs and headmen. Needless to say, this was a very appealing idea to the elderly men present at the *musolu*, as well as to the younger men who had already received general acknowledgment as headmen. It was also an especially appealing idea for the chiefs, because a strengthened tribute system would break their financial dependence on the party and its government by providing them with an alternative means of accumulating resources. Furthermore, it would strengthen the chiefs' relationship with and control over the headmen. Since all tribute would ultimately be collected in the name of the chiefs, the chiefs could then exercise control by deciding who could collect tribute in their names. In other words, having the wherewithal to attract a large following would cease to be the hallmark of headmanship, as it is today. Instead, the authority to collect tribute would became the new symbol of headmanship, and that authority would flow directly from the chiefs. The power of the chiefs would increase greatly if, indeed, a strong tribute system were to be put in place.

The passing of the resolution concerning tribute can easily be understood on one level in terms of its mercenary appeal to the segment of Lunda society that attended the *musolu*. But on another level it can only be understood in light of the atmosphere surrounding the meetings. For three days the participants of the *musolu* were treated to a feast that outdid any other in living memory. Meat and meal were served in prodigious quantities. Honey beer and cassava alcohol flowed like water. Music was constantly in the air. Singers, drummers, and dancers performed with unparalleled beauty. All of this served to elevate the entire event from the level of the profane to the sacred. For three days the participants of the *musolu* were, in a sense, transported to a magical world where no sensual, emotional, or spiritual need went unfulfilled. It was a world no one wanted to leave, a world that the participants felt ordained to bring back to earth, to share with their brothers and sisters in the farthest reaches of the kingdom. But how? In that heady atmosphere answers were simple. The *musolu* represented a past golden era, a Lunda paradise lost. To reclaim paradise the Lunda people had to reclaim their past traditions and customs. They needed a cultural rebirth to rid the kingdom of those modern tendencies that disrupted the basis of Lunda unity, devalued respect for hierarchy, and inhibited the flow of goods and services, destroying traditional notions of rights and responsibilities. Toward that end two major topics dominated the early days of the *musolu*. First it was decided that the chiefs and the people needed to enter into a new social contract. Much of the blame for the poor state of contemporary affairs was placed on the chiefs themselves. Many people argued that chiefs had become like politicians and businessmen, enriching themselves while giving the people only rhetoric in return. Yet it was also acknowledged that these days people gave very little to the chiefs by way of tribute; as a result, the people deserved little from the chiefs in return. The *musolu* demonstrated how joyous things can be when the people and the chiefs share their resources. And just as the *musolu* itself revived an ancient tradition, so too the ancient relationship between the people and the chiefs needed to be revived. Hence the proliferation of resolutions aimed at making the chiefs of today more like the legendary chiefs of old. Their persons should be sacred, their palaces large, their storehouses full and always open to those in need. The chiefs would serve as the social safety net of the chiefdom and people in return would pay tribute.

The second major topic was the need to check the divisive effect of Christianity. Christian elements were increasingly being woven into Lunda ceremonial life. The female maturation ceremony, for example, had previously been accompanied by the robust singing of songs with sexually explicit lyrics taunting the males present in a lighthearted fashion. More and more, however, these songs were being replaced with church hymns. Prayers, Scripture readings, and even modified church services had been incorporated into many maturation ceremonies. The effect had been to give a sectarian tone to ceremonies; at times, primarily Catholics attended certain ceremonial performances and primarily Protestants attended others. The situation had yet to reach the point where one could begin to speak of the existence of something akin to religious clans in Mwinilunga, but there were undoubtedly tendencies in that direction. It was thus decided that ceremonies should take place without the singing of Christian songs. All ceremonies should be open to the general public and thus return to being occasions for reinforcing the essential unity of all Lunda people irrespective of religious affiliation.

One resolution which was widely discussed but eventually voted against was that of giving tributary wives to the chiefs. Interestingly, it was the chiefs themselves who exhibited the most ambiguity on this point. In their private discussions there was much talk about the advantages of receiving tributary wives and the power it would give the chiefs by linking them more concretely with the dominant lineages in the territory, as well as its capacity for quickly integrating lineages who came into Mwinilunga from Angola or Congo. But stories about the behavior of tributary wives of old finally dissuaded the chiefs from pushing the issue. Because these wives symbolized a chief's link with a particular lineage, he was forbidden by custom from ever divorcing them or mistreating them. Stories abounded about tributary wives who refused to work and became involved in numerous adulterous affairs but were nevertheless entitled to a comfortable life at the chief's capital because of their status. Hence the chiefs decided that tributary wives might not be a good idea at the present time.

The final set of issues which was discussed but not resolved aimed at reinforcing separation by gender and age through reinstituting traditional norms governing association. There were strong feelings at the *musolu* that the free mingling of people of different categories ran counter to tradition and to the basic rules of nature. It was deemed by some to be spiritually polluting. Yet despite the high level of emotion centering on the issue of separation, time prevented a full exploration of the multifaceted problem, that is, in light of contemporary pressures toward greater interdependence, how to redesign villages and reorganize labor in order to bring about a more complete separation of sexes and ages. Hence it was decided that individual headmen would continue the debate in their respective villages, and it was hoped that a chiefdom-wide consensus could be reached at the next *musolu*.

One resolution that everyone enthusiastically agreed upon was that henceforth *musolu* must be held annually. Regardless of the resolutions passed each year, or the lack thereof, a new symbol of Lunda unity had come into being. A vehicle had been established whereby for at least a few days each year some members of society could bathe in the euphoria of a past golden age. And judging from the reaction of the participants in the *musolu*, that must be a delightful feeling indeed. But it is equally clear that the chiefs were concerned with more than merely providing their subjects with a brief moment of merriment. They saw the expansion of the party and its government's machinery into the rural area as a serious threat to the limited sovereignty they possessed. They were fighting back to maintain and even expand their range of authority using the most obvious tool at their disposal: the symbolic appeal for ethnic unity. The chiefs were well aware that, despite the relative success of the party and its government at inculcating a sense of national identity in the Lunda people, there was still a lingering undercurrent of suspicion and dissatisfaction at the relatively slow pace of economic development in Mwinilunga in comparison with most other regions of the country. There was a feeling, not often publicly articulated, that perhaps the Lunda were not receiving their fair share of the national pie, that perhaps the government was not sufficiently committed to seriously developing Lunda areas. There seemed to be a general but unspoken understanding at the *musolu* that through unity the Lunda not only could solve many of their own problems but also would be in a more powerful position to confront the government on the question of allocation of national resources. The chiefs were able, therefore, to imbue the *musolu* with a sense of the urgent need for the Lunda to unite in order to confront contemporary problems, even though there was no public expression of animosity toward the political elites or any other Zambian ethnic group. In fact the chiefs publicly pledged their allegiance to the ruling party and the Zambian state on several occasions, exhorted their subjects to be good citizens, and repeatedly expressed the view that the development of their area was to be seen as their contribution to the development of the nation as a whole. Thus, any party member attending the *musolu* who might have been required to report on its proceedings to his superiors would have had little to say that would have portrayed the *musolu* as antiparty or antigovernment or as advocating any actions that ran counter to the national interest. Yet the chiefs had fired a salvo across the bow of the ship of state. They would not be content to serve merely as symbolic props, lending a sense of legitimacy to the hegemonic forces of the party and its government. They served notice that as symbols they still possessed the power to mobilize and motivate the rural population, to capture its imagination in ways the party and its government could not.

Angola and Ethnicity

The shifting nature of the Angolan civil war has influenced the construction of ethnicity among the Kanongesha Lunda. The fortunes of the Zambian economy have waxed and waned repeatedly since independence, and it is currently in a downward spiral, with urban unemployment at an all-time high. Fewer Lunda youth see migration to the city as a viable means of securing a livelihood or of accumulating capital to support a rural-based existence. Lucrative trade opportunities exist, however, on the Angolan side of the border. UNITA rebels, who are in firm control of the region abutting Zambia, have access to precious and semiprecious gems as well as highly prized forest products. Yet, they lack the basic food staples and man-ufactured items more readily available in Zambia. Clandestine exchange across the border is growing by leaps and bounds.

The Zambian government's official position on UNITA has been quite ambiguous. At times it has expressed sympathy with UNITA's aims. At other times it has voiced unequivocal support for the MPLA government. At still other times it has tried to play the role of neutral mediator. UNITA, however, has historically viewed the government of Zambia with much sus-picion. It has frequently accused Zambian intelligence agencies of provid-ing MPLA with vital information on the location and strength of UNITA bases in the border region and has also accused Zambian troops of actually participating in MPLA military operations. For years UNITA's policy has been to detain and hold for questioning any individual of Zambian origin found on Angolan soil. The Kanongesha Lunda have largely managed to avoid such a fate by restricting their cross-border movements to Lundaized areas. They have learned to enter Angola not as Zambians but as Lunda seeking contact with fellow Lunda. Youths, who dominate the trade on both sides of the border, are actively collaborating on the construction of an inclusive identity that naturalizes their activities and mediates against it dan-gers. The identity under development appeals to the same body of oral tra-ditions, the same primordial assemblages that cemented the separate iden-tities on each size of the border. The operative level of connection varies, however, from that of the previous generation. Old debates surrounding the legitimacy of the Sakapenda versus the Kabanda factions to hold the Kanongeshaship have been pushed into the shadows. Shared status as chil-dren of Nkuba, the first Kanongesha, or indeed children of the Mwantiyan-vwa at the Lunda Center, is now the central point of social recognition. That identity is further buttressed by shared feelings of marginality within their respective countries. The Lunda of Angola, like those of Zambia, occupy a region that has long been neglected by their central government. Even as UNITA supporters, the Lunda of Angola recognize that they are but a tiny faction in an essentially ethnic Ovimbundu-dominated political movement. Few of their members occupy any positions of real authority within that movement. Nor will their local interests necessarily be best served by a UNITA victory. Their proximity to the Zambian border and their capacity to funnel Zambian goods to the rebel cause strengthens their bargaining position within the rebel movement.

The cross-border trade is fraught with dangers. Zambians entering Angola must navigate through miles of territory studded with land mines. They run the risk of confrontation with suspicious and often poorly disciplined UNITA troops, of stumbling into areas of active military operations, or of being apprehended by their own government agents for violating customs and immigration laws. Angolans heading to Zambia face an equally onerous array of perils. Yet, the scarcity of other economic options in the region and the potentially lucrative nature of cross-border trade propel both sides forward. The effectiveness of this trade depends on secrecy of the highest order, information of the most precise nature, and personal trust of the most intimate sort. A heightened sense of ethnicity, the feeling of a shared primordial past and a common destiny, provides the basis for assuming and mediating the risk inherent in the trade. It is far too early to speculate about the ultimate outcome of these cultural and economic innovations. Perhaps we are witnessing the formative stage of a process paralleling that described by Cohen concerning the Hausa in Yorubaland, where ethnicity effectively served as a utilitarian device for maintaining control over a lucrative and long-lasting trade network. Perhaps the changing economic fortunes of Angola and Zambia will hinder such a formation. What is clear at the moment, however, is that a new generation of potential culture brokers is attempting to forge a mechanism that they feel best responds to the contemporary structure of opportunities and constraints in which they are embedded. They are sifting through the local cultural assemblage with the aim of inculcating sentiments of primordial connections for instrumental purposes. They are developing a generational style which they hope to justify and indigenize by enveloping it in an aura of tradition.

Summary

Notions of "us" are always developed in tandem with notions of "them," within historically specific streams of needs, wants, constraints, and opportunities. The point of this chapter has been to draw attention to those moments when group identity mattered most to the Lunda. In the absence of powerful imperatives, questions of group identity recede into the background. Distinctions between people and peoples are allowed to become blurred. But when there is an urgent need to gain or contain valued rights and privileges or to acquire or protect control over valued goods, clarity of identity resurfaces as an absolute prerequisite for collective action. In the case of the Lunda, sensitivity to ethnic affiliation also rose in response to the desperate attempt to avoid having their bodies reduced to goods, services, or resources, that is, becoming enslaved. Participation in long-distance trade, avoidance of capture in the slave trade, acquisition of Mbwela land for cassava production, negotiation of colonial relationships, and jockeying for position within the postcolonial state were all accompanied by the energetic drawing of boundaries between "us" and "them." Ethnicity is an instrument with utilitarian value, but its relevance must be convincingly demonstrated; its constituent parts must be cleverly constructed, packaged, and presented by particularly influential individuals. The emergence of astute culture brokers or culture entrepreneurs is required to activate the process of ethnic intensification. It is they who sense the opportunities, articulate the goals, clarify the motives, and dig deeply into the cultural assemblage to pull out seemingly primordial justifications for proposed courses of action. The substance out of which they weave powerful cultural collages, however, is not uniquely their own. The raw material of their constructions is kept alive and ready for use through rather mundane quotidian practices. For example, epic narratives detailing the exploits of past heroes, cautionary tales, morality plays, parables, allegories, and anecdotes are regularly retold simply to while away the hours in frivolous fun during nightly fireside chats. Yet, through such processes valuable information is transmitted from generation to generation—information that can be elevated from the profane to the sacred plane when circumstances require and used to cultivate shared sensibilities about, and orientation toward, significant social phenomena.

Lunda chiefs continue to excel as culture brokers. On the one hand, most have obtained comparatively high levels of formal education and have lived and worked sufficiently long in urban areas to be able to move about comfortably in Zambia's modern political and economic sectors. Yet chiefs are also well steeped in traditional forms of myth-making and myth-using. Most possess *wuhaku,* that combination of oratory skill, historical knowledge, and attentiveness to social impulses that is the distilled essence of leadership among the Lunda. Through the *musolu,* chiefs were able to make manifest the sharp contrast between present suffering and presumed past glory. They

were able to ethnicize the causes and conditions of their social and economic collapse. They were able to ethnicize the solution as well. Chiefs succeeded in mobilizing some momentary support for resisting the ethnically
divisive influences of Christian ideology and practices, the social engineer-
ing policies of a nationalist government, and the economic contingencies of
a cash-driven society. Chiefs have taken on three powerfully hegemonic
forces: church, state, and the global economy. The long-term prognosis
may not look good. But the instrumental construction of primordial connections is ultimately about the here and now. Tomorrow will generate its
own unique challenges and spawn its own bricolage to most usefully depict
the present and the past.

Chapter Eight

This World and the Other World

Ask Me No Secrets . . .
June 1994
Senior Headman Chifunga was a remarkable individual—remarkable and strange. His relationship to time, in particular, was puzzling. It was almost as if he had taken Einstein's theories about the relativity of time one step further than the genius had intended. Chifunga's personal movement of time seemed relative not only to speed but also to any number of other features: space, place, activity, and even mood. He would tell stories of the early days of colonialism in Northern Rhodesia with such vividness and precision of detail that it seemed evident that he had actually been there. By most accounts he had been quite mature, married with big children, working on the docks in South Africa when World War II broke out. Everyone agreed that he was at least seventy years old, perhaps eighty. And, indeed, most of the time he looked the part. He moved about gingerly, leaning heavily on his cane; he was slight of build, almost frail. A strong wind would no doubt have carried him away. But at times, out of the corner of the eye, one would catch Chifunga moving in ways that defied belief. Once, on a hunting trip, he suddenly sprinted off in response to a sound that I could not hear, at a pace that I could not match. He fired his gun before I could catch up, hitting his prey squarely between the eyes at two hundred yards. His catlike movements had frightened me. Others claimed to have seen him jumping across wide rivers, or pushing over trees with his bare hands, or clearing boulders out of his garden as effortlessly as shooing flies. Shaky octogenarian one moment, spry teenager the next, and occasionally, something utterly indescribable. That's the way it was with Chifunga.

Yesterday morning he was working in his garden. Those nearby say he suddenly flew twenty feet into the air, violently hurled by some unseen force. Yet the only sounds were an unearthly roar that Chifunga himself emitted and the thud of his impact. The shock of the landing should have shattered every bone in his body. Yet, he walked away unscathed. Chifunga was unable or unwilling to offer any explanation for what had happened. A couple of people, however, claimed to have heard him mutter something to the effect that he knew who was responsible and would deal with them forthwith.

Dangerous Knowledge and Ambiguous Power

In a society where the living see themselves as directly dependent on their ancestors, power over the living alone cannot suffice. The dead, too, must somehow be tamed—and in this, ritual rather than military means must of necessity be used.

Fairley 1987, 99

Lunda philosophies traditionally revolved around the notion of life as an unbroken chain of linked individuals. The multitude of the living, the many more who have died, and the countless number yet to be born all form a single community. Notions of hierarchy, social responsibility, and moral obligation include them all. The Lunda believe that the *akishi*, spirits of deceased individuals, neither ascend to some heavenly plane nor descend into the depths of some hell but stay in the same geographical region where they lived and died, continue to interact with their kin, and remain an integral part of the corporate community. This is neither particularly profound nor particularly novel. Throughout much of Africa, indeed much of the world, people have deeply held beliefs about ancestors and about their social and moral obligations to them. Yet for the Lunda, such beliefs not only occupy the philosophical domain but also infuse meaning into the webs of relationships that constitute day-to-day life—they are never very far from the surface. The ancestors are present at daily communal meals and must be fed along with the rest. They witness intra- and intervillage disputes and develop their own judgments about the merits of each side of any argument. They assist women through the difficult process of childbirth. They protect and guide men on their hunting forays into the forest domain. They make their displeasure known by inducing illness in those who breach the moral code, those who break promises, those who sow disorder and discord among the living, and those who fail to perform significant acts of remembrance toward the dead.

All the relationships we have explored thus far are underpinned, sanctioned, and sanctified by reference to the ancestors. The ancestors, for example, are central to the relationship between people and the environment. It is they, in fact, who legitimize claims to land. Through conquest one may become *Mwanta Wantu*, owner of the people, but the title *Mwenitunga*, owner of the land, stays with those whose ancestors have resided longest in a particular place. The latter should always be accommodated in some formal fashion, for only they can make peaceful coexistence with resident spirits possible. Ancestors cement the relationship between the individual and the group by reinforcing hierarchies that extend into the afterlife. They recruit and metaphysically bind together groups that are responsible for the collective health of the community. Ancestors are the primordial links that naturalize social identities: "us" and "them." They justify current political alignments and condition the relationship between rich and poor. Ancestors pioneered the proverbial well-worn path—the body of judicial precedence relied upon for social order as well as the repertoire of technical skills upon which daily subsistence is based.

Ancestors, however, are not the only residents of the unseen realm. Other vaguely defined categories of metaphysical beings exist as well. Animals have spirits that roam the earth after the death of the bodies that once held them, just as people do. *Makishi,* demigods or nature spirits, exist in untold numbers. *Andumba, tuyebela, ilomba,* and other entities constitute a vast array of invisible beings that serve as agents for the destructive capacity of witches and sorcerers.

There is little local lore concerning the spirits of animals. A few stories circulate about famous big game hunters of old who had fatal encounters with vengeful animal spirits. But for the most part, notions about animal spirits are poorly elaborated. Such spirits seem not to be the major source of any anxiety, either specific or general. It is widely assumed that spirit men, somehow, possess the power to dominate spirit animals, or to limit their influence. The living need not overly concern themselves with the specificities.

Notions about *makishi,* however, are much more elaborated. At one level they are believed to be disembodied spirits that periodically localize themselves, making their presence known through the masked dancers who used to play a central role in a number of ritual performances, most especially *mukanda* (boys' maturity rites). Certain elderly individuals acquired widespread acclaim for their ability to serve as channels or conduits for particular *makishi.* Yet it is rarely clear why a particular *makishi* spirit consistently chooses to possess a particular masked dancer. Likewise, the

actual origins of *makishi* are unclear. Some contend that the original human creator of a mask returns after death to inhabit that mask and its
wearer in a particular mode. Others contend that the spirits of all those who
have performed well in a particular mask become an expanding body of energy that conjures up its own being and localizes itself in the mask. Still others contend that *makishi* are spirits created in nature who desire contact
with the human world. They grow lonely roaming the forest and thus periodically visit the living through a mask they find particularly appealing.
Perhaps a dozen or so *makishi* have widely agreed upon names, personalities, likes and dislikes, and particular domains of human experience in
which they are most interested and to which they can lend their power.
Some of the best known include Mukaala, Kaluwi, and Ntambu, each of
whom assists men in the area of huntsmanship. Kamwadi is most interested
in dreams and impotence; he helps to interpret the former and alleviate the
latter. Kayong'u specializes in madness, demonic possession, and divination. Njinga and Nukula assist women in all areas of fertility and childbirth.

Andumba are a class of spirits with much more nefarious intent toward
human beings. Their origins are equally speculative. Some contend that
they are simply *makishi* who detest humans for one reason or another. Others claim that *andumba* are the enduring spirits of monsters that once
roamed the earth. They are said to be cat-like demons that lurk along dark
and isolated pathways, waiting to devour lone individuals who happen to
pass by. Still others claim that *andumba* work primarily through human
agents. They invade the bodies of particularly evil individuals, strengthen
them, and use them as vessels to wreak havoc among humans.

Tuyebela are an invisible menagerie of grotesque little beings. They can
be twisted elves with backward-facing feet, or they can be composed of random assemblages of body parts that defy overall description. They are familiar spirits that do evil deeds on behalf of a particular female owner. Supposedly, a *tuyebela*, under instructions from its owner, slowly consumes the
liver of its hapless victim, causing him or her to waste away gradually. But it
is also said that each *tuyebela* must be fed according to its own schedule;
when hungry, it approaches its owner for the name of the next victim.
Should she refuse to give a name, she herself becomes the next victim. Upon
the death of its owner, a *tuyebela* approaches one of her surviving matrilineal female kin. This person, in turn, must either name or become the next
victim. As in the case of the other spirit beings, it is unclear where the *tuyebela* come from or why they select a particular owner/victim. Some say that

those predisposed toward witchcraft tend to attract *tuyebela*. Others feel that the happenstance of being related to a former *tuyebela* owner, combined with the fear of facing one's own death, is responsible for a relationship with one of the spirits.

The familiar spirit most associated with men is the *ilomba*, an invisible water snake that possesses a face, if one could see it, identical to that of its owner. An *ilomba* lives in a river but moves about through a system of huge tunnels that connect its home to that of its owner and to other homes in the area. It can, supposedly, spy on events and overhear conversations, which it reports back to its owner. It can also be sent to devour the livers of its owner's enemies. It is commonly suggested that men created their individual *ilomba* through magic acquired at a dear price from those who know the secret. Those who possess *ilomba* are said to have the power to "see" who else possesses one. The impact of an *ilomba* on the world of the living ceases with the death of its owner.

Other inhabitants of the invisible world crop up in nightly fireside conversations. These beings share with those described above the ambiguities of origin and intent as well as the uncertain meaning of their relationship with the world of living humans. Tales about invisible beings generally lack the authoritative tone of many Lunda orations. They are usually couched in terms such as "it is said," or "I have heard," or "some believe." In a very real sense, it can be dangerous to express too great a certitude about one's knowledge of the "other" world. Only those who have actually peeked into that world are believed to truly know it. And to possess such powers is fraught with many levels of meaning and risk.

The countenances of those who occupy the spirit world are said to be so terrifying that even the briefest glimpse of them would drive ordinary people insane. Indeed, many cases of severe mental illness are thought to have arisen when an individual's gaze, for some unexplained reason, momentarily penetrated the veil that separates the physical and metaphysical worlds. The vision beheld was so incomprehensible, so at odds with all human notions of rationality, that it left such people forever incapable of regaining control of their mental faculties. Yet certain categories of people are believed to possess the power to see the unseeable without suffering horrific consequences. That power evokes envy and loathing, wonder and revilement, desire and disgust. It is a supremely ambiguous power, most often associated with *atutepa* (diviners), *aloji* (witches or sorcerers), and *anyanta* (chiefs). These three categories of individuals, in a sense, stand in the doorway linking two worlds. I explore the changing relationship between this world and the other world through the changing status of these individuals and their impact on the sets of relationships that make up day-to-day life.

Revelation and Divination

Diviners occupy a pivotal position in social and ritual life. They are the ones who are called upon to identify the spiritual agents that are deleteriously affecting the world of the living. It is their task to indicate the specific ritual performance required to placate an angry ancestor, drive away a familiar spirit, alleviate a case of infertility, or reestablish social order. It might seem, therefore, that any study of the changing relationship between this world and the other is necessarily a study of the changing patterns of revelations from diviners. That is only partially true, however, for the power of the diviner is not as absolute as it might at first appear. Diviners' decisions are not always accepted without question. Indeed, diviners have been beaten and supposedly even killed by those outraged by their decisions, particularly by people who have been accused of witchcraft. Local custom also allows anyone doubting a diviner's decision to challenge him to an ordeal by poison. Should the diviner survive the ordeal, he can claim redress from his accuser. Divining is a most precarious occupation, and diviners are often viewed with a measure of suspicion. They tend to be marginal men—strange characters existing at the periphery of society but never really part of it. They are shadowy, solitary figures seen only in brief glimpses, antisocial men who nevertheless seem to know all that transpires in the village. In fact their lack of involvement in and attachment to this world is supposedly the source of their power to peer into the other world. But it is also asserted that there is a close relationship between the power to divine and insanity. Madmen also see things that others do not. Thus diviners are often suspected of having crossed the line to insanity. After all, Kayong'u, the patron spirit of all diviners, is also associated with madness and demonic possession. Yet, orderly social life is dependent on the availability of reliable diviners at particularly stressful moments.

In *Revelation and Divination in Ndembu Ritual* (1975), Victor Turner analyzes both the methods and symbolic content of Lunda divinatory practices. He recorded ten forms of local divination and noted that C. M. N.

White had experience of several others. The most common form of divination according to Turner's and White's as well as my own observation is *ng'ombu yakusekula:* literally, divination by shaking up and tossing objects in a basket. Twenty to thirty small figurines and other symbolic objects (*tuponya*) made of wood, stone, clay, bone, and other materials are shaken into a heap inside a flat winnowing basket. After each shake, the top three or four objects on the heap are examined individually, in combination, and with reference to their relative height in the heap. Each object has a variety of meanings. Each may in some way symbolize persons, social positions, characteristics, thoughts, emotions, and especially desires and ambitions. If the same object or cluster of objects repeatedly appears near the top, the answer to specific questions lies in the cluster of meanings those objects map out. As Turner noted, divinatory symbols are multireferential, and their referents are highly autonomous and readily detachable from one another. The concept here, as in the case of Lunda symbols in other contexts, is that the more they are known, the more they are considered mastered; the less they are known, the more they exert mastery. The prestige and influence of the ritual expert depends on this simple fact. There is power in the unknown (Turner 1975, 209). Although the meanings of some *tuponya* are quite straightforward and widely known, a fully trained diviner necessarily knows a vast amount more than the nonspecialist. But only a diviner fully possessed at the moment by a powerful spirit is capable of infallibly interpreting the *tuponya* pieces. Belief in the existence of spirit possession is essential for belief in divination.

To become a diviner, one must have been *kwata*, caught, by Kayong'u, the principal spirit for all diviners. Being caught produces a violent illness characterized by periods of complete disassociation, frequent seizures, and bouts of trembling. The illness can be successfully treated only by a cult group led by a powerful diviner. Should the patient survive, he becomes eligible to begin training as a diviner, if that is his wish. Very few actually take up the offer. Most acknowledge outright fear of the physical and psychological demands of the job, as well as of the threats to personal safety intrinsic in the position. Those who choose to join the ranks of the diviners pay well for the privilege. In the early 1950s a novice might have paid forty yards of cloth or a cow for knowledge of how to interpret divining objects. It is said that in the past even a slave would have been included in the payment (Turner 1975, 215). The clandestine nature of divination today makes it difficult to generalize about payments. But evidently a cow, a few pieces of good cloth, and a large amount of cash would not be unusually high for the mid-1990s.

Turner viewed diviners as extraordinarily shrewd and practical men, but he did not see them as charlatans. Diviners do indeed believe that they are possessed by spirits when they divine and that their divinatory objects have a certain intrinsic power to reveal that which is hidden. The diviner's task, however, is the practical one of revealing the causes of misfortune or death. His insights are retrospective, not predictive. Ndembu diviners, unlike many southern Bantu diviners, are seldom oracular. Their verdicts, as noted above, are not always accepted without question. Witches, sorcerers, and a range of other beings are credited with extraordinary powers to conceal their presence from the diviner or to envelop the mind of the diviner in false illusions. Even the most powerful diviners must continually fortify themselves with special medicines to combat the forces secretly sent to constrain their vision and confuse their judgment.

The central theme that pervades all Lunda rituals is that of bringing into the open what is hidden or unknown. The process of curing metaphysically induced illnesses, for example, is simply called *kusola* or *kumwekesa*, making known and visible. A spirit is made known through several phases. The first and most obvious is to identify it, name it, or discover by what name it wishes to be called. The second is to acknowledge awareness of that name and to mention it frequently. The third phase is to represent the spirit in some physical form. Only then does the spirit cease to catch, and can itself be caught. The diviner initiates the process by revealing the identity of the spirit. All family and cult members affected by that spirit need to mention the name of the spirit in prayers and invocations in elaborate and long-lasting ritual enactments, as well as in less formal quotidian interactions. The diviner may construct or commission the construction of a new *tuponya*, a figurine or other object to represent that spirit in his basket. One of the next few children to be born in the area might be named after the spirit. It is believed that when a spirit knows that it is truly "known" it emerges from its victim and ceases to cause illness, interfere with fertility, or create instability and disorder in village life.

A diviner proceeds in a step-by-step fashion, ascertaining the answer to one question after another through manipulating his basket. The questions are not put forward by the client. The diviner, instead, proposes questions to himself, proffers an answer, and examines his client's reaction, saying, "you have come for this reason," "such and such has been happening," or "you suspect so-and-so." With increasing specificity the diviner circles around the maze of contending issues before homing in on concrete answers to concrete questions. Unlike in the Western world, where a practitioner expects to receive a complete account of a patient's symptoms and past medical history in order to facilitate diagnosis of an illness, a diviner is expected to arrive at a diagnosis with minimum input from his clients. Clients may even try to trick him by disagreeing or incorrectly agreeing with his answers, all with the aim of testing his divinatory acuity.

The overwhelming majority of illnesses are locally recognized as malaria, colds, flus, or simple aches and pains which can be effectively treated with bed rest, good nutrition, or standard herbal preparations. Only diseases characterized by sudden violent attacks, unrelenting fever, and resistance to even the most powerful herbal treatments are suspected of being metaphysically induced. These are the signs, often accepted only reluctantly, that a diviner might be needed. It appears that in the past, successful diviners had expansive networks of apprentices, supplemented by young boys who regularly brought food sent by former clients as partial payment for the diviners' services. From this network the diviner was probably well apprised of any illness in the area, the background of the sufferer, and the gossip concerning possible causes. Undoubtedly, an effective intelligence network would have been a valuable asset to any diviner. A diviner whose revelations continually ran counter to local suspicions stood little chance of remaining long in business. Many diviners sought the protection of a chief and performed under his auspices near his capital village. Local lore, nevertheless, contains numerous stories of diviners who were shot, bashed, or speared to death because of an unacceptable or intolerable revelation. Yet, divining remains more than the art of lending a mystical aura to already well-formed local suspicions. The messenger may be killed, but the power of those in the other world to send messages is never denied. Orderly social life depends on orderly interaction with the spirit world. It requires individuals who can mediate and negotiate with that world, who can see what is hidden from others. Diviners may be feared and hated because they can condemn. But they also provide the only real mechanism for exoneration, for redress, and for social adjustment with the spirit world.

The precarious position of diviners became even more so with the outlawing of divination by the British colonial government. The threat of imprisonment drove many diviners out of business and others into remote or border regions, out of the reach of colonial officials. Diviners not only became more scarce but, by some accounts, their services became more expensive. People often had to travel great distances to receive revelations that often lacked the degree of specificity common to those of the old village diviner who had his finger on the pulse of the local community. Already in Turner's day, during the early 1950s, nearly one-third of all rituals were performed without the identity of the responsible spiritual agent's being known for certain (Turner 1967). Today, although diviners still more often than not confidently assert the mode of affliction, the precise identity of the afflicting agent is identified in only about half of the cases. Clearly, this has important implications for the process of building a consensus about holding exorcistic rituals. Rituals are rather expensive and time-consuming affairs requiring high levels of physical and fiscal cooperation among large numbers of individuals. If the exact identity of the spiritual focus of the intended ritual is unknown, the prospects for success are correspondingly diminished. In such a context it is undoubtedly difficult to marshal the required consensus for organizing a ritual performance.

The frequency of traditional exorcistic activity precipitously declined after divination was outlawed. In the early 1950s, Turner recorded that the average number of divination rituals that had been performed for a person during their lifetime was 3.3 for adult females and 2.5 for adult males. The corresponding figures for the mid-1980s were 0.52 per female and 0.31 per male, an 87 percent decline in three decades (tables 14–17). This decline no doubt reflects both the scarcity of diviners in general and the lack of precision exhibited by the remaining diviners, which reduced their effectiveness and thus made people less likely to call on them. Diviners increasingly drew clients from extremely large areas about which their knowledge was often limited, so their revelations did not have the personal touch that would lend them an air of unassailable truth.

It is interesting to note that colonial officials, no doubt at the urging of missionaries, chose to outlaw diviners rather than *chimbuki* (herbalists), *mbimbi* (circumcisers), or any other ritual specialists.[1] They must have had at least some knowledge of the key position that diviners occupied in Lunda social discourse. Colonial officials certainly were aware of one fact that few of the early structural-functionalist anthropologists seemed to recognize: rituals are risky business, and rituals dealing with the spirit world are even more so. The arguments over who is responsible for a person's illness, who should contribute funds and energy toward seeking out a diviner, whether or not to proceed on the advice of that diviner, and how to evaluate the outcome of a particular ritual are processes surrounded with such emotional intensity that exorcistic rituals are just as likely to provide the spark that breaks up a village as they are to provide the mechanism for bringing about healing and social order. Colonial officials probably saw diviners more as a threat to the general peace than as a threat to the new political order. In any event, colonial and missionary policies had a far-reaching impact on the Lunda's relationship to the other world.

The spread of Christianity reduced the influence of diviners not so much because it displaced traditional beliefs as because it became incorporated into them. Unlike the foreign-born missionaries, the Lunda did not necessarily view Christianity as an alternative belief system which could be embraced only after previously held beliefs had been rejected. The earliest missionaries, in choosing to use the local term Nzambi to refer to the High God, perhaps unknowingly perpetuated the notion that they were not attempting to introduce a new God but were simply bringing new information about the old Lunda High God. Thus, for many, conversion to Christianity merely meant an acceptance of the new belief that the High God was benevolent and responsive to prayers rather than otiose and uncaring. This acceptance required few modifications to the belief that the world was filled with disembodied spirits who periodically entered the realm of the living to cause illness and social unrest.

Christianity, as a new complex of beliefs, practices, and processes, had much to command the attention of the local population. In addition to the economic opportunities previously noted, Christianity appealed to the Lunda on both an aesthetic and an emotional level. It was centered around a book, a set of scriptures, and a set of rituals that were open and public. Things were not hidden in Christianity. The very will of God was seen as accessible to all—for some, through direct literate engagement with the Bible, for others, through oral engagement via sermons. The Bible itself, particularly the Old Testament, read like a Lunda text. It utilized techniques, traditionally acknowledged as valid, for justifying its authority. It was filled with genealogies linking the people of its time to primordial processes. It located the divisions among peoples in a tale of a collapsing tower that was similar to the tale of the tower of Kaposhi. It was saturated with stories of invisible beings, angels, devils, ancestor spirits, and even a holy ghost that regularly interacted with the living. Rather than transforming local belief, Christianity became an additional tool in the arsenal for engaging the spirit world and for combating the negative impact of nefarious spirits. Christians could appeal directly to the High God for relief from spirit-caused afflictions while continuing to make traditional appeals to the lower-level spirit more directly responsible for an illness.

The major groups of foreign-born missionaries among the Lunda, Catholics and Protestants, established clinics as well as churches, seeing medical work as an effective way to draw the population into the Christian sphere of influence. Christianity and medicine were inextricably linked in the local psyche. The clinics became quite popular, since people tended to view the pharmaceutical drugs they dispensed as akin to traditional herbal preparations, albeit more powerful. Clinic medicines, particularly the injectable types, were believed to be simply more concentrated. Nevertheless, even today most individuals still try one or more herbal preparations before they visit a medical clinic. This is partially so because most traditional medicines can be gathered in the course of daily activities, such as going to the fields and gardens, drawing water from the river, trekking to distant pastures to round up the goats and sheep, or going to the bush to hunt, trap, or fish. Visiting a clinic, however, tends to break up the daily routine, often forcing people to walk great distances and wait in long lines, perhaps to receive only pills rather than the much more highly desired injections.

More significant for the acceptance of the medical system introduced by missionaries, however, was that many Lunda came to see the Western system as parallel to their own two-tiered system. On the one hand it possessed pharmaceutical drugs for addressing routine organic-based illness. On the other it possessed a body of rituals, such as prayer, worship services, baptism, and communion, which facilitated communication with the spiritual world and could supposedly alleviate metaphysically induced illness. Thus Christianity can be seen to have had a dual impact on Lunda treatment strategies, affecting both physical and metaphysical treatment routines. Instead of becoming an alternative to the traditional system, the Christianity–Western medicine nexus became inserted in the middle of a larger action sequence. The old sequence of treatment seeking entailed trying homemade herbal preparations first, before seeking out the more powerful remedies of professional herbalists. If the illness persisted, metaphysical rather than organic causes were suspected, a diviner would be consulted, and exorcistic rituals would be enacted. Christianity has lengthened the sequence. Now, after using homemade and professional herbal remedies without success, some may try clinic medicine before entertaining the possibility of metaphysical involvement. Should pharmaceutical drugs likewise prove unsuccessful, increased participation in church rituals may constitute the first appeal to the spirit world. Only as a last resort do some then proceed to consult a diviner and organize an exorcistic ritual. The contrast between the two sequences can be outlined as follows:

Traditional healing sequence
   home-prepared herbs —▶ professionally prepared herbs —▶ consultation with diviner —▶ exorcistic rituals
Healing sequence with addition of Christianity
   home-prepared herbs —▶ professionally prepared herbs —▶ clinic visit —▶ church rituals —▶ consultation with diviner —▶ exorcistic rituals

The lengthening of the sequence holds important implications for those activities at the end of the chain, particularly divination and rituals. The fact that additional stages are now undertaken before a consensus is reached on the necessity of such activities might well in itself explain the decrease in their frequency. These activities, which traditionally served as options of last resort, are now less frequently seen, either because patients are more often cured at an earlier stage of the treatment sequence, or, quite frankly, because they have died before a consensus could be reached on the necessity of organizing a divination and the performance of complex rituals.

In this overview of the changing place of divination in Lunda social life, which is mostly an explanation of its quantitative decline, I have greatly oversimplified a history rich in responses to metaphysical imperatives. The colonial assault on local diviners took place concomitantly with the national rise of new interpretative frameworks for understanding the metaphysical world and new practices for accessing its power.

The Age of Evil

Lunda old-timers remember the 1920s and 1930s as an era of rampant *wu-loji* (witchcraft). It was a time of cosmic struggle against the forces of evil, a time that brought forth new interpretations and new means of redressing the relationship between this world and the other. Prophetic and antiwitchcraft movements swept across all of Zambia during that era (see van Binsbergen 1981). Although focused on and emanating from particular charismatic individuals, these movements spread like wildfire across ethnic boundaries, appealing to people steeped in diverse historical traditions. Similar movements occurred all over Africa, and the anthropological literature contains numerous hypotheses to explain such phenomena. Some of these explanations rely fundamentally on a cognitive interpretation of events. According to this view, antiwitchcraft movements were primarily an intellectual process that involved the creation of new explanatory devices. They constituted an effort to redefine an overwhelming problem, the problem of powerlessness. With the consolidation of colonial control over Africa through physical means and Africans' recognition of the futility of armed struggle, both the explanatory framework and the subsequent sphere of African resistance moved into the metaphysical realm. Witches, rather than men, machines, or political mechanisms, became the enemy. The identity of those witches had to be made known, and ways had to be generated to circumscribe their influence and activities. A second interpretive track sees prophetic and antiwitchcraft movements as a process of psychological reorientation. The recognition of colonial status was profoundly disturbing to the individual psyche. Rather than seeking to explain it, people sought instead to collectively explain it away: it cannot, it must not be happening. Alternatively, it must mean something other than what it appears to mean: it must be a stage in a more powerful unfolding. Proponents of this viewpoint hold that prophetic and antiwitchcraft movements are perhaps best understood not as having generated effective solutions but as having provided a psychological balm to soothe the battered consciousnesses left in the wake of colonial conquest. The movements provided some individuals with a peaceful interlude as they awaited the coming of a new age, but propelled others into frenzied activity in an effort to bring about that new age. The third dominant interpretive strand focuses on the sociological implications of these movements, calling attention to the organizational constructs generated as they swept across the landscape. The 1920s and 1930s saw new forms of social organization that mapped out new pan-ethnic clusters of individuals, mobilized and animated for action. The thrust of that action was not always clear, and the nature of its impact remains highly contested by both participants and outside interpreters.

The evidence from the Lunda case, scanty though it may be, based for the most part on the reconstructed memories of the very elderly, suggests that the power of prophetic and antiwitchcraft movements lay in their multiplicity of appeals. Such movements were unique in their capacity to create points of overlap between cognitive, psychological, and sociological needs, simultaneously appealing to potentially competing interests. They represented a pool of opportunities which a wide array of innovative actors and organizers could utilize to further an equally broad range of personal and collective ambitions.

One of the earliest prophetic and antiwitchcraft movements in Zambia was that initiated by an individual known as Mupumani. A brief history of his movement and a rigorous analysis of its meaning and historical impact can be found in van Binsbergen's *Religious Change in Zambia* (1981). A few details need be retold here, for in many ways Mupumani's movement became the intellectual, structural, and emotional model for the waves of other movements that followed in rapid succession. His movement made imaginative use of widely held traditional beliefs, repositioned revered symbols in an innovative way, and tapped into deeply felt emotional longings. It was Mupumani's movement that resituated the struggle for meaning in the colonial order on the metaphysical plane. His movement opened up the first real pan-ethnic dialogue about the relationship between this world and the other, and about the role of that relationship in maintaining intolerable colonial conditions.

Mupumani began his prophetic career in 1913, near Nanzela mission in central western Zambia. Within months he was attracting people from as far away as Mwinilunga, and beyond into Angola. Many, inspired during their stay with Mupumani, returned to their home areas to spread the word of his visions, the meaning of his revelations, and the necessity for adopting new practices. Mupumani was in many ways the archetypical prophet, according to van Binsbergen's definition: "We reserve the term 'prophet' for an individual who has had particularly original and direct experiences attributed to the supernatural and who, on that basis, attempts to persuade society to adopt his particular interpretation of the contemporary situation and to embark on new or exceptional practices" (1981, 145). Mupumani possesses the standard biographical profile of Central African religious innovators, a profile widely acknowledged in oral traditions as necessary to justify and legitimize one's claim to special status. It begins, more often than not, with a lingering affliction that baffles all medical specialists, continues with a crisis followed by a short period of death (perhaps a coma), and ends with a rapid and complete recovery. The short death is subsequently interpreted as a period during which the individual has been in communication with the spirit world. We saw virtually this same symbolic sequence in the rites of afflictions discussed earlier and the same metaphysical relations expressed in the recruitment of diviners. But it is the short period of death that signals the potential arrival of a genuine prophet rather than a new diviner or medical specialist. In a sense, a prophet is both, and more. To claim that position, however, one has to convincingly articulate a powerful message that one received while "dead," from a spirit revealed as responsible for one's miraculous recovery. If one could further demonstrate one's transformed status by enacting a miracle or two, one's claim would be all the more recognized.

Mupumani's innovation on this long-standing Central African tradition was his claim to have actually been in the presence of and in communication with the High God Nzambi rather than with the usual *akishi*, ancestor spirit. Mupumani claimed that, through God's eyes, he had seen witches pervading the landscape in all forms of disguise, causing confusion, disorder, and chaos. God revealed the terms under which he would assist people in a grand struggle against evil, reestablish the primacy of the living, and usher in a new age in which Africans would equal or exceed Europeans in existential glory. The first act required was the symbolic recognition of Nzambi as the supreme deity. The large forked stick generally planted in the center of each village circle or in front of the headman's house as a shrine to the founding ancestor had to be reoriented and reconsecrated to Nzambi. It had to be *tookesha*, cleansed or purified—stripped of its bark and made white, revealing its inner core. Prayers would now be offered directly to Nzambi rather than to any other spirit. Second, an antiwitchcraft campaign was to ensue. Witches had to be isolated and identified if their power was to be circumscribed. Two important techniques were offered to humankind to ferret out the witches. The first involved passionate sermons and the vibrant singing of Christian hymns. It was said that the very sound of loud rhythmical praises to Nzambi was offensive and even painful to witches and that regular attendance at worship services would be intolerable for them. Second, witches could not withstand dipping, that is, full-immersion baptism. The water itself would reject them and reveal their identities by causing them to become visibly ill on the spot. Mupumani's converts attempted to corral entire villages into undergoing these tests as a means of exposing the witches in their midst. In areas where they became a dominating force, it became dangerous to refuse participation in these rituals.

As van Binsbergen noted, what was new here was not the conception of the High God itself but rather the attempt to endow this conception with so much splendor, power, and immediate relevance that it would become capable of eclipsing all other religious entities that had previously been so conspicuous. Second, rather than accepting the traditional notion of witchcraft as inevitable and seeking to maintain a tolerable balance between good and evil on earth, Mupumani's followers sought instead a definitive confrontation aimed at eradicating all witchcraft, for all time. The vigor and emotional intensity with which Mupumani's supporters carried out their cosmic struggle against evil inflamed passions throughout much of Zambia. An explosion of witchcraft identifications took place in village after village. Forced attendance at huge open-air religious revivals and forced dippings regularly turned up witches. Some were beaten, some were killed. Others, however, managed to escape punishment by mournfully and repentantly confessing to witchcraft and by agreeing to use their powers to identify other witches. Mupumani's eradication teams swept through villages, confiscating and publicly burning all idols, figurines, and shrine objects associated with any spirit other than Nzambi. People were frequently beaten on the suspicion of hiding such objects. Colonial officials, after some vacillation, finally intervened in the name of public order. Mupumani was imprisoned for vagrancy and false pretensions in 1914, only one year after his movement had begun.

The key had hardly been turned on Mupumani's cell before new prophets began to sprout up everywhere in western Zambia. Each one had experienced a miraculous recovery from a troubling illness. Each one had undergone a short period of death during which he had supposedly had direct communications with Nzambi. Each one reaffirmed the validity of Mupumani's original vision and proclaimed the need to reinvigorate the antiwitchcraft campaign. Numerous such movements appeared among the Kanongesha Lunda. Some were externally inspired, others were locally generated. Most such movements, however, were far too ephemeral to leave their names in the historical record. They simply appeared as hastily assembled groups guided by little-known prophets, demanding the use of their own particular configurations of dipping, hymn singing, and manipulation of the Bible or other material paraphernalia for the identification and cleansing of witches. Often they did not identify themselves as belonging to any specific movement. It was well into the 1930s before the antiwitchcraft fervor began to wane in Mwinilunga and elsewhere. For the most part, the dawning of the nationalist era at that time yanked the strug-

gle against colonial conditions from the metaphysical sphere and resituated it in the physical realm of confrontational politics.

Chiefs

*The conception of chieftainship as sustained by basic, unchallenged
values effectively internalized throughout the societies of Central
Africa increasingly appears to be a myth. The fact that chieftainship often resorted to open, physical violence, and cruelty, and surrounded itself with mystical terror, could well be interpreted as a response to continuous and strong popular counter-currents against
chiefly legitimacy. Chiefs took on witchcraft connotations, which
they could not shake off even if they went to the extent of attempting
to monopolize the right to identify and prosecute witches.*

van Binsbergen 1981, 162

Chiefs occupy symbolic apical positions at the tops of the many social hierarchies that link the living. For this reason they are in greater existential
proximity to the ancestors than are other living beings. This nearness accentuates their ability to see into the other world. But a chief must also tap
into other sources of power. The Kanongesha for example, like most Central African chiefs, is inextricably associated with huntsmanship. His praise
names speak of him as *chibinda chinene*, the big hunter, or *sazomba*, the
supreme tracker. He finds and exerts mastery over animals in the forest as
well as men in the village. Hunting, the quintessential male activity, is the
most dangerous of all activities. It requires one to kill physical bodies yet
to avoid the ire of the spirits contained within those bodies. A big hunter
must have powers paralleling those of a witch, the difference being that a
hunter feeds on the meat of the forest rather than the "meat" of the village;
the latter is a reference to witches' having a taste for the flesh of people. The
big hunter today is invariably a gun hunter. The Kanongesha's elaborately
decorated gun is an essential, widely recognized and talked about item in
his stock of royal paraphernalia. It has come to surpass the ceremonial bow
and arrows and axe as the cardinal symbol of chieftaincy. In fact, *Wuta*, the
gun, is a commonly used synecdoche to refer to a chief in particular or roy-
alty in general. The formal title reserved for a prince or an eldest son of a
chief is *Mwanawuta*, son of the gun. The Kanongesha, however, is said to

possess another gun, which, although rarely seen, is the subject of even more local lore than is his ritually displayed rifle. This is his *wuta wawufuku,* or night gun. It is a powerful weapon whose functional capacity is a regular source of speculation and an occasional source of fear. A night gun is supposedly constructed from the thigh bone of a male who has been ritually sacrificed as part of the enthronement process of a new Kanongesha. Properly "medicated," by techniques known only to the royal family, this gun is said to fire invisible bullets capable of causing death by striking at the very soul of its intended victim.

A chief, more than any other individual, is bound to be the focus of much envy. The affective intensity of envy is neither minimized nor glossed over in Lunda society. It is the central theme of numerous proverbs; it guides the plot in whole categories of traditional tales; it is the moral of many fables; it is localized and represented as a *kaponya* figurine in the diviner's basket. Smoldering resentment from other claimants to the throne is frequently suspected of spilling over into metaphysical attacks on a chief's person. All potential heirs are suspected of knowing, or of being in the process of buying, the secret to the manufacture of *wuta wawufuku.* A chief is believed to be in nightly combat with all those who possess night guns. He must continually fortify himself through medicine and rituals of a most hidden nature if he is to survive for long. Additionally, witches are said to release their familiars immediately and repeatedly on a new chief, if for no other reason than to test his powers, his strength to identify and overcome them. The power possessed by chiefs may provoke envy and enmity among his subjects. Yet, as in the case of diviners, that power is widely acknowledged as a necessary element in maintaining the balance of forces between this world and the other. Some measure of personal excess or idiosyncratic behavior on the part of a chief may be tolerated. The success of his reign will ultimately be evaluated in terms of his capacity to hold witches and other forces that emanate from the other world in check. The lore surrounding the metaphysical power of Chief Kanongesha and the ever-evolving fortunes of his nightly struggle with the forces of evil is voluminous, highly elaborated, and frequently discussed.

Chiefs, however, do not spend all their time on cosmic battles. They are, more often than not, master politicians, shrewd entrepreneurs and cultural innovators who are actively involved in the nitty-gritty of day-to-day life. They stand not only in the metaphysical doorway to the other world but also at the crossroads of village social intercourse. Historically they have been amazingly adaptable, almost chameleon-like in their capacity to blend in with emerging social, political, and religious processes and to reappear well positioned to thrive under new conditions. Chiefs played a powerful role in legitimizing the antiwitchcraft movements of the 1920s and 1930s. The Kanongesha, like many others chiefs, openly aligned himself with the movements. Indeed, he continually struggled to subsume the new-style witch-finders under his authority. Fighting witches, after all, was his traditional domain. He therefore claimed the right to issue or withhold permission for the enactment of antiwitchcraft rituals. The literate Kanongesha of the 1930s became fond of issuing written permits as a symbol of his having authorized and legitimized the activities of the holder. Those without permits could be treated as false prophets intent upon sowing disorder for personal gain. They could be beaten soundly for their pretensions without fear of chiefly intervention.

Antiwitchcraft movements were not static or mechanical phenomena. Each one evolved in accordance with the dialectical relation between the prophet's vision and popular response. Nor did these movements result in a simple bifurcation of society, particularly not between a so-called "modernist" faction pursuing careers within the new colonial economy and a "traditionalist" faction still deeply encased in the precolonial framework. As has often been noted, it was particularly the labor migrants who spread the details of prophetic and antiwitchcraft movements over vast distances. They, along with those in the area who were pursuing modern careers, often initiated and acted as agents for the witchcraft eradication movements in Central Africa. In some cases one finds even the new mission elite, particularly African catechists and lay preachers, leading Christian converts out of the expatriate-established churches and founding their own charismatic movements. These movements may have started out as eschatological movements with millenarian overtones, but they quickly came to resemble what had become an almost standardized version of the antiwitchcraft movement in Central Africa. Subsequently, under pressure from adherents, leaders of these movements would be forced to conjure up medicines that would supposedly provide protection from the power of witches.

For chiefs to retain power, they had to be politically and socially nimble; carefully navigating the dangers of constantly emerging and contradictory social phenomena. They had to be seen protecting the interests of absent migrant workers while serving as champion of the interests of those who stayed behind. They were expected to access the range of benefits that modernity, in the form of Christian missions and government agencies, brought to the land yet continue to be stalwarts of tradition. They were expected to rout out evil yet restrain the divisive forces of anti-witchcraft movements. In short, they were expected to be magical and to use their powers solely for good.

Continuity and Change

Mary Douglas and other anthropologists have suggested that recurrent witch-cleansing cults are part and parcel of the traditional setup of Central African rural society; they argue that witchcraft accusations ebb and flow with levels of social stress. For Zambia in particular, van Binsbergen has suggested that the prophetic and antiwitchcraft movements of the 1920s and 1930s represented a major break with past patterns of witch-cleansing. The most significant element lay not in the frequency of occurrence but rather in the personnel and the idiom of witch-cleansing. In the past, he noted, "sorcery formed the central moral issue. The necessity to control sorcery and to expose and eliminate sorcerers was fully acknowledged. These functions were the prerogatives of those exercising political and religious authority. The battle against sorcery was waged continually, and formed a major test for the amount of protection and well-being those in authority could offer their followers" (van Binsbergen 1981, 285). The notion of a definitive battle to permanently eradicate witchcraft can be viewed as incompatible with previously held beliefs. In particular, the cyclical perception of time, said to characterize precolonial Africa, is discordant with the idea of a coming millennium. Millenarianism and notions of salvation imply a more linear view of the flow of history. All of the standard arguments about African perceptions of time could be inserted at this point. From Evans-Pritchard on ecological and structural time among the Nuer, to Bohannan on time as both a natural and social construct among the Tiv, to works by Mbiti and Fabian, the subject of the transformation of African perceptions of time has been thoroughly dissected. I refer the reader to those texts and move on to restate that the major elements of van Binsbergen's thesis revolve around the personnel involved in the new movements and the symbolic idiom they spoke: "The recruitment of witch-cleansing agents from amongst outsiders divorced from local foci of authority (even if often invited and protected by chiefs), the new symbols (dipping, the High God, hymns and sermons), the massive response which made the populations of entire villages and regions step forward, hand in their sorcery apparatus, and get cleansed—all this suggest not a recurrent 'traditional' phenomenon, but a dramatic attempt at superstructural reconstruction that properly belongs to the chapter of recent religious innovation in Central Africa" (1981, 285).

Yet, it must be noted that many elements of these movements recall, replicate, reinvigorate, or resituate preexisting beliefs and practices of an almost generic Central African variety. Among the Kanongesha Lunda, as elsewhere, the belief that the spirit world exists and that it is a source of power to be tapped is real. Under the stressful conditions of colonialism, we can only presume that some must have been genuinely tempted to access this power. Perhaps those who recognized their own temptation were also more predisposed to believe that others were yielding to the option. People who had no hope of competing using the new tools of advancement, or who had mastered them but still found their path to the top blocked for some reason, are the usual suspects. Throughout Africa, the three categories of individuals who were most frequently at the center of witchcraft accusations as both accused and accusers during the 1920s and 1930s were those Africans who occupied the highest rungs of the colonial ladder, those recognized as trying to crash the new hierarchy, and those most left behind in the new scramble for positions within the colonial order of things. The genuineness of witchcraft beliefs is perhaps best reflected in the overwhelming numbers of people who owned and voluntarily surrendered paraphernalia for interacting with the spirit world. Figurines, fetishes, and medicinal concoctions were assembled and burned by the thousands in campaign after campaign during the antiwitchcraft movements.

The basic nature of preexisting beliefs about witches had not changed. Rather, they were compounded by the novel recognition of the pan-African nature of prevailing conditions. They demanded pan-African rather than localized solutions. The tradition of whites as witches is a long-standing one throughout Africa and relates to the images that Africans had formed of whites early in the history of their interaction. Whites are all wealthy. They have access to wondrous machines they do not create, or at least that no African sees being created. There is much about whites that is mysterious and hidden. Africans do not witness their births, their illnesses, or their funerary practices. Nor do Africans witness the generation of European cash and commodities. Many precolonial tales existed of whites using African bodies to manufacture a range of products. As early as the 1600s it was said that European wine was made from African blood, salted meats from African flesh, cheese from African brains, and gunpowder from the ashes of African bones. The image of Europeans as witches quietly feeding on African bodies fits neatly into local conceptions of witches. The metamessage of prophetic antiwitchcraft movements was that Europeans were now in alliance with local witches. The Witchcraft Ordinance of 1914 (amended in 1948, 1952, 1963, and 1964) made witchcraft accusations, rather than the actual practice of witchcraft, the main culpable offense. From colonial quarters there was a complete refusal even to entertain the notion that witchcraft might be a real phenomenon. From the local perspective, however, the approach of the colonial authorities was evidence at least of profound ignorance, but most likely of outright collusion between European and local witches. This law added to the vulnerability of the diviners and of traditional witch-finding activities. Compliance with the law would leave the local population defenseless and open up uncontested space for witches to operate more freely.

Furthermore, as time passed and a generation of Europeans had actually expired on African soil, their spirits were added to the traditional mix. The spirits of Europeans, like all other spirits, must have wishes and desires. European spirits must endeavor to be known, acknowledged, accommodated, or celebrated in some fashion. Do Africans have a responsibility to address the needs of those European spirits now roaming African territory? Can Africans suffer when European spirits are displeased? How is the presence of European spirits to be revealed, represented, and thus mediated? These are some of the questions that framed the religious innovations of the 1920s and 1930s. The "other world" was expanding in scope and variety. New means for understanding and addressing that world were needed. One route led to increased interaction with those Europeans claiming fullest knowledge of the spirit world, the expatriate priests and pastors. Church attendance boomed in tandem with the spread of antiwitchcraft movements. Christian symbolism became more deeply infused into local life. The other route, however, led to innovation and expansion of the traditional repertoire of rites of affliction. The Kanongesha Lunda associated the coming of Europeans with the emergence of what they recognized as new diseases. New figurines were added to the diviners' baskets, and at least two new rituals, *tukuka* and *masandu*, emerged to appease European spirits causing illness. As Victor Turner noted in the early 1950s, "These two rituals are becoming very popular . . . and are often performed for persons suffering from tuberculosis. The shades [spirits] who cause the disease are said to be those of Europeans or of members of other tribes like the Lwena and part of the treatment consists of giving the patient European foods, served by a 'houseboy,' miming European dancing in couples, wearing European dress, and singing up-to-date songs such as 'We are going in an airplane to Lumwana'" (1967, 15).

The symbolic elements may be novel in themselves, but the framework of meaning in which they are embedded is a long-standing one. The rapid expansion of external trade during the seventeenth and eighteenth centuries, for example, had also spawned rituals to address the new insecurities and diseases that followed the caravan routes across Central Africa. The introduction of new cults of affliction, explicitly associated with and often named after the people among whom the diseases supposedly arose, was a common phenomenon. Senior adepts from such cults might then spread the new interpretation of disease further afield. They, however, were generally regarded as agents of a cult that already existed elsewhere, rather than as creators of a new cult. J. C. Miller, Wyatt MacGaffey, and John Janzen have each explored in some detail the consistency and prevalence of this phenomenon throughout Central Africa.

A second area of continuity lies in the meaning assigned to reversals in power relations. Momentary reversals of status or relationships have long served as a motif in oral traditions, storytelling, and ritual practices to presage an impending change of monumental significance. Within rites of passage, for example, rapid reversals of status between initiates and officiants are core enactments. At certain points the initiates are fed by hand, and at other points they feed their ritual elders. In *mukanda* camps, boys are reduced to the status of animals, stripped of all natural human rights, before being granted the status of men with expanded rights. In *nkanga* ceremonies, girls are ritually reduced to babies before their reproductive capacity is socially recognized. In all ceremonies, initiates undergo a symbolic death before their rebirth in a new status is complete. Schecter's collection of Lunda oral traditions and Turner's collection of rites of affliction both contain many examples of reversals preceding a fundamental reordering. Because colonialism brought such a rapid and profound reversal of conditions, it required an equally powerful interpretation. Slow, steady change can be explained, contained, and indigenized; rapid reversals may indicate not the emergence of a new steady state but rather even greater change to come. The meaning of such reversals may require interpretation, perhaps with assistance from those in the metaphysical world. The fact that many were prepared to believe that the changes brought about by colonialism foretold the coming of the millennium should not be particularly surprising. Nor would such a belief necessarily require a fundamental transformation in notions of time or history. The African concept of the millennium contains many elements of circularity. It is not a linear break with the past, but rather a return to an original point in the past. For the Lunda it would represent a return to the primordial condition of direct and personal contact with the High God Nzambi, a time before human beings discovered witchcraft.

A third level of continuity is in the persistence of the belief that those who have resided longest in an area must be formally recognized as the owners of the land. Traditionally, conquered owners were accorded areas of preeminence in the ritual or religious sphere. Antiwitchcraft movements, at one level, were an assertion of that right. Although in many ways the movements acknowledged European conquest over people, they did pose a direct challenge to Europeans' attempts to dictate the relationship between Africans and the other world. Implicit in much of the rhetoric and many practices associated with antiwitchcraft movements was the desire to compel Europeans to more adequately accommodate the preexisting residents. The movements did not borrow symbols from the newly introduced religions so much as demonstrate the possibility of mastering those symbols, of appropriating them and tapping their power for local use.

The movements of the 1920s and 1930s flowed along many tracks. They provided plausible cognitive interpretations of dramatically changed circumstances; psychological reorientation for the decentered psyche; and methods for organizing people across traditional ethnic boundaries, classes, and occupations. From a more cynical viewpoint, they also provided new pathways to prominence for creative individuals and groups within the colonial order of things. The movements were seminal to the formation of the modern nationalist movement of the 1940s and 1950s, as well as being anticolonial struggles in their own right. They were battles against a particular phase of colonial intrusion—the attempt to interfere with, disturb, or establish control over the relationship between this world and the other.

Structural Adjustment and Spiritual Response

The nationalist era may have served to redirect Africans' attention to the need to struggle in the physical realm. But in many respects, the broad traditional framework for interpreting the metaphysical realm remained remarkably unchanged. The social, political, and economic expansion of the local microcosm and the infusion of new peoples and their spirits into the Lunda sphere of operation may have expanded and enriched Lunda notions and practices vis-à-vis the other world. Colonialism, after all, not only forcefully placed Lundaland within a larger political construct but also repositioned the Lunda within a larger metaphysical world. Nevertheless, few aspects of Lunda interpretations and responses were genuinely novel.

During the dry season of 1993, President Frederick Chiluba embarked on a series of constituency tours to the rural areas of Zambia. The Structural Adjustment Program, implemented at the urgings of the International Monetary Fund (IMF) and the World Bank, was being met with open hostility from many quarters. Consumer prices were skyrocketing as long-standing government subsidies were being removed. Social services were in sharp decline as the size of the federal budget was being reduced. The loosening of import restrictions brought a flood of foreign goods into local markets, challenging manufacturing monopolies and constraining job creation. The more organized segments of urban communities were threatening strikes, boycotts, riots, and general chaos if the government continued its policy of liberalizing and privatizing the formerly state-managed economy. President Chiluba sought to head off similar responses among rural dwellers by persuasively presenting them with the logic of his approach to Zambia's economic woes. In a widely remembered and often quoted speech before thousands of Lunda upon his arrival at the airport in Mwinilunga, President Chiluba compared the Zambian economy to a person afflicted by witchcraft: "We all know what must be done in these sorts of cases, don't we? First we must identify the witches. Then we must keep them away from the patient while we apply the medicine. The medicine will not work if the witches are hovering near the patient." In dramatic fashion he went on to identify the witches as none other than loyalists of UNIP, the party he had defeated in the last election. For about two hours the president developed and embellished his theme of witchcraft, economic misfortune, and the need for traditional exorcistic practices. At one level this speech may be viewed simply as a variant on the age-old political tactic of blaming past administrations for current economic crises. It was a clarion call to root out any lingering influence that UNIP might still possess in the economic sphere. At another level the speech compared IMF/World Bank prescriptions to traditional medicines, which commonly caused pain and even convulsions before eventually effecting a cure. At still another level, Chiluba could be seen as claiming the special status of witch-finder and traditional doctor, albeit on a national scale. He was asserting that his power was more than that of merely the first democratically elected president of Zambia in over two decades—that his moral authority was based on the ability to see what others could not. Zambia's new economic direction seemingly became something other than a contest between competing philosophies or econometric models. It became a metaphysical battle between good and evil. The people need not concern themselves with the intricacies and complexities of economic equations. Theirs was a simple choice between believing or not believing in the special powers of the leader who stood before them. Should they choose to believe, then they would take the medicine. Traditional healers were under no compulsion to explain how their medicines worked. Indeed, President Chiluba offered no such explanation to the people of Mwinilunga that day.

The speech provoked swift and visceral reactions of varying types. UNIP loyalists lashed out angrily at being called witches. Some scrambled for the spiritual high ground, labeling the president himself a false prophet, with evil designs. Others, however, talked of prosecuting the president under chapter 30 of the Laws of the Republic of Zambia, the Witchcraft Ordinance, which made witchcraft accusations a punishable offense. Among the expatriate missionary community in Mwinilunga, the reactions ranged from utter shock to bitter disappointment. Many noted that the speech was delivered without any hint of satire or irony. It appeared to treat witchcraft not as a momentarily useful metaphor but as a real and ever-present phenomenon. It appealed directly to beliefs that missionaries had been struggling to eradicate for almost a century. For some missionaries the speech represented a major setback to their work, while for others it was a painful but clear reminder of the enduring character of witchcraft beliefs. For the vast majority of Lunda present, however, it was a powerful and compelling speech that was endlessly retold and embellished in nightly fireside chats. Chiluba had garnered over 90 percent of the votes cast in Mwinilunga. For many, the speech was further confirmation of the wisdom of their votes.

The intent behind president Chiluba's remarks about witchcraft remains unclear. Perhaps he simply saw the witchcraft motif as a clever way to enliven a potentially dull political stump speech. Perhaps he had higher aims. But the local context into which those remarks flowed is a bit more certain. The reigning traditional authority in Mwinilunga, Senior Chief Kanongesha, had already intensified local sensitivities toward the reality of witches in their midst. For nearly three years the Kanongesha had been openly wielding his metaphysical powers in daily and nightly struggles against the living and the dead. The Kanongesha was ill. At times he would appear on the verge of recovery, only to lapse back into "wasting away." Clearly he was being bewitched. He, and especially his family members, vowed to retaliate. They spoke openly of the metaphysical powers at the disposal of the chief, his command over unspeakable spirit beings, his regiment of zombie guards, and the accuracy of his "night gun." It was said that no one witch would dare attack the chief. His power could be overwhelmed only by a whole coterie of witches acting in concert, all of whom had to be identified and dealt with. N'ganda, the chief's capital village and its residents, was in essence mobilized for spiritual warfare, launching aggressive and widely feared campaigns against those thought responsible for the chief's condition. Subchiefs and senior headmen made pilgrimages to the capital to reaffirm their allegiances and to offer their own power to the struggle as well as that of the major diviners and ritual practitioners in their respective areas. Famous diviners from Angola were invited to take up residence at the capital. A flood of self-styled men and women of power also gravitated toward the capital. Before the elections of 1992, N'ganda had identified several local UNIP party workers as witches. Most of them quickly confessed their sins, gave up politics, and receded into the background. Subsequently, N'ganda made accusations, based on revelations from those who were supposed to be the most powerful diviners, that four individuals from widely dispersed areas of Lundaland were the primary witches assaulting the chief. All were powerful figures, local heroes with large, well-managed villages and plenty of dependents and supporters. Three confessed, promised to stop bewitching the chief, and begged for forgiveness. They were left alone. The fourth, who denounced the accusation as ridiculous, was immediately set upon. His village of nearly twenty buildings was burnt to the ground. His family was badly beaten, and nearly forty individuals were chased from the area with only the clothes on their backs. The chief still did not recover. A period of uneasiness reigned.

In many quarters it was rumored that the Kanongesha had AIDS, that his youthful indiscretions had come back to haunt him. N'ganda, however, reacted particularly harshly to such talk, and drove it underground. On the first of September, 1993, N'ganda announced the death of the Kanonge-sha. Although it was the middle of the hot, dry season, when the sky is usu-ally crystal clear and the air is motionless, the sky turned gray that morning and cold swirling winds swept across the plateau. Animals became disori-ented and ran about wildly. They were said to be chased by the spirits re-leased from captivity upon the death of their master, the Kanongesha. The interregnal period began. Traditionally this has always been a time of insti-tutionalized disorder. Numerous claimants to the throne would arise and would battle one another with knowledge of genealogies and oral tradi-tions by day and with the power of their "night guns" after dark. Two years later, at the time of this writing, the question of succession had yet to be resolved. The area was still alive with talk of witchcraft. Every illness con-tinued to be dissected for its metaphysical implications. Accusations ran rampant.

Here again, events in Angola influence the social dynamics in Zambia. The conflict with Angola has elevated the Kanongesha Lunda's sophistica-tion about the tools of modern warfare and has affected their conceptions of metaphysical war. The notion of a generic "night gun" has been replaced with talk about "night AK-47s" and "night Stinger missiles." On the other hand, the Angolan Lunda have for long been viewed by the Kanongesha Lunda as more "pure," more traditional. Their colonial and postcolonial experiences, although played out as near as a few miles away, were never-theless worlds apart from the experiences of the Kanongesha Lunda under British rule. Under the Portuguese, the Angolan Lunda received far less in the way of schools, clinics, missionary establishments, and government extension services. To a far greater degree they had been forced to orga-nize their existence around traditional, rather than book knowledge. The state of their health was far more dependent on the power of their herbal-ists and ritual practitioners. Their interaction with the spirit world was less intruded upon by Christian doctrines and practices. During the civil war, which has now persisted for nearly three decades, vast numbers have died. The Lunda on the Angolan side of the border have a metaphysical world teeming with recent arrivals. Their connections between this world and the other are fresh and powerful.

The addition of Angolan Lunda into the Kanongesha mix energized the whole range of local metaphysical projects. Medicines or ritual enactments were needed to protect people from the metaphysical fusillade being hurled by those actively engaged in the struggle for the Kanongeshaship. The claimants themselves were said to be continually and desperately seeking out additional sources of power. There were, furthermore, those who used the chaos and uncertainty associated with the chiefly battle to cover their own efforts at settling old scores by metaphysical means. *Andumba, tuyebela,* and *ilomba* were said to have run about unchecked. Then, there were those who were all too ready to interpret the ill effects of the Structural Adjustment Program (SAP) in spiritual terms and to recommend the mobilization of spiritual forces as the only way to negotiate its pitfalls. All across Zambia, the opposition newspapers had become fond of referring to SAP as *Satana Ali Pano:* Satan is here. From the Lunda perspective, the entire metaphysical world seemed to be on the move. People needed protection from the impact of unseen beings and forces, as well as from the impact of witchcraft accusations occurring at all levels of society. Angolans were believed to possess a deeper font of power than the Zambian Lunda, and many eagerly sought them out. On the other hand, a close connection with Angolans could be interpreted as a quest for power. It could be seen to signal one's entry into one or the other of the spiritual frays and thereby provoke preemptive metaphysical strikes. Yet it became increasingly difficult to avoid intimate contact with Angolans. Angola, as noted in chapter 7, represented the new economic frontier, drawing the brave and the adventurous ever deeper into its territory. Furthermore, increasing numbers of Angolans themselves reside in Mwinilunga. More than twenty thousand refugees from the civil war have settled in Mwinilunga during the late 1980s alone. The cheap labor they brought to an area of ample land resources was welcomed. The knowledge they were thought to possess, however, was ambiguous in its implications and impact.

Summary

For over a century, Lunda discourse about the metaphysical world has been enriched by fertile and provocative bodies of beliefs that came in from elsewhere. Some were brought in by Europeans, others by African neighbors, and still others by Lunda people returning from sojourns abroad to raise money for taxes and other requisites of modern life. These beliefs instigated new debates about fundamental issues. Where is the spirit world located? What are the conditions of entry? What is the status of newly arrived vis-à-vis long-residing spirits of various types? For the Lunda of old, things had been relatively simple. The physical and metaphysical worlds occupied different dimensions of the same space. The spirits of the dead neither ascended nor descended into some other realm but continued to move about the same terrain they had trodden while alive. Entry into the metaphysical realm was inevitable and unproblematic. Death severed neither one's connection with the land, nor, it was hoped, one's connection with kin. Lundaland was, thus, a very crowded place with countless spirits jostling about cheek by jowl with the living. The broad outline of relations between this world and the other world was well known to all. Ambiguity and uncertainty surrounded specific details of that relationship, but that was expected and even desirable. After all, only those who had somehow managed to visit the other world and return could speak with absolute authority.

Christianity introduced novel concepts into Lunda thinking about the metaphysical world, most especially into notions of duality and displacement. There were now two metaphysical spaces, heaven and hell, separated from the physical plane by cosmic distances and by a process of judgment. The details of one's life mattered; and they mattered for a very long time. Christianity held out the prospect of an afterlife of eternal bliss or eternal damnation, depending, of course, on the outcome of the final judgment. Traditional beliefs had offered only a rather pleasant but mundane spiritual existence, and only for as long as someone in the world of the living continued to remember a spirit. Christianity, however, raised the stakes to a horrifying or exhilarating degree.

The concept of a judgment day necessarily implies a distinctly nontraditional relationship with the High God. Pre-Christian Nzambi had made no demands, expected no worship, exacted no punishment, and promised no rewards. He was the quintessential otiose African High God. The concept of judgment, however, implies a God who is active and engaged, perhaps jealous and vengeful—one who continually monitors and evaluates human actions. It implies a God who establishes a framework of dos and don'ts within which human behavior must be confined in order to reap divine rewards and avoid everlasting retribution. This relationship with the High God, in turn, displaces the ancestors from their traditional role as the ultimate validators and final arbitrators of moral status. It also signals a significant redirection of ritual activity away from the ancestors and toward the High God.

The Lunda's incorporation into the Central African caravan networks resulted in thousands of people traversing the territory each year. The Lunda's incorporation into a new colonial state, however, resulted in thousands of outsiders actually settling in the territory and, sometimes, dying there. Thus, the spirits of European missionaries, Ovimbundu traders, Bemba bureaucrats, Nyanja veterinarians, Lozi lovers, or perhaps even Kaonde criminals might spend eternity mingling with Lunda spirits. Need they be placated or propitiated, appeased or appealed to? What unknown evil might they unleash on the local population? These were powerful questions that took on increasing urgency as the spirit world became more diverse. And what of the massive numbers of Angolan Lunda entering the spirit realm far too early, as a result of a most tragic war creeping ever too close?

Even in the midst of tumultuous change, some continuity of interpretation remains possible. Life is still an unbroken chain of births and deaths. One's moral status can still have real physical and material consequences. Evil humans do exist and will ever manipulate unseen forces and substances in their bid to acquire power. Spirits have their own hopes, fears, and dreams. The living must, therefore, generate ways of talking with the dead. These are fundamentals that, for some, remain unaffected by the expanding metaphysical microcosm.

But the expansion did make possible new interpretations, open up new courses of action, and suggest the viability of new strategies. Zealous Protestants, Catholics charismatics, Apostolic priests, new-style prophets, and a host of religious innovators attempted to join, or replace, diviners and chiefs as legitimate seers into the other realm. Church ceremonies, ecstatic open-air revivals, dipping, hymn singing, and other idiosyncratic enactments, likewise, offered the ability to reveal and repel old and new forms of evil. Western pharmaceutical medicine was rapidly embraced, at times establishing the biological bases of illnesses that had been misdiagnosed as spiritually induced. The Bible was also embraced for its capacity to manifest the words of the High God and for its revelations about life and the afterlife. Yet, its flexibility of interpretation left plenty of room for human agency. New symbolic elements were inserted in an old framework.

In truth, the Lunda had always been receptive to novel explanations and associated ritual practices. Efficacy, rather than a ritual's place of origin or ethnic association, mattered most. The phenomenon of new people staying in Lundaland long enough to die and join the local spirit world cried out for new paradigms and practices. But these precipitated a struggle—a struggle not just for control over meaning in the physical world, but a struggle for place within the metaphysical world. The Lunda knew that just as their own spirits had overwhelmed those of the indigenous Mbwela, so too the spirits of Europeans and other foreigners could ultimately overwhelm them. The battle had serious implications. Control in the spirit realm legitimized claims to land and power in the physical realm. Thus, everything from personal misfortune to the deterioration of the Zambian economy to the spread of AIDS to the death of the Kanongesha has been attributed to declining control over forces in the metaphysical world. The fear in Mwinilunga is still palpable.

Some have launched a battle not merely to reestablish a balance between the forces of good and evil but to overcome evil once and for all. Night warriors such as Senior Headman Chifunga, however, could not conceive of a world without evil. Without the presence of evil, how could one demonstrate one's own moral righteousness? Without confronting and overcoming evil's temptations to illegitimate power, how could one justify one's claim to legitimate power? Evil must exist. And as long as it does, some might add, so too must men like Chifunga, who serve as living lightning rods for evil, who nightly confront and contain the forces of evil, to the benefit of us all.

Chapter Nine

Style, Change, and Social Transformation

Each of the relationships explored here—between people and the environment, between the individual and the group, between old and young, between males and females, between rich and poor, between "us" and "them," between this world and the other world—presents itself as a protean bricolage of constancy and change. Some of the flux is the inevitable outcome of generational-based strivings for place, meaning, and identity within wide-ranging social formations. Although Central African societies tend to lack the formalized age grades that give structure to intergenerational relations in East Africa, Lunda society can nevertheless be meaningfully viewed as composed of discrete layers of age-mates, collectively moving through time, space, and social positions. This view is not simply a heuristic device that allows the researcher to conveniently periodize and give form to an otherwise unruly mass of cultural moments, movements, motives, and meanings. Indeed, the Lunda themselves apparently find it useful to construct society, through forms of discourse as varied as oral histories, judicial declamations, and even the spatial layout of their villages, in ways that emphasize society's layered and age-centric nature. Among the Lunda, one is without question one's brother's keeper, as well as the keeper, confidant, and comforter of one's sisters, cousins, friends, and other age-mates. Had Evans-Pritchard studied the Lunda rather than the Nuer, he would most likely have still arrived at his famous conclusions about "structural time" in Africa, that is, time reckoned as the movement of groups through hierarchized layers of social structure. While recognizing the injustice that anthropologists have done to both "us" and the "other" by cramming varying notions of time into such strained dichotomies as modern/traditional, linear/cyclical, reversible/irreversible, and qualitative/quantitative, it would nevertheless be an injustice not to note that a good number of Lunda do, indeed, talk about life as sets of cohorts moving through structured time. Each set follows the other from *anyikeki* to *atwanzi* to *atukwenzi* to *akulumpi* to *akishi* (infants to children to adults to elders to ancestors). Succession to political power is adelphic, passing first through an entire line of brothers and male cousins before dropping down to the proximal generation. Each assemblage of cohorts ultimately attempts to leave its mark on local style and aesthetics, on widespread social forms and functions. If not in youth, certainly in later life each set of cohorts endeavors to infuse new meaning into old legends and lore, to impress its own passing upon the physical and social landscape, to leave the names of its members behind as topographical referents or ritual titles long after it has claimed a place of honor in the other world.

Yet, much remains constant in the realms of subsistence acquisition and social relations, an outgrowth of continuity in the domain of taken-for-granted beliefs that may be sufficiently strong to allow us to assert the existence of a local consciousness consistent with a pan-African, or at least a Central African, ecumene of the sort postulated by Vansina, Kopytoff, LeVine, and others. As outlined in more detail in the introduction, this ecumene would include the following beliefs, values, and tendencies:

• High value placed on both local autonomy and widespread social links
• A view of the frontier as a space for social conservation rather than transformation
• A tendency toward fission as a mechanism for dealing with many of life's problems: famine, succession struggles, fear of witchcraft, or even desire for adventure
• Village segmentation carried out by groups such as lineage segments, clans, or sets of brothers
• A constant drive for followers, who, if necessary, are converted into fictive kin, and the corollary drive for patrons
• Maintenance of social distance between those differing in sex and age
• Emphasis on material transactions in interpersonal relations
• Functional diffuseness of authority relations
• Personalization of impersonal forces and concretization of abstract phenomena

Throughout this text we have encountered continuities in the Lunda world that potentially stem from, or at least provide evidence for, the existence of the above ecumene. We saw, for example, the continued immediacy of the Lunda's relationship with the environment and their notion of a world of boundless space waiting to be colonized with meaningful activity. Few social or manufacturing processes separate people and products: "man the hunter" harvests the forest for items of use and trade; "woman the nourisher" sustains the village with the products of farms and fields. Freedom of movement across the landscape is an inalienable right. Movement creates opportunities and generates knowledge. Labor, the meaningful movement of bodies, is the primary creator of value and validator of ownership.

From the days of empire through the era of the one-party nation-state, we find a willingness both to experiment with new products and processes and to accept outsiders as the primary providers of significant elements of daily life. More important, we saw similarities over time in the range of mechanisms utilized to develop personal relations with those outsiders. Newness, rareness, and distinctiveness endure throughout Central Africa as symbols and metaphors for wealth and rank. Imports ranging from cloth to curing rituals, and those who facilitate their flow, remain highly sought after.

We observed the embeddedness of the notion that to be human is to be socially connected while one simultaneously maintains certain inalienable rights as an autonomous individual. One's village remains a fundamental component of identity, while flexibility of residence persists as a basic right. Even the notion of the ideal village as a core set of brothers surrounded by their matrikin continues unchallenged. Throughout their history, the Lunda have spawned a multiplicity of groups with which the individual can choose to affiliate, each group animated and sustained in its own fashion and with its own matrix of rights, duties, expectations, and opportunities. The idiom of age and the image of the elder as both *mukwakuheta* (one with things) and *mukwakwashi* (patron) remain ubiquitous concepts. Individuals are living texts. The elderly are more fully inscribed, providing knowledge, moral guidance, and emotional stability to the group. Throughout every stage of Lunda history we have seen the need, or at least the pressing urge, to construct hierarchies expressed in an age-saturated lexicon that naturalizes the uncertainty and unpredictability of individual achievement, thereby keeping the battle for prestige and remembrance in the afterlife civil and, in fact, constitutive of a pervasive egalitarian ethos.

Even as history presented the Lunda with new opportunities and new labor requirements for engaging the larger world, debates and decisions about the division of labor reflected the continuing strength of notions of *chaambu,* or sexual parallelism. Males and females are thought to possess differing existential statuses and to be at times metaphysically dangerous to one another, and should, therefore, control predominantly different spheres of social activity. We noted, for example, men's continuing responsibility for certain aspects of village maintenance even while they were away as migrant laborers, as well as the corollary, women remaining responsible for a wide range of daily household chores even when they moved into new areas of cash earning.

In the previous chapters, we have frequently encountered the situational and constructed nature of identity. It emerged particularly in the context where limited goods accentuated the need to more precisely define an "us" and an "other" and the relation of each to things of value. The belief is omnipresent that identity in this world is inextricably linked to relationships with and within a vibrant metaphysical world, populated by an incredible array of little-understood beings.

Intergenerational continuities abound. Yet, we have also seen that each generation self-consciously and self-confidently develops its own elements of style. In *Subculture: The Meaning of Style* (1979), Dick Hebdige introduced the idea of style as a form of "refusal": refusal to buy into the dominant paradigm, or the prevailing ethos, or the more widespread cultural practices of one's society. Hebdige focused on forms and rituals of subordinate groups in postwar Britain, such as teddy boys, mods, rockers, skinheads, and punks, in a context where the tension between dominant and subordinate groups became reflected in the surfaces of subcultures, in the styles made up of mundane objects that took on double meanings (1979, 2). Music, motorcycles, and modes of dress were appropriated as markers of dissatisfaction with the state of society and as badges of affiliation with those attempting to bring into being a different future. One could argue that, in contrast, style among the Lunda is more about acceptance than refusal. It is not about rejecting the fundamental shape of society or refusing to play the prevailing game. Rather it is an expression of coming-of-age, and, indeed, a willingness and a preparedness to play a larger role in society as presently constituted. The postwar social dynamics that produced intergenerational conflict in Britain are alien to the Lunda milieu. For the Lunda, the future is not contested space. The young need not enter into battle with the elderly over the form of things to come. The young are acutely aware that with time alone they will inherit this world. Such a recognition allows them to focus their energies on jockeying for position among themselves rather than on intergenerational squabbles. The development of style is, thus, a supremely adult act that is an expression of strength rather than an obliquely subversive act emanating from a position of weakness, generating meanings that need be partially hidden. The ele-

ments of style sharpen the otherwise fuzzy boundaries between generations of cohorts, facilitating the orderly passage of power and purposes.

In addition to being a repertoire of aesthetic frameworks, social habits,
and productive practices, style is also the evolving set of responses to collective life experiences. Like their counterparts in Britain, each generation
of Lunda came to be associated with particular preferences in music, modes
of dress, slang expressions, and social conventions. Yet style may also include the more mundane package of solutions to the problems of daily life,
as well as the set of beliefs that give meaning to that life. Some of these elements, highlighted in the previous pages, include the changing assemblage of crops popular at certain times, e.g. millet, sorghum, cassava,
maize, sunflowers, and pineapples. The entrepreneurial impulses that led
to the adoption of each crop produced new coteries of young bigmen who
led the way in adding the style of their generation to the ongoing cultural
catenation.

It was also noted that generations can be characterized by varying styles
of movement across the landscape: the where, how, and why of movement,
as well as the narratives and symbolic meanings that flow from such movement. We found young Lunda moving as groups in different directions at
different times—south to the frontier; west to the caravans; north to the
opportunities at Christian mission stations; east and south to the mines,
plantations, and ports of southern Africa; and west again to the market at
Cazombo in Angola. The odyssey of each group stands at the core of its
generational epic and serves as the experiential base on which claims to
knowledge of the world reside.

New forms of relationships between the individual and the group
emerge periodically, or, more commonly, new styles of social interaction
develop within old forms of affiliation. Examples explored here include fathers and sons digging fishponds and claiming shared ownership, husbands
and wives applying household resources toward joint economic enterprises, and friends collectively founding villages in locations more aptly
suited to desired activities. Indeed, everywhere we find the young pioneering new ways of becoming *mukwakuheta* while still taking on the responsibilities and the opportunities associated with *mukwakwashi*.

Although each ritual contains a dominant purpose and a dominant set of
acts and symbols that reflect that purpose, much of the embellishment simply emanates from the stylistic propensities of particular ritual organizers.
Elements that can vary from performance to performance without calling

into question the authenticity of the ritual include the length of the ritual, the associated music and dance, the relative importance of particular forms of dress, the degree of isolation required of ritual subjects, the ratio of esoteric to exoteric phases, and so forth. The items used to propitiate the ancestors as well as the bundle of goods deemed acceptable as brideprice have both varied over time. The recent replacement in the lexicon of the generic *wuta wawufuku*, "night gun," with such up-to-date concepts as "night AK-47s" and "night Stinger missiles" would lead one to believe that even those who tap into the power of the metaphysical realm are themselves influenced by evolving military styles in the physical realm.

For the sake of clarity, I have treated observable cultural differences that distinguish one cohort group from another as purely a matter of style or fashion. Only in the case of transgenerational modifications have I spoken of social change. Yet, as noted throughout, such changes are generally justified and indigenized by their conceptual consistency with long-standing cultural principles that reside at a higher level than mere generational markers. Those with *wuhaku*, the ability to convincingly argue for the concordance between the new and the old, are instrumental in this process. Change is most often a matter of upward influence, that is, a younger cohort group impressing its style on an older group. Downward influence is simply continuity, except, perhaps, in cases where an older cohort has modified its own style and then impressed that change upon younger cohorts.

The rapid growth of fish farming in Mwinilunga during the late 1980s was cited as an excellent case a new practice being interpreted in light of long-standing beliefs. The early development of that industry was constrained by the actions of those unwilling to accept water or anything that grew in water as private property. Rampant "poaching" virtually destroyed all incentives for undertaking the arduous and time-consuming task of bringing ponds into production. It took nearly a decade of debate, much *wuhaku*, and a major shift in focus before a consensus was forged around the idea that the labor paradigm of ownership should take precedence over notions of water as common property—that a thing of value brought into being by the labor of individuals should belong, unambiguously, to those individuals.

The widely publicized reaffirmation of labor as the ultimate validator of ownership reverberated throughout other domains of Lunda social life. As noted, young men would increasingly assert that the labor paradigm of ownership also took precedence over the notion of adelphic inheritance, that is, that sets of brothers should automatically inherit one another's goods. Sons would now claim a share in their father's estate not by challenging prevailing matrilineal principles but instead by showing that their labor had been essential in building up their father's estate.

In another vein, the proliferation of new villages might appear to be a fundamental break with past traditions. Rather than waiting patiently for his turn at headmanship of a long-established village, an ambitious individual is increasingly likely to strike off on his own, pursue cash-earning strategies, and, if successful, found his own village, recruit followers, and take on the title of headman. Today, rather than large villages creating powerful individuals, powerful individuals create large villages. Yet, this activity is widely justified as culturally acceptable because it brings into being villages that conform to traditional ideals; these new-style headmen are able to successfully recruit brothers and other matrikin, making the social composition of their new villages virtually indistinguishable from that of traditional, long-established villages. Achievement may appear to have replaced ascription as the basis for headmanship, but in truth the local system of classificatory kinship, particularly the merging of same-sex siblings, tends to produce multiple claimants for every title. Selective remembering, forgetting, and confusion of ages have long been used to insure that the ablest candidate emerges victorious.

Another social change discussed was that of boys moving through *mukanda*, male initiation rites, at an earlier chronological age. Yet, this change could be justified by the need to maintain an acceptable adult male-female ratio relative to the group's labor requirements. The migrant labor system imposed during the colonial era, and the continued movement of young males to town after that period, distorted the gendered division of labor to the disadvantage of females. Not infrequently, 40 percent or more of the local male population was away. Lowering the age of male initiation was one way of redressing the labor imbalance and rapidly adjusting the numbers of those eligible to take on adult male tasks around the village.

The construction of new ethnic stereotypes during colonial wars of pacification and the rise of nation-states and their ethnically based administrative boundaries led to the emergence of new social groupings everywhere in Africa. The development of the Kanongesha Lunda as a distinct and autonomous group is the fortuitous outcome of multifaceted machination among Portuguese, Belgian, and British colonial interests. Although the polity clearly existed before the advent of colonialism, the Kanongesha

Lunda were split in half by new borders, chased from one side to the other, reshuffled during local wars of independence and a subsequent civil war, and ultimately crystallized as simply those Lunda residing in the extreme northwestern corner of Zambia. Yet, the Kanongesha Lunda have naturalized and indigenized the serendipity of their status by reworking history and oral tradition into narratives that both assert and explain their political distinctiveness from surrounding fragments of the ancient Lunda Empire. And they have done so with an empowering rhetoric of succession struggles and peregrinations of ambitious noblemen that minimizes the colonial-centeredness of their present form.

Finally, in chapter eight we noted that Christianity has added much to the local metaphysical mix: new views of the supreme being, new forms of religious organization, the spread of European liturgical practices, the knowledge of new spirits, and the inspiration for new rituals designed to address new diseases believed to be caused by the spirits of dead whites. But, as was shown, there is little about Christianity that does not fit neatly into Lunda cosmology or ontology. The European God was not new. It was simply Nzambi with a more precise delineation of desires and expectations. The spiritual world of Christianity was not wholly different. It was still populated with little-understood beings that desired in some form or fashion to be honored and appreciated by the living. Religious innovators found much within the preexisting Central African repertoire of meanings and practices that allowed them to incorporate or appropriate elements of Christianity in ways that were locally attractive and powerful. Contemporary leaders of African-initiated charismatic churches continue to use Christianity as a rich font of materials for reinforcing, reinvigorating, and reanimating pre-Christian beliefs.

From my perspective, some facets of Lunda society have varied over time in ways that are more substantial than the age-group markers, referred to here as style, or the intergenerational conversions, referred to as social change. There are a number of modifications which might indeed represent genuine social transformation—areas in which the Lunda are (re)-thinking the previously unthinkable, consciously debating issues that had rarely risen to consciousness, and subjecting to scrutiny the taken-for-granted logic underpinning much cultural reasoning. Here we may be witnessing changing paradigms, alterations in explanatory frameworks, or perhaps even shifts in aesthetic preferences. We noted, for example, changes in the spatial layout of villages from concentric circles of houses around a central *chota* to rows of houses along and facing major roads and pathways. This new arrangement obliterates the village as a symbol of enclosure, the center of its own universe, an autonomous social space, a womb from which springs forth future social worlds. It also deletes from the landscape the most visible expression of the opposition of adjacent generations and the alliance of alternate generations, who used to build their houses in the opposite or in the same semicircle, respectively. Perhaps we are witnessing a reconfiguration of notions of place. Does each village see itself as being not at the center but at the periphery of new centers? The metropolitan areas of Zambia are the axes around which the social, economic, and political life of the nation now revolve. By openly aligning themselves along the roads to those centers rather than remaining enclosed in the panopticon of one another's gaze, are the Lunda expressing a recognition of their decenteredness, or an acquiescence to the necessity of more fully participating as citizens in a nation-state that has thus far marginalized their cultural and material production? Or is this a passing fad, the style of the moment that at some future point may become so saturated with symbolic meaning and social significance that it will become revered as deep tradition?

Surely destined to have a more wide-ranging impact than reconfigured village space is the new debate over social space, that is, the continuing relevance of *chaambu*, gender separation. Notions concerning the existential danger of unregulated contact between the sexes seem to exercise less of a hold on the imaginations of this younger generation of Lunda. Most have spent at least a few years studying in coed classrooms, playing together on the schoolyard at recess, and often walking long distances to and from school in one another's company. Conversation and social intercourse between members of the younger generations flow quite easily and naturally. Although specific gender assignments under the prevailing division of labor may not be subject to question, the pragmatic and symbolic necessity of that separation are.

New forms of identity have also emerged that are not easily viewed as permutations on precolonial modes of social reckoning. The ubiquitous national slogan, One Zambia, One Nation, steadfastly chanted at the beginning of every public pronouncement, intoned from radio and television programs, emblazoned on billboards and government buildings, is but one facet of the multilayered effort to develop an identity that supersedes loyalty to place of origin, ethnicity, or present locality. A generation that has grown to adulthood constantly immersed in the symbols of nationhood, such as a flag, an anthem, a government, sports teams, and a synthetic national history, is increasingly comfortable with its Zambian-ness.

The powerful conditioning effect of people's relationships to mode of production has also brought into being new primary loyalties such as that of mineworker, commercial farmer, government functionary, and so forth. Religious groupings, and the propensity of particular denominations to numerically prevail in certain regions, likewise serve as incubators of new identities. Shared religious beliefs and practices have become an acceptable basis for social, political, or economic solidarity. Many deeply religious individuals expend more effort activating social networks among their congregations than among their lineal or affinal kin. Finally, one of the most powerful new identities to arise during the twentieth century, one that evolved in opposition to European colonialism and neocolonialism, is that of "African." Thus, the subject of identity provides more than ample fodder for ruminating on the genuineness of social transformation among the Lunda.

In conclusion, it should be reiterated that new views of the metaphysical world have been constructed that appear to contradict some of the fundamental postulates of traditional cosmology. In the traditional Lunda universe, humans struggled to maintain a balance between the forces of good and evil. Evil was something to guard against, to keep at bay, to overcome. But a universe without evil was inconceivable. Good and evil cease to have meaning in the absence of the other. In a world devoid of temptation, there can be no proof of moral fortitude. Without the presence of unholy power, there can be no demonstration of righteous power. The waves of antiwitchcraft movements during the first half of the twentieth century and the continuing thrust of some evangelical and charismatic churches share the aim of annihilating evil once and for all, of striving for the millennium. Millenarianism and notions of ultimate salvation imply a more linear and cumulative view of history than the older Lunda ontology might support. In any event, the steady appearance of new tools for ridding the world of witches, the regularity with which appeals are made directly to God rather than to the ancestors, and, indeed, the movement of Nzambi from an otiose and inactive being to one assiduously involved in the quotidian struggle against the forces of evil, all represent, in my view, social transformations in the Lunda's relationship with the other world. Yet on a cautionary note, the reader is asked to keep in mind that this and the other social transformations listed above may instead represent a category of activity yet to be fully justified. Or they might represent the limits of my imagination in being able to figure out the correspondence between these new actions and long-standing ones. Perhaps at this very moment, those with *wuhaku* are honing the arguments that will eventually indigenize or traditionalize these new beliefs and practices.

Tradition, however, is more than a clever turn of phrase or the conjuring up of appropriate metaphors. Tradition is a way of making life feel right, of shaving off the rough edges, of soothing the psychic tension produced by the contingent and the unpredictable. Traditions are continually reworked in ways that allow them to represent, or misrepresent, changing paradigms, proclivities, and even productive processes as unchanging and unassailable truths. Tradition naturalizes uncertainty; it sanctions particular strategies and behaviors by reference to their confluence with taken-for-granted beliefs. But tradition is not a unidirectional flow of influence. Tradition is not simply a font from which meanings flow; it is also a repository where cultural desires are stored for safekeeping. The Lunda have conditioned themselves to value the time-honored, to trust the long-standing, to be most comfortable with that which has endured. Tradition remains an exceedingly valuable tool for giving the world that lived-in feeling.

Appendix
Notes
Bibliography
Index

Appendix: Tables Comparing Data Collected during the 1950s and the 1980s

Table 1
Number of Settlements of Different Sizes, 1952 and 1985

Year and Settlement Type	Houses in Settlements																				Total Houses	Total Settlements	Houses per Settlement
	1	2	3	4	5	6	7	8	9	10	11	12	13	14	15	16	17	18	19	20			
1952[a]																							
Registered village	0	0	0	4	2	1	6	1	5	2	3	3	2	3	1	3	5	0	3	6	653	50	13.1
Unregistered village	1	1	0	1	1	2	2	4	1	1	2	1	0	0	0	1	0	0	0	0	139	18	7.5
Farm	3	1	3	1	1	0	0	0	0	0	0	0	0	0	0	0	0	0	0	0	23	9	2.6
1985																							
All villages	8	14	19	20	8	8	6	4	3	3	0	3	2	0	1	3	2	0	0	6	698	110	6.3

[a]*Source:* Turner 1957, table II

Table 2a
Individual Mobility: Natal and Present Village by Age and Sex, 1952

	Males			Females		
Age	Living in Natal Village N (%)	Living in Other Village N (%)	Total	Living in Natal Village N (%)	Living in Other Village N (%)	Total
20–29 years	11 (22.9)	37 (77.1)	48	9 (17.0)	44 (83.0)	53
30–39 years	8 (21.6)	29 (78.4)	37	5 (9.1)	50 (90.9)	55
40–49 years	3 (10.7)	25 (89.3)	28	6 (18.7)	26 (81.3)	32
50–59 years	3 (10.0)	26 (90.0)	29	3 (12.0)	22 (88.0)	25
60–69 years	0 (0.0)	25 (100.0)	25	2 (9.1)	20 (90.9)	22
70–79 years	2 (16.7)	10 (83.3)	12	2 (20.0)	8 (80.0)	10
Total	27 (15.1)	152 (84.9)	179	27 (13.7)	170 (86.3)	197

Source: Turner 1957, table III

Table 2b
Individual Mobility: Natal and Present Village by Age and Sex, 1985

	Males			Females		
Age	Living in Natal Village N (%)	Living in Other Village N (%)	Total	Living in Natal Village N (%)	Living in Other Village N (%)	Total
20–29 years	44 (28.2)	112 (71.8)	156	40 (24.8)	121 (75.2)	161
30–39 years	16 (17.6)	75 (82.4)	91	10 (12.8)	68 (87.2)	78
40–49 years	14 (19.4)	58 (80.6)	72	13 (17.8)	60 (82.2)	73
50–59 years	8 (17.4)	38 (82.6)	46	5 (15.2)	28 (84.8)	33
60–69 years	5 (22.7)	17 (77.3)	22	3 (15.0)	17 (85.0)	20
70–79 years	2 (5.9)	32 (94.1)	34	2 (14.3)	12 (85.7)	14
Total	89 (21.1)	332 (78.9)	421	73 (19.3)	306 (80.7)	379

Table 3a
Individual Mobility: Natal Village and Village of Rearing by Age and Sex, 1952

	Males			Females		
Age	Reared in Natal Village N (%)	Reared in Other Village N (%)	Total	Reared in Natal Village N (%)	Reared in Other Village N (%)	Total
20–29 years	11 (22.9)	37 (77.1)	48	21 (39.6)	32 (60.4)	53
30–39 years	15 (40.5)	22 (59.5)	37	23 (41.8)	32 (58.2)	55
40–49 years	10 (35.7)	18 (64.3)	28	17 (53.1)	15 (46.9)	32
50–59 years	14 (48.3)	15 (51.7)	29	10 (40.0)	15 (60.0)	25
60–69 years	13 (52.0)	12 (48.0)	25	13 (59.1)	9 (40.9)	22
70–79 years	6 (50.0)	6 (50.0)	12	8 (80.0)	2 (20.0)	10
Total	69 (38.6)	110 (61.4)	179	92 (46.9)	105 (53.1)	197

Source: Turner 1957, table IV

Table 3b
Individual Mobility: Natal Village and Village of Rearing by Age and Sex, 1985

Age	Males			Females		
	Reared in Natal Village N (%)	Reared in Other Village N (%)	Total	Reared in Natal Village N (%)	Reared in Other Village N (%)	Total
20–29 years	100 (64.1)	56 (35.9)	156	99 (61.5)	62 (38.5)	161
30–39 years	51 (56.0)	40 (44.0)	91	47 (60.3)	31 (39.7)	78
40–49 years	36 (50.0)	36 (50.0)	72	44 (60.3)	29 (39.7)	73
50–59 years	28 (60.9)	18 (39.1)	46	20 (60.6)	13 (39.4)	33
60–69 years	10 (45.5)	12 (54.5)	22	12 (60.0)	8 (40.0)	20
70–79 years	19 (55.9)	15 (44.1)	34	9 (64.3)	5 (35.7)	14
Total	244 (58.0)	177 (42.0)	421	231 (61.0)	148 (39.0)	379

Table 4a
Individual Mobility: Village of Rearing and Present Village by Age and Sex, 1952

	Males			Females		
Age	Living in Village of Rearing N(%)	Living in Other Village N(%)	Total	Living in Village of Rearing N(%)	Living in Other Village N(%)	Total
20–29 years	15 (31.2)	33 (68.8)	48	3 (5.7)	50 (94.3)	53
30–39 years	9 (24.3)	28 (75.7)	37	10 (18.9)	45 (81.1)	55
40–49 years	5 (17.9)	23 (82.1)	28	2 (6.2)	30 (93.8)	32
50–59 years	2 (6.9)	27 (93.1)	29	5 (20.0)	20 (80.0)	25
60–69 years	6 (24.0)	19 (76.0)	25	1 (4.5)	21 (95.5)	22
70–79 years	0 (0.0)	12 (100.0)	12	0 (0.0)	10 (100.0)	10
Total	37 (20.7)	142 (79.3)	179	21 (10.7)	176 (89.3)	197

Source: Turner 1957, table V

Table 4b
Individual Mobility: Village of Rearing and Present Village by Age and Sex, 1985

Age	Males			Females		
	Living in Village of Rearing N(%)	Living in Other Village N(%)	Total	Living in Village of Rearing N(%)	Living in Other Village N(%)	Total
20–29 years	58 (37.2)	98 (62.8)	156	54 (33.5)	107 (66.5)	161
30–39 years	28 (30.8)	63 (69.2)	91	13 (16.7)	65 (83.3)	78
40–49 years	16 (22.2)	56 (77.8)	72	22 (30.1)	51 (69.9)	73
50–59 years	10 (21.7)	36 (78.3)	46	4 (12.1)	29 (87.9)	33
60–69 years	4 (18.2)	18 (81.8)	22	5 (25.0)	15 (75.0)	20
70–79 years	4 (11.8)	30 (88.2)	34	3 (21.4)	11 (78.6)	14
Total	120 (28.5)	301 (71.5)	421	101 (26.6)	278 (73.4)	379

Table 5a
Individual Mobility through Chiefdoms (Both Males and Females), 1952

Present Chiefdom of Residence	P/R/N[a] %	P/R[b] %	P/N[c] %	O[d] %	Total
Mukangala	69 50.4	15 10.9	3 2.2	50 36.5	137
Ikelenge	16 16.3	17 17.3	2 2.0	63 64.2	98
Nyakaseya	18 23.4	19 24.7	2 2.6	38 49.3	77
Mwiniyilamba	18 29.5	9 14.8	0 0.0	34 55.7	61
Total	121 32.4	60 16.2	7 1.8	185 49.5	373

Source: Turner 1957, table VI
[a]Chiefdom of birth, rearing, and present residence the same
[b]Chiefdom of rearing and present residence the same
[c]Chiefdom of birth and present residence the same
[d]Born and reared outside present chiefdom

Table 5b
Individual Mobility through Chiefdoms and Other Regions (Both Males and Females), 1985

Present Chiefdom of Residence	P/R/N[a] %	P/R[b] %	P/N[c] %	O[d] %	Total
Chiefdoms					
Kanongesha[e]	410 52.1	85 10.8	21 2.8	271 34.4	787
Ikelenge	29 27.9	12 11.5	7 6.7	56 53.9	104
Nyakaseya	8 47.1	0 0.0	1 5.9	8 47.1	17
Mwiniyilamba	6 60.0	0 0.0	0 0.0	4 40.0	10
Chibwika	17 65.4	0 0.0	0 0.0	9 34.6	26
Other regions					
Boma	13 16.9	6 7.8	0 0.0	58 75.3	77
Copperbelt	25 13.6	22 12.0	1 0.5	136 73.9	184
Lusaka	1 2.9	6 17.1	0 0.0	28 80.0	35
Angola	93 86.1	3 2.8	0 0.0	12 11.1	108
Congo	162 82.6	6 3.1	1 0.5	27 13.8	196
Total	764 49.4	140 9.1	31 2.0	609 39.4	1544

[a]Chiefdom or region of birth, rearing, and present residence the same
[b]Chiefdom or region of rearing and present residence the same
[c]Chiefdom or region of birth and present residence the same
[d]Born and reared outside present place of residence
[e]Mukangala ceased to be recognized as a chief and his territory was incorporated into that of Chief Kanongesha in 1947

Table 6a
Divorce Rates, 1952

	N	Number of Divorces	Divorce Rate (%)
All marriages	658	347	52.7
All marriages excluding those ended by death	576	347	61.4

Source: Turner 1957, table VII

Table 6b
Divorce Rates, 1985

	N	Number of Divorces	Divorce Rate (%)
All marriages	1026	231	22.5
All marriages excluding those ended by death	818	231	28.2

Table 7a
Social Composition of Sixty-Eight Settlements, 1952

Social Category	Males		Females		Total	
	N	%	N	%	N	%
Headmen and primary matrilineal kin	172	25.7	72	10.8	244	36.5
Classificatory matrilineal kin	83	12.4	58	8.7	141	21.1
Descendants of headman	53	7.9	23	3.4	76	11.4
Children of male matrilineal kin	29	4.4	9	1.2	38	5.7
Patrilateral siblings and their children	20	2.9	5	0.8	25	3.7
Unspecified kin and affines	16	2.4	3	0.5	19	2.9
Total Kin and Affines	373	55.9	170	25.4	543	81.3
Strangers	97	14.5	28	4.2	125	18.7
Total	470	70.3	198	29.6	668	100.0

Source: Turner 1957, table XI

Table 7b
Social Composition of Ninety-Eight Settlements, 1985

Social Category	Males		Females		Total	
	N	%	N	%	N	%
Headmen and primary matrilineal kin	149	11.7	74	5.8	223	17.5
Classificatory matrilineal kin	26	2.0	32	2.5	58	4.5
Descendants of headman	270	21.1	236	18.5	506	39.6
Children of male matrilineal kin	83	6.5	70	5.5	153	12.0
Patrilateral siblings and their children	2	0.2	2	0.2	4	0.3
Unspecified kin and affines	23	1.8	198	15.5	221	17.3
Total Kin and Affines	553	43.3	612	47.9	1165	91.2
Strangers	55	4.3	58	4.5	113	8.8
Total	608	47.6	670	52.4	1278	100.0

Table 8a

Social Composition of Long-Established Villages Compared with That of Recently Established Villages, 1952

	Social Category	Males		Females		Total	
		N	%	N	%	N	%
Long-Established Villages	Headmen and primary matrilineal kin	52	18.2	23	8.0	75	26.3
	Classificatory matrilineal kin	53	18.6	33	11.6	86	30.2
	Descendants of headman	20	7.0	9	3.2	29	10.2
	Cognatic, patrilateral, unspecified kin, affines	38	13.3	9	3.2	47	16.5
	Strangers	41	14.4	7	2.4	48	16.8
	Total	204	71.6	81	28.4	285	100.0
Recently Established Villages	Headmen and primary matrilineal kin	120	31.3	49	12.8	169	44.1
	Classificatory matrilineal kin	30	7.8	25	6.5	55	14.4
	Descendants of headman	33	8.6	14	3.7	47	12.3
	Cognatic, patrilateral, unspecified kin, affines	27	7.1	8	2.1	35	9.2
	Strangers	56	14.6	21	5.5	77	20.1
	Total	266	69.5	117	30.5	383	100.0
Total	Headmen and primary matrilineal kin	172	25.7	72	10.8	244	36.5
	Classificatory matrilineal kin	83	12.4	58	8.7	141	21.1
	Descendants of headman	53	7.9	23	3.4	76	11.4
	Cognatic, patrilateral, unspecified kin, affines	65	9.7	17	2.5	82	12.3
	Strangers	97	14.5	28	4.2	125	18.7
	Total	470	70.3	198	29.6	668	100.0

Source: Turner 1957, table XII

Table 8b
Social Composition of Long-Established Villages Compared with That of Recently
Established Villages, 1985

		Males		Females		Total	
	Social Category	N	%	N	%	N	%
Long-Established Villages	Headmen and primary matrilineal kin	92	10.7	55	6.4	147	17.0
	Classificatory matrilineal kin	22	2.5	32	3.7	54	6.3
	Descendants of headman	169	19.6	156	18.1	325	37.7
	Cognatic, patrilateral, unspecified kin, affines	73	8.5	172	19.9	245	28.4
	Strangers	43	5.0	49	5.7	92	10.7
	Total	399	46.2	464	53.8	863	100.0
Recently Established Villages	Headmen and primary matrilineal kin	57	13.7	19	4.6	76	18.3
	Classificatory matrilineal kin	4	1.0	0	0.0	4	1.0
	Descendants of headman	101	24.3	80	19.3	181	43.6
	Cognatic, patrilateral unspecified kin, affines	35	8.4	98	23.6	133	32.1
	Strangers	12	2.9	9	2.2	21	5.1
	Total	209	50.4	206	49.6	415	100.0
Total	Headmen and primary matrilineal kin	149	11.7	74	5.8	223	17.4
	Classificatory matrilineal kin	26	2.0	32	2.5	58	4.5
	Descendants of headman	270	21.1	236	18.5	506	39.6
	Cognatic, patrilateral, unspecified kin, affines	108	8.5	270	21.1	378	29.6
	Strangers	55	4.3	58	4.5	113	8.8
	Total	608	47.6	670	52.4	1278	100.0

Table 9a
Relationship of Current Headman to Previous Incumbent, 1952

Relationship	N	Percentage
Brother	20	46.5
Sister's son	15	34.9
Sister's daughter's son	4	9.3
Son	3	7.0
Mother's brother's son	0	0
Mother's brother	0	0
Sister	1	2.3
Total	43	100

Source: Turner 1957, table XVI

Table 9b
Relationship of Current Headman to Previous Incumbent, 1985

Relationship	N	Percentage
Brother	14	12.3
Sister's son	19	16.7
Sister's daughter's son	5	4.4
Son	21	18.4
Unrelated friend	12	10.5
None[a]	41	36.0
Other	2	1.8
Total	114	100

[a]New village with no previous headman

Table 10a
Relationship between Leader of Seceding Group and Previous Headman, 1952

Relationship	N	Percentage
Sister's son	18	54.5
Brother	5	15.2
Son	3	9.1
Mother's brother's son	3	9.1
Mother's brother	2	6.1
Unrelated	2	6.1
Total	33	100

Source: Turner 1957, table XVII

Table 10b
Relationship between Leader of Seceding Group and Previous Headman, 1985

Relationship	N	Percentage
Sister's son	25	25.3
Brother	16	16.2
Son	31	31.3
Sister's daughter's son	9	9.1
Unrelated	18	18.2
Total	99	100

[a]New village with no previous headman

Table 11a
Residence of Husband and Wife, 1952

Residence	N	Percentage
Virilocal	115	69.7
Intravillage	27	16.4
Uxorilocal	12	7.3
Other	11	6.6
Total	165	100

Source: Turner 1957, table XX

Table 11b
Residence of Husband and Wife, 1985

Residence	N	Percentage
Virilocal	296	72.0
Intravillage	19	4.6
Uxorilocal	30	7.3
Other	66	16.1
Total	411	100

Table 12a
Spatial Range of Marriage, 1952

Category of Marriage	N	Percentage
Intravillage cluster	27	16.4
Intrachiefdom	47	28.5
Subtotal	74	44.9
Interchiefdom (Zambia)	47	28.5
Interchiefdom (Congo/Angola)	27	16.4
Other/unknown	17	10.2
Subtotal	91	55.1
Total	165	100

Source: Turner 1957, table XXI

Table 12b
Spatial Range of Marriage, 1985

Category of Marriage	N	Percentage
Intravillage cluster	60	14.7
Intrachiefdom	144	35.4
Subtotal	204	50.1
Interchiefdom (Zambia)	58	14.3
Interchiefdom (Zaire/Angola)	105	25.8
Other/unknown	40	9.8
Subtotal	203	49.4
Total	407	100

Table 13a
Conjugal Status by Age and Sex, 1952

Age	N									Percentage							
	Unw[a]	D[b]	R[c]	Married[d]				Total	Total	Unw	D	R	Married				Total
				1	2	3	4						1	2	3	4	
Males:																	
0–pu[e]	95	—	—	—	—	—	—	—	95	100	—	—	—	—	—	—	—
pu–19	18	—	—	—	—	—	—	—	18	100	—	—	—	—	—	—	—
20–29	15	—	—	31	5	—	—	36	51	29.4	—	—	60.8	9.8	—	—	70.6
30–39	3	2	—	29	5	—	—	34	39	7.7	5.1	—	74.4	12.8	—	—	87.2
40–49	—	3	—	21	6	1	—	28	31	—	9.7	—	67.7	19.4	3.2	—	90.3
50–59	—	—	—	14	14	2	—	30	30	—	—	—	46.7	46.7	6.6	—	100
60–	—	—	5	24	5	—	1	30	35	—	—	14.3	68.5	14.3	—	2.9	85.7
Total	131	5	5	119	35	3	1	158	299	43.8	1.7	1.7	39.8	11.7	1.0	0.3	52.8
Females:																	
0–pu	99	—	—	2	—	—	—	2	101	98.0	—	—	2.0	—	—	—	2.0
pu–19	20	—	—	31	—	—	—	31	51	39.2	—	—	60.8	—	—	—	60.8
20–29	—	8	—	49	—	—	—	49	57	—	14.0	—	86.0	—	—	—	86.0
30–39	—	3	—	52	—	—	—	52	55	—	5.5	—	94.5	—	—	—	94.5
40–49	—	4	1	27	—	—	—	27	32	—	12.5	3.1	84.4	—	—	—	84.4
50–59	—	5	3	19	—	—	—	19	27	—	18.5	11.1	70.4	—	—	—	70.4
60–	—	6	9	10	—	—	—	10	25	—	24.0	36.0	40.0	—	—	—	40.0
Total	119	26	13	190	—	—	—	190	348	34.2	7.5	3.7	54.6	—	—	—	54.6

Source: Turner 1957, table XXII
[a] Unwedded
[b] Divorced
[c] Relict; widower or widow, unmarried
[d] Numbers indicate number of spouses
[e] Puberty

Table 13b
Conjugal Status by Age and Sex, 1985

	N									Percentage							
				Married[d]									Married				
Age	Unw[a]	D[b]	R[c]	1	2	3	4	Total	Total	Unw	D	R	1	2	3	4	Total
Males:																	
–20	99	—	—	2	—	—	—	2	101	98	—	—	2.0	—	—	—	2.0
20–29	76	4	—	52	2	1	—	55	135	56.3	3.0	—	38.5	1.5	0.7	—	40.7
30–39	13	6	—	57	2	1	—	60	79	16.5	7.6	—	72.2	2.5	1.3	—	76.0
40–49	7	1	1	40	5	1	—	46	55	12.7	1.8	1.8	72.7	9.1	1.8	—	83.6
50–59	1	3	3	27	6	1	1	35	42	2.4	7.1	7.1	64.3	14.3	2.4	2.4	83.3
60–69	1	3	—	19	4	1	—	24	28	3.6	10.7	—	67.9	14.3	3.6	—	85.7
70+	—	2	7	21	3	—	—	24	33	—	6.1	21.2	63.6	9.1	—	—	72.7
Total	197	19	11	218	22	5	1	246	473	41.7	4.0	2.3	46.1	4.7	1.1	0.2	52.0
Females:																	
–20	90	4	—	34	—	—	—	34	128	70.3	3.1	—	26.6	—	—	—	26.6
20–29	31	18	2	105	—	—	—	105	156	19.9	11.5	1.3	67.3	—	—	—	67.3
30–39	9	11	2	56	—	—	—	56	78	11.5	14.1	2.6	71.8	—	—	—	71.8
40–49	7	10	2	56	—	—	—	56	75	9.3	13.3	2.7	74.7	—	—	—	74.7
50–59	—	5	5	18	—	—	—	18	28	—	17.9	17.9	64.3	—	—	—	64.3
60–69	1	3	5	14	—	—	—	14	23	4.4	13.0	21.7	60.9	—	—	—	60.9
70+	—	1	5	8	—	—	—	8	14	—	7.1	35.7	57.1	—	—	—	57.1
Total	138	52	21	291	—	—	—	291	502	27.5	4.2	4.2	58.0	—	—	—	58.0

[a]Unwedded
[b]Divorced
[c]Relict; widower or widow, unmarried
[d]Numbers indicate number of spouses

351

Table 14
Number of Rites of Affliction Reported as Having Been Performed for Individual During Lifetime, by Sex, 1986[a]

Reason for Rite and Rite Name	Females	Males	Total
Reproductive troubles			
Nkula	27	3	30
Isoma	25	4	29
Wubwangu	21	15	36
Hunting troubles			
Mukaala		4	4
Chitampakasa		1	1
Kalombu		0	0
Mundeli		0	0
Ntambu		0	0
Other ancestor-caused troubles			
Kayongu	5	12	17
Ihamba	10	18	28
Chihamba	1	0	1
Antiwitchcraft			
Kanenga	22	56	78
Lukupu	2	11	13
Miscellaneous	3	6	9
Total rituals performed	116	130	246
Number of people surveyed	222	421	643
Performances per person	0.52	0.31	0.38

[a]See following list for brief descriptions of selected Lunda rites of affliction.

Brief Descriptions of Selected Lunda Rites of Affliction

• *Nkula*
Performed for menstrual disorders, miscarriages, infertility, or ill health of infants. Core ritual features include an abundance of red symbolic objects, the dressing of patient in hunter's attire, and the carving of a figurine of an infant from a sacred *mukula* tree that is placed into a calabash symbolizing the newly fortified womb of the patient.
• *Isoma*
Performed for still births, menstrual disorders, miscarriages, infertility, or ill health of infants. Core ritual features include the washing of husband and wife with herbal preparations while seated in holes dug at the base of termite mounds, and the sacrifice of chickens.

- *Wubwangu*
Performed upon birth of twins or for menstrual disorders, miscarriages, infertility, or ill health of infants. Core ritual features include symbols representing dualism and the unifying qualities of opposites; prevalence of ribald cross-sexual joking.
- *Mukaala, Chitampakasa, Kalombu, Mundeli,* and *Ntambu*
Performed for lack of hunting success believed to be caused when a spirit either chases game away, makes animals invisible to hunter, or causes hunter to miss aim through trembling. Core ritual features include libations of blood, animal sacrifices, baths with herbal preparations, anthills, and figurines of animals.
- *Kayongu*
Performed for respiratory illnesses believed to be caused by spirit of a diviner. Core ritual features include sacrifices of goats and chickens, ritual trembling, and the finding hidden objects.
- *Ihamba*
Performed for biting pains in body believed to be caused by spirit of a hunter. Core ritual features include ritual trembling, animal sacrifice, and the removal of an upper front incisor tooth from the body of the patient by cupping with an antelope horn.
- *Chihamba*
Performed for any illness, reproductive problem, crop failure, or poor hunting luck. Core ritual features include the appearance of the ritual slaying of a demi-god, and the chasing and interrogation of patients.
- *Kanenga*
Performed for any sudden and severe illness believed to be caused by witchcraft of living person. Core ritual features include the collection of medicinal substances from graveyards and the sacrifice of goats.
- *Lukupu*
Performed for any sudden and severe illness believed to be caused by witchcraft of living person. Core ritual features include splashing of patient with herbal preparations to exorcise offending witch's familiar; hyena figurines.

Table 15
Total Number of Ritual Performances Reported, 1954 and 1986

Year	N	Females	Males	Total
1954[a]	47	87	52	139
1986	643	116	130	246

[a]*Source:* Turner 1968, 303, table 2

Table 16
Average Number of Ritual Performances per Person, 1954 and 1986

Year	Females	Males	Total
1954[a]	3.3	2.5	3.0
1986	0.52	0.31	0.38
Change	−84.2%	−87.6%	−87.3%

[a]*Source:* Turner 1968, 303, table 2

Table 17
Rate of Change in Number of Rituals Performed from 1954 to 1986

Ritual	Females	Males
Fertility class	−80.0%	−90.4%
Hunting class	—	−97.7%
Ihamba	−85.7%	−92.3%
Chihamba	−100%	−100%
Kanenga	−63.0%	−69.8%

Note: Comparative data from 1954 taken from Turner 1968, 303, table 2

Notes

Introduction

1. "Lunda" is the widest term of reference applied to hundreds of ethnolinguistic groups in Zambia, Congo, and Angola who were associated in some fashion with a far-flung sixteenth- to nineteenth-century Central African empire. Myriad terms exist distinguishing one group from another based on geographic placement of local political loyalties. The Lunda of northwestern Zambia, who are the focus of this study, are variously known as the Lunda-Ndembu, the Ndembu, the Kanongesha Lunda, the Zambian Lunda, or just simply the Lunda.

Chapter 1. Histories and Homilies

1. This section draws heavily from the works of Dias de Carvalho 1890; Biebuyck 1957; Crine-Mavar 1961; Miller 1976; Vellut 1972; Schecter 1976; and Hoover 1978.

2. The earliest recorded reference to this fact can be attributed to Dias de Carvalho (1890). The most succinct explication and interpretation is probably that of Miller (1976). See also Cunnison 1956; Biebuyck 1957; and Crine-Mavar 1961.

3. Schecter (1976, chapt. 3) provides a summary of the widespread claims of Lunda origin and of the available evidence that may corroborate such claims. Some of that evidence includes Burton 1873; Dias de Carvalho 1890; and Gamitto 1962.

4. The Mbwela have also been known as Humbu, Lukolwe, or Kawiku. See White 1949.

5. Descriptions of the Central African caravan trade, as well as outlines of specific routes, are contained in Vansina 1963 and the articles in Gray and Birmingham 1970.

6. See Isaacman 1966 for a summary of the evidence on the effects of outlawing the slave trade and abolishing the ivory monopoly.

7. As Roberts (1976), von Oppen (1993), and others have noted, long-distance trade actually continued on a small scale in a clandestine fashion for some time into the colonial era.

8. Personal communication from CMML (Christian Mission in Many Lands) missionaries reflecting on the early 1900s.

9. This system was formalized with the implementation of the Native Authority Ordinances of 1930 and 1936 (Hall 1965, 52–54). See Chipungu 1992 for a detailed account of the imposition of the "Native Authority system" in Zambia.

10. These retainers became known as *kapasus*. They served as the chief's messengers, police, carriers, and bodyguards.

11. At the district level, final legislative, judicial, and executive authority resided with the district commissioner.

12. The notion of kings as "objective outsiders" is a common one throughout Central Africa. See, for example, Miller 1976, 278–79.

13. Perhaps at one level one could assert that a certain sense of continuity existed, in that the British, just like the Lunda chiefs of old, were now the ones dispensing prestigious titles that linked titleholders with the center of power.

14. The obsession with position within lineages, including the intense competition for headmanship, is the dominant theme in Turner 1957.

15. About 1890, during the reign of Kanongesha Ishima Watuta Menji, it was decided to change the Kanongesha mode of succession to matriliny in order to bring it into line with the customs followed in selecting village headmen (Turner 1957, 321).

Chapter 2. People and the Environment

1. Paul Richards has written extensively about the anthropogenic quality of many supposedly natural landscapes. Human action has long played a significant role in favoring or curtailing myriad plant species in vast areas of Africa that were once believed to be virgin forest (Richards 1985, 1986).

2. The plateau is a very ancient land surface formed upon the basement complex of archaean rocks, intensely folded and metamorphosed gneisses or schists, and quartzites with intrusive granites. The visible result is bands of rapidly changing soil types, producing ribbons of distinctive flora patterns.

3. Hospital and clinic records, as well as oral communication with healthcare workers districtwide, confirm the incredible spike in frequency of treatment seeking during April. However, it should be noted that preexisting conditions may be simply ignored or left untreated until cassava planting activities begin to tail off in April, when the rainy season is nearing its end.

4. Personal communication with project coordinators in 1982.

5. In Zambia, a *lima* is a unit of measurement, 100 yards × 100 yards.

6. Cultural differences aside, rarely can the knowledge gains in "women's classes" at mission stations be transferred to the village context. The absence of sinks with running water, refrigerators, stoves with gas burners, and ovens, and the lack of access to certain commodities and foodstuffs prevent village women from implementing techniques learned from missionary women.

7. Livingston 1963, 116. Similar remarks can be found in Baptista 1873, 200; Silva Porto 1885, 24; Vellut 1972, 107; and Madeira Santos 1986, 103.

Chapter 3. The Individual and the Group

1. Audrey Richards is credited with coining the term "matrilineal puzzle." See, especially, Richards 1950.

2. Turner's periods of fieldwork were from December 1950 to February 1952 and from May 1953 to June 1954.

3. The numbers of people per house in 1952 were 2.4 for registered villages, 2.2 for unregistered villages, and 2.5 for farms (Turner 1957, 38); in 1985 the average was 2.2 for all villages.

4. Small scattered villages are far more difficult to supervise and control than

large concentrated ones. The articles in Birmingham and Martin 1983, vol. 2, collectively detail the colonial phenomenon of concentrating the African population in small areas as a major form of labor control. British, French, and Portuguese colonies exhibited similar tendencies in this respect.

5. The most detailed account of the historical relationship among Lunda titleholders can be found in Schecter 1976.

Chapter 4. The Old and the Young

1. See Flanagan and Rayner 1988, introduction by Flanagan and Rayner, 1–16, for a succinct historical overview of the intellectual discourse on egalitarianism in the West.

2. The notion that giving and receiving universally brings into being culturally specific relationships has been well explored in the anthropological literature. From Mauss 1967 to Barth 1965, gift giving has been a central concern.

3. For example, a phrase sometimes heard as part of Chief Kanongesha's praise prose is, *Wanta wasuluka kudi Nzambi kuMwanta kuanyanind* (Authority [dominion, power] comes down from God, to the chief, to his children).

4. Although the definition of power used here is modeled on that of Adams (1977), the distinction between power as coercion and power as influence is both widespread and long-standing in the literature of political anthropology. See, for example, Cohen and Middleton 1970.

5. See Crehan 1994 for a different view on gender relations that extends from her work among the Lunda's eastern neighbors, the Kaonde.

6. Chapter 7 addresses in more detail the relationship between Mwinilunga and the state.

7. In some respects one could talk of separate male and female hierarchies, folded into a unitary prestige system at one level, yet retaining unique elements of meaning at other levels. This begins to hint at gendered notions of egalitarianism. For example, female notions of egalitarianism reflect a system in which there are, in a sense, as many valued positions in society as there are individuals qualified to assume them. But male notions of egalitarianism have more to do with equality of opportunity to succeed within competition, although only a limited number will achieve widely recognized success at any point in time. Thus, as might be expected, the female hierarchy is not permeated with intense emotional sensitivities in the way that the male hierarchy is. One does not see women fighting along the road over acts of disrespect by other women. In both cases, however, hierarchy is put forward as the most effective mechanism for smoothing the way toward conflict resolution.

8. Both males and females possess a range of residential options. Males, however, are far more likely than females to reside alone or to start a new village.

9. It has long been accepted that larger villages lead to a more efficient division of labor and a more effective social safety net. Turner (1957) frequently mentions the social importance attached to membership in large villages.

10. References to joking relationships are ubiquitous in ethnographies on Africa. Individuals involved in such relationships may dispense with the usual social for-

malities and jokingly hurl insults or obscenities at one another that would be wholly inappropriate under any other circumstances. In some cases such relationships are confined to affines of one's own generation. In other cases, a group may view an entire neighboring group as their joking cousins.

11. One could refer to such beliefs as being religious in nature, or as forming part of Lunda cosmological notions. Victor Turner contends that Lunda religion consists mainly of rituals laden with symbolic messages that have an impact at the subconscious level. The types of beliefs that I am referring to here, however, are definitely a conscious part of human strategic behavior.

12. For evidence of early Lunda social organization see, especially, Dias de Carvalho 1890; McCulloch 1951; Miller 1969, 1976; and Schecter 1976.

13. Under the framework of so-called indirect rule, the British created a certain number of highly desirable positions, the Native Authority chiefs, which were open to those with verifiable claims to "traditional" authority (see chapter 1). Indirect rule gave added importance to the local descent system and surely exaggerated the role of ascriptive qualities in reckoning precolonial leadership among the Lunda. See Chipungu 1992; and, on migrant labor, Meebelo 1971.

14. Male spirits, like female ones, can cast illnesses upon their living kin. But spirits can only afflict the living with disorders that they themselves experienced during their lives. Female spirits tend to afflict their kin with reproductive disorders. Such disorders threaten the survival of the group and thus effectively serve to move the entire group to action. The afflictions brought by males spirits, however, tend to be viewed as being more restricted to the individual sufferer, and thus less a matter of urgent group concern.

15. It is said that in the past *nkanga* lasted six to twelve months.

16. Slippery foods are said to increase the possibility of spontaneous abortions; red foods, difficult menstrual periods; and the meat from spotted animals, leprosy; other foods dry up milk.

Chapter 5. Females and Males

1. In truth, a good deal of productive activity takes place in the *chota*. Even while talking, men may be engaged in whittling tool handles, trimming bark fibers, sharpening arrows, or constructing traps. Much useful information is also exchanged in the *chota*.

2. Ault (1983), Chanock (1983, 1985), Geisler (1990), and Chipungu (1992) continue the theme of gender negotiations for other parts of Zambia during the colonial period.

3. I conducted a survey of two thousand individuals residing in the one-hundred-square-mile area centered around Chief Kanongesha's capital village, which represents approximately two-thirds of the population over age ten residing in Kanongesha ward, i.e., the territory under his personal rule, not assigned to any of his subchiefs.

4. See Fortes 1970, 251, for an extended discussion on the ways in which obligatory generosity figures in African thought and social practice.

5. The most recent formulation was spelled out in the Inheritance Act of 1984.

Fifty percent of an individual's estate goes to the surviving spouse, 20 percent to offspring, 20 percent to parents, and 10 percent to siblings.

6. Since the election of Frederick Chiluba in 1992, government policy has changed abruptly toward fostering a free market economy.

Chapter 6. The Rich and the Poor

1. Evidence of these networks can be gleaned from the diaries of the earliest literate travelers in Central Africa, such as the Portuguese explorer Dr. de Lacerda in 1789 and the *pombeiros* P. J. Baptista and Amaro Jose (Burton 1873). See also V. L. Cameron (1877) and Serpa Pinto (1881).

2. Such tales still circulate in Lunda oral traditions, but usually concerning famous chiefs of old.

3. Many of these historians contributed to the volume edited by Chipungu (1992), *Guardians in Their Time: Experiences of Zambians under Colonial Rule, 1890–1964.*

4. Many of Walter Fisher's offspring remain in Zambia today; the largest number still reside in Mwinilunga. See Fisher 1991.

5. Personal communication from Fr. Adrian Peck, the first Catholic missionary in Mwinilunga

6. This story was frequently told of the irascible Mr. Paterson, who settled on Matonchi plateau, the present location of Chifunga village, back in the 1920s.

Chapter 7. Us and Them

1. Leroy Vail's *The Creation of Tribalism in Southern Africa* (1989) contains perhaps the clearest articulation to date of these major theoretical positions on ethnicity, as well as richly illustrative case material.

Chapter 8. This World and the Other World

1. The Witchcraft Ordinance of 1914 actually made the accusation, rather the practice of witchcraft, a crime. Diviners were at the center of most accusations.

Bibliography

Aberle, D. 1961. "Matrilineal Descent in Cross-Cultural Perspective." In *Matrilineal kinship*, ed. D. Schneider and K. Gough, 655–727. Berkeley.

Abrahams, R. D. 1983. *African Folktales*. New York.

Adams, R. 1977. "Power in Human Societies: A Synthesis." In *The Anthropology of Power*, ed. R. Fogelson and R. Adams, 387–410. New York.

Allan, W. 1965. *The African Husbandman*. Edinburgh.

Alpers, E. A. 1975. *Ivory and Slaves in East Central Africa: Changing Patterns of International Trade to the Later Nineteenth Century*. Berkeley.

Ardener, S., ed. 1978. *Defining Females: The Nature of Women in Society*. London.

Arens, W., and I. Karp, eds. 1989. *Creativity of Power: Cosmology and Action in African Societies*. Washington, D.C.

Arnot, F. S. 1893. *Bihe and Garenganze*. London.

Arnot, F. S. [1889] 1969. *Garenganze or Seven Years of Pioneer Mission Work in Central Africa*. London.

Asad, T. 1973. *Anthropology and the Colonial Encounter*. London.

Ashley, K. M. 1990. Introduction to *Victor Turner and the Construction of Cultural Criticism: Between Literature and Anthropology*, ed. K. M. Ashley, ix–xxii. New York.

Ault, J. M. 1983. "Making 'Modern' Marriage 'Traditional': State Power and the Regulation of Marriage in Colonial Zambia." *Theory and Society* 12(2).

Bachofen, J. J. [1861] 1992. *Das Mutterrecht*. In *Myth, Religion, and Mother Right: Selected Writings of J. J. Bachofen*. Trans. Ralph Manheim. Princeton, N.J.

Banton, M. 1966. *Anthropological Approaches to the Study of Religion*. London.

Baptista, J. 1873. "Journey of the Pombeiros." In *Lacerda's Journey to Cazembe, and Journey of Pombeiros*, ed. R. F. Burton. London.

Barrett, S. 1984. *The Rebirth of Anthropological Theory*. Toronto.

Barth, F. 1965. *Political Leadership among Swat Pathans*. New York.

Baxter, P. T. W., and U. Almagor, eds. 1978. *Age, Generation and Time: Some Features of East African Age Organisations*. New York.

Beattie, J., and J. Middleton, eds. 1969. *Spirit Possession and Society in Africa*. London.

Berger, E. L. 1974. *Labour, Race and Colonial Rule*. Oxford.

Berry, S. 1993. *No Condition is Permanent: The Social Dynamics of Agrarian Change in Sub-Saharan Africa*. Madison, Wisc.

Biebuyck, D. 1957. "Fondements de l'organisation politique des Luunda du Mwaantayaav en territoire de Katanga." *Zaire* 11(9): 789–817.

Biebuyck, D., ed. 1961. *African Agrarian Systems*. London.

Birmingham, D. 1965. "The Date and Significance of the Imbangala Invasion of Angola." *Journal of African History* 6(2): 143–52.

Birmingham, D. 1966. *Trade and Conflict in Angola: The Mbundu and Their Neighbours under the Influence of the Portuguese, 1483–1790.* Oxford.

Birmingham, D. 1983. "Society and Economy before A.D. 1400." In *History of Central Africa,* ed. D. Birmingham and P. M. Martin, 1–29. Vol. 1. London.

Birmingham, D., and P. M. Martin, eds. 1983. *History of Central Africa.* 2 vols. London.

Bisson, M. S. 1975. "Copper Currency in Central Africa: The Archaeological Evidence." *World Archaeology* 6:272–92.

Bleek, D. F. 1928. "The Bushmen of Central Angola." *Bantu Studies* 3:105–25. Johannesburg.

Bloch, M. 1989. *Ritual, History and Power: Selected Papers in Anthropology.* London.

Bohannan, P. 1953. *The Tiv of Central Nigeria.* London.

Boxer, C. R. 1969. *The Portuguese Seaborne Empire, 1415–1825.* New York.

Bratton, M. 1980. *The Local Politics of Rural Development: Peasants and Party-State in Zambia.* Hanover, N.H.

British South Africa Company (BSAC). *Report on the Administration of the Rhodesias, 1900-1902.* Zambia National Archives. Lusaka.

Brokensha, D., D. Warren, and O. Werner, eds. 1980. *Indigenous Knowledge Systems and Development.* Washington, D.C.

Burdette, M. 1988. *Zambia: Between Two Worlds.* Boulder, Colo.

Burton, R. F. 1860. *The Lake Regions of Central Africa.* 2 vols. London.

Burton, R. F., ed. 1873. *Lacerda's Journey to Cazembe, and Journey of Pombeiros.* London.

Bustin, E. 1975. *Lunda under Belgian Rule: The Politics of Ethnicity.* Cambridge, Mass.

Cameron, V. L. 1877. *Across Africa.* 2 vols. London.

Capello, H., and R. Ivens. 1882. *From Benguella to the Territory of Yacca.* 2 vols. London.

Carvalhais, J. 1915. *Uma Diligência e expedição Comercial à Mona Quimbundo em 1912.* Luanda.

Chambers, R. 1983. *Rural Development: Putting the Last First.* London.

Chanock, M. 1983. "Making Customary Law: Men, Women, and Courts in Colonial Northern Rhodesia." In *African Women and the Law: Historial Perspectives,* ed. M. J. Hay and M. Wright. Boston University Papers on Africa, no. 8.

Chanock, M. 1985. *Law, Custom, and Social Order: The Colonial Experience in Malawi and Zambia.* Cambridge.

Cheke Cultural Writers Association. 1994. *The History and Cultural Life of the Mbunda Speaking Peoples.* Ed. R. Papstein. Lusaka.

Chibanza, S. J. 1961. "Kaonde History." (Central Bantu Historical Texts.) *Rhodes-Livingstone Institute Communications,* no. 22.

Childs, G. 1949. *Umbundu Kinship and Character.* London.

Chinyama, T. 1945. *The Early History of the Balove Lunda*. Lusaka.

Chipungu, S. 1992. "Accumulation from within: The Boma Class and the Native Treasury in Colonial Zambia," in *Guardians in Their Time: Experiences of Zambians under Colonial Rule, 1890–1964,* ed. S. Chipungu, 74–96.

Chipungu, S., ed. 1992. *Guardians in Their Time: Experiences of Zambians under Colonial Rule, 1890–1964.* London.

Chiwale, J. 1962. "Royal Praises and Praise Names of the Lunda Kazembe of Northern Rhodesia, the Meaning and Historical Background." (Central Bantu Historical Texts.) *Rhodes-Livingstone Institute Communications,* no. 25.

Clarence-Smith, W. G. 1979. *Slaves, Peasants, and Capitalists in Southern Angola, 1840–1926.* Cambridge.

Clarence-Smith, W. G., ed. 1989. *The Economics of the Indian Ocean Slave Trade in the Nineteenth Century.* London.

Clark, J. D. 1970. *The Prehistory of Africa.* London.

Clay, G. C. R. 1945. "History of the Mankoya District." *Rhodes-Livingstone Institute Communications,* no. 4. Lusaka.

Cohen, A. 1969. *Custom and Politics in Urban Africa: A Study of Hausa Migrants in Yoruba Towns.* Berkeley.

Cohen, R., and J. Middleton, eds. 1970. *From Tribe to Nation in Africa: Studies in Incorporation Processes.* Scranton, Penn.

Coillard, F. 1897. *On the Threshold of Central Africa.* London.

Colson, E. 1960. *Social Organization of the Gwembe Tonga.* Manchester.

Colson, E. 1962. *The Plateau Tonga of Northern Rhodesia.* Manchester.

Colson, E. 1969. "Spirit Possession among the Tonga of Zambia." In *Spirit Mediumship and Society in Africa,* ed. J. Beattie and J. Middleton, 69–103. London.

Colson, E., and M. Gluckman, eds. 1951. *Seven Tribes in British Central Africa.* Manchester.

Comaroff, J. 1985. *Body of Power, Spirit of Resistance.* Chicago.

Comaroff, J., and J. Comaroff. 1991. *Of Revelation and Revolution: Christianity, Colonialism, and Consciousness in South Africa.* Vol. 1. Chicago.

Comaroff, J., and J. Comaroff, eds. 1993. *Modernity and Its Malcontents: Ritual and Power in Postcolonial Africa.* Chicago.

Cooper, F. 1977. *Plantation Slavery on the East Coast of Africa.* New Haven, Conn.

Crawford, D. 1912. *Thinking Black: 22 Years without a Break in the Long Grass of Central Africa.* London.

Crehan, K. 1987. "Production, Reproduction, and Gender in North-Western Zambia: A Case Study." Ph.D. dissertation, University of Manchester.

Crehan, K. 1994. "Land, Labour and Gender: Matriliny in 1980s Rural Zambia." African Studies Association Paper, Toronto.

Crehan, K. 1997. *The Fractured Community: Landscapes of Power and Gender in Rural Zambia.* Berkeley.

Crehan, K., and A. von Oppen. 1988. "Understandings of Development: An Arena of Struggle. The Story of a Development Project in Zambia." *Sociologia Ruralis* 28(2/3): 113–45.

Crine-Mavar, F. 1961. "Aspects politico-sociaux du système de tenure des Lunda septentrionaux." in *African Agrarian Systems,* ed. D. Biebuyck. London.

Cunnison, I. 1950. *Kinship and Local Organization on the Luapula.* Lusaka.

Cunnison, I. 1956. "Perpetual Kinship: A Political Institution of the Luapula Peoples." *Rhodes-Livingstone Journal,* no. 20:28–48.

Cunnison, I. 1961. "Kazembe and the Portuguese, 1798–1832." *Journal of African History* 2(1): 61–76.

Curtin, D., S. Feierman, L. Thompson, and J. Vansina. 1978. *African History.* Boston.

de Cadornega, A. 1940. *História das Guerras Angolanas.* Lisbon.

de Heusch, L. 1975. "What Shall We Do with the Drunken King?" *Africa* 45, 4:363–72.

Delgado, R. 1945. *O Reino de Benguela.* Lisbon.

de Maret, P. 1975. "A Carbon-14 Date from Zaire." *Antiquity* 49:133–37.

de Oliveira Marques, A. 1976. *History of Portugal.* 2nd ed. New York.

Derricourt, R. M., and R. J. Papstein. 1977. "Lukolwe and the Mbwela of North-Western Zambia." *Azania* 11:169–75.

DeVos, G. A., ed. 1976. *Responses to Change: Society, Culture, and Personality.* New York.

Dias, G. S. 1938. *Viagem que eu fiz as Remotas Partes de Cassange.* Lisboa.

Dias de Carvalho, H. 1890. *Ethnographia e História Tradicional Dos Povos da Lunda.* Lisbon.

Dias de Carvalho, H. 1892. *Descrição da Viagem à Mussumba.* Lisbon.

Dodge, D. 1977. "Agricultural Policy and Performance in Zambia: History, Prospects, and Proposals for Change." University of California, Berkeley, Institute of International Studies Research Series, no. 32. Berkeley.

dos Santos, J. 1964. "Ethiopia Oriental." In *Records of South-Eastern Africa,* ed. G. M. Theal. Reprint, Capetown.

Douglas, M. 1963. *The Lele of the Kasai.* London.

Douglas, M. 1964. "Matriliny and Pawnship in Central Africa." *Africa* 34(4): 301–13.

Douglas, M. 1969. "Is Matriliny Doomed in Africa?" In *Man in Africa,* ed. M. Douglas and P. Kaberry. London.

Durkheim, E. [1912] 1961. *The Elementary Forms of the Religious Life.* New York.

Durkheim, E. [1933] 1984. *The Division of Labor in Society.* Trans. W. D. Halls. New York.

Duysters, L. 1958. "Histoire des Aluunda." *Problèmes d'Afrique centrale* 12:75–98.

Engels, F. 1892. *Origins of the Family, Private Property, and the State.* 4th ed. London.

Epstein, A. L. 1958. *Politics in an Urban African Community.* Manchester.

Evans-Pritchard, E. E. 1937. *Witchcraft, Oracles, and Magic among the Azande.* London.

Evans-Pritchard, E. E. 1940. *The Nuer.* Oxford.

Evans-Pritchard, E. E. 1948. *The Divine Kingship of the Shilluk of the Nilotic Sudan.* Cambridge.

Evans-Pritchard, E. E. 1956. *Nuer Religion.* Oxford.

Evans-Pritchard, E. E. 1965. *Theories of Primitive Religion.* Oxford.

Fabian, J. 1983. *Time and the Other: How Anthropology Makes Its Object.* New York.

Fagan, B. 1966. *A Short History of Zambia: From the Earliest Times until A.D. 1900.* Oxford.

Fairley, N. 1987. "Ideology and State Formation: The Ekie of Southern Zaire." In *The African Frontier: The Reproduction of Traditional African Societies,* ed. I. Kopytoff, 89–100. Bloomington, Ind.

Feierman, S. 1990. *Peasant Intellectuals: Anthropology and History in Tanzania.* Madison, Wisc.

Ferguson, J. 1990a. "Mobile Workers, Modernist Narratives: A Critique of the Historiography of Transition on the Zambian Copperbelt." Part 1. *Journal of Southern African Studies* 16(3): 385–412.

Ferguson, J. 1990b. "Mobile Workers, Modernist Narratives: A Critique of the Historiography of Transition on the Zambian Copperbelt." Part 2. *Journal of Southern African Studies* 16(4): 603–21.

Fernandez, J. W. 1978. "African Religious Movements." *Annual Review of Anthropology* 7:198–234.

Firth, R. 1959. *Social Change in Tikopia: Re-Study of a Polynesian Community after a Generation.* New York.

Fisher, M. 1991. *Nswana the Heir: The Life and Times of Charles Fisher, a Surgeon in Central Africa.* Ndola, Zambia.

Fisher, W. S., and J. Hoyte. 1948. *Africa Looks Ahead: The Life Stories of Walter and Anna Fisher of Central Africa.* London.

Flanagan, J. G., and S. Rayner, eds. 1988. *Rules, Decisions, and Inequality in Egalitarian Societies.* Aldershot, U.K.

Fortes, M., and E. E. Evans-Pritchard, eds. 1940. *African Political Systems.* London.

Fortes, M. 1949. *Social Structure.* Oxford.

Fortes, M. 1970. *Kinship and the Social Order: The Legacy of Lewis Henry Morgan.* Chicago.

Frankenberg, R. 1969. "Man, Society, and Health." *African Social Research* 8: 573–87.

Freeman-Grenville, G. S. P. 1962. *The East African Coast.* Oxford.

Fuller, C. J. 1976. *The Nayars Today.* New York.

Gago Coutinho, C. V. 1915. "Impressões Das Duas Viagens Atraves d'Africa entre Angola e Moçambique." *Boletim da Sociedade de Geographia de Lisboa,* 33a série (5–6): 181–208.

Galbraith, J. S. 1974. *Crown and Charter: The Early Years of the British South Africa Company.* Berkeley.

Gamitto, A. C. P. 1962. *King Kazembe and Marave, Cheva, Bisa, Bemba, Lunda, and Other Peoples of Southern Africa, Being the Diary of the Portuguese Expedition to that Potentate in the Years 1831 and 1832.* Trans. I. Cunnison. Lisbon.

Gann, L. 1954. "The End of the Slave Trade in British Central Africa." *The Rhodes-Livingstone Journal,* no. 16.

Gann, L. 1964. *A History of Northern Rhodesia: Early Days to 1953.* New York.

Geertz, C. 1966. "Religion as a Cultural System." in *Anthropological Approaches to the Study of Religion,* ed. M. Banton, 1–46. London.

Geisler, G. 1990. "Moving with Tradition: The Politics of Marriage amongst the Toka of Zambia." Chr. Michelsen Institute Working Paper, D:14.

Gertzel, C. J., C. Baylies, and M. Szeftel, eds. 1984. *The Dynamics of the One-Party State in Zambia.* Manchester.

Gifford, P., and W. R. Louis, eds. 1971. *France and Britain in Africa: Imperial Rivalry and Colonial Rule.* New Haven, Conn.

Gilsenan, M. 1972. "Myth and the History of African Religion." *The Historical Study of African Religion,* ed. T. O. Ranger and I. N. Kimambo, 50–79. Berkeley.

Gluckman, M. 1955. *The Judicial Process among the Barotse of Northern Rhodesia.* Manchester.

Gluckman, M. 1956. *Custom and Conflict in Africa.* Oxford.

Gluckman, M. 1963. *Order and Rebellion in Tribal Africa.* London.

Goody, J. 1961. "Religion and Ritual: The Definition Problem." *British Journal of Sociology* 12:142–64.

Goody, J., ed. 1958. *The Developmental Cycle in Domestic Groups.* Cambridge.

Gough, K. 1961a. "Variation in Preferential Marriage." In *Matrilineal Kinship,* ed. D. Schneider and K. Gough, 614–30. Berkeley.

Gough, K. 1961b. "The Modern Disintegration of Matrilineal Descent Groups." In *Matrilineal Kinship,* ed. D. Schneider and K. Gough, 631–52. Berkely.

Graça, J. R. 1890. "Expedição ao Muatayanvua. Diario de Joaquim Rodriques Graça." *Boletim da Sociedade de Geographia de Lisboa,* 9a série:365–468.

Gray, R., and D. Birmingham, eds. 1970. *Pre-Colonial African Trade: Essays on Trade in Central and Eastern Africa before 1900.* London.

Hall, R. 1965. *Zambia, 1890–1964.* London.

Hambly, W. D. 1934. *The Ovimbundu of Angola.* Chicago.

Hansen, A. 1976. "When the Running Stops: The Social and Economic Incorporation of Angolan Refugees into Zambian Border Villages." Ph.D. dissertation, Cornell University.

Harms, R. 1978. "Competition and Capitalism: The Bobangi Role in Equatorial Africa's Trade Revolution, ca. 1750–1900." Ph.D. dissertation, University of Wisconsin.

Harms, R. 1981. *River of Wealth, River of Sorrow: The Central Zaire Basin in the Era of the Slave and Ivory Trade, 1500–1891.* New Haven, Conn.

Harms, R. 1987. *Games against Nature: An Eco-Cultural History of the Nunu of Equatorial Africa.* Cambridge.

Hebdige, D. 1979. *Subculture: The Meaning of Style.* London.

Heimer, F.-W., ed. 1973. *Social Change in Angola.* Munich.

Henige, D. 1974. *The Chronology of Oral Tradition: Quest for a Chimera.* Oxford.

Hilton, A. 1985. *The Kingdom of Kongo.* Oxford.

Hilton-Simpson, M. W. [1911] 1969. *Land and Peoples of the Kasai, Being a Narrative of a Two Years' Journey among the Cannibals of the Equatorial Forest and Other Savage Tribes of the South-Western Congo.* Reprint, New York.

Hinde, S. L. [1897] 1969. *The Fall of the Congo Arabs.* Reprint, New York.

Hobsbawm, E., and T. O. Ranger. 1986. *The Invention of Tradition.* Cambridge.

Holy, L. 1986. *Strategies and Norms in a Changing Matrilineal Society.* Cambridge.

Hoover, J. 1978. "The Seduction of Ruwej: Reconstructing Ruund History." Ph.D. dissertation, Yale University.

Hoppers, W. 1981. *Education in a Rural Society: Primary Pupils and School Leavers in Mwinilunga, Zambia.* The Hague.

Hutchinson, S. 1996. *Nuer Dilemmas: Coping with Money, War, and the State.* Berkeley.

International Labor Office. 1981. "Basic Needs in an Economy Under Pressure." Findings and Recommendations of an ILO/JASPA Basic Needs Mission to Zambia. Addis Ababa.

Isaacman, A. 1966. *An Economic History of Angola, 1835–1867.* Master's thesis, University of Wisconsin.

James, W. 1978. "Matrifocus on African Women." In *Defining Females: The Nature of Women in Society,* ed. S. Ardener, 140–62. London.

Janzen, J. 1978. *The Quest for Therapy in Lower Zaire.* Berkeley.

Janzen, J. 1982. *Lemba, 1650–1930: A Drum of Affliction in Africa and the New World.* New York.

Janzen, J. 1992. *Ngoma: Discourses of Healing in Central and Southern Africa.* Berkeley.

Jones, W. O. 1959. *Manioc in Africa.* Stanford, Calif.

Kakoma, B. K. 1971. "Colonial Administration in Northern Rhodesia: A Case Study of Colonial Policy in the Mwinilunga District of Zambia, 1901–1939." Master's thesis, University of Auckland, New Zealand.

Kaunda, K. D. 1967. *Humanism in Zambia.* Lusaka.

Kaunda, K. D. 1974. *Humanism in Zambia II.* Lusaka.

Kazembe XIV, Mwata. 1985. "My Ancestors and My People." Trans. I. Cunnison. (Central Bantu Historical Texts.) *Rhodes-Livingstone Institute Communications,* no. 23. Lusaka.

Kelly, R. C. 1985. *The Nuer Conquest: The Structure and Development of an Expansionist System.* Ann Arbor, Mich.

Keyes, C. F. 1981. *Ethnic Change.* Seattle.

Kopytoff, I., ed. 1987. *The African Frontier: The Reproduction of Traditional African Societies.* Bloomington, Ind.

Kuper, A. 1973. *Anthropologists and Anthropology: The Modern British School, 1922–1972.* New York.

LaFontaine, J. S. 1985. *Initiation.* New York.

Leach, E.. 1969. *Virgin Birth in Genesis as Myth and Other Essays.* London.

LeVine, R. A. 1976. "Patterns of Personality in Africa." In *Responses to Change: Society, Culture, and Personality,* ed. G. A. DeVos, 112–36. New York.

Lévi-Strauss, C. [1949] 1969. *The Elementary Structures of Kinship.* Rev. ed. Boston.

Livingstone, D. 1857. *Missionary Travels and Researches in South Africa.* London.

Livingstone, D. 1863. *Livingstone's African Journal, 1853–1856,* ed. I. Schapera. London.

Long, N. 1968. *Social Change and the Individual.* Manchester.

Luchembe, C. 1992. "Ethnic stereotypes, violence and labour in early colonial Zambia, 1889–1924." In *Guardians in Their Time: Experiences of Zambians under Colonial Rule, 1890–1964,* ed. S. Chipungu, 30–49. London.

MacGaffey, W. 1983. *Modern Kongo Prophets.* Bloomington, Ind.

MacGaffey, W. 1986. *Religion and Society in Central Africa: The BaKongo of Lower Zaire.* Chicago.

Macpherson, F. 1981. *Anatomy of a Conquest: The British Occupation of Zambia, 1884–1924.* London.

Mamdani, M. 1996. *Citizen and Subject: Contemporary Africa and the Legacy of Late Colonialism.* Princeton, N.J.

Marter, A. 1978. *Cassava or Maize: A Comparative Study of the Economics of Production and Market Potential of Cassava and Maize in Zambia.* Rural Development Studies Bureau. Lusaka.

Martin, P. M. 1986. "Power, Cloth, and Currency on the Loango Coast." *African Economic History* 15:1–12.

Marx, K. 1964. *Pre-Capitalist Economic Formation.* Ed. E. J. Hobsbawm. London.

Mauss, M. 1967. *The Gift: Forms and Functions of Exchange in Archaic Societies.* Trans. I. Cunnison. New York.

Mbiti, J. 1970. *African Religions and Philosophy.* New York.

McCulloch, M. 1951. *The Southern Lunda and Related Peoples.* London.

Meebelo, H. S. 1971. *Reaction to Colonialism: A Prelude to the Politics of Independence in Northern Zambia, 1839–1939.* Manchester.

Melland, F. 1923. *In Witch-Bound Africa: An Account of the Primitive Kaonde Tribe and Their Beliefs.* London.

Miller, J. C. 1969. *Chokwe Expansion, 1850–1900.* Master's thesis, University of Wisconsin.

Miller, J. C. 1976. *Kings and Kinsmen: Early Mbundu States in Angola.* Madison, Wisc.

Miller, J. C. 1982. "The Significance of Drought, Disease, and Famine in the Agriculturally Marginal Zones of West-Central Africa." *Journal of African History* 23(1): 17–61.

Miller, J. C. 1988. *Way of Death: Merchant Capitalism and the Angolan Slave Trade, 1730–1830.* Madison, Wisc.

Miracle, M. P. 1967. *Agriculture in the Congo Basin.* Madison, Wisc.

Mitchell, J. C. 1954. *African Urbanization in Ndola and Luanshya.* Lusaka.

Moore, H. L., and M. Vaughan. 1994. *Cutting Down Trees: Gender, Nutrition, and Agricultural Change in the Northern Province of Zambia, 1890–1990.* Portsmouth, N.H.

Mulford, D. 1967. *Zambia: The Politics of Independence, 1957–1964.* London.
Murdock, G. P. 1957. "World Ethnographic Sample." *American Anthropologist* 59:664–87.
Murdock, G. P. [1949] 1960. *Social Structure.* New York.
Mwanza, I. 1990. *Bibliography of Zambiana Theses and Dissertations, 1930s–1989.* Lusaka.
Mwondela, W. R. 1972. *Mukanda and Makishi: Traditional Education in North Western Zambia.* Lusaka.
Nenquin, J. 1963. *Excavation at Sanga 1957.* Tervuren, Belgium.
Oliver, R., and J. D. Fage. 1962. *A Short History of Africa.* New York.
Ollawa, P. 1979. *Participatory Democracy in Zambia.* Devon.
Palmer, R., and N. Parsons, eds. 1977. *The Roots of Rural Poverty in Central and Southern Africa.* London.
Papstein, R. 1978. "The Upper Zambezi: A History of the Luvale People." Ph.D. diss., University of California, Los Angeles.
Parpart, J. L. 1986. "Sexuality and Power on the Zambian Copperbelt, 1926– 1964." *Working Papers in African Studies,* no. 120. African Studies Center, Boston University.
Phillipson, D. W. 1977. *The Later Prehistory of Eastern and Southern Africa.* London.
Phillipson, D. W. 1985. *African Archaeology.* Cambridge.
Poewe, K. 1981. *Matrilineal Ideology: Male-Female Dynamics in Luapula, Zambia.* London.
Porter, D., B. Allen, and G. Thompson. 1991. *Development in Practice: Paved with Good Intentions.* London.
Pritchett, J. A. 1990. "External Strategies and Local Perceptions: Rural Development in Mwinilunga, Zambia." Presented paper, Walter Rodney Seminar Series, Boston University.
Radcliffe-Brown, A. R. 1952. *Structure and Function in Primitive Society.* London.
Radcliffe-Brown, A. R., and D. Forde, eds. 1950. *African Systems of Kinship and Marriage.* London.
Ranger, T. O. 1986. Chapter 6 in *The Invention of Tradition,* ed. E. Hobsbawm and T. O. Ranger, 211–62. Cambridge.
Ranger, T. O., and I. N. Kimambo, eds. 1972. *The Historical Study of African Religion.* Berkeley.
Ravenstein, E. G. 1901. *The Strange Adventures of Andrew Battell of Leigh in Angola and the Adjoining Regions.* London.
Reefe, T. Q. 1981. *The Rainbow and the Kings: A History of the Luba Empire to 1891.* Berkeley.
Richards, A. 1935. "A Modern Movement of Witch-Finders," *Africa* 8(4): 448–61.
Richards, A. 1939. *Land, Labour and Diet in Northern Rhodesia: An Economic Study of the Bemba Tribe.* London.
Richards, A. 1950. "Some Types of Family Structure amongst the Central Bantu." In *African Systems of Kinship and Marriage,* ed. A. R. Radcliffe-Brown and D. Forde, 207–51. London.

Richards, A. 1956. *Chisungu: A Girls' Initiation Ceremony among the Bemba of Northern Rhodesia.* London.

Richards, P. 1985. *Indigenous Agricultural Revolution.* Boulder, Colo.

Richards, P. 1986. *Coping with Hunger: Hazard and Experiment in an African Rice-Farming System.* London.

Roberts, A. 1976. *A History of Zambia.* New York.

Rotberg, R. I. 1964. "Plymouth Brethren and the Occupation of Katanga." *Journal of African History* 5:285–97.

Rotberg, R. I. 1967. *The Rise of Nationalism in Central Africa.* Cambridge, Mass.

Sangambo, M. K. 1979. *The History of the Luvale People and Their Chieftainship.* Los Angeles.

Santos, M. E. Madeira dos. 1986. *Viagens e Apontamentos de um Portuense em África. Diario de António Francisco Ferreira da Silva Porto.* Coimbra.

Schecter, R. 1976. "History and Historiography on a Frontier of Lunda Expansion: The Origins and Early Development of the Kanongesha." Ph.D. diss., University of Wisconsin.

Schneider, D. 1961. "Introduction: The Distinctive Features of Matrilineal Descent Groups." In *Matrilineal Kinship,* ed. D. Schneider and K. Gough, 1–29. Berkely.

Schneider, D., and K. Gough, eds. 1961. *Matrilineal Kinship.* Berkeley.

Scudder, T., and E. Colson. 1980. *Secondary Education and the Formation of an Elite: The Impact of Education on Gwembe District, Zambia.* New York.

Seleti, Y. 1992. "Entrepreneurship in Colonial Zambia," in *Guardians in Their Time: Experiences of Zambians under Colonial Rule, 1890–1964,* ed. S. Chipungu, 147–79.

Serpa Pinto, A. 1881. *How I Crossed Africa.* 2 vols. London.

Silva Porto, A. 1885. "Novas Jornadas de Silva Porto nos Sertões Africanos," *Boletim da Sociedade de Geographia e da História de Lisboa,* 5a série, no. 1: 3–36, no. 3: 145–72, no. 9: 569–86, no. 10: 603–42.

Smith, W., and A. P. Wood. 1984. "Patterns of Agricultural Development and Foreign Aid to Zambia." *Development and Change* 15(3): 405–34.

Spring, A. 1976. "Women's Rituals and Natality among the Luvale of Zambia." Ph.D. diss., Cornell University.

Spring, A., and A. Hansen. 1985. "The Underside of Development: Agricultural Development and Women in Zambia." *Agriculture and Human Values* 2(1): 60–67.

Stöhr, W. B., and D. R. F. Taylor. 1981. Chapter 18 in *Development from Above or Below? The Dialectics of Regional Planning in Developing Countries,* ed. W. B. Stöhr and D. R. F. Taylor, 453–80. Chichester, U.K.

Sundkler, B. G. 1948. *Bantu Prophets in South Africa.* London.

Sutton, J. E. G. 1973. *Early Trade in Eastern Africa.* Nairobi.

Taylor, D., and F. Mackenzie, eds. 1992. *Development from Within: Survival in Rural Africa.* London.

Theal, G. M., ed. 1964. *Records of South-Eastern Africa.* Reprint, Capetown.

Thornton, J. 1981. "The Chronology and Causes of Lunda Expansion to the West, c. 1700–1852." *Zambia Journal of History* 1:1–14.

Thornton, J. 1983. *The Kingdom of the Kongo*. Madison, Wisc.

Tilsley, G. E. 1929. *Dan Crawford, Missionary and Pioneer in Central Africa*. London.

Tordoff, W., ed. 1974. *Politics in Zambia*. Manchester.

Tordoff, W. 1980. *Administration in Zambia*. Manchester.

Trapnell, C. G. and J. N. Clothier. 1937. *The Soils, Vegetation and Agricultural Systems of North Western Rhodesia: A Report of the Ecological Survey*. Lusaka.

Turner, E. L. B., and V. W. Turner. 1955. "Money Economy among the Mwinilunga Ndembu: A Study of Some Individual Cash Budgets." *Rhodes-Livingstone Journal: Human Problems in British Central Africa*, no. 18:19–37. Manchester.

Turner, V. W. 1952. *The Lozi People of North-Western Rhodesia*. London.

Turner, V. W. 1953. "Lunda Rites and Ceremonies." *Occasional Papers of the Rhodes-Livingstone Museum*, no. 10. Lusaka.

Turner, V. W. 1955. "A Lunda Love Song and Its Consequences." *Rhodes-Livingstone Journal*, no. 19. Lusaka.

Turner, V. W. 1957. *Schism and Continuity in an African Society: A Study of Ndembu Village Life*. Manchester.

Turner, V. W. 1961. "Ritual Symbolism, Morality, and Social Structure among the Ndembu." *Rhodes-Livingstone Journal*, no. 30. Lusaka.

Turner, V. W. 1963. "Lunda Medicine and the Treatment of Disease." *Occasional Papers of the Rhodes-Livingstone Museum*. no. 15. Lusaka.

Turner, V. W. 1964. "Witchcraft and Sorcery: Taxonomy Versus Dynamics," *Africa* 34:314–24.

Turner, V. W. 1967. *The Forest of Symbols*. Ithaca, N.Y.

Turner, V. W. 1968. *The Drums of Affliction: A Study of Religious Processes among the Ndembu of Zambia*. Oxford.

Turner, V. W. 1969. *The Ritual Process*. Ithaca, N.Y.

Turner, V. W. 1975. *Revelation and Divination in Ndembu Ritual*. Ithaca, N.Y.

Turok, B., ed. 1979. *Development in Zambia*. London.

Vail, H. L., ed. 1989. *The Creation of Tribalism in Southern Africa*. Berkeley.

van Binsbergen, W. M. J. 1981. *Religious Change in Zambia*. London.

van Binsbergen, W. M. J. 1992. *Tears of Rain: Ethnicity and History in Central Western Zambia*. London.

van Binsbergen, W. M. J., and P. Geschiere, eds. 1985. *Old Modes of Production and Capitalist Encroachment: Anthropological Explorations in Africa*. London.

van Binsbergen, W. M. J., and M. Schoffeleers, eds. 1985. *Theoretical Explorations in African Religion*. London.

Van Gennep, A. 1960. *The Rites of Passage*. London.

Vansina, J. 1963. "The Foundation of the Kingdom of Kasanje." *Journal of African History* 4 (3): 355–74.

Vansina, J. 1966. *Kingdoms of the Savanna*. Madison, Wisc.

Vansina, J. 1973. *The Tio Kingdom of the Middle Congo, 1880–1892*. New York.

Vansina, J. 1985. *Oral Tradition as History*. Madison, Wisc.

Vansina, J. 1990. *Paths in the Rainforests: Toward a History of Political Tradition in Equatorial Africa.* Madison, Wisc.

Vellut, J.-L. 1972. "Notes sur le Lunda et la frontière Luso-Africaine, 1700–1900." *Études d'Histoire Africaine* 3:61–166.

Verbeken, A. 1953. *La Première Traversée du Katanga en 1806.* Brussels.

Verhulpen, E. 1936. *Baluba et Balubaises de Katanga.* Anvers.

Vickery, K. P. 1985. "Saving Settlers: Maize Control in Northern Rhodesia." *Journal of Southern African Studies* 11(2): 212–34.

von Oppen, A. 1993. *Terms of Trade and Terms of Trust: The History and Context of Pre-Colonial Market Production around the Upper Zambezi and Kasai.* Münster.

Watson, W. 1959. *Tribal Cohesion in a Money Economy.* Manchester.

Watts, M. 1989. "The Agrarian Question in Africa: Debating the Crisis." *Progress in Human Geography* 13(1) :1–41.

Weeks, J. 1971. "Does Employment Matter?" *Manpower and Unemployment Research in Africa* 4(1): 67–70.

Wele, P. 1987. *Kaunda and the Mushala Rebellion.* Lusaka.

Werbner, R. P. 1984. "The Manchester School in South-Central Africa." *Annual Review of Anthropology* 13:157–85.

White, C. M. N. 1948. "The Material Culture of the Lunda-Luvale People." *Occasional Papers of the Rhodes-Livingstone Museum,* no. 3. Lusaka.

White, C. M. N. 1949. "The Balovale People and Their Historical Background." *Rhodes-Livingstone Journal* 8:26–41.

White, C. M. N. 1960. "An Outline of Luvale Social and Political Organization." *Rhodes-Livingstone Paper,* no. 30. Lusaka.

Wilkin, P. D. 1983. "To the Bottom of the Heap: Educational Deprivation and Its Social Implications in the Northwestern Province of Zambia, 1906–1945." Ph.D. dissertation, Syracuse University.

World Bank 1990. "Poverty: World Development Indicators." *World Development Report.* Published for the World Bank by Oxford University Press. New York.

Yoder, J. C. 1992. *The Kanyok of Zaire: An Institutional and Ideological History to 1895.* Cambridge.

Zambia. Central Statistical Office. 1980. *Census of Population and Housing.* Lusaka.

Zambia. Central Statistical Office. 1990. *Census of Population and Housing.* Lusaka.

Zambia. 1976. *Working Paper on Customary Law of Succession* (December). Lusaka.

Index

Aberle, David, 172
Abrahams, Roger D., 18
Affinal relations, 111, 112, 117, 127, 184
African National Congress (ANC), 272
Agricultural resettlement scheme (Dutch), 54–55, 70–71
AIDS, 204, 313, 318
Akishi (ancestral spirits), 287, 301
Alcoholic beverages: types, 196
Andumba (evil spirit), 288, 289, 315
Anthropogenic landscapes, 356*n1*
Antiwitchcraft movements, 298–99, 300–310, 328
Appropriate technology projects, 56
Archaeology: of Central Africa, 20–22
Atlantic trade bloc, 207, 215
Atutepa. See Diviners
Avoidance: social practice of, 12, 178

Bachofen, Johann Jakob, 170, 171
Bakapasu (messengers, *kapasu*), 233, 235, 247, 274, 355*n10*
Beehives: artificial, 231
Bemba (ethnic group), 231, 257, 259, 267, 317
Bigmanship (*iyala muneni*), 140–42, 192, 195
Bigwomanship (*mumbanda muneni*), 140–42, 150, 162, 166, 192
Bihean (traders/porters), 216
Bloch, Maurice, 142
Bohannan, Paul, 306
Boma (rural government center), 48, 101
Boma class, 232–38
Boys' initiation rite. *See Mukanda*
Bridewealth, 184, 228, 237, 241
British South Africa Company (BSAC): loss of charter in 1924, 35; mentioned, 33, 34, 35, 228–32, 239, 266, 267
Brother Joe, 44

Cameron, Vernon, 5, 213, 218, 219, 220, 222, 224, 227
Caravans: system ends, 33; selling cassava to, 51; rates of pay for porters, 222–23; theft from, 223, 224, 225; trade items 226, 227; mentioned, 28, 31, 36, 58, 62, 71, 73, 89, 129, 140, 182, 183, 184, 185, 211–28, 262, 317, 355*n5*
Cash: shortage of, 62–63, 67–68
Cassava: adoption, 29, 215; processing, 52; export to Copperbelt, 59; general marketing of, 60, 194, 196, 221, 231, 234; and role of women, 182–83
Catholic Church: presence in Mwinilunga, 192
Central Africa: as a single cultural unit, 8; connections to West Africa, 8
Central African ecumene, 7–11, 320
Chaambu (gender separation), 177, 178, 181, 187, 189, 191, 192, 202, 277, 280, 321, 327
Chibinda Ilunga (Luba hunter), 257
Chiefs: Lunda, formally recognized, 5, 37, 40, 249; agents of colonialism, 40, 41; agents of independent government, 43; courts of, 273; female, 186; as objective outsiders, 274; as magicians, 290
Chifunga (Senior Headman Isaac Nkemba): tradition of origin, 258–59, 261; mentioned, xiii, 156, 168, 186, 205, 255, 286, 318
Children: as labor pool, 143, 147, 167, 179; as communications network, 179
Chiluba, President Frederick, 311, 312, 359*n6*
Chimbuki (ritual doctor), 114, 115, 116, 245, 295, 312
Chinese pottery: in Central Africa, 20, 21
Chinguli. *See* Kinguri
Chinyama. *See* Kinyama
Chipenge, 32